Opposing the Imām

Islam's fourth caliph, ʿAlī, can be considered one of the most revered figures in Islamic history. His nearly universal portrayal in Muslim literature as a pious authority obscures centuries of contestation and the eventual rehabilitation of his character. In this book, Nebil Husayn examines the enduring legacy of the *nawāṣib*, early Muslims who disliked ʿAlī and his descendants. The *nawāṣib* participated in politics and discussions on religion at least until the ninth century. However, their virtual disappearance in Muslim societies has led many to ignore their existence and the subtle ways in which their views subsequently affected Islamic historiography and theology. By surveying medieval Muslim literature across multiple genres and traditions including the Sunnī, Muʿtazilī, and Ibāḍī, Husayn reconstructs the claims and arguments of the *nawāṣib* and illuminates the methods that Sunnī scholars employed to gradually rehabilitate the image of ʿAlī from a villainous character to a righteous one.

Nebil Husayn is Assistant Professor of Religious Studies at the University of Miami, where his research considers the development of Islamic theology, historiography, and debates on the caliphate. Husayn obtained his Ph.D. in Near Eastern Studies from Princeton University.

Cambridge Studies in Islamic Civilization

Other titles in the series are listed at the back of the book.

Opposing the Imām

The Legacy of the Nawāṣib *in Islamic Literature*

NEBIL HUSAYN
University of Miami

CAMBRIDGE
UNIVERSITY PRESS

CAMBRIDGE
UNIVERSITY PRESS

University Printing House, Cambridge CB2 8BS, United Kingdom

One Liberty Plaza, 20th Floor, New York, NY 10006, USA

477 Williamstown Road, Port Melbourne, VIC 3207, Australia

314–321, 3rd Floor, Plot 3, Splendor Forum, Jasola District Centre, New Delhi – 110025, India

79 Anson Road, #06–04/06, Singapore 079906

Cambridge University Press is part of the University of Cambridge.

It furthers the University's mission by disseminating knowledge in the pursuit of education, learning, and research at the highest international levels of excellence.

www.cambridge.org
Information on this title: www.cambridge.org/9781108832816
DOI: 10.1017/9781108966061

First published 2021

A catalogue record for this publication is available from the British Library.

Library of Congress Cataloging-in-Publication Data
Names: Husayn, Nebil, author.
Title: Opposing the Imam : the legacy of the Nawasib in Islamic literature / Nebil Husayn.
Description: 1. | New York : Cambridge University Press, 2021. | Series: Cambridge studies in Islamic civilization | Includes bibliographical references and index.
Identifiers: LCCN 2020057992 (print) | LCCN 2020057993 (ebook) | ISBN 9781108832816 (hardback) | ISBN 9781108965767 (paperback) | ISBN 9781108966061 (ebook)
Subjects: LCSH: Shīʿah – Relations – Sunnites. | Sunnites – Relations – Shīʿah. | ʿAlī ibn Abī Ṭālib, Caliph, approximately 600–661 – Imamate. | Shīʿah – Apologetic works. | Sunnites – Controversial literature.
Classification: LCC BP194.16 .H87 2021 (print) | LCC BP194.16 (ebook) | DDC 297.8/042–dc23
LC record available at https://lccn.loc.gov/2020057992
LC ebook record available at https://lccn.loc.gov/2020057993

ISBN 978-1-108-83281-6 Hardback

"Beware of mentioning ʿAlī and Fāṭima, for people detest nothing more than the mention of ʿAlī and Fāṭima."

-A prominent chieftain among the descendants of ʿAlī
A little more than a century after the Prophet's death

Contents

Acknowledgments

This project would not exist without the guidance and support of Hossein Modarressi who served as my advisor at Princeton University. He inspired me with his erudition and humility. I seized his office hours as opportunities to query him about anything and everything. He patiently answered my questions with wisdom and occasional humor. I am honored to have received the opportunity to sit with such a fine scholar.

Michael Cook's commitment to his students seemingly possessed no bounds and he graciously accommodated all of my requests. I never doubted that he was invested in my future success. I thank him for his scholarship, teaching, and encouragement.

I would like to express my deep gratitude to a few scholars who agreed to read early draft chapters of this work: Sean Anthony, Michael Dann, Adam Gaiser, Najam Haider, Nancy Khalek, Jack Tannous, Wasim Shiliwala, and Hanna Siurua. Their comments and criticisms were critical to the development and completion of this book.

I would like to thank the editors and staff at Cambridge University Press for their support and patience. I must also thank the publisher for permission to use, in revised form, "The Rehabilitation of ʿAlī in Sunnī Ḥadīth and Historiography," *Journal of the Royal Asiatic Society*, Series 3, 29, 4 (2019).

I am indebted to the faculty and administration of the Department of Near Eastern Studies at Princeton University who generously provided financial and logistical support in the research, writing, and completion of essential aspects of this work that appeared in my doctoral dissertation.

I wrote many chapters of this book as a Visiting Assistant Professor at the Near Eastern Languages and Civilizations (NELC) Department at

Harvard University. I am indebted to the administration and faculty of the Harvard Business School, the NELC Department, specifically, Ali Asani, Shaye Cohen, and Khaled El-Rouayheb for providing me with the opportunity to teach and research at Harvard.

I could not have pursued publication of this work without the generosity and good will of my colleagues in the Department of Religious Studies at the University of Miami who took a chance on me. I am blessed to share good laughs and great conversations with everyone here in Miami. Our department's chair, David Kling, greatly facilitated the writing of this book by supporting my requests for research and family leave each semester that necessitated one. I am particularly indebted to Daniel Pals and Dexter Callender who kindly read proposals and draft chapters of this work. Thank you, Dexter, for encouraging me to move ahead with the project when I considered postponing it another year – or two! A 2018–2019 University of Miami Fellowship in the Arts and Humanities greatly assisted me in the writing of this book.

Patricia Crone and Shahab Ahmed were two brilliant scholars that I held in the highest esteem. Both of them smiled when I mentioned the idea of this project to them years ago. When I solicited her thoughts about my proposal to study depictions of ʿAlī among the ʿUthmāniyya, Patricia joked, "Well, they certainly didn't like him." Perhaps Patricia and Shahab would have found something agreeable in this work, now that it is complete.

What is life without family? My mother is a woman of unconditional love and compassion. Her love has sustained me every day of my life. My father taught me honesty and an unyielding work ethic; Nejat, a fierce spirit. Each day that I share with all of my young siblings – Jemila, Ala, Jafar, and Aman – gives me great joy. The Hussen, Abdella, and Hussam families have all nurtured my intellectual and spiritual growth with their love and support, but none more than my wife Reshma. With her I learned to listen to the forest.

Note on Conventions

The transliteration of Arabic names and phrases is based on the guidelines of the third edition of Brill's *Encyclopaedia of Islam*. The death dates of medieval Muslim scholars appear in the Islamic *hijrī* calendar (AH), followed by the Common Era date (CE). Otherwise, I refer to dates in the Common Era. I forgo citation of the *bāb*, *ḥadīth* number, or first line of a report; conventions that are inconsistently used in western scholarship on *ḥadīth*. I simply cite the volume and page number of a classical Sunnī or Shīʿī *ḥadīth* collection. To aid researchers seeking to follow up these references in Arabic, I cite editions that coincide with those digitized and made freely available on www.shiaonlinelibrary.com. All translations from the Arabic are my own.

Introduction

A few verses of the Qur'ān (33:6, 33:53) instruct Muslims to revere the Prophet's wives as the "mothers" of the faithful. Men should always respect their private spaces. One should ask permission before entering their homes and stay behind a partition when interacting with them. Over the centuries, those who despised the Prophet's son-in-law, ʿAlī, claimed that he scandalously flouted such commandments. According to these story-tellers, ʿAlī would secretly climb the walls of the home belonging to a wife of the Prophet to see her. They narrated that ʿAlī did this so frequently that his fingernails were reduced to stubs.[1]

This book examines the stories that some Muslims shared about a respected caliph in Islamic history, ʿAlī b. Abī Ṭālib (d. 40/661). The unique aspect of this study is that none of these tales come from his admirers. Rather, our informants will be individuals who considered him a man prone to error and misguidance. Evidently, from the example above, some portrayed him as a peeping Tom.

ʿAlī can be considered one of the most contested figures in Islamic history. Within a few centuries of his death, he had become a respected authority in both Sunnī and Shīʿī Islam, with the latter tradition especially dedicated to his veneration. However, his nearly universal portrayal in Muslim literature as a pious authority obscures a centuries-long process of contestation and rehabilitation. In fact, ʿAlī's revered status in Muslim theology and historiography is surprising in view of the early

[1] Abū 'l-Shaykh, *Ṭabaqāt al-muḥaddithīn bi-Iṣbahān*, 3:303; al-Dhahabī, *Taʾrīkh*, 23:517; Ibn ʿAdī, *al-Kāmil*, 4:266. In some versions of this report, the names of ʿAlī and Umm Salama are omitted: see al-Dhahabī, *Siyar*, 13:229; al-Dhahabī, *Tadhkirat al-ḥuffāẓ*, 2:771.

successes of two separate parties that essentially destroyed him, namely, the Khawārij (sing. Khārijī) and the Umayyads. The former declared ʿAlī an infidel and managed to assassinate him. Their ideology survived and persisted throughout Islamic history in the doctrines of a small sect, the Ibāḍīs. The Umayyads (r. 40–132/661–750) were ʿAlī's political rivals and staunchly denounced him, his legacy, his descendants, and his partisans as criminals, both in his lifetime and after his death. Shortly after his assassination, they succeeded in obtaining the reins of the caliphate and establishing a dynasty based in Syria that lasted close to a century. Medieval sources indicate that rhetoric and propaganda hostile to ʿAlī once permeated all public discourse. When the Umayyad state fell, it is generally assumed that hostility to the legacy of ʿAlī was swept away with it as the Umayyads were replaced by a new dynasty, the ʿAbbāsids, that venerated him. The real story, of course, is not so simple.

This book considers the enduring legacy of early Muslims who were hostile to ʿAlī and his descendants, the ʿAlids. Later Muslim authors acknowledged the existence of such figures associated with "anti-ʿAlid sentiment" (*naṣb*) up to the ninth century. Later representatives of both Sunnī and Shīʿī orthodoxy condemned anti-ʿAlid sentiment as heretical, but many of these anti-ʿAlids nonetheless became revered figures in Sunnī Islam. They made literary contributions that subsequent Sunnī authorities transmitted, and circulated views about ʿAlī that later Sunnīs partially accepted as accurate. This book identifies those anti-ʿAlids and the ways in which their beliefs have impacted Sunnī Islam.

Anti-ʿAlid sentiment has received little scholarly attention for a number of reasons. First, unlike pro-ʿAlid sentiment, which found intellectual backing in Shīʿism, anti-ʿAlid sentiment in its most radical form was not represented by a parallel independent and enduring sect. Radical anti-ʿAlids participated in a variety of ideological and political circles, but it seems that the sects that flourished did not fully embrace their doctrines. Sunnīs adopted only the more moderate beliefs espoused by anti-ʿAlids active in pro-Umayyad and ʿUthmānī circles. The same can be said about Ibāḍism, the sole surviving branch of the Khārijī community that once encompassed numerous rival factions. The Ibāḍīs denounced other, now extinct Khārijī sects as extremists and hence did not preserve the literary works of their rivals. Although Ibāḍīs today mildly condemn ʿAlī and reject any veneration of him, Khārijī anti-ʿAlidism was much more pronounced in previous centuries. Consequently, heresiographers writing in later centuries did not dedicate separate chapters to anti-ʿAlids.

Second, there was a sectarian incentive for Sunnīs to deny the existence of anti-ʿAlid sentiment among the leading personalities who were popularly depicted as harboring such beliefs. The acknowledgment of anti-ʿAlid feelings on the part of any Companion of Muḥammad was irreconcilable with belief in the righteousness of *all* Companions and in the superiority of the earliest generations of Muslims, positions that became orthodox in Sunnism. Certain historical precedents, such as the ritual cursing of ʿAlī from Umayyad pulpits, were undeniably anti-ʿAlid. In these cases, many Sunnīs advised against discussing the problematic events altogether.[2] Scholars argued that such discussions were divisive and had the potential to lead Muslims astray by causing them to dislike some Companions and other venerable predecessors. This kind of history fell under the rubric of *fitna* (civil war: lit., "sedition") and was best avoided. An obvious source of concern for anti-Shīʿī polemicists was that the Sunnī *ḥadīth* corpus occasionally validated Shīʿī arguments about the sinfulness of some Companions and other early authorities.

Sunnī historiography preserves accounts in which Companions, Followers (*tābiʿūn*), caliphs, and other respected authorities appear hostile to ʿAlī. The *Ansāb al-ashrāf* of al-Balādhurī (d. 279/892), for example, includes numerous reports depicting ʿAlī's pro-Umayyad and ʿUthmānī rivals as anti-ʿAlid. The transmitters of these reports likely did not deem it necessary to interpret conflicts between Companions charitably so as to make all of the participants appear righteous. In these sources, Companions are capable of sins and crimes.[3] Loathing ʿAlī is one sin among others that include the sale and consumption of intoxicants,[4] lying,[5] adultery,[6] and mass

[2] Ibn Abī 'l-Ḥadīd, *Sharḥ*, 20:10–12; al-Qurṭubī, *Tafsīr*, 16:321–322.

[3] One example is al-Balādhurī's treatment of ʿUthmān: see Keaney, *Medieval Islamic Historiography*, 30.

[4] For reports about Samura b. Jundab selling intoxicants and Muʿāwiya serving intoxicants to guests, see Aḥmad b. Ḥanbal, *al-Musnad*, 1:25, 5:347. For a report about Muʿāwiya selling them during the caliphate of ʿUthmān, see Abū Nuʿaym al-Iṣbahānī, *Maʿrifat al-ṣaḥāba*, 4:828. In later sources, Muʿāwiya's name is omitted so that the owner of the alcohol remains anonymous: see Ibn ʿAsākir, *Taʾrīkh*, 34:420; Ibn al-Athīr, *Usd al-ghāba*, 3:299.

[5] Ṭalḥa and al-Zubayr pledge allegiance to ʿAlī and ask him permission to leave Medina for pilgrimage when their real intentions are to launch a rebellion: see Ibn Abī 'l-Ḥadīd, *Sharḥ*, 10:248. The two are described as swearing false oaths to ʿĀʾisha in the course of their rebellion: see ibid., 9:311; al-Iskāfī, *al-Miʿyār*, 56; al-Masʿūdī, *Murūj al-dhahab*, 2:358. For a report about Ibn al-Zubayr doing the same, see Abū 'l-Fidāʾ, *Tārīkh*, 1:173; Ibn Aʿtham al-Kūfī, *al-Futūḥ*, 2:458; al-Samʿānī, *al-Ansāb*, 2:286.

[6] For the case involving al-Mughīra b. Shuʿba and Umm Jamīl, see ʿAbd al-Razzāq al-Ṣanʿānī, *al-Muṣannaf*, 7:384; al-Bayhaqī, *al-Sunan al-kubrā*, 8:234–235; Ibn Abī Shayba, *al-Muṣannaf*, 6:560; Ibn Ḥajar al-ʿAsqalānī, *Fatḥ al-bārī*, 5:187.

murder.[7] But by the end of the ninth century, proto-Sunnīs had generally come to reject or reinterpret such reports to avoid identifying their own religious and political authorities as anti-ʿAlid.[8] Such identification would have not only validated the complaints of ʿAlid insurrectionists, who were considered enemies of the state, but also vindicated the claims of their partisans (Shīʿīs), who believed that non-Shīʿīs persistently ignored the rights of ʿAlids and treated them unjustly. Thus, Sunnīs had an incentive to deny the historicity of accounts that depicted certain Companions as anti-ʿAlids. Whenever possible, Sunnī biographers and theologians interpreted reports about anti-ʿAlids so that their actions did not entail animosity for ʿAlī. For example, they portray the rebellion of ʿAlī's most famous antagonist, the future Umayyad caliph Muʿāwiya b. Abī Sufyān (r. 41–60/661–80), as prompted by a simple misunderstanding between the two.[9] In other reports, Muʿāwiya is described as openly admiring and weeping for ʿAlī.[10] As a result, anti-ʿAlid sentiment came to possess an *erased history* in Sunnī Islam.[11] Influential *ḥadīth* scholars of the ninth century began to condemn and cease transmitting many early anti-ʿAlid doctrines that had enjoyed popularity in the Umayyad period. The erasure of the history of anti-ʿAlid sentiment entailed not only its disappearance, but also a denial that it had ever existed among the Companions or their partisans. The suppression of earlier depictions becomes apparent only with a sustained reading of *ḥadīth*, biographical dictionaries, and theological texts.

The absence of anti-ʿAlidism as an independent sect in heresiographies explains the fact that secondary literature generally contains only brief, tangential notes about individuals accused of anti-ʿAlid sentiment without providing a framework to contextualize and judge such claims.

[7] Busr b. Abī Arṭāt is infamous for the murderous raids he led near the end of ʿAlī's caliphate: see Madelung, *Succession*, 299–307.

[8] One can compare portrayals of ʿAlī's political rivals in al-Balādhurī's *Ansāb al-ashrāf* (or Madelung's *The Succession to Muḥammad*) to their presentation in Aḥmad b. Ḥanbal, *Kitāb Faḍāʾil al-ṣaḥāba*. For a passionate defense of the righteousness of Companions and a refutation of their alleged sins, see Ibn al-ʿArabī, *al-ʿAwāṣim*, 280–281, 289, 340. For studies on the historiography of Companions, see Lucas, *Constructive Critics*, 221–285; Osman, "ʿAdālat al-Ṣaḥāba."

[9] According to these Sunnīs, Muʿāwiya and other rebels wanted to punish ʿUthmān's murderers right away, while ʿAlī desired to delay such action until civil strife had subsided. Some Sunnīs speculated that Muʿāwiya believed that the punishment of murderers was a collective obligation (*farḍ kafāʾī*) that anyone could carry out independent of a ruling authority, while ʿAlī believed otherwise: see Amaḥzūn, *Taḥqīq mawāqif al-ṣaḥāba fī ʾl-fitna*, 454; al-Khamīs, *Ḥiqba min al-tārīkh*, 117–120.

[10] Ibn ʿAsākir, *Taʾrīkh*, 24:401–402.

[11] On erased histories, identity politics, and their relationship to memories of pain, see Brown, "Wounded Attachments."

Asma Afsaruddin, Abbas Barzegar, Patricia Crone, Wilferd Madelung, Christopher Melchert, and Muhammad Qasim Zaman have all commented on early anti-ʿAlid attitudes in the nascent Sunnī community, but they have offered neither a comprehensive rubric nor a chronological narrative for understanding the phenomenon.[12] This work aims to fill this lacuna in the study of anti-ʿAlid sentiment in Islamic history.

I survey medieval Muslim literature (from the eighth to the thirteenth centuries) across a number of genres, including *ḥadīth*, biographical, historical, and theological works. References to anti-ʿAlids are frequently elusive and brief. Nonetheless, the diversity of the sources provides rich portrayals of a few key anti-ʿAlid figures and their alleged beliefs. I consider common themes in these texts and the reception of this literature among prominent medieval Muslim scholars who discussed them.

Chapter 1 identifies the phenomenon of anti-ʿAlid sentiment in its varied expressions in early Muslim political and intellectual history. The chapter also provides a framework for researchers to locate and contextualize anti-ʿAlid doctrines that appear in later Sunnī and Ibāḍī historiography. I identify six distinct positions on ʿAlī held by Muslims, and I arrange these doctrines on a spectrum from the ardently pro-ʿAlid to the radically anti-ʿAlid to enable readers to (1) interpret literary depictions of ʿAlī and (2) situate authors who engaged in theological discussions about ʿAlī with like-minded peers even when they were separated by sectarian boundaries, geography, and hundreds of years. The remainder of the book is devoted to the study of influential personalities in Islamic history who articulated anti-ʿAlid doctrines or showed sympathy for them. These case studies are organized chronologically.

Chapter 2 examines the doctrines of two sociopolitical factions that influenced later Sunnī thought: the Umayyads and the ʿUthmāniyya. These two factions were most active in the earliest periods of Islamic history (the seventh and eighth centuries). Historians have attributed the earliest expressions of anti-ʿAlid sentiment to members of these groups (alongside the Khawārij). Since anti-ʿAlids active before the fall of the Umayyads did not leave primary documents discussing ʿAlī, this chapter relies on *ḥadīth* and on biographical and historical literature to elucidate the doctrines of the two groups. The historicity of these portrayals is not of primary importance for this literary survey. At the very least, this literature

[12] *EI*^{2}, s.v. "Imāma" (W. Madelung), "ʿUthmāniyya" (P. Crone); Afsaruddin, *Excellence*, 14–23; Barzegar, "Remembering Community"; Crone, *God's Rule*, 20–32; Melchert, "The Rightly Guided Caliphs," 65–68; Zaman, *Religion and Politics*, 49–63.

documents for us the memories of later Muslims about this early period. Subsequent chapters access the views of influential authors and the religious communities that they represented primarily through the texts they penned themselves.

The case studies in Chapter 2 include Companions of the Prophet and other early Muslims who were portrayed as anti-ʿAlids. A commitment to the belief in the righteousness of the Companions played an important role in the reception of anti-ʿAlid *ḥadīth* in Sunnī Islam. It created an incentive for scholars to reject or charitably reinterpret not only texts that disparaged ʿAlī but also those that portrayed other Companions despising him.

Chapter 3 examines the views of ʿAmr b. Baḥr al-Jāḥiẓ (d. 255/869), a Muʿtazilī bellettrist who lived in a period in which anti-ʿAlid sentiment still ran high in various parts of the Muslim world. His *Risālat al-ʿUthmāniyya* examines the views of one of the factions introduced in the previous chapter and constitutes a seminal text for understanding this anti-ʿAlid current in early Islam. The work of al-Jāḥiẓ foreshadows that of another author, Ibn Taymiyya (d. 728/1328), discussed in Chapter 5. Both provide comprehensive arguments and many proofs in favor of anti-ʿAlid doctrines while claiming to be Muslims who respected ʿAlī. Al-Jāḥiẓ's treatise triggered a number of rebuttals from authors who condemned him as an anti-ʿAlid.

Chapter 4 discusses the literary heritage of one of the least discussed sects in Islamic history, Ibāḍism. The Ibāḍīs portray ʿAlī as having been a righteous Muslim and a legitimate caliph until the end of the battle of Ṣiffīn.[13] At that point, they believe, he fell from grace in his quest for power. This image of ʿAlī differs from ʿUthmānī and Umayyad portrayals of him as vicious and sinful throughout his life. This chapter draws primarily on the *Kitāb al-Dalīl* of Abū Yaʿqūb Yūsuf al-Wārjalānī (d. 570/1175), an influential Ibāḍī scholar, complemented by expressions of anti-ʿAlid views in other authoritative Ibāḍī historical works. Ibāḍī communities in Oman, Zanzibar, and North Africa still rely on such works to understand history and this suggests that the Khārijī legacy of anti-ʿAlidism survives even in the contemporary world.

Chapter 5 examines the writings of the highly influential Sunnī scholar Ibn Taymiyya and those of some of his detractors, who accused him of advocating anti-ʿAlid doctrines. Ibn Taymiyya discussed his views of ʿAlī and anti-ʿAlids in his multivolume anti-Shīʿī work *Minhāj al-sunna al-nabawiyya*. His anti-ʿAlid and anti-Shīʿī claims illuminate the tension

[13] Al-Kāshif, ed., *al-Siyar*, 1:97–104, 371, 375; al-Wārjalānī, *Kitāb al-Dalīl*, 1:28.

that some Sunnīs (and their predecessors such as al-Jāḥiẓ) faced in opposing Shīʿism while simultaneously rejecting anti-ʿAlid sentiments.

The concluding chapter reconsiders certain important assumptions about anti-ʿAlid sentiment: namely, that it was limited to the early Umayyads and Khawārij, and that it played no role in shaping Sunnī theology. Instead, my literary excavation reveals strong indications of an enduring legacy that continued to shape medieval and contemporary Sunnī views about ʿAlī. The conclusion also discusses the methods that Sunnīs used to transform ʿAlī from a villainous character to a righteous one. I draw on canonical *ḥadīth* and parallel recensions in other works to argue that Sunnī writers actively engaged in the process of rehabilitating ʿAlī by censoring, reinterpreting, and emending texts that portrayed him negatively and by circulating counterclaims that exalted him. Scholars also selectively appropriated anti-ʿAlid reports to modulate ʿAlī's image. They tempered the pro-ʿAlid (and Shīʿī) portrayal of ʿAlī as an impeccable saint via reports that portrayed him as sinful or frequently mistaken. On the whole, we can consider Sunnī efforts to construct an image of ʿAlī that differed from both Shīʿī and anti-ʿAlid views to have been successful. After three centuries of contestation, Sunnīs came to value ʿAlī b. Abī Ṭālib universally as nothing less than a knowledgeable Companion, a valiant warrior, and the fourth rightly guided caliph. Most Sunnīs subsequently understood the succession of rightly guided caliphs to indicate their spiritual ranks in the sight of God. Accordingly, ʿAlī could not have acceded to the caliphate before ʿUthmān, ʿUmar, or Abū Bakr since God had ensured that those with the most merit would rule first. However, beyond this simple picture lies an intense history of debate among Muslims both inside and outside the Sunnī community.[14]

Sectarianism between Sunnīs and Shīʿīs is widespread in the Middle East, and continues to affect the region's geopolitics. Public figures in the Middle East aiming to stir up fear or outrage among their supporters may cite historical fault lines between sects in order to drum up opposition to "the other." For example, Arab Shīʿīs are accused of being agents of Iran. Shīʿīs commonly describe Sunnīs supportive of anti-Shīʿī doctrines as "anti-ʿAlids" (*nawāṣib*). Sunnīs vigorously deny the accusation while nevertheless condemning Shīʿī devotion to ʿAlī as misguided. Obviously, there is a longstanding debate on what can and cannot be categorized as "anti-ʿAlid." For example, some Sunnīs deny that the esteemed

14 For an excellent study of debates regarding spiritual precedence, merit, and their relationship to Muslim debates on the caliphate, see Afsaruddin, *Excellence*.

personalities discussed in Chapters 2 and 5 were truly anti-ʿAlids. This book notes these debates and theorizes a framework for resolving such identity questions. I have aimed to make its writing style accessible to a wider audience while providing extensive references to engage with current scholarship.[15] Appendices to Chapters 1, 2, and 5 offer extracts from anti-ʿAlid texts in English translation as illustrative supplements to the themes discussed in their respective chapters.

EARLY PORTRAYALS OF ʿALĪ

This study is not a biography of ʿAlī, although Muslim historiography regarding his life is central to it. Rather, it is an attempt to understand unfavorable depictions of ʿAlī popular in the Umayyad era and their subsequent transmission and reception among Muslim scholars. Despite the warranted objections to the term "proto-Sunnī,"[16] I use it to refer to authorities who lived between the eighth and tenth centuries and appear in influential Sunnī *ḥadīth* collections and legal texts. In spite of their differences, these proto-Sunnī authorities generally considered the first three caliphs to have been legitimate, and apparently abstained from attending Khārijī and Shīʿī circles of learning. Some proto-Sunnīs considered ʿAlī's life to have been one of complete wisdom, whereas others condemned his conduct. Contestation within the Sunnī community regarding ʿAlī's place in history, law, and theology is an important indication of his prominence in the literature.

The author of *Kitāb Sulaym b. Qays* was a Kūfan Shīʿī who denounced the majority of Muslims as misguided for following political leaders other than ʿAlī. Although the narratives in this polemical and hagiographical

15 For simplicity's sake, I reference *ḥadīth* as I do any other literature: I refer to the title of the collection, volume, and page number. Free online access to many of the editions I use is readily available with an Arabic-language search. One website, www.shiaonlinelibrary.com, has digitized essential texts from both the Shīʿī and Sunnī traditions. Those wishing to follow up my citation of a *ḥadīth* from a famous collection (e.g., al-Bukhārī, *Ṣaḥīḥ*, 7:73 or al-Kulaynī, *al-Kāfī*, 8:58) will find that they correspond to these digitized editions. To accommodate various editions of a single collection, academic conventions in the citation of *ḥadīth* have changed over the years to include *bāb*, *ḥadīth* number, or the first sentence of the text. One drawback to implementing these conventions is their inconsistent adoption for some *ḥadīth* collections and not others. For these reasons, I avoid their use and hope the above alternative meets the needs of those desiring to perform Arabic-language searches of *ḥadīth*.

16 For a discussion of the methodological problems associated with the term, see Dann, "Contested Boundaries," 8–14.

Shīʿī text do not seem to offer any reliable historical information, its reproduction of a sermon of ʿAlī's summarizing the edicts of the first three caliphs deserves some attention.[17] The sermon depicts ʿAlī as a nonconformist, frequently disagreeing with the judgments of his predecessors and thus diverging from other Companions who adopted the opinions of the first three caliphs.[18] Shīʿī writers emphasized the motif of ʿAlī's nonconformism to the point of making it seem that ʿAlī never agreed with the actions of the other caliphs; but this depiction is not entirely faithful to the sources. Twelver Shīʿī law and ethics, which claim to reflect the opinions of ʿAlī, converge so frequently with Sunnism and the views of other Companions that the claim that ʿAlī *always* disagreed with his peers is unwarranted.

Nonetheless, this Umayyad-era portrayal of ʿAlī as a dissident is echoed by prominent proto-Sunnī *ḥadīth* transmitters, who depict him or his family members contradicting the first three caliphs on a variety of issues. They also report that ʿAlī considered himself to be the most qualified person to lead the community after the Prophet's death. *Naṣb* (anti-ʿAlid sentiment) and *tashayyuʿ* (pro-ʿAlid sentiment) stood against each other as currents in the nascent Sunnī community, always in perpetual conflict, both politically and intellectually. Anti-ʿAlids considered ʿAlī the worst calamity to befall the community, whereas his partisans saw him as a peerless and charismatic leader. A third group consisted of Muslims who were ambivalent about ʿAlī's personality and treated him simply as a Companion no different from other Companions of the Prophet. For them, ʿAlī was liable to making mistakes, but he was not evil. This middle ground between the warring factions eventually became the hallmark of Sunnism, and it enshrined the Sunni view of ʿAlī as a nondescript personality among many righteous peers.

Various Sunnī and Shīʿī sources have depicted ʿAlī's kin, close friends in Medina, and disciples in Kūfa as the earliest individuals who championed

[17] *Kitāb Sulaym*, 262–265; al-Kulaynī, *al-Kāfī*, 8:58–63 (for one relevant commentary). See also al-ʿAskarī, *Maʿālim*, 2:352–356.

[18] For discussions regarding ʿAlī's views on the caliphate and the Prophet's estates, see *Encyclopaedia Islamica*, s.v. "ʿAlī b. Abī Ṭālib" (F. Manouchehri, M. Melvin-Koushki, R. Shah-Kazemi, et al.); Jafri, *Origins*; Madelung, *Succession.* For the divergent opinions of ʿAlī and his family on the origin of the *adhān*, the phrase "come to the best of works," *sahm dhī 'l-qurba*, the waiting period of a widow who is pregnant, and certain rituals related to the pilgrimage, see Abū Yaʿlā al-Mawṣilī, *Musnad*, 5:123–124; Aḥmad b. Ḥanbal, *al-Musnad*, 1:135; al-Bayhaqī, *al-Sunan al-kubrā*, 1:425; Ibn Abī Shayba, *al-Muṣannaf*, 1:244, 3:342, 374, 393–394, 4:341; Ibn Ḥibbān, *Ṣaḥīḥ*, 11:155–156; Ibn Shāhīn, *Nāsikh al-ḥadīth wa mansūkhuh*, 272–275.

his views and resolutely followed them despite their divergence from the community's normative practice. This pro-ʿAlid faction generally believed that the community had wronged ʿAlī in rebelling against him during his reign as caliph, while some considered him the direct heir of the Prophet's authority. Shīʿism eventually came to represent the sentiments of the latter group and developed its own literary tradition that embellished (sometimes clearly ahistorical) anecdotes in which ʿAlī would display his superior wisdom at the expense of the first three caliphs.[19] However, the same motif exists implicitly in Sunnī sources as well.[20] Theological, historical, and biographical works written in Sunnī and Shīʿī circles alike mention individuals and groups who believed in the superiority of ʿAlī (*tafḍīl ʿAlī*) in relation to other Companions. For example, members of ʿAlī's own clan (the Hāshimids), a number of Companions, and Kūfans who fought for him all appear as proponents of *tafḍīl ʿAlī* in various genres of Sunnī literature. Some Muʿtazilī and Sufi scholars became proponents of *tafḍīl ʿAlī* in later centuries. It is frequently unclear whether this *tafḍīl* was spiritual, political, or both.[21] The scope of this book, however, is limited to the study of anti-ʿAlid sentiment.

Anti-ʿAlidism appears to have been fairly common among some populations before its suppression and virtual extinction among Sunnīs. Early anti-ʿAlids despised the personality of ʿAlī and considered him to have been evil. They likewise condemned those who cherished the memory of ʿAlī as heretics. On the other hand, influential *ḥadīth* scholars of the ninth century, such as Aḥmad b. Ḥanbal (d. 241/855), are reported to have expressed public discontent with peers and predecessors who had displayed anti-ʿAlid sentiment.[22] The formation of Sunnism as a social and intellectual tradition seems to have encouraged the censure of eccentric views at both the pro-ʿAlid and the anti-ʿAlid end of the spectrum.

THE SIGNIFICANCE OF MUSLIM HISTORIOGRAPHY

This book does not attempt to provide a definitive narrative of the life of ʿAlī or to judge the historicity of the reports on which it draws. The historicity of accounts describing events in the life of the Prophet and his

[19] For example, see Ibn Shahrāshūb, *Manāqib*, 2:178–194.

[20] For example, see Abū Dāwūd al-Sijistānī, *Sunan*, 2:339; al-Ḥākim al-Naysābūrī, *al-Mustadrak*, 1:457; al-Khuwārizmī, *al-Manāqib*, 80–81, 95–96, 99–101.

[21] For a comprehensive study of *tafḍīl ʿAlī*, see Mamdūḥ, *Ghāyat al-tabjīl*, 113–205.

[22] See Chapter 6.

Companions, including ʿAlī, has been subject to vigorous academic debate. Jonathan Brown and other scholars have accurately described many of the tensions and methodological issues involved in utilizing classical Muslim historiography and *ḥadīth* as sources for history.[23] The tendency of pro-ʿAlid Sunnī and Shīʿī writers to exalt ʿAlī and, conversely, that of the ʿUthmāniyya to laud ʿAlī's political rivals certainly problematize efforts to establish an "objective" historical description of events. As a result, most claims to objective historical truth about this early period should be viewed with caution.[24] A comparative reading of the past may yield valuable information by revealing points of agreement between sources representing mutually antagonistic views.[25] However, the possibility of opposing factions simply sharing some cultural myths engenders some uncertainty in even these historical kernels.[26] Our understanding of the past is inevitably conditioned by the memories, narrative techniques, and interpretations of right and wrong of the authors who produce those accounts. Thus, modern historians of Islam have begun to use documentary evidence such as coins, Arabic papyri, and inscriptions on mountains and tombstones to check and supplement literary sources.[27]

The work of Abbas Barzegar, Najam Haider, Tayeb El-Hibri, Erling Petersen, and Denise Spellberg reflects an important turn away from debates about historicity.[28] These scholars have engaged with Muslim historiography to better understand the values of the communities that produced those disputed narratives about the past. This book adopts a similar methodological approach, which views *ḥadīth* and Muslim historiography as attempts to produce collective identities and the historical narratives that validate them.[29] To what extent those narratives reflect historical reality is a debate I leave to other historians who may wish to pursue it. The literary analysis of such texts, however, provides rich information regarding the beliefs of the agents who produced them.

[23] Brown, *Hadith*, 197–275; Donner, *Narratives*; Noth and Conrad, *Early Arabic Historical Tradition*; Spellberg, *Politics, Gender, and the Islamic Past*, 1–25.

[24] For references to studies that understand historical narratives as a particular type of cultural memory, see Kansteiner, "Finding Meaning in Memory," 184.

[25] Donner, *Narratives*, 25–31, 138–141, 285–290; Husayn, "Scepticism and Uncontested History"; Sadeghi and Bergmann, "Codex of a Companion," 364–366.

[26] Gedi and Elam, "Collective Memory."

[27] Saifullah and David, "The Codex of a Companion of the Prophet."

[28] Barzegar, "Remembering Community"; Haider, *The Rebel and the Imām*; El-Hibri, *Parable and Politics*; Petersen, *ʿAlī and Muʿāwiya*; Spellberg, *Politics, Gender, and the Islamic Past.*

[29] Barzegar, "Remembering Community," 19–43; Keaney, *Medieval Islamic Historiography*, 3–5, 19; Spellberg, *Politics, Gender, and the Islamic Past*, 11.

Further insight can be gleaned from the social and intellectual history of scholars who shared in the authorial enterprise of *ḥadīth* by composing biographical dictionaries. In addition to providing prosopographical details, biographical entries show how later *ḥadīth* specialists negotiated the identity and contributions of controversial predecessors in the community. Thus, for example, I analyze the reports of Sayf b. ʿUmar al-Tamīmī (d. ca. 180/796) about the caliphate of ʿAlī not for a better understanding of ʿAlī, but for what they reveal about ways in which Kūfan ʿUthmānīs of the eighth century narrated early political conflicts and judged the characters of ʿAlī, his disciples, and his rivals.

When a *ḥadīth* appears in multiple collections, a comparison of the variants can also provide information about the sensibilities of early Muslim historians. When one documents the transmission and reception of a report about a legal dispute involving ʿAlī across multiple sources, it quickly becomes apparent which compilers frequently made use of their editorial privilege by censoring material they considered objectionable. For example, Muḥammad b. Ismāʿīl al-Bukhārī (d. 256/869), who compiled the most revered collection of canonical *ḥadīth* in the Sunnī tradition,[30] was strongly inclined to omit dialogue that his predecessors and contemporaries preserved. According to the canonical collection of Muslim b. al-Ḥajjāj (d. 261/875), the second caliph, ʿUmar b. al-Khaṭṭāb (d. 23/644), criticized ʿAlī for calling him and Abū Bakr (d. 13/634) sinful and deceitful, but in al-Bukhārī's collection ʿAlī is criticized vaguely for claiming "this and that" (*kadhā wa kadhā*).[31] Al-Bukhārī thus omitted ʿAlī's explicit affront to the honor of the first and second caliphs. Even if respected proto-Sunnī transmitters of the previous century had accepted the historicity of the described exchange, al-Bukhārī was careful not to include material that would vindicate Shīʿī sentiments about the first two caliphs or ʿAlī. Such case studies demonstrate the important role that the editorial enterprise played in constructing orthodoxy in Sunnism in the ninth century.

It is not uncommon to find contemporary researchers affirming the particular historical vision of Sunnī *ḥadīth* specialists as "orthodox," "unbiased," or "neutral." In doing so, pro-ʿAlid reports were automatically suspect, biased, and labeled as Shīʿī contributions. For example, in a study of interpretations of a qurʾānic verse (Q33:33) regarding the Prophet's family, a modern author characterizes ʿUthmānī (and possibly Khārijī) reports on the verse as "exegetically neutral," in contrast to pro-ʿAlid

[30] See Brown, *Canonization*. [31] See Chapter 6.

and Hāshimid reports, which have "political and factional undertones."[32] In this case, it was the pro-ʿAlid reports that eventually entered Sunnī canonical *ḥadīth* collections.[33] These reports lauded the purity of Fāṭima, the daughter of the Prophet, and her household. The anti-ʿAlid reports that claimed the verse had nothing to do with ʿAlī and his family were in fact polemical ʿUthmānī rebuttals. Neither the ʿUthmānī nor the pro-ʿAlid reports can be described as neutral, since they represent fundamentally different scriptural hermeneutics and the exaltation of saints in competing communities. As Barzegar notes: "Historical narration, that is, any speech act that lays claim towards the recollection [of] past events, contains a moralizing impulse and produces a legitimating function, because it posits one interpretation over and against another. Even in its singularity, a solitary historical account is always part of a debate."[34] Scholars debated Q33:33's relationship to ʿAlī and his family by transmitting those reports that agreed with their sensibilities. Some participants in this debate were pro-ʿAlid, while others were not.

Thus, a narrative about the past can always "be read as an argument between groups."[35] The ethos of a community is built on mythmaking and storytelling. A representative of any community holds himself accountable in narrating its view of the past. Although the collective memory of a community can be described as a "metanarrative" or a "myth," myth does not necessarily denote something fantastic or false.[36] Rather, myth is "ideology in narrative form."[37] Therefore, we must understand historical reporting as a discursive tradition that produces communities through the articulation and transmission of their ideologies. In Muslim historiography and *ḥadīth*, competing subcommunities argued for their particular narratives of the past through agents who eulogized certain predecessors while explicitly or implicitly discrediting their rivals. Through selected case studies, this book analyzes the methods that Muslims utilized to contest the image of ʿAlī in theological, legal, historical, biographical, and *ḥadīth* literature.

This investigation also lies at the intersection of studies on Sunnī orthodoxy, *ḥadīth*, and identity formation. Since the crystallization of

[32] Sharon, "Ahl al-Bayt," 174–175. Many of the anti-ʿAlid reports are transmitted on the authority of ʿIkrama, the client of ʿAbd Allāh ibn ʿAbbās who reportedly became a Khārijī: see Ibn ʿAsākir, *Taʾrīkh*, 41:120.

[33] Al-Fīrūzābādī, *Faḍāʾil al-khamsa*, 1:224–243; Ibn Kathīr, *Tafsīr al-Qurʾān al-ʿaẓīm*, 3:491–492; Muslim, *Ṣaḥīḥ*, 7:130.

[34] Barzegar, "Remembering Community," 25. [35] Ibid.

[36] Barzegar, "Remembering Community," 26; Gedi and Elam, "Collective Memory."

[37] Barzegar, "Remembering Community," 26; Lincoln, *Theorizing Myth*, 147.

Sunnism in the eleventh century, debates regarding the precedence of ʿAlī in Sunnī theology have largely subsided. The suppression of anti-ʿAlid sentiment coincided with Sunnī efforts to promote a four-caliph theory that accepted ʿAlī as rightly guided after centuries of defamation in many regions. I discuss the impact of the four-caliph theory on the memory of ʿAlī in the Conclusion.

I

ʿAlī: A Contested Legacy

There was once a famous scholar who agreed to tutor the young sons of a caliph. He would travel to a palace located in the deserts of Syria to share his knowledge of *ḥadīth* and instruct the royal family in religion. One day, the tutor found the head of the Muslim community, the caliph himself, reading the Qurʾān. The caliph stopped on the verse, "Surely those who committed slander were a gang among you … Each one shall have his share of the sin that he has earned. As for the one who initiated it, he shall have a grievous chastisement" (Q24:11).

The Umayyad caliph was familiar with this story, in which members of the community falsely accuse the Prophet's wife of infidelity. But the ensuing exchange between the caliph and the tutor shows that in the Umayyads' telling of the tale, the role of the unnamed villain who initiated the slander and would consequently face a "grievous chastisement" was played by the Prophet's son-in-law ʿAlī.[1] Only a few sources report the conversation between the tutor and the caliph, but these sources include *Ṣaḥīḥ al-Bukhārī*, the most revered *ḥadīth* collection in Sunnism.[2] Thus, the belief of some early Muslims that ʿAlī had been capable of such a deed is preserved as canon in Sunnī Islam.

Anti-ʿAlid sentiment constitutes one end of a spectrum. As the early Muslim community split into rival factions, many grappled with ʿAlī's

[1] ʿAbd al-Razzāq al-Ṣanʿānī, *Tafsīr al-Qurʾān*, 3:51–52; al-Bukhārī, *Ṣaḥīḥ*, 5:60; Ibn Ḥajar al-ʿAsqalānī, *Fatḥ al-bārī*, 7:335–337.

[2] Al-Bukhārī only provides a brief excerpt of the report, omitting portions wherein the caliph declares ʿAlī to be the real source of all the slander. In al-Bukhārī's report, the caliph only asks the tutor if he came across versions of the story in which ʿAlī had been a culprit: see al-Bukhārī, *Ṣaḥīḥ*, 5:60.

legacy and arrived at divergent conclusions. Was ʿAlī a sinner or a saint? A legitimate caliph or a pretender? A Shīʿī imām or an ordinary Companion? Despite the normative Sunnī practice of dismissing Shīʿism as heresy, over the centuries Sunnī *ḥadīth* specialists devoted many works to enumerating the merits of ʿAlī and his family.[3] The Sunnī *ḥadīth* tradition was complemented by various Sufi orders that granted ʿAlī a preeminent role in their cosmology and spirituality.[4] Although Shīʿism as a sect was particularly devoted to the veneration of ʿAlī and his progeny (the ʿAlids), by the twelfth century pro-ʿAlid sentiment had become a trans-sectarian phenomenon. Sunnīs in many regions and living under various empires revered the Prophet's family, and sometimes recognized his kin as having succeeded him in spiritual authority. But such near-universal approval of ʿAlī was a later development: it is clear that some early Muslims viewed ʿAlī with contempt, and they left a legacy of doctrines and texts in Sunnī Islam that warrants consideration.

Shortly after ʿAlī's death, the Umayyads ascended to power, and medieval sources indicate that they publicly endorsed and disseminated anti-ʿAlid rhetoric. Umayyad governors reportedly cursed him from the pulpits on Fridays.[5] In the Umayyad period, non-Shīʿī scholars of *ḥadīth* and law distanced themselves from prominent ʿAlids lest they be labeled Shīʿīs themselves and face persecution.[6] Poets also publicly denied the merits of ʿAlids – not only to please their royal benefactors, but also to influence public opinion on the matter.[7] As a result of political developments and rivalries, certain towns, such as Damascus and Baṣra, became famous for their populations' outspoken anti-ʿAlid sentiment.[8]

[3] For example, al-Ījī, *Tawḍīḥ al-dalāʾil*; al-Kanjī, *Kifāyat al-ṭālib*; al-Nasāʾī, *Khaṣāʾiṣ*.

[4] Nasr, "Shiʿism and Sufism"; Rahim, "Perfection Manifested"; Yildirim, "Shīʿitisation of the Futuwwa Tradition in the Fifteenth Century," 53–70.

[5] See Chapter 2. See also Ibn Abī ʾl-Ḥadīd, *Sharḥ*, 4:56–63; van Ess, "Political Ideas," 154 n. 20.

[6] Al-Dhahabī, *Siyar*, 7:130–131 (for a report that al-Awzaʿī and scholars of the Umayyad court were coerced to swear that ʿAlī was a hypocrite to receive their stipends); Ibn Abī ʾl-Ḥadīd, *Sharḥ*, 6:44–47; Ibn Ḥajar al-ʿAsqalānī, *Tahdhīb al-Tahdhīb*, 9:116 (for the murder of the Companion Muḥammad b. Maslama because he refused to help Muʿāwiya in his wars); Ibn Qutayba, *al-Ikhtilāf*, 54. See also Muḥammad b. ʿAqīl al-ʿAlawī, *al-ʿAtb al-jamīl*, 116–118; al-Kuthayrī, *al-Salafiyya*, 609–610.

[7] Ibn Sukkara al-Hāshimī (d. 385/995) was an ʿAbbāsid who allegedly claimed in his poetry that ʿAlī unjustly rebelled (*baghā*) against Muʿāwiya and that the Umayyads justifiably killed al-Ḥusayn: see al-Amīnī, *al-Ghadīr*, 4:90 (who cites an unpublished copy of the *Diwān Ibn al-Ḥajjāj*); al-Muʿallim, *al-Nuṣb wa ʾl-nawāṣib*, 463. For geographic regions and cities that publicly expressed animosity toward ʿAlī, see al-Muʿallim, *al-Nuṣb wa ʾl-nawāṣib*, 229–244.

[8] The people of Baṣra were known to have contempt for ʿAlī: see Ibn Abī ʾl-Ḥadīd, *Sharḥ*, 4:103 (who cites Abū Jaʿfar al-Iskāfī); al-Thaqafī, *al-Ghārāt*, 2:554. In one narrative,

BLURRED LINES

It is often difficult to distinguish between zealous Sunnī pro-ʿAlid sentiment and Shīʿism. Pro-ʿAlid Sunnīs in the premodern and contemporary period are frequently accused of heresy and crypto-Shīʿism.[9] Their veneration of and beliefs about the Prophet's Household (*ahl al-bayt*) complicate sectarian boundaries and undermine simplistic assumptions about Sunnī and Shīʿī Islam. A similar problem arises in analyzing the work of polemicists engaged in the refutation of Shīʿism. Sometimes such refutations appeared to veer from opposition to Shīʿism toward contempt for ʿAlī and his progeny. Although these polemicists acknowledged ʿAlī's piety and the importance of honoring him, in their efforts to discredit Shīʿism they occasionally appealed to the arguments of early anti-ʿAlids who had sought to tarnish ʿAlī's reputation. Although the two appear to be mutually exclusive, some Shīʿīs defined *naṣb* (anti-ʿAlid sentiment) to include anti-Shīʿī sentiment as a symptom.[10]

Since the crystallization of Twelver Shīʿism occurred within a broader community of Imāmīs that had historically maintained belief in the divine appointment of imāms, theologians sometimes referred to Twelvers as Imāmīs. Twelvers occasionally lambasted other Muslims who rejected Imāmī doctrine as anti-ʿAlids. For example, some early pro-ʿAlids in Kūfa reportedly revered Abū Bakr, ʿUmar, and other Companions. Zaydīs who followed their example by expressing respect for the first two caliphs were either accused of anti-ʿAlid sentiment or cursed in Imāmī literature.[11] For Imāmīs, a Zaydī's devotion to ʿAlī and his progeny did not suffice to absolve him of the charge of anti-ʿAlidism if he showed

a group of Baṣrans command a narrator to desist from transmitting any of Jaʿfar al-Ṣādiq's *ḥadīth* to them: see Ibn Ḥajar al-ʿAsqalānī, *Tahdhīb al-Tahdhīb*, 1:312. See also al-Muʿallim, *al-Nuṣb wa ʾl-nawāṣib*, 232–234. Baṣrans also joined Muʿāwiya in opposition to the caliphate of al-Ḥasan b. ʿAlī: see *EI*², s.v. "ʿUthmāniyya" (P. Crone). For Damascus, see al-Dhahabī, *Siyar*, 3:128, 15:476, 18:617.

9 One premodern example is Sibṭ ibn al-Jawzī (d. 654/1256): see Ibn Ḥajar al-ʿAsqalānī, *Lisān al-Mīzān*, 6:328. For the case of Ḥasan b. Farḥān al-Mālikī (b. 1390/1970), see ʿAbbād al-Badr, *al-Intiṣār*, 13–20.

10 In a report attributed to Jaʿfar al-Ṣādiq, he explains that anti-ʿAlids can no longer denigrate the Prophet's kin in public, so they indirectly do so by denigrating their loyal partisans: see al-Baḥrānī, *al-Ḥadāʾiq al-nāḍira*, 5:177, 185, 10:361–362; Ibn Bābawayh, *ʿIlal al-sharāʾiʿ*, 2:601; al-Ṭurayḥī, *Majmaʿ al-baḥrayn*, 2:173–174.

11 For example, Sālim b. Abī Ḥafṣa and Kathīr al-Nawwāʾ are Batrīs criticized and cursed in the literature: see al-Kulaynī, *al-Kāfī*, 2:403; al-Māzandarānī, *Sharḥ Usūl al-Kāfī*, 10:56–57; al-Ṭūsī, *Ikhtiyār maʿrifat al-rijāl*, 2:503–505.

contempt for the Twelver imāms or Imāmī theology.[12] Over the centuries, Twelvers also described Mu'tazilīs and Sunnīs who penned refutations of Shī'ism, such as al-Jāḥiẓ and Ibn Ḥajar al-Haytamī (d. 974/1566), as anti-'Alids.[13]

In essence, Shī'ism is distinguished by its restriction of ultimate authority to 'Alids, who are understood to be the Prophet's rightful successors. By contrast, pro-'Alid attitudes among non-Shī'īs (e.g., Sunnīs and Mu'tazilīs) encompassed a variety of beliefs ranging from hostility to Mu'āwiya to belief in the divine selection of 'Alids for religious authority and esoteric knowledge. Non-Shī'īs who were zealous pro-'Alids still recognized the Companions and other early jurists as authoritative sources of law and practice. Can one venerate and love the Prophet's family but despise Shī'ism? Can one oppose the special veneration of 'Alī without harboring hatred for him as well? The existence of both pro-'Alid and nonpartisan Sunnīs who exalted any and every Companion seems to answer both questions in the affirmative.

TRAVERSING THE SPECTRUM

Muslims of the eighth and ninth centuries can be classified into six broad categories according to their pro- and anti-'Alid sentiments.

*Group 1 Anti-'Alids (*Nawāṣib*) Openly Hostile to 'Alī and his Progeny*

The explicitly anti-'Alid Group 1 consisted mainly of Umayyads, Khawārij, and early 'Uthmānīs who supported the first three caliphs and joined 'Ā'isha's army (against 'Alī) in the battle of the Camel in 36/656. Members of these factions disparaged 'Alī and his family, sought

[12] For portrayals of 'Alids upset with al-Ḥusayn b. 'Alī and Ja'far al-Ṣādiq, see al-Kulaynī, *al-Kāfī*, 1:359, 362–363. For Zaydī attacks on Imāmī conceptions of the imāmate and the competency of child imāms such as Muḥammad al-Jawād, see al-Rassī, *al-Radd 'alā 'l-rāfiḍa*, 98–101.

[13] Ibn Ṭāwūs, *Binā' al-maqāla*, 59; al-Tustarī, *Maṣā'ib al-nawāṣib*, 1:60, 89, 234, 2:73; al-Tustarī, *al-Ṣawārim al-murhiqa*, 329. For Shī'ī condemnation of other prominent thinkers such as Wāṣil b. 'Aṭā' (d. 131/748), Abū 'Alī al-Jubbā'ī (d. 303/915), al-Qāḍī Abū Bakr al-Bāqillānī (d. 403/1013), al-Qāḍī 'Abd al-Jabbār (d. 415/1025), Ibn Khaldūn (d. 808/1406), and the exegete Shihāb al-Dīn al-Ālūsī (d. 1270/1854), see al-Mu'allim, *al-Nuṣb wa 'l-nawāṣib*, 264, 279–280, 350, 353, 459, 464, 478, 512.

deliberately to cause pain to members of the Prophet's Household, and considered ʿAlī a criminal.

Group 2 Those Opposed to any Special Veneration of ʿAlī

The second category comprised *ahl al-ḥadīth*, anti-Shīʿī politicians and polemicists, some Ḥanbalīs, and individuals with no knowledge of or interest in ʿAlī's biography. The members of this group generally venerated other Companions in place of ʿAlī. They did not condemn ʿAlī as a person, but their political and theological allegiances kept them from revering him. They typically voiced reservations about ʿAlī's conduct as caliph or about the appropriateness of treating him as a uniquely special person. Ibn Taymiyya, for example, did both.[14]

The Ḥanbalīs in this group may have objected to veneration of ʿAlī on the grounds that venerating any objects or persons other than God was fundamentally wrong. Others refused to accept the validity of any Shīʿī beliefs or practices. For them, all Companions were equally righteous and deserving of adoration, and there was no difference in this regard between those who were related to the Prophet and those who were not. In their zeal to defend Sunnī orthodoxy, some Sunnīs stridently denied the authenticity of *ḥadīth* about the merits (*manāqib*, *faḍāʾil*) of the *ahl al-bayt* and attached no substantive meaning or value to kinship with the Prophet.

Group 3 Those Opposed to Tafḍīl ʿAlī

The members of the third group ranked ʿAlī as the Prophet's greatest Companion after Abū Bakr, ʿUmar, and ʿUthmān. This quintessential Sunnī doctrine allowed scholars to accept and transmit some pro-ʿAlid *ḥadīth* alongside Umayyad and ʿUthmānī reports. However, the members of this group usually objected to *tafḍīl ʿAlī*, or belief in ʿAlī's superiority to all others after the Prophet.[15] Belief in the legitimacy of the first three caliphs, in the righteousness of Companions who waged war against ʿAlī (e.g., ʿĀʾisha and Muʿāwiya), and in the integrity of Sunnī canonical *ḥadīth* led members of this group to reject some distinctions ascribed to ʿAlī and to interpret the actions of his rivals charitably. Others, such as Ibn

14 Ibn Taymiyya, *Minhāj*, 4:389, 392, 5:6–7.

15 Ibn Abī Yaʿlā, *Ṭabaqāt al-Ḥanābila*, 1:172, 2:120; Ibn ʿAsākir, *Taʾrīkh*, 39:506. For Sunnī debates on *tafḍīl*, see Mamdūḥ, *Ghāyat al-tabjīl*.

ʿAbd al-Barr (d. 463/1071), acknowledged that a few Companions and early figures respected as *ḥadīth* authorities considered ʿAlī and his family the most meritorious Muslims after the Prophet.[16] Although these authors were not proponents of *tafḍīl ʿAlī*, they abstained from condemning it as heresy.

Many Sunnī scholars who believed in the merits of ʿAlī and the *ahl al-bayt* considered ʿAlī's family to be a special group but would not allow this belief to contradict their view of the first three caliphs or other Companions. For most Sunnīs, allegiance to the early caliphs required an affirmation of their merits over those of ʿAlī.

Group 4 Those Opposed to the Veneration of ʿAlī as a Miraculous Imām

The members of Group 4 ranked ʿAlī as the greatest Muslim after the Prophet Muḥammad, affirming the doctrine of *tafḍīl ʿAlī*. But they opposed popular Imāmī depictions of ʿAlī and his descendants as individuals endowed with miraculous abilities, clairvoyance, familiarity with alchemy, knowledge of all languages (including communication with various types of animals), and power over the natural world.

Muslims in this group held ʿAlī to have been the best candidate for the caliphate after the Prophet and superior to all of his peers in merit. Some believed that God had designated ʿAlī to succeed the Prophet directly as an imām, a legatee (*waṣī*), or a spiritual master and saint (*walī*). The political significance attributed to this succession differed between various types of Muslims. This group encompassed some early Imāmīs, Zaydīs, Muʿtazilīs, pro-ʿAlid Sufis, and a small number of other Sunnīs.[17]

Group 5 Those Opposed to ʿAlī's Deification

Group 5 consisted mostly of Imāmīs who rejected only ʿAlī's deification. Imāmī *ḥadīth* literature is full of reports in which various groups and their leaders are cursed and condemned as *ghulāt* (radical Shīʿīs) for ascribing divinity to ʿAlī.[18] Although the previous four groups also opposed the deification of any member of the Household, Group 5 was distinguished

[16] Ibn ʿAbd al-Barr, *al-Istīʿāb*, 2:799, 3:1090, 1116.

[17] For an overview of Muslim doctrines on ʿAlī, see *Encyclopaedia Islamica*, s.v. "ʿAlī b. Abī Ṭālib" (F. Manouchehri, M. Melvin-Koushki, R. Shah-Kazemi, et al.).

[18] Kohlberg, "Barāʾa in Shīʿī Doctrine," 164–167.

by its portrayal of ʿAlī and his descendants as endowed with miraculous powers over the natural world. In their view, the imāms possessed expertise in divination and the occult, infallibility that shielded them from all types of mistakes, and some level of omniscience that was not learned but inspired.

Group 6 Ghulāt

The members of this final group deified the Household of the Prophet as manifestations of God. This group included people whom the Imāmīs described as *ghulāt*, *mufawwiḍa* (who believed that God had bestowed His divine responsibilities on the imāms), and Nuṣayrīs.[19] Many of them believed that the Prophet and the imāms were endowed with divine abilities, such as the power to manage the affairs of the universe. These beliefs put them at odds with other early Imāmīs who denied that the imāms possessed divine capabilities.[20] There is also evidence that these groups were exclusivist and cast non-Shīʿīs and members of other groups as infidels.[21]

ANTI-SHĪʿĪ OR ANTI-ʿALID?

This book focuses principally on individuals whom later writers classified into Groups 1 and 2. Historically, some members of Group 2 may have hated ʿAlī and his progeny in addition to opposing their veneration. However, when a person dismissed as false claims of ʿAlid exceptionalism but refrained from attacking ʿAlī and his family as evil, I consider the two sentiments to be mutually exclusive. Such a person only appears to be a member of Group 2. Group 2's opposition to the veneration of ʿAlids should be differentiated from Group 1's open contempt for them. Ibn Taymiyya's detractors cite his many radically anti-Shīʿī dialectical positions as evidence of his membership in Group 1 or 2. Although Ibn

19 Ibn Shahrāshūb, *Manāqib*, 1:228 (for a description of the Nuṣayrīs). See also Friedman, "al-Husayn ibn Hamdān al-Khasībī." Isḥāq al-Aḥmar (d. 286/899) reportedly believed that ʿAlī was God incarnate. He was considered an authority of the *ghulāt* and close to Nuṣayrīs in doctrine: see al-Dhahabī, *Mīzān al-iʿtidāl*, 1:196–197.

20 For a summary of this historical tension in the Imāmī community, see Modarressi, *Crisis*, 20–51.

21 In one narrative, Abū al-Khaṭṭāb argues that non-Shīʿīs were *kāfirūn*: see Dakake, *Charismatic Community*, 188. For the groups associated with him, see *EI*², s.v. "Khaṭṭābiyya" (W. Madelung).

Taymiyya did not have high regard for ʿAlī's political career, he nonetheless claimed to uphold the values of Group 3, the vanguard of orthodox Sunnism.[22] Among Sunnīs, Ibn Ḥajar al-ʿAsqalānī (d. 852/1449) was a respected *ḥadīth* scholar with nonpartisan (rather than pro-ʿAlid) sensibilities. He criticized Ibn Taymiyya in the following terms:

> I examined [Ibn Taymiyya's *Minhāj al-sunna*] … but I found it extremely prejudiced and unfair (*kathīr al-taḥāmul*) in achieving its purpose of refuting the *ḥadīth* that Ibn al-Muṭahhar mentioned, even if the majority of them were fabricated and baseless. In the process, he refuted a multitude of *ḥadīth* considered first-rate (*jiyād*) … One cannot count the number of times that excessively discrediting the *rāfiḍī*'s words led him to belittle (*tanqīṣ*) ʿAlī.[23]

Ibn Taymiyya held that ʿAlī possessed no unique merit in the Islamic tradition.[24] Al-Bukhārī, Ibn Ḥazm (d. 456/1064), and Muḥammad b. Yaʿqūb al-Fīrūzābādī (d. 817/1415), too, denied the uniqueness and authenticity of ʿAlī's alleged merits in their respective works, as did the Muʿtazilī al-Jāḥiẓ in his treatise on the doctrines of the ʿUthmāniyya. The contributions of these authors are surveyed later in this chapter and in the chapters that follow.

Pro-ʿAlid Sunnīs exalted ʿAlī by transmitting hundreds of *ḥadīth* about his alleged distinctions with chains of transmission that they considered acceptable. Some Sunnīs, such as Aḥmad b. Jalāl al-Dīn al-Ījī (active ca. 820/1417), extolled ʿAlī out of strong pro-ʿAlid proclivities, whereas others, such as Aḥmad b. Ḥanbal, did so as part of a culture that collectively honored all of the Prophet's Companions. Chapters 3 and 5 engage with a selection of ʿUthmānī and anti-Shīʿī arguments found in the works of al-Jāḥiẓ and Ibn Taymiyya. I examine the writings of these two authors because they joined other members of Group 2 in rejecting the authenticity of most *ḥadīth* about ʿAlī's merits or reasoning that his merits were neither significant nor unique.

Al-Bukhārī mentions six *ḥadīth* about ʿAlī in his chapter dedicated to ʿAlī's merits, but only three can be characterized as pro-ʿAlid reports intended to praise him. According to al-Bukhārī, the Prophet said to ʿAlī, "I am from you and you are from me" and "You are unto me like Aaron unto Moses," and he described ʿAlī as a man whom God and His Prophet loved before giving him the banner at the battle of Khaybar.[25]

[22] He states that no one was more meritorious than ʿAlī except for the three caliphs who preceded him: see Ibn Taymiyya, *Minhāj*, 4:396.

[23] Ibn Ḥajar al-ʿAsqalānī, *Lisān al-Mīzān*, 1:319–320.

[24] For more on Ibn Taymiyya, see Chapter 5.

[25] Al-Bukhārī, *Ṣaḥīḥ*, 4:207–209.

But al-Bukhārī excludes hundreds of favorable reports about ʿAlī that his predecessor Aḥmad b. Ḥanbal had considered acceptable for transmission.[26] He justifies this omission by appealing to the authority of Ibn Sīrīn (d. 110/728): "Ibn Sīrīn considered most of that which is narrated regarding ʿAlī to be false."[27] In his analysis, a Moroccan Sufi scholar of *ḥadīth* who professed *tafḍīl ʿAlī*, Aḥmad b. al-Ṣiddīq al-Ghumārī (d. 1380/1960), accused al-Bukhārī of harboring anti-ʿAlid sentiment.[28] Although al-Ghumārī did not explain the basis for his assessment, it is likely related to al-Bukhārī's decision to omit most reports about ʿAlī's merits from his collection and his support for Ibn Sīrīn's assessment of that corpus.

Like al-Jāḥiẓ before him, Ibn Ḥazm devalued ʿAlī's military prowess, conversion as a young boy, asceticism, expertise in religion, and other merits by reinterpreting them so as to ensure that ʿAlī did not appear to surpass the first three caliphs in excellence. Ibn Ḥazm also rejected the authenticity of many reports that exalted ʿAlī.[29] Some historians have criticized Ibn Ḥazm for downplaying ʿAlī's stature while lauding the Umayyads, to whom he was related through clientage.[30] Ibn Ḥazm summed up his view of ʿAlī's status as follows:

> The merits of ʿAlī that are authentic consist of the Prophet's words "You are unto me like Aaron unto Moses, except that there is no prophet after me," and his statement, "I shall give the banner to a man who loves God and His Prophet while God and His Prophet love him too," but this is a characteristic of every believer and person of merit. [There is] also his promise to ʿAlī that only a person of faith will love him and only a hypocrite will despise him, but this distinction is also authentically reported about the *anṣār* ... As for [the *ḥadīth*] "ʿAlī is the *mawlā* of whosoever considers me his *mawlā*," it is not authentically reported through any reliable chain of transmitters. As for all the other *ḥadīth* that the *rāfiḍa* usually cite, they are fabricated. Anyone with the slightest bit of knowledge regarding historical reports (*akhbār*) and their transmission already knows this.[31]

[26] For Aḥmad's reports about ʿAlī, see Aḥmad b. Ḥanbal, *Faḍāʾil Amīr al-Muʾminīn*. A Shīʿī author takes al-Bukhārī to task for his decision to exclude most *ḥadīth* about ʿAlī's merits: see al-Najmī, *Aḍwāʾ ʿalā ʾl-Ṣaḥīḥayn*, 108–109.

[27] Al-Bukhārī, *Ṣaḥīḥ*, 4:209. [28] Al-ʿAwwād, *al-Naṣb*, 431.

[29] Ibn Ḥazm, *al-Fiṣal*, 4:78, 107, 110–112, 114–116. See also Afsaruddin, *Excellence*, 69, 99, 102–104.

[30] Al-Dhahabī, *Siyar*, 18:184, 201; Ibn Ḥazm, *Rasāʾil*, 1:91, 208, 2:22 al-Ṣafadī, *al-Wāfī*, 20:93, 96. See also al-ʿAwwād, *al-Naṣb*, 471, 476; al-Ghumārī, *al-Jawāb al-mufīd*, 67; al-Mālikī, *Naḥwa inqādh al-tārīkh*, 136, 288.

[31] Ibn Ḥazm, *al-Fiṣal*, 4:116.

Both Ibn Taymiyya and al-Fīrūzābādī concur with Ibn Ḥazm and make similar statements to this effect.[32]

A representative of the Muʿtazilī school of Baghdad, Abū Jaʿfar al-Iskāfī (d. 240/854), similarly commented on his contemporaries' tendency to either reject, refrain from mentioning, or reinterpret reports concerning the merits of ʿAlī to deprive them of significance.[33] Al-Iskāfī considered al-Jāḥiẓ, for example, guilty of anti-ʿAlid sentiment and/or ignorance on such grounds.[34] Al-Jāḥiẓ himself mentioned a contemporary who had accused him of *naṣb* after reading his treatise on ʿUthmānīs (ʿUthmāniyya).[35] However, al-Jāḥiẓ denied feeling any contempt for ʿAlī. Likewise, the four Sunnī authorities mentioned above (al-Bukhārī, Ibn Ḥazm, Ibn Taymiyya, and al-Fīrūzābādī) would have denied disliking ʿAlī, despite the claims of their critics.

Aḥmad b. Jalāl al-Dīn al-Ījī was a Shāfiʿī who composed a work about the merits of ʿAlī and implicitly argued for his superiority (*tafḍīl*). He referred to an unnamed contemporary who had written a work that denied most of ʿAlī's merits. Al-Ījī was dismayed that someone could either reject or devalue most of the *ḥadīth* about ʿAlī's merits and claim that only three such *ḥadīth* were authentic. Al-Ījī seems to be referring to al-Fīrūzābādī, whom he described as so prejudiced against Shīʿism that it led him to object to verses of the Qurʾān and *ḥadīth* that praise the Prophet's family.[36]

The characterization of a statement as anti-ʿAlid when it was originally made to discredit Shīʿism was contentious. Sunnism contained a spectrum of pro-ʿAlid beliefs, and the proponents of each trend criticized those of the others. Pro-ʿAlid Sufis who regarded ʿAlī as the legatee and inheritor of the Prophet's spiritual knowledge were offended by anti-Shīʿī polemicists who rejected most *ḥadīth* about ʿAlī. Although Sufis typically viewed Ibn Taymiyya as anti-ʿAlid, others, influenced by him, considered him an exemplary, orthodox Sunnī. Al-Jāḥiẓ, al-Bukhārī, Ibn Ḥazm, Ibn Taymiyya, and al-Fīrūzābādī were all proponents of the four-caliph theory; nonetheless, they promote the views of early ʿUthmānīs who never recognized ʿAlī as a legitimate caliph in their tracts against Shīʿism.

32 Al-Fīrūzābādī, *al-Radd ʿalā ʾl-rāfiḍa*, 66–68; Ibn Taymiyya, *Minhāj*, 7:120, 199, 320–321, 354–355, 8:420–421.
33 Al-Iskāfī, "Naqḍ al-ʿUthmāniyya," 282.
34 See ibid., 297, 302–305, 318, 320; al-Jāḥiẓ, *al-Rasāʾil al-siyāsiyya*, 26–27. See also Afsaruddin, *Excellence*, 7, 23–25.
35 Al-Jāḥiẓ, *Kitāb al-Ḥayawān*, 1:13.
36 Al-Ījī, *Tawḍīḥ al-dalāʾil*, 225; cf. al-Fīrūzābādī, *al-Radd ʿalā ʾl-rāfiḍa*, 66.

The difficulty in categorizing Ibn Taymiyya and other anti-Shīʿī polemicists who shared his sensibilities is that they appeal to arguments and individuals characteristic of Groups 1 and 2. Their reliance on such arguments reflects a Sunnī tendency to reach into an anti-ʿAlid tradition that it both appropriated and suppressed. Sunnī scholars had to negotiate between teachings characteristic of Group 1 (anti-ʿAlids) and those of Group 4 (proponents of *tafḍīl ʿAlī*), since Sunnī *ḥadīth* compilations preserved contributions from *ḥadīth* transmitters representing both of these rival groups. The divergence between Ḥarīz b. ʿUthmān (d. 163/779), who despised ʿAlī for killing his ancestors at Ṣiffīn, and ʿUbayd Allāh b. Mūsā (d. 213/828), who ranked ʿAlī higher than Abū Bakr, is clear in their biographical entries and evident in some of the *ḥadīth* they narrated,[37] but both nevertheless appear in Sunnī canonical collections such as al-Bukhārī's *Ṣaḥīḥ*.[38] Group 4's overtly pro-ʿAlid stance within the proto-Sunnī tradition has continued even into the modern period. Contemporary pro-ʿAlids argue that the compilers of Sunnī biographical dictionaries tended to be more lenient with anti-ʿAlids. By contrast, they point out, biographical entries on members of Groups 4 and 5 would usually include criticism and condemnation of their subjects' beliefs.[39]

ANTI-ʿALID SENTIMENT DEFINED

Muslim scholars referred to expressions of anti-ʿAlid sentiment as *naṣb*.[40] They described proponents of *naṣb* (sing. *nāṣibī*, pl. *nawāṣib*, *nāṣiba*, or *nuṣṣāb*) in at least three ways. First, anti-ʿAlids held ʿAlī and, by extension, his family in contempt (*bughḍ*). Some Imāmī sources extended *naṣb* to include hatred for Shīʿīs.[41] Second, *nawāṣib* sought to cause pain to the

37 For reports about Ḥarīz, see Ibn Ḥajar al-ʿAsqalānī, *Tahdhīb al-Tahdhīb*, 2:20–210. ʿUbayd Allāh narrates a *ḥadīth* in which the Prophet describes ʿAlī as his *waṣī* and the best of those he would leave behind: see Ibn ʿAdī, *al-Kāmil*, 6:397; Ibn ʿAsākir, *Taʾrīkh*, 42:57. For entries about ʿUbayd Allāh that mention his pro-ʿAlid leanings, see Ibn Saʿd, *al-Ṭabaqāt al-kubrā*, 6:400; al-Mizzī, *Tahdhīb al-Kamāl*, 18:59.

38 Al-Bukhārī, *Ṣaḥīḥ*, 1:8, 4:164. For more on this phenomenon, see Melchert, "Sectaries in the Six Books."

39 Muḥammad b. ʿAqīl al-ʿAlawī argued this point in a famous treatise: see Muḥammad b. ʿAqīl al-ʿAlawī, *al-ʿAtb al-jamīl*.

40 The linguistic root *naṣaba* possesses numerous meanings, including (1) to designate, (2) to establish, and (3) to have enmity: see al-Ṭurayḥī, *Majmaʿ al-Baḥrayn*, 2:171–174.

41 Al-Baḥrānī, *al-Ḥadāʾiq al-nāḍira*, 5:177, 185, 10:361–362; Ibn Bābawayh, *ʿIlal al-sharāʾiʿ*, 2:601; al-Ṭurayḥī, *Majmaʿ al-Baḥrayn*, 2:173–174.

Household of the Prophet through words or deeds.[42] And third, they not only possessed animosity toward ʿAlī but also justified their stance within a theological framework (*dīn*) or as a virtuous principle.[43] These descriptions differentiated *nawāṣib* who considered ʿAlids heretics or evil in the sight of God from those who were simply political rivals of ʿAlī or of his descendants. The malicious nature of *naṣb* best distinguishes this sentiment from two similar, concurrent tendencies, *khilāf* and *taqṣīr*, which are described later in this chapter.

After the Prophet's death, a number of conflicts pitted ʿAlī and his family against other leading Companions. According to Sunnī and Shīʿī sources, Hāshimids withheld their oath of fealty to the first caliph for a time; the Prophet's daughter, Fāṭima, unsuccessfully claimed rights to her father's estate; and years later, leading Companions faced ʿAlī and his sons at the battle of the Camel.[44] Umayyad and ʿUthmānī *ḥadīth* transmitters subsequently blamed ʿAlī and his partisans for fomenting civil war, whereas Shīʿī historiography depicted almost everyone who opposed ʿAlī and his family as villains. Sunnī orthodoxy faced a major dilemma in interpreting these conflicts once ʿAlī had been rehabilitated from misguided pretender to rightly guided caliph. Previous narrators of this early history had despised ʿAlī and portrayed his rivals as detesting him, but now historians could no longer accommodate such views. Sunnīs could not legitimize *naṣb* or accept tales in which venerated Companions appeared as *nawāṣib*, because such acceptance would have directly undermined Sunnī belief in these Companions' righteousness. Although Sunnī orthodoxy favored rejecting such historiography as false, scholars could not censor or reinterpret the entire body of literary evidence that portrayed some contemporaries of the Prophet as hating ʿAlī. As a result, *ḥadīth* transmitters consciously avoided transmitting such reports and encouraged the faithful to avoid discussions about conflicts between Companions.[45] By the end of the tenth century, Sunnī orthodoxy appealed

[42] Ibn Taymiyya, *Majmūʿ fatāwā*, 3:154.

[43] Al-Fīrūzābādī, *al-Qāmūs al-muḥīṭ*, 1:132. *Dīn* in its various notions includes *ḥukm*, *madhhab*, and *milla*, which are translated as judgment, doctrine and religious community. *Dīn* implies "faith, obedience, and the practice of a given belief." The affairs and the concept of *dīn* were sometimes cited in contradistinction to *dunyā*: see *EI*[2], s.v. "Dīn" (L. Gardet).

[44] For studies on these conflicts, see Husayn, "*Aḥkām* concerning the *Ahl al-Bayt*"; Jafri, *Origins*, 58–100; Lucas, *Constructive Critics*, 226–237; Madelung, *Succession*.

[45] Al-Ābī al-Azharī, *al-Thamar al-dānī*, 23; al-ʿAynī, *ʿUmdat al-qārī*, 1:212; Ibn Ḥajar al-Haytamī, *al-Ṣawāʿiq al-muḥriqa*, 216; ʿIyāḍ, *al-Shifā*, 2:52; al-Nawawī, *Sharḥ Ṣaḥīḥ Muslim*, 18:11; al-Ṭabarī, *al-Riyāḍ al-naḍira*, 1:23.

to the concept of *ijtihād* to explain the actions of those Companions who went to war against ʿAlī.[46]

In the Islamic legal tradition, a *mujtahid* is a jurist with the necessary authority and expertise to undertake *ijtihād*, the derivation of new law based on the sacred sources. Sunnīs charitably regarded the political decisions of ʿAlī's rivals as a type of *ijtihād*. Faced with changing political and social circumstances, some Companions raised an army independent of ʿAlī because they believed that this was the right course of action. Many Sunnīs were convinced that ʿĀʾisha and Muʿāwiya fought ʿAlī's army with the best of intentions and that they were forced into the conflict by nefarious figures in ʿAlī's army who were fomenting war and civil unrest. Since they possessed the necessary authority and justifications to take action, ʿAlī's opponents were *mujtahids*.[47] Ibn Ḥazm even identifies Ibn Muljam, ʿAlī's assassin, as a *mujtahid*.[48] In some cases, Sunnīs further considered ʿAlī and his family mistaken in their opinions and actions. For example, in the dispute between Fāṭima and Abū Bakr about the legal status of the Prophet's estate, Sunnīs agreed with Abū Bakr's ruling that such lands had become public endowments upon the Prophet's death.[49]

Proto-Sunnī efforts to reinterpret the conflicts between Companions in a favorable light followed a period of intense factionalism in which many Muslims had sharply attacked the leaders and members of rival groups. *Ḥadīth* transmitters sympathetic to Zubayrid, Umayyad, or Hāshimid claims to authority depicted the favored group's opponents as corrupt in their narratives about the conflicts of the seventh century. For partisans of ʿAlī, his rivals were motivated by envy and a desire for power, wealth, honor, or vengeance.[50] The Umayyads, for example, are portrayed in pro-

[46] Ibn al-Fūrak, *Maqālāt*, 195; Ibn Ḥajar al-ʿAsqalānī, *Fatḥ al-bārī*, 1:451; Ibn Ḥazm, *al-Fiṣal*, 4:125; Ibn Kathīr, *al-Bidāya wa ʾl-nihāya*, 8:135; al-Juwaynī, *Kitāb al-Irshād*, 433.

[47] For cases in which a scholar claims ʿĀʾisha, Ṭalḥa, al-Zubayr, Muʿāwiya, and ʿAmr b. al-ʿĀṣ utilized *ijtihād* in their decision to rebel against ʿAlī, see Ibn Ḥazm, *al-Fiṣal*, 4:124; Ibn Taymiyya, *Minhāj*, 4:320; al-Qurṭubī, *Tafsīr*, 14:182. See also al-ʿAskarī, *Maʿālim*, 2:66–75; Sharif, "Baghy in Islamic Law," 299–301.

[48] Ibn Ḥazm, *al-Muḥallā*, 10:484. See also Ansari, "Ibn Ḥazm selon certains savants shīʿites," 655.

[49] For the dispute about Fadak, see Ibn Abī ʾl-Ḥadīd, *Sharḥ*, 6:46–50, 16:208–284; al-Nawawī, *Sharḥ Ṣaḥīḥ Muslim*, 12:69–82. See also Husayn, "*Aḥkam* concerning the *Ahl al-Bayt*."

[50] For example, al-Zubayr admits that (political) ambitions led him to the battle of the Camel: see Ibn Abī Shayba, *al-Muṣannaf*, 7:258, 8:712. One Ḥanafī theologian explains that ʿĀʾisha disliked ʿAlī because she was envious of him: see Ibn Abī ʾl-Ḥadīd, *Sharḥ*, 9:192–199. For more examples of other Companions, see also Madelung, *Succession*.

ʿAlid sources as collectively seeking vengeance from ʿAlī for the deaths of ʿUthmān and other Umayyads.[51] In one report, Marwān b. al-Ḥakam (r. 64–645/684–685) admits in private that the Umayyads publicly lambasted ʿAlī as a political stratagem: he served as a symbolic scapegoat for the civil unrest that plagued the community after ʿUthmān's death.[52] Muʿāwiya is also quoted as admitting openly that he rebelled against ʿAlī only to establish his own right to rule.[53] On the basis of such early source material, Shīʿīs considered the Companions capable of committing any vice or crime.[54]

Umayyad-era Shīʿī literature, such as *Kitāb Sulaym b. Qays*, describes most individuals who disagreed with ʿAlid imāms as anti-ʿAlids. It is unlikely that everyone who diverged from ʿAlī or his descendants was in fact anti-ʿAlid. But other factions of the early eighth century (the ʿUthmānīs, the Umayyads, the Khawārij, etc.) propounded similarly inflexible views regarding "others." After the ninth century, many proto-Sunnī *ḥadīth* transmitters and scholars attempted to recast the disputes between ʿAlī and his rivals into a benign history in which disagreements always culminated in reconciliation.[55] An implausible reinterpretation of history in which well-meaning Companions accidentally fought with their peers or became the victims of a mischievous Jew named Ibn Sabaʾ who sought to covertly destroy the Muslim community became the hallmark Sunnī response to polarizing debates regarding conflicts between Companions.[56] In this framework, it was Ibn Sabaʾ, desperate to cause

[51] For example, the Umayyads appear this way in al-Zubayr b. Bakkār's *al-Mufākharāt*, which is no longer extant. For relevant fragments of the text, see Ibn Abī 'l-Ḥadīd, *Sharḥ*, 6:285–288.

[52] Al-Dhahabī, *Taʾrīkh*, 3:460–461; Ibn ʿAsākir, *Taʾrīkh*, 42:438; al-Iskāfī, "Naqḍ al-ʿUthmāniyya," 283. See also Madelung, *Succession*, 334.

[53] Abū 'l-Faraj al-Iṣbahānī, *Maqātil al-Ṭālibiyyīn*, 45; Ibn ʿAsākir, *Taʾrīkh*, 59:150–151; Ibn Kathīr, *al-Bidāya wa 'l-nihāya*, 8:140.

[54] Shīʿī polemical texts portrayed the Companions, including early caliphs, as explicitly expressing contempt for ʿAlī and his household. See the portrayal of Companions in *Kitāb Sulaym*, 150–155, 162–163. See also Kohlberg, "Some Imāmī Shīʿī Views on the *Ṣahaba*."

[55] For example, according to one report, Fāṭima reconciled with Abū Bakr before she died: see al-Bayhaqī, *al-Sunan al-kubrā*, 6:301; Ibn Kathīr, *al-Bidāya wa 'l-nihāya*, 5:310. See also Madelung, *Succession*, 52 n. 67; van Ess, "Political Ideas," 155–156 (on how the wars between Companions were charitably reinterpreted).

[56] See Anthony, *The Caliph and the Heretic*; Barzegar, "Remembering Community." The Sunnī theological tenet of *ʿadālat al-ṣaḥāba* (the righteousness of the Companions) required Muslims to believe that they were all just and to read all actions attributed to them charitably: see Ibn ʿAbd al-Barr, *al-Istidhkār*, 3:301; Ibn Ḥibbān, *Ṣaḥīḥ*, 1:162; al-Nawawī, *al-Majmuʿ*, 6:190, 348. See also al-ʿAskarī, *Maʿālim*, 1:95–97; van Ess, "Political

havoc in the Muslim community, who initiated the battle of the Camel by attacking ʿĀʾisha's army in the middle of the night;[57] ʿĀʾisha would have never fought ʿAlī without such a provocation. Likewise, after ʿAlī's death, when Muʿāwiya learned of his merits, he wept[58] and exclaimed that had he known about them earlier, he would have become ʿAlī's faithful servant.[59] In other reports, Muʿāwiya is depicted as testifying to the Prophet that he loves ʿAlī.[60]

DISAGREEING (*KHILĀF*) WITHOUT *NAṢB*

Various authorities active in the eighth century and after it, including other ʿAlids, are portrayed as respecting the Twelver Shīʿī imāms while disagreeing with their legal opinions.[61] Although Shīʿīs generally considered *khilāf*, disagreement with ʿAlī and the Shīʿī imāms, to be tantamount to contesting the command of God and His Prophet,[62] non-Shīʿīs obviously did not. In the latter's view, ʿAlī and his family expressed their legal opinions, but other Companions and jurists were entitled to their own opinions as well. For non-Shīʿīs, religious authority became dispersed in the community after the Prophet's death. Consequently, there was no harm in disagreeing with the judgments of ʿAlī and his family.

Ideas," 155–156. For modern Sunnī criticisms of *ʿadālat al-ṣaḥāba*, see Abū Rayya, *Aḍwāʾ ʿalā ʾl-sunna al-Muḥammadiyya*, 339–363; al-Mālikī, *al-Ṣuḥba wa ʾl-ṣaḥaba*, 90–126.

57 Ibn Kathīr, *al-Bidāya wa ʾl-nihāya*, 7:265–267.

58 Ibn ʿAsākir, *Taʾrīkh*, 24:401.

59 Ibid., 20:360–361; Ibn Kathīr, *al-Bidāya wa ʾl-nihāya*, 8:84.

60 Ibn ʿAsākir, *Taʾrīkh*, 59:139–140.

61 Although al-Awzaʿī is listed as one who transmitted from al-Bāqir, the former disagreed with a number of opinions associated with jurists in the Ḥijāz and the Imāmī community, including combining prayers without an excuse and temporary marriage: see al-Dhahabī, *Siyar*, 7:131. One prominent ʿAlid who publicly differed with Jaʿfar al-Ṣādiq and gave his own legal opinions was ʿAbd Allāh b. al-Ḥasan b. al-Ḥasan (d. 145/762): see al-Kulaynī, *al-Kāfī*, 1:349–351, 359 (where he is upset with al-Ḥusayn for excluding Ḥasanids from the imāmate), 2:155, 3:507, 8:363–364. See also al-Khūʾī, *Muʿjam rijāl al-ḥadīth*, 11:170–175; Modarressi, *Crisis*, 53. For non-Shīʿī contemporaries who praised Muḥammad al-Bāqir, but did not necessarily follow his rulings, see Lalani, *Early Shīʿī Thought*, 96–102. For case studies that compare eighth-century Imāmī legal rulings to other schools, see Haider, *Origins*, 57–186; Lalani, *Early Shīʿī Thought*, 120–126.

62 Some Shīʿī jurists considered such folk impure (*najis*) and no better than polytheists: see al-Baḥrānī, *al-Ḥadāʾiq al-nāḍira*, 5:175–190. See also Kohlberg, "Barāʾa in Shīʿī Doctrine," 154. The term *mukhālif* in these contexts sometimes referred to *nawāṣib*. The latter were not considered Muslims in Shīʿī law. Other times the term referred to any scholar who was not a Twelver Shīʿī. There was a radical current in the Imāmī community that considered all non-Imāmīs as enemies of the Household, but this was not universal: see Dakake, *Charismatic Community*, 132–139, 151–155.

Shīʿīs accused of *naṣb* in Imāmī literature were generally involved in a dispute regarding the imāmate with other Shīʿīs or an ʿAlid imām.[63] Imāmī factions frequently condemned each other for disagreeing on the identity of the true imām. For example, some Zaydīs and Wāqifī Imāmīs are denounced by their rivals as "worse than *nuṣṣāb*."[64] It appears that these Shīʿīs were more appropriately guilty of *khilāf* rather than *naṣb*, but the nature of these disagreements lies outside the scope of this book as they usually did not involve anti-ʿAlid sentiment.[65]

In Sunnī and Shīʿī literature, only a few Companions and their students appear as Shīʿīs or ardent partisans of ʿAlī.[66] Most Companions freely disagreed with the opinions of ʿAlids, directed their devotion and allegiance to other individuals and clans, or adopted a nonpartisan stance. Eventually, the later Sunnī community recognized the need to rehabilitate ʿAlī and to legitimize their own beliefs by citing texts in which ʿAlī and his family members repudiated Shīʿī historical claims, doctrines, or laws.[67] In one report, for example, ʿAlī denies possessing more merit than Abū Bakr or ʿUmar and threatens to whip anyone who considers him superior to them.[68] Elsewhere, he rejects the idea that he or the *ahl al-bayt* received any special knowledge from the Prophet.[69] Sunnī polemicists such as Ibn Taymiyya vigorously disassociated the later Shīʿī imāms from Shīʿism and claimed that the imāms in fact followed the beliefs and practices of the Sunnī community despite their relative absence from Sunnī *ḥadīth* and legal texts.[70]

REPUDIATING ʿALID RIGHTS (*TAQṢĪR*)

After nearly a century of rule, the Umayyad dynasty fell to the ʿAbbāsids, who attempted to replace the Umayyads' anti-ʿAlid propaganda with an

[63] Al-Baḥrānī, *al-Ḥadāʾiq al-nāḍira*, 5:189–190. See also Kohlberg, "Barāʾa in Shīʿī Doctrine," 158–163.

[64] Al-Baḥrānī, *al-Ḥadāʾiq al-nāḍira*, 5:189–190; al-Ṭūsī, *Tahdhīb al-aḥkām*, 4:53. See also Kohlberg, "Barāʾa in Shīʿī Doctrine," 163.

[65] In one uprising, however, Zaydīs reportedly showed contempt for Jaʿfar al-Ṣādiq by violently imprisoning him and confiscating wealth belonging to him and his family: see al-Kulaynī, *al-Kāfī*, 1:362–363. I am indebted to Hossein Modarressi for this reference.

[66] See Muḥammad b. ʿAqīl al-ʿAlawī, *al-Naṣāʾiḥ al-kāfiya*, 296–298; Sharaf al-Dīn, *al-Fuṣūl al-muhimma*, 189–200; Sharaf al-Dīn, *al-Murājaʿāt*, 105–182.

[67] For more on ʿAlī's rehabilitation, see Chapter 6. See also *EI*², s.v. "Imāma" (W. Madelung), "ʿUthmāniyya" (P. Crone).

[68] Aḥmad b. Ḥanbal, *Faḍāʾil al-ṣaḥāba*, 1:83; Ibn Kathīr, *al-Bidāya wa ʾl-nihāya*, 10:303; Ibn Taymiyya, *Minhāj*, 1:308, 6:135–138; al-Ṭabarī, *al-Riyāḍ al-naḍira*, 1:90.

[69] Aḥmad b. Ḥanbal, *al-Musnad*, 1:118, 152; al-Bukhārī, *Ṣaḥīḥ*, 4:30.

[70] For example, see Ibn Taymiyya, *Jāmiʿ al-Masāʾil*, 3:87–88.

attitude that was pro-Hāshimid and occasionally pro-ʿAlid as well.[71] But the ʿAbbāsids eventually had to defend their legitimacy against ʿAlid rivals to the caliphate by devising, or sometimes reverting to, arguments that denied the merits of ʿAlī and his household. The ʿAbbāsids, like their political predecessors, endeavored to prove that ʿAlids had no special legal or theological claim to authority in Islam.[72] ʿAbbās and his descendants became the Prophet's *ahl al-bayt* and his legitimate heirs.[73] ʿAbbāsid repudiation of ʿAlid claims to the Prophet's legacy closely resembled the tendency among other rivals of the ʿAlids to reject any special reverence for ʿAlī and his household or to deny their rights (*ḥaqq*, pl. *ḥuqūq*) or merits (*khaṣāʾiṣ*, *faḍāʾil*, *manāqib*). Pro-ʿAlids such as the Baghdādī Muʿtazila referred to this tendency as *taqṣīr* and considered it an indicator of anti-ʿAlid sentiment.[74] Among Sunnīs, those who rejected the merits and achievements of ʿAlī and his family when reports affirming them were widely transmitted and preserved in Sunnī *ḥadīth* collections were accused of *tabkhīs* (devaluing ʿAlī)[75] and *tanqīṣ* (diminishing his stature).[76]

As mentioned earlier, Abū Jaʿfar al-Iskāfī, the Baghdādī Muʿtazilī, accused some of his contemporaries of seeking to refute ʿAlī's merits (*naqḍ faḍāʾilahu*) and rejecting the authenticity of any *ḥadīth* mentioning them.[77] Although al-Iskāfī is probably referring to ʿUthmānīs and to *ḥadīth* transmitters committed to the cult of Muʿāwiya,[78] in subsequent centuries Sunnī scholars who attempted to refute Shīʿism were also accused of going

[71] The ʿAbbāsids utilized reverence for ʿAlī, al-Ḥusayn, and Zayd b. ʿAlī as well as an ʿAlid *waṣiyya* in their favor as tools to legitimizing their rule: see, for example, al-Balādhurī, *Ansāb al-ashrāf*, 3:273–275; Ibn Abī ʾl-Ḥadīd, *Sharḥ*, 7:131; Ibn Ḥajar al-Haytamī, *al-Ṣawāʿiq al-muḥriqa*, 247; Ibn Qutayba, *ʿUyūn al-akhbār*, 2:275; al-Masʿūdī, *Murūj al-dhahab*, 3:257. See also Haider, "The *Waṣiyya* of Abū Hāshim," 49–77; Zaman, *Religion and Politics*, 33–35.

[72] Zaman, *Religion and Politics*, 43–48.

[73] In an ʿAbbāsid version of the *ḥadīth al-kisāʾ*, the Prophet refers to ʿAbbās and his sons as "my household (*ahl baytī*)": see al-Balādhurī, *Ansāb al-ashrāf*, 4:5; al-Ṭabarānī, *al-Muʿjam al-kabīr*, 19:263. See also Sharon, "Ahl al-Bayt," 176–177.

[74] *Taqṣīr*, lit. to shorten; diminish; fail to reach: al-Iskāfī, *al-Miʿyār*, 32–33 (also cited in Modarressi, *Crisis*, 36 n. 105). Although Ibn al-Nadīm attributes the text to Ibn al-Iskāfī, ʿAbd al-ʿAzīz al-Ṭabāṭabāʾī and Hassan Ansari note that every manuscript copy attributes the text to the father instead of the son: see Ansari, *Bar rasīhā-yi tārīkhī*, 493–506.

[75] Ibn Qutayba, *al-Ikhtilāf*, 54. The Qurʾān condemns *bakhs* a number of times: see Q7:85, Q11:85, and Q26:183.

[76] Ibn Ḥajar, *Lisān al-mīzān*, 1:319–320; al-Iskāfī, *al-Miʿyār*, 33–34.

[77] Al-Iskāfī, "Naqḍ al-ʿUthmāniyya," 282.

[78] Many reports from Abū ʾl-Qāsim al-Saqaṭī (d. 406/1015) indicate his strong devotion to Muʿāwiya. For a sample of these reports, see Ibn ʿAsākir, *Taʾrīkh*, 14:113–114, 59:70–71, 87, 89, 93, 104–105, 142, 211–212. See also Barzegar, "Remembering Community," 178, 193–195.

too far in downplaying ʿAlī's merits. Sunnīs who engaged in anti-Shīʿī polemics recognized the existence of a spectrum of beliefs about ʿAlī. However, many did not consider the extent to which the doctrinal and textual legacy of anti-ʿAlids was partially incorporated in the Sunnī literary tradition. Their use of arguments and texts that their pro-ʿAlid Sunnī and Shīʿī interlocutors considered anti-ʿAlid appears to have pulled these polemicists unwittingly closer to that end of the spectrum. These dynamics are evident in the case of al-Jāḥiẓ, Ibn Ḥazm, Ibn Taymiyya, al-Fīrūzābādī, and others who sought to discredit Shīʿism in their literary work.

Radical Shīʿīs such as the *mufawwiḍa* and the *ghulāt* accused non-Shīʿīs and moderate Shīʿīs of *taqṣīr* if they did not uphold certain doctrines regarding the imāmate. For example, the *mufawwiḍa* claimed that Shīʿīs who limited the scope of the imāms' knowledge, miraculous ability, or infallibility were guilty of *taqṣīr*.[79] Although *taqṣīr* and *naṣb* were often used synonymously in the premodern period,[80] contemporary researchers should attempt to distinguish the two, since many individuals accused of *taqṣīr* were in fact pro-ʿAlid or Shīʿī.

SURVEYING MUSLIM LITERATURE FOR ANTI-ʿALID SENTIMENT

Historically, the most staunchly anti-ʿAlid individuals were part of larger collectives of Muslims who did not necessarily agree with all of their views. These groups might have been found in a pro-Umayyad mosque in eighth-century Kūfa, in proto-Sunnī *ḥadīth* circles, or in an army that fought against ʿAlī and his descendants.[81] An investigation of non-Shīʿī personalities accused of *khilāf* and *tanqīṣ* can help identify the beliefs of anti-ʿAlids, even if those personalities did not actually despise ʿAlī. Individuals with varying degrees of anti-ʿAlid sentiment could belong to the same political and social group. In these cases, the group would respond to the views of its most extreme members with silence or perhaps some criticism, but not excommunication. Thus, al-Dhahabī (d. 748/1348) and Ibn Ḥajar al-ʿAsqalānī note dozens of instances in which *ḥadīth* transmitters up to the tenth century disparaged ʿAlī but were still accepted as authorities by the compilers of the canonical Sunnī *ḥadīth* collections and other scholars.[82]

[79] Modarressi, *Crisis*, 36–51.
[80] For example, al-Iskāfī, *al-Miʿyār*, 32. See also Modarressi, *Crisis*, 36 n. 103 and n. 105.
[81] For a topography of mosques infamous for anti-ʿAlid sentiment in Kūfa, see Haider, *Origins*, 232–242.
[82] For a list of over a hundred examples, see al-ʿUqaylī, *Muʿjam nawāṣib al-muḥaddithīn*.

Consequently, *ḥadīth* transmitters who were not anti-ʿAlid themselves would nonetheless record the claims of their anti-ʿAlid peers in biographical dictionaries or *ḥadīth* compilations. Some anti-ʿAlid *ḥadīth* even appear in the canonical work of al-Bukhārī and other influential Sunnī *ḥadīth* collections. However, as anti-ʿAlid sentiment lost favor among *ḥadīth* transmitters, the contributions of *nawāṣib* were emended or fell out of circulation.[83] Because of the extinction of overt *naṣb*, a methodology that distinguishes it from *taqṣīr* and *khilāf* and surveys the reception of anti-ʿAlid sentiment in *ḥadīth* and biographical literature is particularly valuable since it allows the recapture of the claims of *nawāṣib* partially preserved in Sunnī literature. The results of such a survey can then either problematize or substantiate descriptions of anti-ʿAlids in works of history and theology.

In the literature that they produced, scholars such as Aḥmad b. Ḥanbal, Muḥammad b. Saʿd (d. 230/845), and their successors attempted to minimize the early partisan divisions that existed within the Sunnī community.[84] This process required not only the incorporation of pro-ʿAlid sentiments but also the repudiation of anti-ʿAlid elements in the greater non-Shīʿī community. The Sunnī intellectual tradition sought to include individuals accused of *khilāf* and *bughḍ/naṣb* by censoring, discrediting, or charitably reinterpreting objectionable elements in reports about them. Some historians of the eighth century were discernibly more partisan than others. Sectarian works are exemplified by the works of the unabashedly anti-Shīʿī storyteller Sayf b. ʿUmar, his *Kitāb al-Jamal wa masīr ʿĀʾisha wa ʿAlī*, and his reports about ʿAlī that are reproduced in al-Ṭabarī's (d. 310/923) famous chronicle. Another example is *Kitāb Sulaym b. Qays*, a book that was clearly an early Shīʿī apologia. On the other hand, many Sunnī *ḥadīth* collections did not attempt to provide a cohesive narrative.

Many ʿAbbāsid-era works of history and *ḥadīth* served as receptacles for various sentiments of the time. One finds anti-ʿAlid, pro-ʿAlid, and nonpartisan *ḥadīth* in the same collections, despite the attempts of Sunnī orthodoxy to propagate only the last type. For example, the histories of al-Ṭabarī and al-Balādhurī and the *ḥadīth* collections of Aḥmad b. Ḥanbal and al-Ṭabarānī (d. 360/971) contain diverse currents, including pro-ʿAlid and anti-ʿAlid ones, despite some censorship of the most extreme elements. The compilers of Sunnī *ḥadīth* collections after Aḥmad b. Ḥanbal seem to have supported a nonpartisan reading of history, attempting to

[83] For more on the Sunnī reception of anti-ʿAlid reports, see Chapter 6.
[84] See Lucas, *Constructive Critics*.

deemphasize the historical partisan identities of the Companions and defending them all as one pious group. For example, al-Qāḍī Abū Bakr b. al-ʿArabī (d. 543/1148) was criticized by some Sunnīs for his defense of Umayyads accused of *naṣb* and other crimes, but he maintained that this defense was part of an overall worldview that judged all Companions to be blameless.[85] Thus, Ibn al-ʿArabī equally rejected any insinuation that ʿAlī or any other Companion was responsible for the death of ʿUthmān.[86] Similarly, Muḥammad b. Ṭūlūn (d. 953/1548) paradoxically wrote a treatise in defense of Yazīd b. Muʿāwiya (r. 60–64/680–683)[87] and another exalting the Twelver imāms.[88] The dual pro-ʿAlid and pro-Umayyad commitments of these Sunnī authors are rooted in the belief that all Companions deserve reverence and that any texts that appear to denigrate early Muslims should be rejected or reinterpreted more charitably. Instead of showing fidelity to any particular political faction, these authors exemplified allegiance to Sunnism as a sect that, after Aḥmad b. Ḥanbal, gradually came to oppose any criticism of early Muslim political figures.

Eighth-century literary sources on the political history of Iraq describe people's diverse allegiances in relation to the ʿAlids, the Umayyads, and others. However, the sources do not fully explicate the nature of these allegiances, specifically their theological dimensions.[89] This lack of clarity complicates any characterization of anti-ʿAlid and anti-Shīʿī sentiments during this period. Some Shīʿī sources denounce any disagreement with ʿAlī's opinions as *naṣb*, without regard for the identity of the culprit or the relative significance of the issue. For example, al-Ḥasan III b. al-Ḥasan b. al-Ḥasan b. ʿAlī is condemned essentially for failing to follow Jaʿfar al-Ṣādiq (d. 148/765) and the Imāmī community.[90] I differentiate between *khilāf*, *taqṣīr*, and *naṣb* in order to identify historically clear expressions of the latter and to pave the way for future academic inquiries into the phenomenon. My investigation does not assume the portrayal of any given anti-ʿAlid to be historically accurate; what matters is that later Muslims associated the individual with such beliefs. Although the prevalence of

[85] For criticisms, see al-Ālūsī, *Rūḥ al-maʿānī*, 26:73–74; Ibn Khaldūn, *Tārīkh*, 1:217; al-Munāwī, *Fayḍ al-qadīr*, 1:265, 5:313.

[86] Ibn al-ʿArabī, *al-ʿAwāṣim*, 280–281, 298.

[87] Ibn Ṭūlūn, *Qayd al-sharīd min akhbār Yazīd*.

[88] Ibn Ṭūlūn, *al-Aʾimmat al-ithnā ʿashar*.

[89] Dakake, *Charismatic Community*, 3–5.

[90] Al-Khūʾī, *Muʿjam rijāl al-ḥadīth*, 5:289. Animosity toward Ḥasanids or other ʿAlids in Imāmī sources was most likely due to their claims to the caliphate during the early ʿAbbāsid era: see Kohlberg, "Barāʾa in Shīʿī Doctrine," 162–163 (for animosity toward ʿAbd Allāh b. Jaʿfar al-Ṣādiq); Modarressi, *Crisis*, 53 (for the rivalry between the Ḥasanids and the Shīʿī Imāms).

khilāf and *taqṣīr* in the first three centuries of Islamic history is not a contentious claim, the existence of *naṣb* requires further discussion.[91] A sample of supporting sources in translation is provided in the appendix. The rest of this chapter provides a brief summary of those sources.

ANTI-ʿALID TEXTS

Because both Sunnī and Shīʿī sources describe *nawāṣib* as extremists, their extinction as a group has led to the disappearance of most primary source materials from anti-ʿAlid writers. However, the authors of *ḥadīth* collections and biographical dictionaries include quotations from *ḥadīth* transmitters who were considered *nawāṣib* by their peers. These quotations thus constitute a fragmentary form of primary source material. In some cases, the teachings of *nawāṣib* were subject to censorship and revision by other scholars. Thus, the theological treatise of al-Jāḥiẓ (discussed in Chapter 3) and other early ninth-century literature on anti-ʿAlidism offer contemporaneous testimony of the views of some *nawāṣib*. Nonetheless, they are secondary sources, since they only reproduce reports from anti-ʿAlids or provide information about them and their beliefs. In the following section I provide a framework for identifying and organizing expressions of anti-ʿAlid sentiment in Muslim literature. Thus far, there have been no scholarly attempts to analyze this subject as a theme in early Muslim historiography.

Anti-ʿAlid arguments put forward during the first three centuries of Islamic history by ʿUthmānīs, Umayyads, Khawārij, and ʿAbbāsids included anti-ʿAlid interpretations of Qurʾān, law, and *ḥadīth*. The surviving evidence of such arguments can be divided into the following eight categories, with sample texts provided in the appendix:

1. Statements that defend the motives for the murder, persecution, or physical harming of ʿAlī and members of his household.
2. Texts describing individuals who cursed ʿAlī or members of his family.
3. Accusations of heresy, evil, or intentional disobedience to God or His Prophet leveled at ʿAlī or his family members.
4. Statements disparaging ʿAlids as individuals lacking any merits.

[91] No one generally denies that multiple factions went to war with ʿAlī during his caliphate or that he was assassinated. The parties that fought him obviously exemplified *khilāf* because each war was predicated upon a disagreement. The assassin's belief that ʿAlī should be killed plainly constitutes *taqṣīr*, or a disregard for ʿAlī's rights as a caliph and Muslim.

5. Texts criticizing the actions and opinions of ʿAlī and his sons as unwise or mistaken.
6. Texts disputing the trustworthiness of ʿAlids as transmitters of religious knowledge.
7. Staunch defenses or endorsements of the piety of individuals who fought against or disagreed with the Household.
8. Statements condemning the companions of ʿAlī as evil.

TENSIONS IN DEVELOPING A FRAMEWORK FOR *NAṢB*

Some *mufawwiḍa* used the term *naṣb* disparagingly to describe anyone who disagreed with them concerning the divine nature of the imāms.[92] Their use of the term would include Twelver Shīʿīs who rejected the divinity of the imāms, Shīʿīs who recognized other imāms (e.g., the Zaydīs), Sunnīs who respected the ʿAlids, and even ʿAlids who disagreed with any of the twelve imāms. Some Imāmīs were even accused of anti-ʿAlid sentiment or unbelief because they failed to recognize a particular line of ʿAlid imāms. Political and theological disputes in the early period fueled sectarian tendencies and narratives that sought to discredit rival factions. Although Twelver Shīʿīs denounced many of their adversaries as *nawāṣib*, not all of their opponents harbored contempt for ʿAlī or his family. Disagreements with ʿAlids ranged from benign to violent. It is likely that the true *nawāṣib* were mostly found among those who waged war against ʿAlī and his household or blamed them for civil strife in the community.

The methods and motivations of Shīʿī and Sunnī authors in identifying expressions of *naṣb* in ʿAlī's lifetime and in the Umayyad period varied greatly, reflecting sectarian incentives to defend the integrity of their respective creeds and frameworks. Outright hatred of ʿAlī was unequivocally condemned in the most revered Sunnī *ḥadīth* collections, so individuals known to have harbored such hatred generally could not retain a respected status.[93] As a consequence, both Sunnīs and Imāmīs were forced to develop charitable reinterpretations of instances in which Companions or other distinguished figures had disagreed with the Shīʿī imāms. Historical reports that predate the life of Aḥmad b. Ḥanbal and

[92] Modarressi, *Crisis*, 36 nn. 102–103.

[93] Although Ibrāhīm al-Jūzajānī and others are famous exceptions: see al-ʿUqaylī, *Muʿjam nawāṣib al-muḥaddithīn*.

his peers in proto-Sunnī *ḥadīth* circles describe animosity toward ʿAlī as arising from envy, greed, and pride. In addition, Shīʿī and pro-ʿAlid Muʿtazilī writers argued that many Muslims were jealous of ʿAlī's close relationship to the Prophet, his marriage to Fāṭima, and his victories in battle during the lifetime of the Prophet. After the Prophet's death, ʿAlī's rivals sought to obtain power, wealth, and land, which led them to reject any pro-ʿAlid arguments for his authority or preeminence.[94] According to pro-ʿAlids and Shīʿīs, his contemporaries refused to recognize his right to the caliphate because his pious and egalitarian methods of governance hindered their aspirations for upward mobility. Recognition of any of ʿAlī's merits would have delegitimized a rival's own claim to authority. Some Umayyads and other late converts to Islam are further portrayed as detesting ʿAlī for his role in killing their kin in the battles led by the Prophet. Finally, Khawārij are commonly described as condemning ʿAlī as an infidel for agreeing to arbitration of his dispute with Muʿāwiya. During ʿAlī's lifetime, an individual's contempt for him may have originated from any of these varied motivations. After his death, anti-ʿAlid sentiment may have flourished due to Umayyad and ʿAbbāsid propaganda that was both anti-ʿAlid and anti-Shīʿī. To avoid provoking the ire of anti-ʿAlids, the descendants of ʿAlī sometimes concealed their identities when traveling. One of the most prominent ʿAlid chieftains and jurists of the eighth century, Jaʿfar al-Ṣādiq, is quoted as cautioning his contemporaries, "Beware of mentioning ʿAlī and Fāṭima, for people detest nothing more than the mention of ʿAlī and Fāṭima."[95] It seems that the statement would have been pertinent to ʿAlids living under the Umayyads or the ʿAbbāsids.

The historical tensions among Companions, ʿAlids, and caliphs, among competing Shīʿī factions, between pro-ʿAlid and anti-ʿAlid currents in Sunnism, and finally between Shīʿīs and Sunnīs complicate the classification of individuals as *nawāṣib* and our understanding of *naṣb*. Identifying these tensions helps to contextualize the doctrines and personalities in Islamic history that have been associated with *naṣb*. The next chapter examines historical reports about the earliest proponents of *naṣb*: the Umayyads and the ʿUthmānīs. The case studies that follow (in Chapters 3 to 5) offer a broad overview of anti-ʿAlid beliefs as they appear

94 See Ibn Abī ʾl-Ḥadīd, *Sharḥ* (and the historical sources that the author uses); al-Sharīf al-Murtaḍā, *al-Shāfī fī ʾl-imāma*. For English narratives, see also Jafri, *Origins*; Madelung, *Succession*.

95 Al-Kulaynī, *al-Kāfī*, 8:159. I am indebted to Hossein Modarressi for this reference.

in the works of influential authors who were accused of harboring anti-ʿAlid sentiment themselves. As the reception of their works and the translated excerpts demonstrate, Sunnī theologians faced a major challenge in discrediting Shīʿism without disrespecting ʿAlī in the eyes of their coreligionists with pro-ʿAlid commitments.

2

The Umayyads and the ʿUthmānīs

Praise the Lord who made the truth manifest and . . . killed the liar, son of a liar Ḥusayn, the son of ʿAlī and his partisans

—Ibn Ziyād (d. 67/686)[1]

Those who fought against ʿAlī and his descendants (or participated in their massacre) in early Islamic history are usually characterized as anti-ʿAlid in pro-ʿAlid Kūfan *ḥadīth*, Muʿtazilī historical accounts, and Shīʿī literature. Umayyads, Zubayrids, ʿAbbāsids, and their partisans largely serve as the villains in such narratives. Shīʿīs were keen to include among the villains Companions who not only emerged as rivals to ʿAlī after the death of the Prophet but also allegedly expressed antipathy to ʿAlī during the Prophet's lifetime. Shīʿī authors used certain cues to inform their readers that a particular person was anti-ʿAlid without using the word *naṣb* by portraying the character as maliciously plotting to oppose the ʿAlids or as confessing his hatred of them. Such individuals were also described as hypocrites or as marked by envy (*ḥasad*).

The political careers of many of the figures discussed in this chapter demonstrate their opposition to the restriction of religious and political authority to ʿAlī and his descendants. Although these figures are depicted in historical literature as disagreeing with Shīʿī doctrines, this investigation does not assume the historicity of the anti-ʿAlid sentiments attributed to them. Rather, the literature I discuss confirms that at least some Muslims in both proto-Sunnī and Shīʿī circles believed that these reports accurately

[1] Al-Ṭabarī, *Tārīkh*, 4:350–351.

reflected the past. These authors accepted the presumption that some Companions and their partisans were anti-ʿAlid.

LEADING ELDERS OF THE TRIBE OF QURAYSH

Wilferd Madelung has listed numerous passages in the works of al-Balādhurī, Ibn Abī ʾl-Ḥadīd (d. 656/1258), and well-known biographical dictionaries in the Sunnī tradition that indicate that ʿAlī and al-Ḥasan believed that the tribe of Quraysh collectively refused to recognize their right to rule.[2] "Quraysh" seems to refer primarily to Abū Bakr, ʿUmar, ʿUthmān, and their partisans; in other words, ʿUthmānīs (ʿUthmāniyya). Pro-ʿAlids in Sunnī *ḥadīth* and Muʿtazilī circles occasionally interpreted opposition to ʿAlī's claim to the caliphate as stemming from anti-ʿAlid sentiment. Madelung's extensive examples of ʿUthmānī and pro-Umayyad attitudes in the early community are not repeated here to avoid redundancy, but this section provides additional indications of Qurashī anti-ʿAlidism.

Both ʿUmar and Muʿāwiya are portrayed as acknowledging, on behalf of the elders of Quraysh, that "they detested the idea of prophethood and the caliphate remaining in one family."[3] In one report, ʿUmar explains that ʿAlī is disliked because of his youth and his love for his Hāshimid kinsmen.[4] Other comments from ʿUmar suggest that he was acutely aware that ʿAlī considered himself and his family the rightful heirs to the caliphate.[5]

According to Caetani and Madelung, the interests of the leaders of Quraysh who sought political power and hegemony over the Islamic empire were virtually identical to those of the Umayyads.[6] These leaders generally pursued policies that did not benefit Hāshimids, Arabs of other tribes, or non-Arabs. ʿUthmānīs who supported the Quraysh extolled the virtues of Abū Bakr, ʿUmar, and the commanders of the army that faced

[2] These views are expressed in their alleged letters to Muʿāwiya: see Madelung, *Succession*, 213–214 (for ʿAlī), 314 (for Ḥasan). For Shīʿī *iḥtijāj* literature of this type, see al-Ṭabrisī, *al-Iḥtijāj*. See also Ḥasan, *Munāẓarāt fī ʾl-imāma*.

[3] Al-Balādhurī, *Ansāb al-ashrāf*, 10:378; al-Suyūṭī, *al-Durr al-manthūr*, 2:173; al-Ṭabarī, *Tārīkh*, 3:288. Al-Balādhurī and al-Ṭabarī cited al-Madāʾinī as their source. See also Madelung, *Succession*, 67–68.

[4] Madelung, *Succession*, 68. [5] Ibid., 28–29, 72–73.

[6] Ibid., 96 (also citing Caetani). The dominance of Quraysh in the reign of the first three caliphs can be observed from the ascendancy of the Umayyads and their partisans during ʿUthmān's rule.

ʿAlī at the battle of the Camel.[7] This party also defended the legacy of ʿUthmān after his death in spite of their opposition to Umayyad ascendancy near the end of his life. After the battle of the Camel, ʿUthmānīs in Yemen sought the patronage of Muʿāwiya.[8] The Zubayrids revived their claim to the caliphate and the interests of Qurashī aristocrats after Muʿāwiya's death.

ʿĀʾisha

Sunnī literature occasionally portrayed ʿĀʾisha, the daughter of Abū Bakr and the wife of the Prophet, as loathing ʿAlī, some of his close kin, and his disciples. For example, al-Zuhrī (d. 124/742) and Maʿmar b. Rāshid (d. 153/770) quote Ibn ʿAbbās (d. ca. 68/687) as explaining that ʿĀʾisha was reluctant to refer to ʿAlī in favorable terms.[9]

She is also portrayed as jealous of the Prophet's love for and devotion to others. The amount of affection and time the Prophet gave to others is a central source of tension and competition in narratives regarding ʿĀʾisha, and this preoccupation may help explain her alleged resentment toward ʿAlī. For example, exegetes of the Qurʾān report that after the Prophet began to prolong his visits to his wife Zaynab bt. Jaḥsh, ʿĀʾisha became jealous and devised a plan that would embarrass him and cause him to refrain from visiting Zaynab so frequently.[10] On another occasion, ʿĀʾisha criticized the Prophet for spending too much time with ʿAlī.[11] In an argument with the Prophet she complained, "By God, I have come to know that you love ʿAlī more than you love my father and me."[12] The

[7] Ibid., 147. The inhabitants of Mecca, the historical home of Quraysh, also refused to pledge allegiance to ʿAlī and supported ʿĀʾisha at the battle of the Camel: see ibid., 155.

[8] Ibid., 298 (for Ṣanʿāʾ), 305 (for Ḥaḍramawt).

[9] Al-ʿAynī, *ʿUmdat al-qārī*, 5:192; al-Balādhurī, *Ansāb al-ashrāf*, 1:545; Ibn Ḥajar al-ʿAsqalānī, *Fatḥ al-bārī*, 2:131; al-Ṭabarī, *Tārīkh*, 2:433. For a canonical report in which ʿĀʾisha refused to mention the name of ʿAlī, see al-Bukhārī, *Ṣaḥīḥ*, 1:162, 3:135, 5:140; Muslim, *Ṣaḥīḥ*, 2:22.

[10] Abū Dāwūd al-Sijistānī, *Sunan*, 2:191; Aḥmad b. Ḥanbal, *al-Musnad*, 6:221; al-Bukhārī, *Ṣaḥīḥ*, 6:68, 167; Muslim, *Ṣaḥīḥ*, 4:184; al-Nasāʾī, *Sunan al-Nasāʾī*, 6:151, 7:13, 71; al-Suyūṭī, *al-Durr al-manthūr*, 6:239. For further references, consult works of exegesis for Q66:1–12.

[11] Ibn Abī ʾl-Ḥadīd, *Sharḥ*, 9: 195.

[12] Aḥmad b. Ḥanbal, *al-Musnad*, 4:275; al-Haythamī, *Majmaʿ al-zawāʾid*, 9:126–127; Ibn Ḥajar al-ʿAsqalānī, *Fatḥ al-bārī*, 7:19; al-Nasāʾī, *al-Sunan al-kubrā*, 5:139, 365. Note that some *ḥadīth* transmitters suppressed all references to the Prophet's love of ʿAlī in some recensions of the report: see Abū Dāwūd al-Sijistānī, *Sunan*, 2:477.

Prophet's other wives reportedly felt that ʿĀʾisha sought to monopolize his time.[13]

The Prophet is portrayed as having loved his first wife, Khadīja, deeply and as having refrained from marrying another woman in her lifetime. ʿĀʾisha reportedly admitted to being jealous of the Prophet's lifelong devotion to Khadīja's memory and his praise of her.[14] The fact that Khadīja bore him children was a source of great happiness for the Prophet,[15] but it may have been a source of resentment for ʿĀʾisha, who never became a mother. In ʿĀʾisha's feuds with Fāṭima, the latter became a living reminder of Khadīja in the Prophet's home.[16] According to pro-ʿAlid *ḥadīth*, ʿĀʾisha acknowledged that Fāṭima and her husband were the people most beloved by the Prophet.[17] Once the couple began to have children, the Prophet may have increased the amount of time he spent with them, to ʿĀʾisha's disappointment.

Ibn Abī ʾl-Ḥadīd provides an explanation for ʿĀʾisha's dislike of ʿAlī from one of his teachers, the Ḥanafī Abū Yaʿqūb Yūsuf b. Ismāʿīl al-Lamghānī (d. 606/1209), another Muʿtazilī who upheld *tafḍīl ʿAlī*. The two provide the following account:

> The more the Prophet praised Fāṭima, the more ʿAʾisha resented her. [According to Sunnī *ḥadīth*,] ʿAlī encouraged the Prophet to marry other women in place of ʿĀʾisha during a scandal in which she was accused of infidelity.[18] This event is cited as a reason for her resentment toward ʿAlī. Furthermore, when the Prophet closed Abū Bakr's door to the mosque, he then opened ʿAlī's. Later, he sent her father with [the chapter of the Qurʾān entitled] *al-Barāʾa* [Q9] to Mecca but then forbade him from presenting it and sent ʿAlī in his place. During the Prophet's final illness, ʿAlī believed that both ʿĀʾisha and Ḥafṣa rushed to have their fathers [Abū Bakr and ʿUmar] lead the community's prayers. When the Prophet realized their ambitions he became upset and said, "You are like the women of Joseph!"[19]

13 Aḥmad b. Ḥanbal, *al-Musnad*, 6:88; Muslim, *Ṣaḥīḥ*, 7:136.

14 According to Sunnī canonical *ḥadīth* she states that she never envied anyone more than Khadīja: see Aḥmad b. Ḥanbal, *al-Musnad*, 6:58, 202; al-Bukhārī, *Ṣaḥīḥ*, 4:230–231; Muslim, *Ṣaḥīḥ*, 7:133–134.

15 Al-Bukhārī, *Ṣaḥīḥ*, 4:231.

16 Ibn Abī ʾl-Ḥadīd argued that it would only have been natural for Fāṭima to have resented her stepmother and ʿĀʾisha to have resented the daughter of Khadīja: see Ibn Abī ʾl-Ḥadīd, *Sharḥ*, 9:192–193.

17 Al-Ḥākim al-Naysābūrī, *al-Mustadrak*, 3:157; Ibn ʿAbd al-Barr, *al-Istīʿāb*, 4:1897; Ibn ʿAsākir, *Taʾrīkh*, 42:261–263; al-Nasāʾī, *Khaṣāʾis*, 109; al-Nasāʾī, *al-Sunan al-kubrā*, 5:139–140; al-Tirmidhī, *Sunan*, 5:362.

18 Al-Bukhārī, *Ṣaḥīḥ*, 3:155; Muslim, *Ṣaḥīḥ*, 8:115; al-Suyūṭī, *al-Durr al-manthūr*, 5:25. Imāmī literature did not narrate this episode and some Shīʿī scholars doubt its historicity: see al-Amīn, *Aʿyān al-Shīʿa*, 1:393; al-ʿAskarī, *Aḥādīth Umm al-Muʾminīn ʿĀʾisha*, 2:165–184.

19 A reference to Q12:30–33, 50–51. ʿUthmānī *ḥadīth* noted that the Prophet said these words when ʿĀʾisha piously protested his resolute desire for Abū Bakr to lead the prayers.

Fāṭima and ʿAlī refused to join the community in pledging allegiance to ʿĀʾisha's father after the death of the Prophet. Fāṭima further disputed with Abū Bakr regarding the inheritance of the Prophet, her ownership of various estates, and a designated share in the spoils of war. It seems that ʿAlī only reluctantly pledged allegiance a few months later after Fāṭima passed away. ʿĀʾisha, in turn, publicly refused to recognize the legitimacy of ʿAlī's caliphate and led an army against him after the death of ʿUthmān.[20]

The views of al-Lamghānī and Ibn Abī 'l-Ḥadīd are representative of many pro-ʿAlids who lived before the widespread acceptance of Sunnī creeds and methodologies such as belief in the righteousness of all Companions and the tendency to refrain from transmitting reports about their misdeeds. It seems that some Shāfiʿīs and Ḥanafis who were Muʿtazilīs continued to reject these tenets well into the thirteenth century. They freely narrated eighth-century reports that portrayed Companions acting sinfully. Although they considered the soldiers who fought against ʿAlī at the battle of the Camel to be doomed, they excepted the commanders from hellfire. Since these Sunnī Muʿtazilīs affirmed the merits of Ṭalḥa, al-Zubayr, and ʿĀʾisha as preserved in Sunnī literature, they also accepted reports about their repentance and reasoned that all of them were inhabitants of Heaven.[21]

Al-Bukhārī and others also transmit reports which confirm that the Umayyads identified ʿAlī as one of the slanderers of ʿĀʾisha in the *Ifk* incident.[22] This belief provided a persuasive explanation for the poor relations between ʿAlī and ʿĀʾisha.

ʿAbd Allāh b. al-Zubayr and the Zubayrids

Some historical literature portrays ʿAbd Allāh b. al-Zubayr (d. 73/692) as despising ʿAlī and his household.[23] After ʿAlī became caliph, Ibn al-Zubayr and his family led a rebellion against ʿAlī. In fact, as a grandson of the first caliph, Abū Bakr, Ibn al-Zubayr had an even greater interest in opposing

The pro-Abū Bakr reports are widely reported; for a small selection of the material, see ʿAbd al-Razzāq al-Ṣanʿānī, *al-Muṣannaf*, 5:433 (in this version ʿĀʾisha's concern is her father's social standing); Aḥmad b. Ḥanbal, *al-Musnad*, 6:34, 96:159, 202; al-Bukhārī, *Ṣaḥīḥ*, 162, 165–166, 4:122; al-Tirmidhī, *Sunan*, 5:275–6; Ibn Abī Shayba, *Muṣannaf*, 2:228; Ibn Māja, *Sunan*, 1:390; Mālik, *al-Muwaṭṭa*ʾ, 1:170–171; Muslim, *Ṣaḥīḥ*, 2:22–23, 25.

20 For additional arguments and the full text, see Ibn Abī 'l-Ḥadīd, *Sharḥ*, 9:192–199.

21 Ibid., 6:214, 17:254. For references to ʿĀʾisha's repentance in Sunnī literature, see Spellberg, *Politics, Gender, and the Islamic Past*, 119–120.

22 Al-Bukhārī, *Ṣaḥīḥ*, 5:60; Ibn Ḥajar al-ʿAsqalānī, *Fatḥ al-bārī*, 7:335–337.

23 For reports from ʿUmar ibn Shabba and other sources now lost, see Ibn Abī 'l-Ḥadīd, *Sharḥ*, 4:61ff.

ʿAlī than his own father, al-Zubayr (d. 36/656).[24] The commanders at the battle of the Camel may have viewed themselves as representatives of the family of Abū Bakr and appealed to his memory for authority. All three daughters of Abū Bakr as well as ʿAbd al-Raḥmān, one of his two surviving sons, were present in the army against ʿAlī. ʿĀʾisha, Abū Bakr's second daughter, possessed the most clout as the Prophet's widow. His eldest daughter, Asmāʾ, was married to one commander of the army, al-Zubayr, and his youngest daughter, Umm Kulthūm, was married to the other, Ṭalḥa b. ʿUbayd Allāh (d. 36/656). Further, Ṭalḥa's father and Abū Bakr were brothers, making Ṭalḥa a son-in-law and nephew to the first caliph. The war thus pitted Abū Bakr's family against ʿAlī's kin, consisting of al-Ḥasan, al-Ḥusayn, Muḥammad b. al-Ḥanafiyya, ʿAbd Allāh b. ʿAbbās, other Hāshimids, and their supporters. Abū Bakr's youngest son, Muḥammad b. Abī Bakr (d. 38/658), who had been raised in ʿAlī's home as a stepson, joined ʿAlī's army as an ardent pro-ʿAlid. ʿĀʾisha reportedly considered ʿAlī and his partisans responsible for ʿUthmān's death and believed the third caliph to have been unequivocally better than ʿAlī.[25] The soldiers in her army also voiced anti-ʿAlid sentiments by blaming the Hāshimids for ʿUthmān's death.[26]

As a grandson of Abū Bakr, Ibn al-Zubayr was well positioned to revive the family's claim to the caliphate two decades after their defeat at the battle of the Camel. When the Hāshimids of Mecca refused to pledge allegiance to Ibn al-Zubayr, he is reported to have shown public animosity toward them, having previously concealed his true feelings for decades.[27] According to the sources, he felt that whenever the Prophet was mentioned, the Hāshimids would display excessive pride in their kinship to him. Consequently, he made a conscious effort to refrain from mentioning Muḥammad's name in his sermons:[28]

[24] For indications that Ibn al-Zubayr vigorously opposed ʿAlī, in contrast to his father, see al-Balādhurī, *Ansāb al-ashrāf*, 2:255; Ibn ʿAbd al-Barr, *al-Istīʿāb*, 3:906; Ibn Abī Shayba, *al-Muṣannaf*, 7:271; Ibn ʿAsākir, *Taʾrīkh*, 18:404; Ibn al-Athīr, *Usd al-ghāba*, 3:162–163. When al-Zubayr promised ʿAlī that he would desist from participating in the war, Ibn al-Zubayr became upset with him and urged him to break his oath, even mocking him as afraid of ʿAlī's military prowess and the prospect of death in some recensions: see al-Balādhurī, *Ansāb al-ashrāf*, 2:255; al-Bayhaqī, *Dalāʾil al-nubuwwa*, 6:415; al-Ḥākim al-Naysābūrī, *al-Mustadrak*, 3:366; Ibn ʿAsākir, *Taʾrīkh*, 18:410; Ibn Aʿtham al-Kūfī, *al-Futūḥ*, 2:470; Ibn Kathīr, *al-Bidāya wa ʾl-nihāya*, 6:238; al-Ṭabarī, *Tārīkh*, 3:520–521. See also Madelung, *Succession*, 105.

[25] Madelung, *Succession*, 107.

[26] Ibid., 156 (for a Meccan aristocrat who accuses the Hāshimids of ʿUthmān's murder).

[27] Al-Balādhurī, *Ansāb al-ashrāf*, 3:291.

[28] Ibid., 3:291, 7:133; Ibn Abī ʾl-Ḥadīd, *Sharḥ*, 4:61–62. See also Athamina, "The Sources," 259.

By God, I ceased to mention [the Prophet] publicly but continued to do so in private and abundantly. I did this when I saw that the Hāshimids would rejoice whenever they heard his name. By God, I will never give them any reason to rejoice! It is my desire to confine them to an enclosure made of firewood and burn them alive. Were I to kill them, I have no doubt that I would be killing sinful and unbelieving men who only bewitch others (*āthiman kaffāran saḥḥāran*). May God diminish them in number and never give them grace! They are an evil clan ... The Prophet of God left nothing [or no one] good among them ... They are the most deceitful of men.[29]

Ibn al-Zubayr also imprisoned Ibn al-Ḥanafiyya and Ibn ʿAbbās.[30] They were rescued after he threatened to burn them alive and made relevant arrangements.[31]

After the fall of the Zubayrid caliphate, members of the family continued to flourish in the community as *ḥadīth* transmitters and scholars. A few, such as Muṣʿab al-Zubayrī (d. 236/851) and his father, were criticized for anti-ʿAlid sentiment.[32] A prolific and respected *ḥadīth* transmitter, ʿUrwa b. al-Zubayr (d. 94/712–13), was portrayed as an anti-ʿAlid in pro-ʿAlid Muʿtazilī circles. According to Abū Jaʿfar al-Iskāfī and Ibn Abī ʾl-Ḥadīd, ʿUrwa belonged to a group of transmitters who fabricated reports to defame ʿAlī.[33] ʿUrwa claimed, for instance, that ʿĀʾisha had told him, "I was with the Messenger of God when he saw ʿAbbās and ʿAlī. He said, 'O ʿĀʾisha, indeed these two shall not die as members of my community (*millatī*).' He may have said, 'my religion (*dīnī*).'" ʿUrwa also quoted ʿĀʾisha as having said, "I was with the Prophet when he saw ʿAbbās and ʿAlī. He said, 'If you would like to take pleasure in looking at two men from the people of Hell, then look at these two who have just appeared.'"[34]

THE UMAYYADS

There is evidence that the Umayyads claimed to be the Prophet's kin and his heirs. According to some reports, when the ʿAbbāsids entered the

[29] The text is a fragment from the writings of al-Madāʾinī: see Ibn Abī ʾl-Ḥadīd, *Sharḥ*, 20:127–128.

[30] Al-ʿAynī, *ʿUmdat al-qārī*, 18:267; al-Balādhurī, *Ansāb al-ashrāf*, 5:317; Ibn Ḥajar al-ʿAsqalānī, *Fatḥ al-bārī*, 8:245. See also Anthony, "The Meccan Prison," 10–22; Athamina, "The Sources," 259 n. 138.

[31] Al-Balādhurī, *Ansāb al-ashrāf*, 3:282; al-Ṭabarī, *Tārīkh*, 4:545. See also Anthony, "The Meccan Prison," 11, 13.

[32] Ibn Abī ʾl-Ḥadīd, *Sharḥ*, 19:91–94 (for a hagiographical report in which Yaḥyā al-Daylamī curses the father and causes his death); Ibn al-Athīr, *al-Kāmil*, 7:57. Muṣʿab was the son of ʿAbd Allāh b. Muṣʿab b. Thābit b. ʿAbd Allāh b. al-Zubayr.

[33] Ibn Abī ʾl-Ḥadīd, *Sharḥ*, 4:63–64. [34] Ibid.

Levant, some Syrians were confused by their claims to represent the Prophet's family, saying that they had not known the Prophet to possess relatives other than the Umayyads.[35] In their efforts to discredit the claims of their ʿAlid rivals, the Umayyads were keen to erase any distinction between the Hāshimids and other members of Quraysh. They hoped to persuade the Muslim community to consider the descendants of Hāshim and ʿAbd Shams equivalent in their kinship to the Prophet. The two progenitors were brothers and equal sons of ʿAbd Manāf; thus, the Umayyads argued, one branch could not claim superiority over the other.[36] Since the Umayyads viewed ʿAlids and their partisans as a threat to their authority, they killed many of ʿAlī's most famous companions, publicly cursed the ʿAlids, and portrayed them as heretics. For example, Ḥujr b. ʿAdī (d. 51/671) and Maytham b. Yaḥyā al-Tammār (d. 60/692) were two disciples of ʿAlī who were executed for publicly opposing the anti-ʿAlid rhetoric of the Umayyads.[37]

It seems that some Umayyads harbored rancor for ʿAlī because he had killed their relatives in the Prophet's wars with Quraysh.[38] For example, ʿAlī was responsible for the deaths of many of Muʿāwiya's relatives.[39] But only Yazīd b. Muʿāwiya is quoted as acknowledging openly that he had avenged the deaths of his kinsmen who died at Badr by killing Hāshimids and residents of Medina in turn.[40] Muʿāwiya justified his rebellion against ʿAlī by claiming to be the rightful successor to ʿUthmān and the member of his family most capable of avenging his death. Since the Umayyads considered ʿAlī culpable in ʿUthmān's murder, they collectively rejected him as a pretender to the caliphate.[41] After ʿAlī's assassination, the Umayyads succeeded in reclaiming the authority they had previously wielded during

[35] Ibn Abī 'l-Ḥadīd, *Sharḥ*, 7:159; al-Maqrīzī, *al-Nizāʿ wa 'l-takhāṣum*, 68. See also Sharon, "Umayyads as Ahl al-Bayt," 120.

[36] Al-Jāḥiẓ, "Faḍl Hāshim ʿalā ʿAbd Shams," 455. See also Sharon, "Umayyads as Ahl al-Bayt," 139 n. 49.

[37] Madelung, *Succession*, 334–339. Ḥujr b. ʿAdī and Maytham were two companions of ʿAlī who refused to disassociate from him. For a further discussion of disassociation (*barāʾa*) and references to these two individuals, see Kohlberg, "Barāʾa in Shīʿī Doctrine," 156.

[38] According to Shīʿīs and those who upheld *tafḍīl ʿAlī* this was a reason why many members of Quraysh and other Arabs did not wish ʿAlī to succeed the Prophet as caliph, but al-Jāḥiẓ dismisses this argument: see al-Jāḥiẓ,"Risālat al-ʿUthmāniyya," 164.

[39] Madelung, *Succession*, 218 n. 300.

[40] Al-Balādhurī, *Ansāb al-ashrāf*, 5:333; al-Dīnawarī, *al-Akhbār al-ṭiwāl*, 267; Ibn Aʿtham al-Kūfī, *al-Futūḥ*, 5:129; Ibn al-Jawzī, *al-Muntaẓam*, 5:343; Ibn Kathīr, *al-Bidāya wa 'l-nihāya*, 8:209; Ibn Ṭayfūr, *Kitāb balāghāt al-nisāʾ*, 21; al-Ṭabarī, *Tārīkh*, 8:187–188.

[41] That Muʿāwiya and his party never recognized ʿAlī as caliph is evident even in narratives of the arbitration in which they refused the inclusion of his title "Commander of the Faithful" in the treaty: see Madelung, *Succession*, 242.

the reign of ʿUthmān. Although al-Ḥasan b. ʿAlī briefly managed to rally a coalition of supporters to wage war against Muʿāwiya, a mutiny within his army and a number of other setbacks led him to negotiate a surrender and seek a general amnesty for his followers.[42] Muʿāwiya was reportedly delighted when al-Ḥasan died some years later, since al-Ḥasan's absence facilitated Yazīd's succession.[43] Umayyad hostility to the Prophet's grandsons is also apparent in Marwān b. al-Ḥakam's successful effort to prevent the burial of al-Ḥasan next to Muḥammad. Marwān reportedly sought to please Muʿāwiya by gathering a police force and blocking the funeral procession from reaching the site of Muḥammad's grave.[44] Although al-Ḥusayn b. ʿAlī (d. 61/680) took great offense, he refrained from clashing with the Umayyad forces, and commanded the procession to bury his brother in the great cemetery of Medina instead.

According to al-Jāḥiẓ and al-Maqrīzī (d. 845/1442), the Umayyads assaulted Hāshimids without justification on numerous occasions. These attacks included going to war against ʿAlī, poisoning al-Ḥasan, and sending Busr b. Abī Arṭāt on raids that led to the murder of two young sons of ʿUbayd Allāh b. ʿAbbās.[45] Although some authors sought to defend Yazīd as a pious Muslim,[46] he is explicitly described as a *nāṣibī* in other biographies.[47] Historians generally criticized him for causing the deaths of al-Ḥusayn and of the sons of ʿAlī and ʿAqīl b. Abī Ṭālib at Karbalāʾ, killing many Medinese Hāshimids at the battle of al-Ḥarra, taking the Prophet's female descendants captive, disrobing ʿAlī b. al-Ḥusayn (d. ca. 94/712) and threatening to execute him, and poking al-Ḥusayn's decapitated head with his cane.[48]

42 For a monograph on al-Ḥasan's caliphate and details regarding his surrender, see Āl Yāsīn, *Ṣulḥ al-Ḥasan*.

43 Abū Dāwūd al-Sijistānī, *Sunan*, 2:275 (although this recension omits Muʿāwiya's name); al-Jāḥiẓ, *al-Bayān wa 'l-tabyīn*, 592; al-Ṭabarānī, *al-Muʿjam al-kabīr*, 3:43, 20:269; Aḥmad b. Ḥanbal, *al-Musnad*, 4:132.

44 Al-Dhahabī, *Siyar*, 2:605; Ibn ʿAsākir, *Taʾrīkh*, 13:290–291, 67:355; Ibn Kathīr, *al-Bidāya wa 'l-nihāya*, 8:116. See also al-ʿAwwād, *al-Naṣb*, 679. In Shīʿī sources, ʿĀʾisha also objects to al-Ḥasan's burial next to the Prophet: see Spellberg, *Politics, Gender, and the Islamic Past*, 117–118.

45 Al-Jāḥiẓ, "Faḍl Hāshim ʿalā ʿAbd Shams," 421–423; al-Maqrīzī, *al-Nizāʿ wa 'l-takhāṣum*, 27–34 (for a list of the crimes Umayyads perpetuated against Hāshimids).

46 Murtaḍā al-ʿAskarī references three positive opinions of Yazīd in the Sunnī intellectual tradition: (1) some prohibited cursing him and considered him a believer; (2) some declared him a *mujtahid* and an imām who was justified in attacking dissenters; and (3) others considered his actions to be acceptable errors: see al-ʿAskarī, *Maʿālim*, 2:75.

47 Al-Dhahabī, *Siyar*, 4:37.

48 Al-Jāḥiẓ, "Faḍl Hāshim ʿalā ʿAbd Shams," 421–422; Maqrīzī, *al-Nizāʿ wa 'l-takhāṣum*, 27–34.

Near the end of ʿAlī's caliphate, Busr b. Abī Arṭāt infamously led raids to terrorize citizens who pledged allegiance to ʿAlī and to obtain support for Muʿāwiya.[49] As a loyal Umayyad soldier he considered everyone who was not a partisan of ʿUthmān to share in the guilt for ʿUthmān's death, and he thus included Hāshimids and the inhabitants of Medina among the culprits.[50] The Hāshimids he killed included descendants of Abū Lahab and the children of ʿUbayd Allāh b. ʿAbbās.[51] After al-Ḥasan's abdication, Muʿāwiya made Busr the governor of Baṣra. In his first sermon as governor, Busr used foul language (*shatama*) to disparage ʿAlī.[52] Despite the campaign of terror, murder, and looting that he carried out under orders from Muʿāwiya, Ibn Taymiyya considered Busr a reliable transmitter of *ḥadīth*.[53]

The following sections examine the circulation and reception of portrayals of specific Umayyads as anti-ʿAlids in Sunnī literature.

Marwān b. al-Ḥakam Cursing ʿAlī

A number of reports claim that Marwān b. al-Ḥakam cursed ʿAlī in public during his term as governor of Medina because he believed that the practice strengthened partisanship and support for the Umayyad dynasty.[54] The following section presents four different types of texts related to Marwān's devotion to cursing ʿAlī from the pulpit. The tendency of transmitters to exclude certain details in their narrations indicates their attitudes and concerns about Marwān. I present the most explicit reports first; the increasingly indirect nature of the subsequent reports suggests a gradual process of censorship.

Aḥmad b. Ḥanbal reported from Isḥāq b. ʿUmayr, a resident of Medina during the reign of Muʿāwiya, that "Marwān was our governor for six years, and he would revile (*yasubb*) ʿAlī every Friday [during the sermon]. Then he was dismissed and replaced with Saʿīd b. al-ʿĀṣ (d. ca 59/678–9), who governed for two years. He would not verbally abuse [ʿAlī]. Later Marwān was reappointed, and the cursing continued."[55]

[49] For details regarding his violent raids, see Madelung, *Succession*, 299–307.

[50] Ibid., 301–302. [51] Ibid., 301, 303–304.

[52] Ibn al-Athīr, *al-Kāmil*, 3:414; Ibn al-Jawzī, *al-Muntaẓam*, 5:186; al-Ṭabarī, *Tārīkh*, 4:128.

[53] Ibn Taymiyya, *Minhāj*, 1:456.

[54] Al-Dhahabī, *Taʾrīkh*, 3:460–461; Ibn ʿAsākir, *Taʾrīkh*, 42:438; al-Iskāfī, "Naqḍ al-ʿUthmāniyya," 283. See also Madelung, *Succession*, 334.

[55] Aḥmad b. Ḥanbal, *al-ʿIlal*, 3:176; Ibn ʿAsākir, *Taʾrīkh*, 57:243; Ibn Kathīr, *al-Bidāya wa ʾl-nihāya*, 8:284.

A second report, included in *Ṣaḥīḥ Muslim*, describes a governor of Medina "from the family of Marwān" who not only cursed ʿAlī but also ordered a revered Companion and member of the Medinese aristocracy, Sahl b. Saʿd al-Anṣārī (d. ca. 91/710), to do so publicly as well. The governor to whom the report refers was Marwān b. al-Ḥakam himself, but the recension does not name him out of respect for both pro-Umayyad sensibilities and Sunnī creed which upheld the righteousness of all Companions. The report states:

> A member of the family of Marwān became the governor of Medina. He once requested the presence of Sahl b. Saʿd. After [Sahl appeared, they engaged in a conversation in] which he [the governor] ordered him to insult (*yashtam*) ʿAlī [in a public gathering]. Sahl refused. [The governor] said, "If you will not do this, then [at least] proclaim, 'God damn (*laʿana Allāh*) Abū Turāb.'"[56]

Al-Bukhārī included a heavily censored version of the report in his *Ṣaḥīḥ*. The name of the governor, Sahl's direct witnessing of the governor's anti-ʿAlid sentiment, the governor's order to direct explicit language toward ʿAlī, and his final compromising request to damn ʿAlī with a short invocation are all omitted. Al-Bukhārī's version reads as follows:

> A man came to Sahl b. Saʿd and said, "So-and-so, the governor of Medina, *yadʿū ʿAliyyan* from the pulpit."
> Sahl asked, "What does he say?"
> The man said, "He says Abū Turāb ("Father of Dust")."
> Sahl laughed, "By God, it was the Prophet who gave him that name."[57]

According to Sibṭ b. al-Jawzī (d. 654/1256), the unnamed man said, "He says Abū Turāb and damns (*yalʿan*) Abū Turāb";[58] but al-Bukhārī's wording, *yadʿū ʿAliyyan*, is both slightly ambiguous and seemingly innocuous. The phrase could be understood as "he mentions ʿAlī by another name." Without any context, the reader is left with the impression that an anonymous and ignorant person mentioned to Sahl that he had heard the governor refer to ʿAlī with a strange nickname, and that Sahl jovially explained that the governor had done nothing wrong, since the Prophet himself gave the nickname to ʿAlī. A reader aware of the Umayyad practice of cursing ʿAlī from the pulpits could read the phrase as "he invokes evil upon ʿAlī" (*yadʿū* [*ʿalā*] *ʿAlī*). However, both of these readings

[56] Al-Bayhaqī, *al-Sunan al-kubrā*, 2:446; al-Ḥākim al-Naysābūrī, *al-Mustadrak*, 211; Ibn ʿAsākir, *Taʾrīkh*, 42:17; Muslim, *Ṣaḥīḥ*, 7:123–124. See also al-Mālikī, *Naḥwa inqādh al-tārīkh*, 21–27.

[57] Al-Bukhārī, *Ṣaḥīḥ*, 4:207–208. [58] Sibṭ Ibn al-Jawzī, *Tadhkirat al-khawāṣṣ*, 16.

are probably incorrect. As Ibn Ḥajar al-ʿAsqalānī notes in his commentary, the phrase *yadʿū ʿAliyyan* may have been shortened from *yadʿūka li-tasubb ʿAliyyan* ("he invites you to curse ʿAlī"), which is the phrasing found in other recensions of this report.[59]

Finally, in one parallel recension, all references to any disparagement of ʿAlī have been removed, and Sahl's explanation that the Prophet called ʿAlī Abū Turāb appears as the first element. Al-Bukhārī and others reported a story from Sahl b. Saʿd in which the Prophet visits Fāṭima after she has a disagreement with ʿAlī and the latter leaves the home. When the Prophet finds ʿAlī at the mosque covered in dust, he addresses him with the nickname.[60] It is probable that *ḥadīth* transmitters omitted any reference to the Umayyad practice of cursing ʿAlī from this recension to placate Muslims in the early ʿAbbāsid period who refused to hear or transmit reports that portrayed the Umayyads negatively.

Ibn Ḥajar al-Haytamī argues that no *ṣaḥīḥ* report exists in which Marwān curses ʿAlī and his family. However, in another work he himself cites reports that depict Marwān doing just that.[61]

Al-Mughīra Cursing ʿAlī

A number of sources depict al-Mughīra b. Shuʿba (d. 50/670) as ritually cursing and disparaging ʿAlī in his sermons when he served as the governor of Kūfa during Muʿāwiya's reign.[62] The motif appears in two recensions of a famous Sunnī *ḥadīth* about the ten Companions who were granted paradise. In these reports, witnesses state that "al-Mughīra b. Shuʿba began to deliver a sermon and then disparaged (*nāla*) ʿAlī. This prompted Saʿīd b. Zayd to stand up [and interrupt him] . . ."[63]

Aḥmad b. Ḥanbal and al-Ḥākim al-Naysabūrī (d. 405/1014) report that al-Mughīra b. Shuʿba cursed (*sabba*) ʿAlī in a speech, causing Zayd b. Arqam (d. 66/686 or 68/688) to stand up and address him thus: "Indeed you know that the Messenger of God prohibited the cursing of the

[59] Ibn Ḥajar al-ʿAsqalānī, *Fatḥ al-bārī*, 7:58.

[60] Al-Bukhārī, *al-Adab al-mufrad*, 183; al-Ījī, *Tawḍīḥ al-dalāʾil*, 163; Muḥibb al-Dīn al-Ṭabarī, *Dhakhāʾir al-ʿuqbā*, 57.

[61] Ibn Ḥajar al-Haytamī, *al-Ṣawāʿiq al-muḥriqa*, 55, 139; Ibn Ḥajar al-Haytamī, *Taṭhīr al-janān*, 95–96.

[62] Al-Dhahabī, *Siyar*, 3:31; al-Ḥākim al-Naysābūrī, *al-Mustadrak*, 3:450; Ibn al-Jawzī, *al-Muntaẓam*, 5:241.

[63] Abū Dāwūd al-Ṭayālisī, *Musnad*, 32; Abū Yaʿlā al-Mawṣilī, *Musnad*, 2:259; Aḥmad b. Ḥanbal, *al-ʿIlal*, 1:188; Aḥmad b. Ḥanbal, *al-Musnad*, 1:188.

deceased. Why do you curse (*tasubb*; lit., verbally abuse) ʿAlī when he is dead?"[64]

Muʿāwiya Cursing ʿAlī

Various proto-Sunnī *ḥadīth* transmitters in the early ʿAbbāsid period as well as later Sunnīs such as Ibn Taymiyya accepted reports about ʿAlī, Muʿāwiya, and their partisans mutually supplicating for the damnation of one another.[65] For example, both Abū Yūsuf (d. 182/798) and al-Shaybānī (d. 189/804) narrate from Abū Ḥanīfa (d. 150/767) that ʿAlī would supplicate against Muʿāwiya in his *qunūt* and vice versa: "ʿAlī began to supplicate against Muʿāwiya in his prayers when he confronted him in war. The Kūfans then followed him in this practice. Likewise, Muʿāwiya began to supplicate against ʿAlī in his prayers, and the Syrians followed him in this practice."[66]

Al-Balādhurī, al-Ṭabarī, Ibn al-Athīr (d. 630/1233), and Ibn Khaldūn (d. 808/1406) transmit a similar report:

> When ʿAlī offered his dawn prayers, he would supplicate [in the course of his *qunūt*], "O God, damn (*ilʿan*) Muʿāwiya, ʿAmr, Abū 'l-Aʿwar al-Sulamī, Ḥabīb [b. Maslama al-Fihrī], ʿAbd al-Raḥmān b. Khālid [b. al-Walīd], al-Ḍaḥḥāk b. Qays, and al-Walīd [b. ʿUqba]." When news of this reached Muʿāwiya, he would, when offering *qunūt*, damn ʿAlī, Ibn ʿAbbās, [Mālik] al-Ashtar, al-Ḥasan, and al-Ḥusayn.[67]

In his refutation of al-ʿAllāma al-Ḥillī's (d. 726/1326) claims about history, Ibn Taymiyya argues that one should not assume that Muʿāwiya and his partisans were alone in cursing their rivals. The practice may have fallen under the heading of *ijtihād*, or it might have been a sin. Either way, Ibn Taymiyya implies that since ʿAlī and his party also engaged in the practice, Muʿāwiya should not be denounced for it:

> As for what he [al-ʿAllāma al-Ḥillī] has mentioned regarding invocations for the damnation of ʿAlī [from Umayyad pulpits]: both parties engaged in supplications against one another, just as they mutually engaged in war. Each party would supplicate for the damnation of the leaders of the rival faction. Furthermore, it is narrated that each faction would use the *qunūt* to supplicate against the other. In

[64] Aḥmad b. Ḥanbal, *al-Musnad*, 4:369; al-Ḥākim al-Naysābūrī, *al-Mustadrak*, 1:385.
[65] Ibn Taymiyya, *Minhāj*, 4:468.
[66] Abū Yūsuf, *Kitāb al-Āthār*, 71; al-Shaybānī, *al-Āthār*, 1:595–599.
[67] Al-Balādhurī, *Ansāb al-ashrāf*, 2:352; Ibn al-Athīr, *al-Kāmil*, 3:333; Ibn Khaldūn, *Tārīkh*, 2.II: 178; al-Ṭabarī, *Tārīkh*, 4:52.

any case, armed conflict is graver than mutual cursing (*al-talāʿun*), which is only speech. Whether it is considered a sin or *ijtihād*, God forgives all of it through repentance.[68]

Once Muʿāwiya became caliph, he is reported to have issued the following supplication from the pulpit every Friday: "May God damn Abū Turāb; indeed, he has become heretical in his practice of Your religion and has obstructed the path to You. Damn him grievously and punish him severely!"[69]

Anti-Shīʿī polemicists generally reject reports that Muʿāwiya cursed ʿAlī from the pulpit or instituted the practice of doing so. One group of scholars insists that the claim that he did either is a Shīʿī fabrication that appears only in untrustworthy works of history, not in the canonical Sunnī *ḥadīth* collections that are regarded as containing authentic reports about the past.[70] A second group recognizes the existence of such reports in the canonical collections but argues that one should interpret these reports charitably. For example, Aḥmad b. ʿUmar al-Qurṭubī (d. 656/1258) suggested that Muʿāwiya may have merely criticized ʿAlī's alleged association with ʿUthmān's assassins and his decision to wage war against other Muslims, instead of cursing him; later *ḥadīth* transmitters then misidentified this criticism as *sabb*.[71] Al-Nawawī (d. 676/1277) argued that Muʿāwiya simply asked another Companion, Saʿd b. Abī Waqqāṣ (d. ca. 50–8/670–8), amicably and without rancor, why he refrained from cursing ʿAlī.[72] Reports about this incident are discussed further in the next section. Finally, a third group of scholars asserts that both historical works and canonical *ḥadīth* collections such as *Ṣaḥīḥ Muslim* contain fabricated reports about Muʿāwiya cursing ʿAlī.[73] Some scholars, such as Maḥmūd

[68] Ibn Taymiyya, *Minhāj*, 4:468.

[69] Ibn Abī 'l-Ḥadīd, *Sharḥ*, 4:56–57 (citing an unspecified work of al-Jāḥiẓ as his source).

[70] ʿUmar al-Bāḥith and ʿAbd al-Ḥalīm ʿUways argue along these lines: see al-Bāḥith, "Firyat amr Muʿāwiya ibn Abī Sufyān"; al-Mālikī, *Naḥwa inqādh al-tārīkh*, 20.

[71] Al-Qurṭubī, *al-Mufhim*, 6:278–279.

[72] Al-Nawawī, *Sharḥ Ṣaḥīḥ Muslim*, 15:175–176; al-Qurṭubī, *al-Mufhim*, 6:278–279. See also al-Madkhalī, "Bayān manāqib Muʿāwiya raḍiya Allāh ʿanhu wa 'l-dhabb ʿan *Ṣaḥīḥ Muslim*."

[73] ʿUmar al-Bāḥith limits his analysis to a report which Nāṣir al-Dīn al-Albānī considered *ṣaḥīḥ* in *Sunan Ibn Māja*. His argument that the report, despite appearing in a canonical compilation, has narrators who have been criticized in biographical sources could hypothetically be extended to *Ṣaḥīḥ Muslim*, as Suhayla Ḥammād has done. A leading Wahhābī cleric, Rabīʿ al-Madkhalī, has taken Ḥammād to task for rejecting the authenticity of these reports found in *Ṣaḥīḥ Muslim*: see al-Bāḥith, "Firyat Muʿāwiya yanālu min ʿAlī ibn Abī Ṭālib"; al-Ḥammād, "Muʿāwiya raḍiya Allāh ʿanhu al-muftarā ʿalayhi"; al-Madkhalī, "Bayān manāqib Muʿāwiya."

Shukrī al-Ālūsī (d. 1342/1924), vacillate between the three approaches. On one occasion, he claims that all reports about Muʿāwiya's cursing of ʿAlī were false; on another, he admits that although *ṣaḥīḥ ḥadīth* attesting to such cursing do exist, they should be interpreted charitably to preserve Muʿāwiya's honor. And in a third instance, he advises readers to refrain from accepting as authentic any apparently *ṣaḥīḥ ḥadīth* that make such claims about Muʿāwiya.[74] All of these defenses rest on the theological principle that Muʿāwiya, like any other Muslim who met the Prophet Muḥammad, is above reproach and therefore could never have cursed ʿAlī.

Adopting the first approach, the popular contemporary Salafī jurist Muḥammad Ṣāliḥ al-Munajjid characterizes reports according to which Muʿāwiya cursed ʿAlī as fabrications. However, his opinion is based on a misrepresentation of the sources; he does not acknowledge the existence of a report in *Ṣaḥīḥ Muslim* that problematizes his claims.[75] He appeals to the authority of "al-Ālūsī" but does not make it clear that he is referring to a scholar of the twentieth century instead of the celebrated exegete of the Qurʾān, Shihāb al-Dīn al-Ālūsī (d. 1270/1854). He also omits some of the commentary provided by al-Qurṭubī and Maḥmūd Shukrī al-Ālūsī that contradicts his thesis.[76] Reports about Muʿāwiya's cursing of ʿAlī evidently forced Sunnīs to address their theological and epistemological assumptions regarding accounts that depict Companions as villains, the principle of interpreting charitably any reports about their misconduct, and the authenticity of *ḥadīth* that appear in both canonical and noncanonical collections. Since both Sunnīs and Shīʿīs were invested in discrediting each other's historical narratives, the Sunnī authors discussed here were ever vigilant in their efforts to ensure that Shīʿīs could not effectively use Sunnī literature to substantiate their doctrines. The greatest sources of tension lay in the Sunnīs' defense of blanket statements such as "all Companions are righteous" and their balancing of sectarian allegiances

[74] Maḥmūd Shukrī al-Ālūsī, *Ṣabb al-ʿadhāb*, 421–422, cf. 427.

[75] Although he mentions a similar report transmitted by al-Ḥākim and al-Nasāʾī, their recensions (conveniently for him) exclude an introductory sentence found in Muslim's version where Muʿāwiya appears to command Saʿd to curse ʿAlī: see Muslim, *Ṣaḥīḥ*, 7:120; cf. al-Ḥākim al-Naysābūrī, *al-Mustadrak*, 3:108; al-Munajjid, "Lam yathbut ʿan Muʿāwiya sabb ʿAlī"; al-Nasāʾī, *Khaṣāʾis*, 48, 81.

[76] Al-Munajjid does not acknowledge to the reader that al-Qurṭubī admitted that Muʿāwiya may have criticized ʿAlī in a way that others may have described as *sabb* or that al-Ālūsī recognized the existence of *ṣaḥīḥ* reports, but consciously rejected their contents: see al-Munajjid, "Lam yathbut ʿan Muʿāwiya sabb ʿAlī"; cf. al-Ālūsī, *Ṣabb al-ʿadhāb*, 422; al-Qurṭubī, *al-Mufhim*, 6:278–279.

(i.e., the assumption that Shīʿī claims are generally false)[77] with epistemic ones (i.e., the axiom that only the Qurʾān surpasses the *Ṣaḥīḥayn* in the authenticity of its contents)[78] when these principles occasionally contradicted each other.

Muʿāwiya Cursing ʿAlī in the Presence of Saʿd b. Abī Waqqāṣ

Saʿd b. Abī Waqqāṣ was a member of the electoral council that elected the third caliph, but he subsequently joined neither ʿAlī's army nor any of the factions that rebelled against him. According to some historians, Muʿāwiya attempted to secure political support from Saʿd or, at the very least, a public condemnation of ʿAlī. Saʿd refused all his advances, but Sunnī *ḥadīth*, biographical, and historical sources reproduce a story in which Muʿāwiya curses ʿAlī in the presence of this prominent Companion. A comparison of the five different extant versions of this story demonstrates how elements of it were censored to reflect the sensibilities of the transmitters and consumers of Sunnī *ḥadīth*.

The first three versions of the story appear to reflect environments in which transmitters did not wish to be seen as dishonoring Muʿāwiya or sympathizing with Shīʿism. The first version suppresses both Muʿāwiya's identity and his command to curse ʿAlī. According to one report in *Ṣaḥīḥ Muslim*, ʿĀmir b. Saʿd simply reported from his father that the Prophet had praised ʿAlī as possessing the rank of Aaron, the brother of Moses. The report makes no reference to the public cursing of ʿAlī or to the historical context that led Saʿd to narrate this *ḥadīth*.[79] This distinction conferred by the Prophet on ʿAlī is mentioned along with two others in all of the parallel recensions below. In other versions of the report, however, there are subtle allusions to Muʿāwiya's request that Saʿd curse ʿAlī:

According to Aḥmad b. Ibrāhīm al-Dawraqī (d. 246/860), ʿĀmir b. Saʿd reported the following from his father: "Saʿd joined *the company of a man* who asked, "What keeps you from cursing *so-and-so*?" He said, "I remember three things that the Messenger of God said to him, and therefore I will never curse him . . ."[80]

According to Ibn al-Bāghandī (d. 312/925), ʿĀmir b. Saʿd reported that "*a man passed by* Saʿd and asked, 'What keeps you from cursing Abū Turāb?'"[81]

[77] Ibn Taymiyya's *Minhāj al-sunna* is exemplary in reflecting this tenet.
[78] Ibn Ḥajar al-ʿAsqalānī, *Taghlīq al-taʿlīq*, 5:423–426; Ibn Ṣalāḥ, *Muqaddimah*, 19–21. See also Brown, *Canonization*.
[79] Muslim, *Ṣaḥīḥ*, 7:120. [80] Al-Dawraqī, *Musnad Saʿd ibn Abī Waqqāṣ*, 51.
[81] Ibn ʿAsākir, *Taʾrīkh*, 42:112. It seems *amara* became *marra* in a few recensions.

According to the Ḥanafī jurist Muḥammad b. Yūsuf al-Zarandī (d. 750/1347), ʿĀmir b. Saʿd reported from his father that *a head of state* asked him, "What keeps you from cursing Abū Turāb?" He said, "I remember three things that the Messenger of God said to him, and therefore I will never curse him . . ."[82]

It is unclear to what extent the above three authors censored their own transmissions or were genuinely unaware that the questioner in this incident was Muʿāwiya. In the case of al-Zarandī, it is relatively unlikely that he redacted the text himself since his book contains other reports that portray Muʿāwiya unfavorably.[83] He cites *Sunan al-Tirmidhī* as his source, but this source names Muʿāwiya as the questioner. It is possible that other authors received their narrations from sources that were sensitive to negative portrayals of Muʿāwiya, but this is not the case with al-Zarandī. Perhaps al-Zarandī or a later copyist omitted Muʿāwiya's name here out of respect for the sensibilities of his audience. The same may be said of al-Dawraqī, who lived in ninth-century Baghdad when pro-Muʿāwiya sentiment was popular among some residents.

Al-Ḥākim al-Naysābūrī and al-Nasāʾī (d. 303/915) transmit the second version of the story which reveals Muʿāwiya's identity but omits the command to curse ʿAlī: "ʿĀmir b. Saʿd reported that Muʿāwiya once asked Saʿd, 'What keeps you from cursing Abū Turāb?'"[84]

In the third version, Muʿāwiya's command appears in the text, but it is partially censored with the removal of the second verb: ʿĀmir b. Saʿd reported that "Muʿāwiya b. Abī Sufyān ordered Saʿd [. . .]. Then he asked, 'What keeps you from cursing Abū Turāb?'"[85] The lacuna in the text appears to be an incomplete deletion of Muʿāwiya's command to curse ʿAlī. This is the version that appears in Muslim's *Ṣaḥīḥ*.

The fourth version contains Muʿāwiya's command in full, but it provides no further detail about the historical setting of the incident. This version appears only in thirteenth- and fourteenth-century *ḥadīth* collections dedicated to the merits of ʿAlī. This report is transmitted on the authority of Saʿd b. Abī Waqqāṣ: "Muʿāwiya commanded Saʿd to curse Abū Turāb. However, [Saʿd] objected, saying, 'But I remember three things

82 Al-Zarandī, *Naẓm durar al-simṭayn*, 107.

83 Al-Zarandī points to reports where ʿAlī disparages him, Muʿāwiya keeps the company of someone who curses ʿAlī, and another report in which he wishes to dishonor al-Ḥasan: see ibid., 97, 108, 200–201.

84 Al-Ḥākim al-Naysābūrī, *al-Mustadrak*, 3:108; al-Nasāʾī, *Khaṣāʾis Amīr al-Muʾminīn*, 81.

85 Al-Bāʿūnī, *Jawāhir al-maṭālib*, 1:171; al-Dhahabī, *Taʾrīkh*, 3:627; Ibn ʿAsākir, *Taʾrīkh*, 42:111; Ibn Kathīr, *al-Bidāya wa ʾl-nihāya*, 7:376; Muslim, *Ṣaḥīḥ*, 7:120; al-Nasāʾī, *al-Sunan al-kubrā*, 5:107–108; al-Tirmidhī, *Sunan*, 5:301.

that the Prophet said to him [ʿAlī] ...”[86] Ibn al-Biṭrīq's (d. ca. 600/1203) transmission from *Ṣaḥīḥ Muslim* differs slightly from the other recensions in that it quotes Muʿāwiya's command in the first person: “Muʿāwiya ordered Saʿd,[87] ‘I command you to curse Abū Turāb.’ He [Saʿd] answered, ‘But I remember three things that the Prophet said to him that ensure I will never curse him ...’”[88] Ibn al-Biṭrīq's recension thus complements versions that reproduce Muʿāwiya's command in the third person.

The fifth, final version of the story quotes Muʿāwiya either disparaging ʿAlī himself or explicitly commanding Saʿd to curse him, and it provides a context for Saʿd's response. In this version, found in the *Sunan* of Ibn Māja, ʿĀmir b. Saʿd reported from his father that Muʿāwiya visited *dār al-nadwa*[89] near the Kaʿba on one of his pilgrimages. Saʿd soon joined the gathering, and those present started discussing ʿAlī. Muʿāwiya disparaged ʿAlī, causing Saʿd to become angry and say, “You talk this way about a man of whom I heard the Messenger of God say, ‘ʿAlī is the *mawlā* of whoever considered me his *mawlā* ...’”[90] Ibn ʿAsākir (d. 571/1176) and Ibn Kathīr (d. 774/1373) transmit a more detailed version of the incident:

> ʿĀmir b. Saʿd reported from his father that during his pilgrimage, Muʿāwiya took the hand of Saʿd b. Abī Waqqāṣ and said, “O Abū Isḥāq! Conquest has prohibited us from carrying out the pilgrimage for so long that we have almost forgotten some of its rites ...” Once he [Saʿd] completed the rites, [Muʿāwiya] invited him to enter the *dār al-nadwa* and sit next to him on his throne. Then he mentioned ʿAlī b. Abī Ṭālib and vilified him (*waqaʿa fīhi*). [Saʿd] responded, “You invited me to your private residence and sat me on your throne, then you proceed to vilify [ʿAlī] and insult him (*tashtumuhu*)?”[91]

The first two versions of the story best reflect the efforts of transmitters to narrate material that did not implicate Companions in any scandalous behavior. The third version indicates that Muʿāwiya commanded Saʿd to carry out an action, but the verb that should have appeared after the command (*amara Muʿāwiya ...*) is missing and leaves the sentence incomplete. A hypothetical *urtext* would have included this verb as well as Saʿd's refusal to fulfill the command (i.e., *amara Muʿāwiya Saʿd b. Abī*

[86] Al-Ījī, *Tawḍīḥ al-dalāʾil*, 312; Muḥibb al-Dīn al-Ṭabarī, *al-Riyāḍ al-naḍira*, 3:152; al-Qundūzī, *Yanābīʿ al-mawadda*, 2:119.

[87] Either a copyist or the Shīʿī Ibn al-Biṭrīq adds here, “and may God damn him (Muʿāwiya).”

[88] Ibn al-Biṭrīq, *Khaṣāʾiṣ al-waḥy al-mubīn*, 126.

[89] Originally a meeting place of Quraysh, later a place of residence for nobility (e.g., the caliphs in the Umayyad and ʿAbbāsid periods) near the Kaʿba.

[90] Ibn Māja, *Sunan*, 1:45.

[91] Ibn ʿAsākir, *Taʾrīkh*, 42:119; Ibn Kathīr, *al-Bidāya wa ʾl-nihāya*, 7:376.

Waqqāṣ an yasubb 'Aliyyan fa-abā). The deletion of both the second verb and Saʿd's reaction may serve as an example of discreet censorship that occurred in the transmission of *ḥadīth*. It is unclear whether eighth-century transmitters who appear as informants in *Ṣaḥīḥ Muslim*, the compiler, or subsequent copyists of this collection played a role in modifying this report.

The fourth version of this report appears to leave the complete command intact (*amara Muʿāwiya Saʿdan an yasubb Abā Turāb*). Version four appears in relatively late sources such as the *ḥadīth* compilations of Aḥmad b. Jalāl al-Dīn al-Ījī and Muḥibb al-Dīn al-Ṭabarī (d. 694/1295). Although version four provides greater coherence to Muʿāwiya's alleged command to Saʿd, it displays a few irregularities which suggest that it is only a shortened form of version three.[92] One indication is that all of the authors who report version four cite earlier collections that only report version three. In version four, the speaker (Saʿd) also awkwardly switches from the third to the first person, a corruption that was introduced in the text's revision.

The fifth version reflects the type of report transmitted in circles that were generally concerned with history (*akhbār*) rather than *ḥadīth*. It provides the most details, a coherent narrative, and some historical context regarding the meeting between Saʿd and Muʿāwiya. Muḥammad b. Isḥāq (d. 150/767) is listed as a source of this version, and he probably included the story in his history of the caliphate.

The above versions of Muʿāwiya's encounter with Saʿd reflect some of the ways Sunnīs dealt with texts that portrayed Muʿāwiya disparaging ʿAlī. Some authors such as Ibn Isḥāq and Ibn ʿAsākir were willing to transmit *akhbār* that did not appear in *ḥadīth* collections. Other *ḥadīth* transmitters were circumspect in the material that they narrated, and omitted references to Muʿāwiya's name or his disparagement of ʿAlī.

Ibn Ḥajar al-Haytamī scoured numerous Sunnī *ḥadīth* collections for obscure reports about the *faḍā'il* of Muʿāwiya and carefully responded to a number of criticisms about his character. However, in his monograph dedicated to the rehabilitation of Muʿāwiya, he oddly never addresses the reports preserved in revered *ḥadīth* collections (such as *Ṣaḥīḥ Muslim*) that depict Muʿāwiya disparaging ʿAlī or ordering others to curse him. The absence of any discussion of the topic is conspicuous and may indicate

[92] Version four is missing the portion [*fa-qāla mā yamnaʿuk*] and *tasubb* is mistakenly emended to *yasubb*. Shams al-Dīn al-Bāʿūnī (d. 871/1467) reports version four of the *ḥadīth*, but the editor of his work corrects it to version three: see al-Bāʿūnī, *Jawāhir al-maṭālib*, 1:171.

al-Haytamī's hesitancy to deal with evidence that directly contradicts his thesis that Muʿāwiya revered ʿAlī and never questioned his merits or superiority.[93]

It seems that al-Haytamī wanted his audience to subsume any claim about Muʿāwiya cursing ʿAlī under the heading of false reports about Muʿāwiya. Had he chosen to discuss the reports on the subject that appear in *Ṣaḥīḥ Muslim*, al-Haytamī could have followed al-Nawawī in interpreting them in a favorable light to deny that Muʿāwiya ever explicitly cursed ʿAlī or called on others to do so.[94] Hypothetically, al-Haytamī could have argued that even if Muʿāwiya did curse ʿAlī, he was a Companion and a *mujtahid* with only good intentions (and thus free of any anti-ʿAlid sentiment) and must have made a mistake in doing so. Consequently, God would still reward him with paradise, and Muslims should overlook his honest mistake. Al-Haytamī employed a similar argument when discussing Muʿāwiya's rebellion against ʿAlī.[95] The modern anti-Shīʿī and anti-Sufi polemicist ʿAbd al-Raḥmān al-Dimashqiyya (b. 1957) argues along such lines. He acknowledges that a few *ṣaḥīḥ* reports seem to indicate that al-Mughīra b. Shuʿba and Muʿāwiya cursed ʿAlī, but he claims that once other Companions explained the prohibition against cursing ʿAlī, Muʿāwiya and al-Mughīra realized the error of their ways and ceased cursing him.[96]

The Umayyads and al-Ḥasan b. ʿAlī

Al-Zubayr b. Bakkār (d. 256/870), Ibn Abī 'l-Ḥadīd, and Shams al-Dīn Muḥammad b. Aḥmad al-Bāʿūnī (d. 871/1466) narrate an ostensibly pro-ʿAlid report in which al-Ḥasan b. ʿAlī and his rivals are portrayed as arguing against one another until al-Ḥasan succeeds in shaming his interlocutors for accusing him and his father of any misconduct.[97] Despite the hagiographic nature of this report and the fact that al-Ḥasan emerges as

93 Ibn Ḥajar al-Haytamī, *Taṭhīr al-janān*, 77.
94 Al-Nawawī, *Sharḥ Ṣaḥīḥ Muslim*, 15:175–176.
95 Ibn Ḥajar al-Haytamī, *Taṭhīr al-janān*, 77.
96 Dimashqiyya, "Ibṭāl daʿwā 'l-rāfiḍa anna 'l-dawlat al-umawiyya wa baʿḍ al-ṣaḥāba kānū yalʿanūn sayyidanā ʿAlī ibn Abī Ṭālib."
97 Al-Bāʿūnī, *Jawāhir al-maṭālib*, 2:217–220; Ibn Abī 'l-Ḥadīd, *Sharḥ*, 6:285–294. The Egyptian writer Muḥammad Diyāb al-Itlīdī (active 1100/1689) narrates the report without mentioning his source: see al-Itlīdī, *Nawādir al-khulafāʾ*, 27–29. For other anecdotes with a similar theme, see al-Jāḥiẓ (attr.), *al-Maḥāsin wa 'l-aḍdād*, 133–142; Sibṭ Ibn al-Jawzī, *Tadhkirat al-khawāṣṣ*, 182–184.

the victor in it, the ʿUthmānī and Umayyad reports discussed in this chapter (and in the appendix) suggest that the anti-ʿAlid views expressed by al-Ḥasan's opponents in this report enjoyed relatively uncensored currency until the era of al-Jāḥiẓ. According to Ibn Abī 'l-Ḥadīd's copy[98] of al-Zubayr b. Bakkār's *al-Mufākharāt* (which is no longer extant), Muʿāwiya told al-Ḥasan, "We invited you here so that you may concede that ʿUthmān was murdered unlawfully and that your father killed him . . ." Then ʿAmr b. al-ʿĀṣ (d. ca. 43/663) began to censure ʿAlī, claiming that "ʿAlī disparaged Abū Bakr and loathed his succession; he refused to pledge allegiance to him until he was coerced; he was partially responsible for ʿUmar's assassination; he unlawfully murdered ʿUthmān; and then he falsely claimed a right to the caliphate."[99] ʿAmr then blamed ʿAlī for his conduct in the civil wars and argued that God would not grant the Hāshimids any political authority because they hankered after power, had the blood of caliphs and innocent people on their hands, and had committed other sinful acts to obtain it. He continued:

As for you, O al-Ḥasan . . . You have neither the fortitude nor the intellect to rule as caliph. God has removed your intellect and made you the idiot of your tribe (*aḥmaq Quraysh*) . . . as a consequence of the sins of your father. We have brought you here to disgrace you and your father. As for your father, God decided to take care of him for us. As for you . . . if we executed you, neither would God consider it a sin nor would society censure us for it.[100]

Al-Walīd b. ʿUqba, ʿUtba b. Abī Sufyān, and al-Mughīra b. Shuʿba all reiterated the accusation that ʿAlī killed ʿUthmān or, more precisely, that he was culpable in ʿUthmān's death since, they believed, his assassins were mostly obedient to ʿAlī. Al-Walīd also exclaimed, "O children of Hāshim, you were the maternal uncles of ʿUthmān . . . but the first to become jealous of him, so your father killed him wrongfully . . ."[101] ʿUtba b. Abī Sufyān, for his part, told al-Ḥasan:

O al-Ḥasan, your father was the worst Qurashī to afflict the tribe of Quraysh. He shed their blood the most. He had a shameful sword and tongue. He killed the living and would disparage the dead . . . Indeed you participated in ʿUthmān's murder and we will execute you in retaliation . . . As for your desire for the caliphate, you are clearly unqualified . . . O children of Hāshim, you killed ʿUthmān and it is our right to execute you and your brother [al-Ḥusayn] in retaliation . . ."[102]

[98] Ibn Abī 'l-Ḥadīd, *Sharḥ*, 6:285–294. [99] Ibid., 6:287. [100] Ibid.
[101] Ibid., 6:287–288. [102] Ibid., 6:288.

THE ʿUTHMĀNĪS

ʿUthmānī Ḥadīth *Transmitters*

In early proto-Sunnī circles, the ʿUthmānīs seem to have fostered a culture that criticized narrators who transmitted pro-ʿAlid reports lauding ʿAlī and his household. Some ʿUthmānīs despised ʿAlī because their forebears had died fighting him (e.g., Abū Labīd al-Baṣrī and Thawr b. Yazīd al-Ḥimṣī).[103] Since they did not consider ʿAlī a legitimate caliph, they frequently viewed those who venerated him with suspicion and accused them of Shīʿism. For example, Yaḥyā b. Maʿīn (d. 233/847) studied with Wakīʿ b. al-Jarrāh (d. 197/812–13) for an extended period and noted that his teacher consciously refrained from narrating *ḥadīth* about the merits of ʿAlī. Finally, Ibn Maʿīn asked, "Why do you refrain from narrating such reports?" Wakīʿ answered, "These people will resent us for [discussing ʿAlī's merits]."[104] Wakīʿ went on to narrate a few reports on the subject to appease Ibn Maʿīn. Other *ḥadīth* transmitters, such as al-Aʿmash (d. 148/765), similarly complained of mosque attendees who prevented scholars from openly narrating reports on ʿAlī's merits.[105] Reports from much later periods describe Sunnīs as objecting in a public outburst and leaving a gathering when the lecturer turns to the subject of ʿAlī's merits. For example, Abū 'l-Faḍl al-Sulaymānī (d. 404/1013) was a Sunnī *ḥadīth* transmitter who became angry and walked out when Abū Bakr al-Dihqān (d. 350/961) began transmitting reports about ʿAlī's merits in a gathering that he attended.[106] In the introduction to his book on ʿAlī, Muḥammad b. Yūsuf al-Kanjī (d. 658/1260) explains that he decided to compose the book after experiencing a similar disruption in 647/1249. Al-Kanjī was lecturing to an audience that included nobility at the *dār al-ḥadīth* in Mosul and decided to conclude his lecture by reciting reports concerning ʿAlī's merits. However, he was dismayed when a member of the audience whom he considered ignorant of *ḥadīth* began to argue against the authenticity of some of the reports.[107]

Providing further evidence of *ḥadīth* scholars' reluctance to discuss ʿAlī's merits, Ibn Ḥibbān reports, "I have not recorded a single *ḥadīth*

[103] See Chapter 2 Appendix, nn. 30–38. [104] Ibn Maʿīn, *Tārīkh*, 1:320.

[105] Al-Fasawī, *al-Maʿrifa wa 'l-taʾrīkh*, 2:764. I am indebted to Hossein Modarressi for this reference.

[106] The transmitter of the report interpreted al-Sulaymānī's actions charitably and argued that he left due to anti-Shīʿī, rather than any anti-ʿAlid, sentiment: see al-Dhahabī, *Siyar*, 15:524; al-Dhahabī, *Taʾrīkh*, 25:450. See also al-ʿAwwād, *al-Naṣb*, 627.

[107] Al-Kanjī, *Kifāyat al-ṭālib*, 36–37.

about the merits of ʿAlī from all that Mālik and al-Zuhrī transmitted."[108] It seems that al-Zuhrī's pro-Marwānid stance[109] and Mālik's ʿUthmānī sympathies[110] led them to reject the authenticity of pro-ʿAlid reports or to refrain from narrating them.[111] Mālik (d. 179/795) believed that ʿAlī desired the caliphate, whereas his predecessors piously did not. According to Mālik, this fact made ʿAlī at the very least inferior to his predecessors,[112] if not altogether illegitimate as a ruler.[113] Al-Bukhārī transmitted a report from Mālik and al-Zuhrī that describes ʿAlī as coveting the caliphate (*wa huwa ʿalā ṭamaʿ*) after ʿUmar's death.[114] Asked about ʿAlī's departure from Medina to engage his rivals at the battle of the Camel and his decision to move the center of his government to Kūfa, where he enjoyed greater support, Mālik reportedly opined, "His *khurūj* was an error."[115] As a follower of Ibn ʿUmar's opinions, Mālik seems to have approved of the former's decision to refrain from participating in ʿAlī's military conflicts with other Muslims in the wake of ʿUthmān's assassination.

ʿUthmānī *ḥadīth* transmitters who denounced and cursed ʿAlī but nonetheless appear in Sunnī *ḥadīth* collections include Qays b. Abī Ḥāzim al-Bajalī (d. 98/717),[116] ʿAbd Allāh b. Shaqīq al-Baṣrī (d. ca. 100/719),[117] Abū Qilāba al-Jarmī (ʿAbd Allāh b. Zayd) al-Baṣrī (d. ca. 104–7/722–25),[118] Maymūn b. Mihrān al-Raqqī (resident of Raqqa,

[108] Ibn Ḥibbān, *Kitāb al-Majrūḥīn*, 1:258.

[109] Al-Balkhī, *Qubūl al-akhbār*, 1:269; Ibn ʿAsākir, *Taʾrīkh*, 42:228.

[110] For the ʿUthmānī sentiments of Mālik and his ancestors, see ʿIyāḍ, *Tartīb al-madārik*, 48, 90.

[111] Mālik reportedly gave the excuse that Ibn ʿAbbās, ʿAlī and their partisans lived in other lands, so he did not rely on them as authorities: see al-Suyūṭī, *Tanwīr al-ḥawālik*, 1:7; al-Zurqānī, *Sharḥ ʿalā Muwaṭṭaʾ*, 1:9.

[112] ʿIyāḍ, *Tartīb al-madārik*, 90.

[113] Although Mālik may not have narrated the maxim, other Sunnīs and Mālikīs believed that a person who coveted authority was not suitable for it: see ʿAbd al-Razzāq al-Ṣanʿānī, *al-Muṣannaf*, 11:320; Abū Dāwūd al-Sijistānī, *Sunan*, 2:13, 159; Aḥmad b. Ḥanbal, *al-Musnad*, 4:409, 5:62–63; al-Bukhārī, *Ṣaḥīḥ*, 3:48, 7:216, 240, 8:50; Ḥaṭṭāb, *Mawāhib al-Jalīl*, 8:69, 85; Ibn ʿAbd al-Barr, *al-Tamhīd*, 21:244; Muslim, *Ṣaḥīḥ*, 5:86, 6:5–6; al-Nasāʾī, *al-Sunan al-kubrā*, 1:64, 3:463–464; al-Qurṭubī, *Tafsīr*, 9:216; al-Tirmidhī, *Sunan*, 3:42.

[114] Al-Bukhārī, *Ṣaḥīḥ*, 8:123. For a report where ʿUmar describes ʿAlī as coveting the caliphate, see Ibn Aʿtham al-Kūfī, *al-Futūḥ*, 2:325.

[115] I am reading *khurūj* as referring not only to ʿAlī's "departure" from the city, but also to his decision to engage in warfare: see ʿAbd al-Malik ibn Ḥabīb, *Kitāb al-taʾrīkh*, 115; al-Qāḍī al-Nuʿmān, *The Eloquent Clarification*, 11, 14.

[116] Ibn Ḥajar al-ʿAsqalānī, *Fatḥ al-bārī*, 10:352; al-Mizzī, *Tahdhīb al-Kamāl*, 24:14.

[117] *wa kāna yaḥmil ʿalā ʿAlī...wa kāna ʿUthmāniyyan ... yubghiḍ ʿAliyyan.* See Ibn ʿAsākir, *Taʾrīkh*, 29:161; al-Mizzī, *Tahdhīb al-Kamāl*, 15:91.

[118] Ibn Ḥajar al-ʿAsqalānī, *Tahdhīb al-Tahdhīb*, 5:198.

d. 118/736),[119] Azhar b. Saʿīd al-Ḥarrāzī al-Ḥimṣī (d. ca. 129/746),[120] Isḥāq b. Suwayd al-ʿAdawī al-Baṣrī (d. 131/748),[121] Mughīra b. Miqsam al-Kūfī (d. 136/753),[122] Asad b. Wadāʿa (d. ca. 136/753),[123] Nuʿāym b. Abī Hind (d. 211/827),[124] Ḥuṣayn b. Numayr al-Wāṣiṭī,[125] and many others. As late as the ninth century, *ḥadīth* transmitters such as the Baṣran Aḥmad b. ʿAbdah al-Ḍabbī (d. 245/859) are described as despising ʿAlī.[126]

ʿUthmānī Muʿtazilīs

A few heresiographies portray early Muʿtazilīs as declining to condemn either army that participated in the battle of the Camel, while acknowledging that one of them must have been in error. Wāṣil b. ʿAṭāʾ, ʿAmr b. ʿUbayd, Ḍirār b. ʿAmr, and Abū ʾl-Hudhayl are mentioned as proponents of this view.[127] The sources attribute anti-ʿAlid sentiment to some early Baṣran Muʿtazilīs, including Abū Bakr al-Aṣamm (d. ca. 201/816) and Hishām al-Fuwaṭī (d. ca. 227–32/842–7), and claim that they rejected the legitimacy of ʿAlī's caliphate altogether. Like other ʿUthmānīs, al-Fuwaṭī believed that ʿAlī's claim to the caliphate was invalid because it had been ratified during a period of sedition and civil war.[128]

Abū Bakr al-Aṣamm staunchly supported Muʿāwiya in his conflict with ʿAlī.[129] He argued that Abū Bakr, ʿUmar, ʿUthmān, and Muʿāwiya had

119 Ibn ʿAsākir, *Taʾrīkh*, 61:348; Ibn Ḥajar al-ʿAsqalānī, *Tahdhīb al-Tahdhīb*, 10:349; al-Mizzī, *Tahdhīb al-Kamāl*, 29:214.

120 Abū Dāwūd al-Sijistānī, *Suʾālāt Abī ʿUbayd*, 2:253; Ibn Ḥajar al-ʿAsqalānī, *Lisān al-Mīzān*, 1:385; Ibn Ḥajar al-ʿAsqalānī, *Tahdhīb al-Tahdhīb*, 1:179; Ibn Maʿīn, *Tārīkh*, 2:326.

121 *kāna yaḥmil ʿalā ʿAlī*. He also reportedly said, "I have no love for ʿAlī." See Ibn Ḥajar al-ʿAsqalānī, *Hady al-sārī*, 387; Ibn Ḥajar al-ʿAsqalānī, *Tahdhīb al-Tahdhīb*, 1:207.

122 Al-Mizzī, *Tahdhīb al-Kamāl*, 28:401.

123 Abū Dāwūd al-Sijistānī, *Suʾālāt Abī ʿUbayd*, 2:253; Ibn Ḥajar al-ʿAsqalānī, *Lisān al-Mīzān*, 1:385; Ibn Maʿīn, *Tārīkh*, 2:326.

124 *kāna yatanāwal ʿAliyyan*. See al-Dhahabī, *Mīzān al-iʿtidāl*, 4:271; Ibn Ḥajar al-ʿAsqalānī, *Tahdhīb al-Tahdhīb*, 10:418.

125 Ibn Ḥajar al-ʿAsqalānī, *Hady al-sārī*, 396; Ibn Ḥajar al-ʿAsqalānī, *Tahdhīb al-Tahdhīb*, 2:337.

126 Melchert, "The Life and Works of Abū Dāwūd," 42. For two modern studies devoted to cataloging Muslims accused of anti-ʿAlid sentiment, see al-Muʿallim, *al-Nuṣb wa ʾl-nawāṣib* and al-ʿUqaylī, *Muʿjam nawāṣib al-muḥaddithīn*.

127 Al-Baghdādī, *Uṣūl al-dīn*, 335; al-Khaṭīb al-Baghdādī, *Taʾrīkh Baghdād*, 12:175. See also al-ʿAwwād, *al-Naṣb*, 634–637. It should be noted that Muʿtazilīs did not consider Ḍirār b. ʿAmr to have been a Muʿtazilī.

128 Al-Baghdādī, *Uṣūl al-dīn*, 272.

129 Ibid., 291; al-Nāshiʾ al-Akbar (attrib.), "Masāʾil al-imāma," 60.

been legitimate caliphs, in contrast to ʿAlī, since political authority could be established only through consensus.[130] Since ʿAlī failed to secure such consensus, his claim to power was invalid.

For al-Aṣamm, Muʿāwiya's legitimacy was confirmed through his appointment as governor of Syria by ʿUmar and ʿUthmān, both of whom had acceded to the caliphate through consensus. As a legitimate governor, Muʿāwiya had no choice but to defend his territory against ʿAlī, an illegitimate pretender, who desired to oust him. Al-Aṣamm also believed that Abū Mūsā al-Ashʿarī (d. ca. 48/668) and ʿAmr b. al-ʿĀṣ had been correct to renounce ʿAlī's caliphate, since it facilitated an eventual consensus in favor of Muʿāwiya.[131]

THE ʿABBĀSIDS

ʿAlid challenges to ʿAbbāsid rule prompted a number of caliphs and their entourages to persecute and wage war against ʿAlids. Similarly, in lands ruled by Zaydīs, ʿAlids regularly fought against one another. In many of these cases, both parties held ʿAlī, Fāṭima, and their children in high esteem but considered their ʿAlid rivals misguided for refusing to recognize their right to rule. Arguably, these political conflicts do not reflect a person's support for anti-ʿAlidism. In a few cases, however, ʿAbbāsid caliphs were known to loathe ʿAlī and his sons.[132] For example, biographers portray al-Mutawakkil (r. 232–247/847–861) as an ardent anti-ʿAlid who mocked ʿAlī for the sake of entertainment and razed the shrine of al-Ḥusayn to the ground.[133] The history of anti-ʿAlid sentiment among ʿAbbāsid caliphs lies beyond the scope of this study.

CONCLUSION

In order to identify pro- and anti-ʿAlid sentiments in Sunnī literature, a schema that recognizes the existence of rival ideological factions in Sunnī Islam on matters related to ʿAlī is helpful. The schema I have

130 Al-Baghdādī, *Uṣūl al-dīn*, 287; al-Nāshiʾ al-Akbar (attrib.), "Masāʾil al-imāma," 59.
131 Al-Baghdādī, *Uṣūl al-dīn*, 292.
132 For poets who lampooned ʿAlids to the delight of some ʿAbbāsids, see Chapter 1 Appendix.
133 Abū ʾl-Fidāʾ, *Tārīkh*, 2:38; al-Dhahabī, *Siyar*, 12:18, 35; al-Dhahabī, *Taʾrīkh*, 18:552; Ibn al-Athīr, *al-Kāmil*, 7:55–56; Ibn Khallikān, *Wafayāt al-aʿyān*, 3:365; al-Qalqashandī, *Maʾāthir al-ināfa*, 1:230–231. See also Modarressi, *Crisis*, 16.

sketched in this chapter provides the context for the following chapters' case studies of the circulation and censorship of reports that portray leading Companions as anti-ʿAlids. The varied reception of *ḥadīth* about ʿAlī and his rivals reflects a process of negotiation among Sunnīs with competing theological commitments that persists even in the modern period. Sunnī theologians with pro-ʿAlid proclivities have accepted the historicity of these portrayals and utilized them to exalt ʿAlī and his family members as righteous figures who faced profound enmity from hostile villains. Meanwhile, Sunnīs committed to the preservation of the dominant orthodoxy denied the historicity of such reports, charitably reinterpreted them, or circulated abridged versions that omitted the objectionable elements. Anti-Shīʿī polemics played an important role in encouraging Sunnīs to deny anti-ʿAlid sentiment among the Companions and to reject *ḥadīth* about ʿAlī's putative merits.

The survey offered in this chapter reveals that a vigorous debate regarding the piety and character of early political leaders raged over many centuries among Muʿtazilī theologians, historians, and Sunnī *ḥadīth* specialists. By the ninth century, the locus of conflict between the competing factions had shifted from the battlefield to *ḥadīth* collections and texts describing the history of the early community. The new weapons of choice included an authorial enterprise that actively chose to portray ʿAlī and his rivals as either villains or saints and an editorial privilege that selected certain texts for preservation while censoring others.

3

The Muʿtazilī: al-Jāḥiẓ

As the previous chapter noted, some Muʿtazilī theologians were ʿUthmānī, while others were pro-ʿAlid. The most enigmatic Muʿtazilī in terms of his political philosophy was the belletrist ʿAmr b. Baḥr al-Jāḥiẓ, who can be described as both. In his *Risālat al-ʿUthmāniyya*, he polemically devalues every possible quality, *ḥadīth*, or verse of the Qurʾān that pro-ʿAlids and Shīʿīs utilized to exalt ʿAlī over Abū Bakr. He then systematically argues in favor of Abū Bakr's preeminence over ʿAlī and all other Muslims after the Prophet.[1] At times al-Jāḥiẓ's arguments are so far-fetched that the reader wonders whether al-Jāḥiẓ believed his own claims. Nonetheless, al-Jāḥiẓ's claims support a thesis that became orthodoxy in Sunnī Islam: each of the early four caliphs was the most virtuous candidate in the community at the time of his accession. In terms of rank, Abū Bakr was superior to ʿUmar, the latter was superior to ʿUthmān, and the latter, in turn, was superior to ʿAlī. In his treatise, al-Jāḥiẓ seeks to dismantle any evidence that could be used to support *tafḍīl ʿAlī*.

The puzzling feature about al-Jāḥiẓ, however, is that elsewhere he utilizes his polemical style to defend the exalted image of ʿAlī that he practically destroys in his *Risālat al-ʿUthmāniyya*. In his *Risālat al-Ḥakamayn* and other works, al-Jāḥiẓ stridently defends ʿAlī's sagacity and piety as a caliph.[2] He does not shy away from recognizing the same

[1] For more on this work, see Afsaruddin, *Excellence*, 13–14. The thesis of his work is that "ʿAlī does not possess a merit except that Abū Bakr possesses one that is superior either in that same regard or another. In addition, Abū Bakr possessed distinctions that neither ʿAlī nor any other person shared with him": see al-Jāḥiẓ, "Risālat al-ʿUthmāniyya," 152.

[2] For his praise of ʿAlī and affirmation of his merits, see al-Jāḥiẓ, "Risālat al-awṭān wa 'l-buldān," 109; al-Jāḥiẓ, "Risālat al-Ḥakamayn," 355, 357, 360, 363, 365, 377, 398.

ʿAlid distinctions that he previously rejected in his *Risālat al-ʿUthmāniyya*. In the *Risālat al-ʿUthmāniyya*, for example, he questions ʿAlī's expertise as a jurist, but in the *Risālat al-Ḥakamayn*, he deems ʿAlī to be flawless in his judgments.[3] Al-Jāḥiẓ himself acknowledges the apparent contradictions between his treatises on the imāmate and explains that he is both ʿUthmānī and pro-ʿAlid at the same time.[4] Although he does not elaborate on what it meant to him to identify with these two competing loyalties, it is apparent from his writings that he revered ʿAlī as the legitimate caliph of the community after the death of ʿUthmān, and also harbored strong anti-Umayyad sentiments. Al-Jāḥiẓ criticizes those who rebelled against ʿAlī, such as Muʿāwiya and the Khawārij, as misguided, and characterizes ʿAlī's words and actions as caliph as politically astute and correct. As I have previously noted, Sunnī orthodoxy sought to interpret the civil wars that occurred during the caliphate of ʿAlī charitably in order to safeguard the reputation of the Companions involved in these conflicts.[5] Once Sunnīs accepted ʿAlī as a legitimate caliph, it was also important to defend ʿĀʾisha and Muʿāwiya as pious participants in their wars against him. For example, in the Sunnī orthodox view, the leaders of the battle of the Camel (ʿĀʾisha, Ṭalḥa, and al-Zubayr) never intended to wage war against ʿAlī. Instead, they sought to capture the assassins of ʿUthmān, and relied on expert juridical reasoning (*ijtihād*) in deciding to raise an army against ʿAlī.[6] So even though ʿAlī is described as having been in the right in the matter, the actions of his opponents can also be considered justified and worthy of God's reward.[7] Some Sunnīs emphasize that the commanders of both armies in the battle of the Camel regretted their participation in the war.[8] From this perspective, ʿAlī does not fare any better than his rivals in terms of his role in the conflict. He is neither superior to his rivals nor confident that his actions were justified according to the law. This image of ʿAlī contradicts the one that appears among pro-ʿAlids.

[3] For al-Jāḥiẓ's critiques of ʿAlī's legal opinions, see al-Jāḥiẓ, "Risālat al-ʿUthmāniyya," 186–188. For his strident defense of ʿAlī's judgments as a leader, see al-Jāḥiẓ, "Risālat al-Ḥakamayn," 355, 357, 360, 363, 365, 377.

[4] Al-Jāḥiẓ, "Risālat al-Ḥakamayn," 369.

[5] See Chapter 1 nn. 46–47.

[6] Ibn al-Fūrak, *Maqālāt*, 194–195; Ibn Ḥazm, *al-Fiṣal*, 4:123; Ibn Taymiyya, *Minhāj*, 4:320; al-Juwaynī, *Kitab al-Irshād*, 433.

[7] Ibn Ḥazm, *al-Fiṣal*, 4:123.

[8] Al-Ḥākim al-Naysābūrī, *al-Mustadrak*, 3:104, 119; Ibn Abī Shayba, *al-Muṣannaf*, 8:718–719. In these reports, ʿAlī is depicted as failing to heed the warnings of his son, al-Ḥasan, to refrain from fighting his opponents in the battle of the Camel. After the war, ʿAlī regrets his actions: see also Ibn ʿAsākir, *Taʾrīkh*, 42:458; Ibn Kathīr, *al-Bidāya wa ʾl-nihāya*, 7:268.

A hallmark of pro-ʿAlids (even among Sunnīs and Muʿtazilīs) is the tendency to regard all rebellions against ʿAlī as errors and acts of disobedience against God and the caliph. Pro-ʿAlids resisted attempts to diminish the gravity of such rebellions or to charitably interpret the intentions of the rebels. Pro-ʿAlid Sunnīs and Muʿtazilīs who wished to refrain from condemning the characters of ʿĀʾisha, Ṭalḥa, and al-Zubayr appealed to reports that indicated that these three personalities repented of their role in waging war against ʿAlī.[9] For pro-ʿAlids, none of the ʿUthmānī or orthodox Sunnī justifications for fighting against ʿAlī were valid. Nonetheless, pro-ʿAlids considered the leaders of the battle of the Camel to have been saved from God's wrath because they realized the legitimacy of ʿAlī's authority and the error of their actions before their deaths. For pro-ʿAlids, ʿAlī was the wise caliph who rightfully put an end to their unlawful rebellion.

Al-Jāḥiẓ's defense of ʿAlī's conduct as caliph and his condemnation of Muʿāwiya ground him firmly as a pro-ʿAlid. The apparent contradiction lies in the juxtaposition of this pro-ʿAlidism with al-Jāḥiẓ's endorsement of the ʿUthmānī position in his other treatise. However, the two positions can be harmonized by recognizing that al-Jāḥiẓ opposed any attempts to elevate ʿAlī above Abū Bakr, ʿUmar, or ʿUthmān. To acknowledge ʿAlī's primacy over his predecessors would have meant that both God and the Muslim community had failed to appoint the best candidate to the position of authority. By holding this view, al-Jāḥiẓ is effectively representing the Baṣran tradition; Baṣrans were famously ʿUthmānī and hostile to Shīʿism. He provides a glimpse into how some ʿUthmānīs may have responded to arguments in support of *tafḍīl ʿAlī*. Al-Jāḥiẓ opposed *tafḍīl ʿAlī* because he believed that the doctrine entailed criticism of Abū Bakr's accession to the caliphate. For al-Jāḥiẓ, the doctrine reflected Shīʿī (or, more precisely, *rāfiḍī*) attempts to defame Abū Bakr and delegitimize his caliphate altogether, which was heresy. Since a defense of ʿAlī's conduct as caliph did not impugn the legitimacy of his predecessors, al-Jāḥiẓ felt free to defend ʿAlī creatively in the *Risālat al-Ḥakamayn*, as he did with Abū Bakr in the *Risālat al-ʿUthmāniyya*.

Al-Jāḥiẓ lived in the eighth and ninth centuries, a period central to the genesis of the Sunnī community. In these two centuries, Muslims witnessed

[9] For the claim that Ṭalḥa and al-Zubayr repented of their participation in the battle of the Camel, see Ibn al-Fūrak, *Maqālāt*, 195. For ʿĀʾisha, see al-Ḥākim al-Naysābūrī, *al-Mustadrak*, 3:119; Ibn Abī Shayba, *al-Muṣannaf*, 8:718; Ibn al-Athīr, *Usd al-ghāba*, 3:284.

the fall of the Umayyad dynasty, an attempt at a Sufyānid restoration,[10] the rise of the scholars of *ḥadīth* and the articulation of Sunnī orthodoxy, and the rejection of overt anti-ʿAlidism in the intellectual tradition. Like the much later Sunnī scholar Ibn Taymiyya, al-Jāḥiẓ wrote extensively about the beliefs of anti-ʿAlids (*nawāṣib*) in the early Muslim community, and sometimes validated them to the extent that both he and Ibn Taymiyya were themselves accused of *naṣb*. In this chapter, I consider some of the doctrines that al-Jāḥiẓ propounds in his *Risālat al-ʿUthmāniyya* that earned him a reputation as an anti-ʿAlid, although he and his admirers considered the accusation unfounded. I discuss the work of Ibn Taymiyya in Chapter 5.

Al-Jāḥiẓ won favor at the ʿAbbāsid court from the reign of al-Maʾmūn (r. 198–218/813–833) to that of al-Mutawakkil.[11] His interest in an encyclopedic array of intellectual questions and in rationalist disputation, and his close acquaintance with the beliefs of his contemporaries, are important assets to this investigation. He was born at the end of the eighth century and flourished in the ninth, a period in which a few Umayyad revolts, led by descendants of Muʿāwiya b. Abī Sufyān, occurred in Syria and pro-Umayyad *ḥadīth* transmitters and theologians rose to great prominence. Al-Jāḥiẓ's exposition of ʿUthmānī and Umayyad views provides important details regarding the anti-ʿAlid and anti-Shīʿī arguments that these groups may have utilized. The Sufyānid revolts at the end of the eighth century indicate that Syria was still a bastion of pro-Muʿāwiya and pro-Umayyad sentiment despite decades of ʿAbbāsid rule. A century later al-Nasāʾī was violently expelled from the Umayyad mosque in Damascus after he attempted to narrate *ḥadīth* about the merits of ʿAlī and refused to entertain his audience's love for legends about Muʿāwiya. He eventually died of the injuries sustained in the Syrian mob's attack.[12] Likewise, the people of Damascus expelled the famous grammarian al-Zajjājī (d. 340/952) from the city for statements that he made in praise of ʿAlī.[13] The expulsions of al-Nasāʾī and al-Zajjājī indicate that anti-ʿAlid sentiment was still prevalent in traditionally pro-Umayyad areas in the tenth century.

In his *Risālat al-ʿUthmāniyya*, al-Jāḥiẓ systematically makes the case that ʿAlī cannot be considered superior to Abū Bakr or to any other

[10] For Syrian attempts at a Sufyānid restoration, see Cobb, *White Banners*; Madelung, "Abū ʾl-ʿAmayṭar the Sufyānī"; Madelung, "The Sufyānī between Tradition and History."

[11] *EI*[2], s.v "Djāḥiẓ" (C. Pellat).

[12] Al-Dhahabī, *Siyar*, 14:132–133; Yāqūt al-Ḥamawī, *Muʿjam al-buldān*, 5:282. See also Melchert, "The Life and Works of al-Nasāʾī," 403–404.

[13] Al-Dhahabī, *Siyar*, 15:476.

Companion. This argument served the ʿUthmānīs, who considered the succession of the first three caliphs legitimate but who doubted or opposed the legitimacy of ʿAlī's caliphate. The partisans of the first three caliphs are referred to as Bakriyya, ʿUmariyya, and ʿUthmāniyya in some heresiographies, but, as in the case of many other so-called sects in Islamic history, it is unclear to what extent the first two groups existed as discrete communities.[14] Biographical entries on *ḥadīth* transmitters and texts composed in the eighth and ninth centuries indicate that those who generally upheld the legitimacy of the first three caliphs were known as ʿUthmānīs (ʿUthmāniyya).

Umayyad partisanship drew strength from and grew out of a partisanship to ʿUthmān, but not all ʿUthmānīs were pro-Umayyads. For example, the Zubayrids and their partisans were both ʿUthmānī and anti-Umayyad. By the time of al-Jāḥiẓ, the only theologians who refused to recognize ʿAlī as a legitimate caliph were pro-Umayyads who revered Muʿāwiya.[15] Aḥmad b. Ḥanbal and other influential early Sunnī scholars had rehabilitated ʿAlī in ʿUthmānī circles to the point that he was widely accepted as the fourth caliph.[16] By contrast, pro-Umayyads identified the rightly guided caliphs in the following order: Abū Bakr, ʿUmar, ʿUthmān, and then Muʿāwiya.[17] When eighth- and ninth-century non-Muslim historians writing in Greek and Syriac listed Muslim rulers, they likewise excluded ʿAlī from their chronicles.[18] Their informants were undoubtedly pro-Umayyads who had considered him a pretender. Al-Jāḥiẓ's *Risālat al-Ḥakamayn* and *Risāla fī ʾl-Nābita* serve as evidence that an ʿUthmānī such as al-Jāḥiẓ could accept ʿAlī as a legitimate caliph after ʿUthmān and remain staunchly anti-Umayyad.[19]

In addition to detailing ʿUthmānī and pro-ʿAlid arguments, al-Jāḥiẓ writes eloquently as a partisan of the Umayyads in his *Risālat al-Ḥakamayn*. Testifying to his caliber as a dialectician, he did not shy away

[14] Al-Mīlānī, *Sharḥ Minhāj al-karāma*, 1:127–128 (for the Bakriyya). Al-Jāḥiẓ refers to the Bakriyya as a group independent of the ʿUmariyya: see al-Jāḥiẓ, "Risālat al-Ḥakamayn," 368. The term Bakriyya may refer to a sect that formed within or separate from the proto-Sunnī community. According to some sources, the Bakriyya believed that the Prophet explicitly designated Abū Bakr to succeed him as caliph: see Afsaruddin, *Excellence*, 29.

[15] Al-Jāḥiẓ, "Risālat al-Ḥakamayn," 385–390. [16] Afsaruddin, *Excellence*, 18.

[17] Al-Ashʿarī, *Maqālāt al-Islāmīyyīn*, 2:144–145; Ibn Taymiyya, *Minhāj*, 4:400–401; Sāmirī, *Samaritan Chronicle*, 53–54, 125–126.

[18] Borrut, "Vanishing Syria," 48–50; Hoyland, *Seeing Islam as Others Saw it*, 394–397, 434–436, 617–618; Wolf, *Conquerors and Chroniclers*, 94–96, 99.

[19] For al-Jāḥiẓ's praise of ʿAlī, see al-Jāḥiẓ, "Risālat al-Ḥakamayn," 398. For his condemnation of Muʿāwiya, see al-Jāḥiẓ, "Risāla fī ʾl-Nābita," 2:241–242.

from articulating coherent and comprehensive arguments in support of the views of interlocutors with whom he disagreed. Al-Jāḥiẓ held that the best dialectician was someone who could expound the views of his rivals and even formulate proofs that they themselves had not considered, and then systematically refute them.[20] If he could argue the views of his rivals more convincingly than their best theologians could, al-Jāḥiẓ reasoned, his own arguments would be all the stronger and his decisive victory in debates with his opponents would be assured.[21] However, herein lies a question that can never be answered with certainty: to what extent did al-Jāḥiẓ agree with the arguments he formulated to represent the views of the various sects he discussed? His presentation was, after all, aimed first and foremost at satisfying his audience, not at expressing his own convictions. The pro-ʿAlid al-Maʾmūn may have reveled in al-Jāḥiẓ's depiction of ʿAlī as a peerless leader in his *Risālat al-Ḥakamayn* and his treatise on the Zaydīs,[22] whereas al-Mutawakkil is likely to have responded most positively to the portrayal of ʿAlī in al-Jāḥiẓ's *Risālat al-ʿUthmāniyya*. As long as he positioned himself as someone who simply relayed the views of others, al-Jāḥiẓ could benefit from anyone's patronage. This was a significant advantage in the turbulent life of the royal court. It was common for governors and members of the court to lose favor whenever a caliph died and a new one succeeded him. In spite of the power such courtiers wielded, their positions were quite precarious. The new caliph could confiscate all of their property, imprison them, or execute them at any moment. To insulate himself from the dramatic changes in fortune that befell his peers, al-Jāḥiẓ thus consciously refrained from explicitly articulating his own beliefs in certain matters pertaining to Islamic political history. This approach allowed him to maintain a degree of deniability as caliphs and their attitudes toward ʿAlī and Shīʿīs changed throughout his life.

The response of a contemporary, Abū Jaʿfar al-Iskāfī, and many others to al-Jāḥiẓ's *al-ʿUthmāniyya* indicates that the latter was widely read and his interlocutors strongly believed it warranted refutations.[23] Al-Jāḥiẓ was reportedly offended by al-Iskāfī's refutation of *Risālat al-ʿUthmāniyya*

[20] Al-Jāḥiẓ, "Risālat al-Ḥakamayn," 393; al-Jāḥiẓ, "Risālat al-ʿUthmāniyya," 328. See also El-ʿAṭṭār, "al-Jāḥiẓ," 1:133.

[21] Al-Jāḥiẓ, "Risālat al-Ḥakamayn," 393.

[22] For his treatise on the Zaydīs and their best arguments in support of *tafḍīl ʿAlī*, see al-Jāḥiẓ, "Istiḥqāq al-imāma," 179–183.

[23] Afsaruddin, *Excellence*, 7, 23–25.

and by others who identified him with the views expressed in the treatise and accused him of harboring malice for ʿAlī.[24]

Ironically, al-Jāḥiẓ's pro-Hāshimid treatises also generated criticism among his contemporaries.[25] However, he claimed that he wrote his pro-Hāshimid and ʿUthmānī treatises only to detail these groups' beliefs and to provide readers with their most compelling arguments. On multiple occasions he denied that the views of these sects represented his personal beliefs.[26]

In one treatise, he readily acknowledges that Muʿāwiya and his companions themselves never made use of some of the pro-Umayyad arguments that he presents in his work. He explains that these arguments are drawn from "accursed *nāṣiba*" of later generations who despised ʿAlī, from Muʿtazilī theologians who rationally reconstructed pro-Umayyad theories before refuting them, or from his own mind.[27] Thus, one can never be sure to what extent al-Jāḥiẓ's arguments are dependent on informants or reflect his own creative thinking. The following is a summary of arguments that may have been agreeable to *nawāṣib* in his representation of the views of the ʿUthmānīs, the Umayyads, and the Khawārij.

ON THE DOCTRINES OF THE ʿUTHMĀNĪS

It is clear from the topics that al-Jāḥiẓ discusses in his *Risālat al-ʿUthmāniyya* that the primary bone of contention between the ʿUthmānīs and the Shīʿīs was whether Abū Bakr or ʿAlī possessed a greater right to succeed the Prophet as his caliph. Most Muslims agreed that Abū Bakr was the superior candidate, but Shīʿīs and a minority of pro-ʿAlids favored ʿAlī. Al-Jāḥiẓ considers a series of ʿAlī's qualities put forward by his partisans and reaches the same conclusion in each case: ʿAlī's partisans have misinterpreted and exaggerated the significance of his merits, or outright fabricated their claims. In the course of arguing that claims about ʿAlī's merits have been misinterpreted, al-Jāḥiẓ further points to evidence singling out Abū Bakr or other Companions as truly distinguished. Asma Afsaruddin has closely examined a number of these instances.[28]

[24] Al-Jāḥiẓ, *Kitāb al-Ḥayawān*, 1:13; al-Jāḥiẓ, *al-Rasāʾil al-siyāsiyya*, 26–27. See also Afsaruddin, *Excellence*, 24.

[25] Al-Jāḥiẓ, *Kitāb al-Ḥayawān*, 1:9, 10.

[26] Ibid., 1:9, 10, 13; al-Jāḥiẓ, "Risālat al-ʿUthmāniyya," 259.

[27] Al-Jāḥiẓ, "Risālat al-Ḥakamayn," 393.

[28] Afsaruddin, *Excellence*, 52–56, 81–82, 84–96, 114–120, 148–159, 184–186, 198–202, 243–248.

For example, al-Jāḥiẓ argues that ʿAlī's conversion as a child was not equal to the conversion of a rational adult, as he probably did not perceive the gravity of his action.[29] ʿAlī resembled children born of Muslim parents who are reared to follow the religion of their households. As a consequence, his conversion at a young age should not be considered particularly praiseworthy. By contrast, Abū Bakr and other adult Companions converted as a result of reasoned reflection inspired by faith. Their conversion entailed a great cost to their social status and financial well-being, whereas ʿAlī neither risked nor lost any wealth or social standing through his conversion. Al-Jāḥiẓ argues that ʿAlī did not need to fear persecution thanks to the protection afforded to him by his father, Abū Ṭālib, and his status as a Hāshimid. Abū Ṭālib was a respected elder in Mecca and chief of the Hāshimid clan. For many years, Hāshimid converts to Islam appeared to enjoy sufficient social standing to escape direct persecution. By contrast, according to al-Jāḥiẓ, most Companions could not expect such protection and were frequently punished for associating with Muḥammad. Adult converts sacrificed their wealth to free Muslim slaves and to provide other services, whereas ʿAlī did not have the means to carry out such deeds.[30]

Al-Jāḥiẓ seeks to convince his readers that ʿAlī's conversion as a child carried no great significance for the community and served no one – not even ʿAlī. Theologians and jurists commonly hold that children are not accountable for any deeds they commit before the age of majority or puberty. A maxim attributed to the Prophet states that angels do not begin to write in a person's registry of deeds until the person comes of age.[31] If the reports that ʿAlī converted as a young child are accepted, his conversion took place at a time when he possessed no real autonomy or legal responsibility for his actions. Thus, his decision to convert should not be compared to that of Abū Bakr or other adults. Al-Jāḥiẓ adds that no one converted to Islam as a result of ʿAlī's missionary efforts, whereas many did so at the hands of Abū Bakr.[32] The reader can only conclude that Abū Bakr's conversion and membership in the community were more valuable than ʿAlī's.

[29] Al-Jāḥiẓ, "Risālat al-ʿUthmāniyya," 129–138. See also Afsaruddin, *Excellence*, 52–56.

[30] Al-Jāḥiẓ, "Risālat al-ʿUthmāniyya," 142, 144, 146, 148. Al-Jāḥiẓ argues that other Companions either utilized those things in the service of Islam or were forced to relinquish them due to their conversion.

[31] Abū Dāwūd al-Sijistānī, *Sunan*, 2:338–339; Aḥmad b. Ḥanbal, *al-Musnad*, 1:116, 118, 140; al-Bukhārī, *Ṣaḥīḥ*, 6:169, 8:21; al-Tirmidhī, *Sunan*, 2:438.

[32] Al-Jāḥiẓ, "Risālat al-ʿUthmāniyya," 146–150.

After devaluing ʿAlī's childhood conversion, al-Jāḥiẓ turns to his supposed merits as an adult. Al-Jāḥiẓ notes that the Prophet praised the righteousness and faith of other individuals, and famously gave them particular titles to honor them. These titles were so well known that one could refer to a person by means of his title in place of his name and the reference would be unambiguous. As his key example, al-Jāḥiẓ points to Abū Bakr, whom the Prophet called al-Ṣiddīq ("the trusting").[33] ʿAlī, by contrast, received no such title. For ʿUthmānīs, this difference is an indication of Abū Bakr's superiority to ʿAlī and the former's unique status in the community. ʿAlī's piety and faith cannot be compared with those of Abū Bakr.

Pro-ʿAlids consider ʿAlī the most knowledgeable person after the Prophet in matters of religion and the most ascetic of the Prophet's Companions, but al-Jāḥiẓ rejects both of these claims. He maintains that other Companions shared equally in these merits, or even surpassed ʿAlī in some cases.[34] Unlike Zayd b. Thābit (d. 45/665), ʿAlī is never mentioned as someone who memorized the Qurʾān in the lifetime of the Prophet. Neither was ʿAlī a key authority in teaching its recitation, script, or exegesis to the rest of the community, according to al-Jāḥiẓ.[35] When the early community sought the aid of experts in matters relating to the Qurʾān, they turned to Zayd b. Thābit, Ubayy b. Kaʿb (d. 30/651–2), and ʿAbd Allāh b. Masʿūd (d. 32/653) rather than ʿAlī. Other Companions were clearly superior to him in knowledge of *ḥadīth* and Islamic law as well. For this reason, they had more students and left a more enduring legacy.[36] The correctness of their judgments can also be gauged by the extent to which other jurists adopted their pronouncements. Al-Jāḥiẓ observes that members of the community mostly follow the legal opinions of ʿĀʾisha and ʿAbd Allāh b. ʿUmar (d. 73/693) over those of ʿAlī.

[33] Ibid., 211–212.

[34] For claims that others surpassed ʿAlī in their valor in war, see al-Jāḥiẓ, "Risālat al-ʿUthmāniyya," 157. For the superiority to ʿAlī in knowledge, see ibid., 175, 185, 189–190. For matters relating to governance and asceticism, see ibid., 190–192.

[35] Al-Jāḥiẓ obviously wrote for the ʿAbbāsid court. His pro-ʿAbbāsid sentiment is evident in his writing: see al-Jāḥiẓ, "Faḍl Hāshim ʿalā ʿAbd Shams," 419–460, al-Jāḥiẓ, "Risālat al-ʿAbbāsiyya"; al-Jāḥiẓ, "Risālat al-ʿUthmāniyya," 210–211.

[36] Al-Jāḥiẓ, "Risālat al-ʿUthmāniyya," 189–190. Al-Jāḥiẓ qualifies his attack on the precedence of ʿAlī in Islamic scholarship by admitting that ʿAlī was indeed "a jurist, scholar, and one who had knowledge in each (aforementioned) field." This acknowledgement, al-Jāḥiẓ contended, was in contrast to (Imāmī) Shīʿīs who refused to recognize the scholarly capacities of the first three caliphs.

Imāmī Shīʿīs considered ʿAlī's knowledge of the Qurʾān and Islamic law to be perfect. By the ninth century, the Imāmīs maintained that such perfect knowledge made ʿAlī and the imāms after him infallible. This meant that any legal opinion issued by ʿAlī necessarily represented the correct ruling on the matter. Al-Jāḥiẓ attempts to challenge this conviction about ʿAlī by portraying him as a person who would change his mind on legal questions. For a time, ʿAlī reportedly agreed with ʿUmar's opinion that a concubine who gives birth to her master's child cannot be resold, but he subsequently adopted the contrary view.[37] Al-Jāḥiẓ mentions this issue along with other legal opinions reportedly held by ʿAlī that disagree with normative legal doctrines.[38] For example, he says, ʿAlī would sever the fingers of a thief in punishment instead of amputating the entire hand. Al-Jāḥiẓ also points to rulings that he deems absurd. Although children are not understood to possess legal responsibility (*taklīf*), al-Jāḥiẓ reports that ʿAlī would punish child offenders.[39] In each case, al-Jāḥiẓ refers to well-known rulings of ʿAlī discussed among Sunnī and Shīʿī jurists.

In literature about the wars that occurred in the lifetime of the Prophet Muḥammad and in biographies of ʿAlī, the latter is described as peerless in combat. Although al-Jāḥiẓ cannot point to a single mention of Abū Bakr's exceptional military prowess, this does not deter him from imagining how Abū Bakr might nonetheless theoretically have been superior to ʿAlī in warfare. Abū Bakr is the only Companion believed to have stood with the Prophet under a covered arbor to observe the sequence of battles.[40] For al-Jāḥiẓ, this distinction is an indication of Abū Bakr's unique status in the community. He was second only to the Prophet and played a key advisory role in times of war and peace alike.[41] On numerous occasions, Abū Bakr was the first to voice his determination to go to war.[42] Although al-Jāḥiẓ concedes that ʿAlī was considered invincible in close combat, he argues that this skill cannot be deemed a requisite of heads of state or an indication of ʿAlī's right to the caliphate. Rather, he contends, the commanders of armies and heads of state must be capable of military strategy and of safeguarding the collective welfare of their

37 ʿAbd al-Razzāq al-Ṣanʿānī, *al-Muṣannaf*, 7:291; Ibn Qudāma, *al-Mughnī*, 12:492–493; al-Sarakhsī, *al-Mabsūṭ*, 7:150.

38 Al-Jāḥiẓ, "Risālat al-ʿUthmāniyya," 186–188.

39 Ibid., 187. In Shīʿī *ḥadīth*, ʿAlī acknowledges that he alone among the Companions of the Prophet employed discretionary punishments with thieves who were minors, so he cites a case brought before the Prophet as justification: see al-Kulaynī, *al-Kāfī*, 7:232–233.

40 Ibn Hishām, *Sīrat al-Nabī*, 2:456–457; Ibn Kathīr, *al-Bidāya wa ʾl-nihāya*, 3:347; Ibn Saʿd, *al-Ṭabaqāt al-kubrā*, 2:15.

41 Al-Jāḥiẓ, "Risālat al-ʿUthmāniyya," 158–161.

42 Ibid., 162, 166–168.

followers.[43] Soldiers skilled in combat do not necessarily have leadership skills. Therefore, Abū Bakr's standing with the Prophet in his arbor is a far better indication of his qualifications to succeed the Prophet in authority and of the Prophet's high opinion of him.

In their defenses of *tafḍīl ʿAlī*, pro-ʿAlids and Shīʿīs appeal to a number of incidents in which the Prophet singled ʿAlī out for praise or a verse of the Qurʾān that points to his saintly status and authority. Al-Jāḥiẓ responds that these pro-ʿAlid reports, which appear in exegetical and *ḥadīth* literature, are uncorroborated by others and narrated by individuals who are considered untrustworthy.[44] If such reports were true, a greater number of Companions and scholars would have transmitted them.[45] In some cases, when a historical fact about ʿAlī is uncontested or al-Jāḥiẓ is willing to accept that the Prophet said something in praise of ʿAlī, al-Jāḥiẓ offers a reason to devalue the significance of the reported statement. ʿAlī may have been the first male convert to Islam, but al-Jāḥiẓ belittles the conversion of a child so forcefully that it no longer seems to constitute a merit. Although ʿAlī was widely regarded as an extraordinarily talented warrior, al-Jāḥiẓ portrays this quality as inconsequential.

Al-Jāḥiẓ utilizes a similar technique when discussing the Prophet's migration from Mecca to Medina and ʿAlī's decision to stay behind and serve as a decoy in his home. The Prophet fled Mecca only after learning that the Meccans had made arrangements to enter his home and assassinate him on that particular evening. To facilitate the Prophet's escape and deceive the assassins surrounding his home, ʿAlī agreed to wrap himself in the Prophet's robes and wait for the Meccans to storm the house. Believing the Prophet to be asleep, the attackers waited until the middle of the night and then entered his home with their swords drawn. It is unclear from the sources what exactly occurred when they found ʿAlī.[46] The assassins may have attacked ʿAlī, who skillfully defended himself and fought them off, or they may have collectively decided not to kill him since he was not their intended target.

Pro-ʿAlids revere ʿAlī for courageously agreeing to face the assassins and possibly sacrifice his life to facilitate the Prophet's escape. However,

[43] Ibid., 155–156, 158. [44] Ibid., 206, 227–41. [45] Ibid., 209–210.

[46] In most sources, narrators do not provide any details about what happens to ʿAlī after the Meccans find him: see Aḥmad b. Ḥanbal, *al-Musnad*, 1:331; al-Ḥākim al-Naysābūrī, *al-Mustadrak*, 3:133; Ibn Kathīr, *al-Bidāya wa 'l-nihāya*, 3:221. According to one source, the Meccans delayed their search for the Prophet because they believed that he would not leave the city without ʿAlī: see Ibn al-Athīr, *Usd al-ghāba*, 4:19. In one Shīʿī source, the Meccans assault ʿAlī, but in another they leave him alone: see Ibn Bābawayh, *al-Khiṣāl*, 560; al-Ṭūsī, *al-Amālī*, 447.

al-Jāḥiẓ responds that one need not consider ʿAlī's actions particularly brave or praiseworthy because there are indications that he was never truly in danger. He claims that the Meccans would not have considered ʿAlī a person of sufficient importance to warrant harming him. At that point, ʿAlī was still a young man who had not provoked the Meccans in any way. In addition, according to al-Jāḥiẓ, before his departure the Prophet had promised ʿAlī that no harm would come to him at that time.[47] To strengthen his argument, al-Jāḥiẓ points to corroborating reports from Shīʿīs who claim that the Prophet prophesied the wars that ʿAlī would fight as caliph.[48] Al-Jāḥiẓ claims that ʿAlī did not in fact sacrifice anything since he was assured that no harm would come to him and that he would succeed the Prophet as caliph and fight future wars. Consequently, ʿAlī's decision to serve as the Prophet's decoy that night was not particularly meritorious. In devaluing the significance of this event in history, al-Jāḥiẓ aims to support the ʿUthmānī thesis that Abū Bakr's role as the Prophet's traveling companion during his migration to Medina required far more valor. Muslims should thus revere Abū Bakr, not ʿAlī, as the real hero of this episode.

When considering the *ḥadīth al-manzila* – a famous statement of the Prophet in which he likens ʿAlī to Aaron, the brother of Moses – al-Jāḥiẓ argues that the report must be understood within its proper context. Drawing on qurʾānic verses that describe Aaron as Moses's vizier and a brother who assisted him in guiding the Israelites, pro-ʿAlids argue that ʿAlī uniquely occupied an analogous position in relation to the Prophet. In another report, the Prophet selects ʿAlī as his spiritual brother after pairing off other Companions as "brothers" to one another.[49] Al-Jāḥiẓ, however, outright rejects the authenticity of the reports that name ʿAlī as the Prophet's spiritual brother.[50] He doubts the authenticity of the *ḥadīth al-manzila*, but considers the *ḥadīth*'s implications if the Prophet indeed made such a statement.[51]

As in his analysis of ʿAlī's conversion and his role in facilitating the Prophet's escape from Mecca, al-Jāḥiẓ argues that Shīʿīs have misconstrued and exaggerated the *ḥadīth*'s importance. Throughout his life, the Prophet selected numerous Companions to serve as his deputies in Medina when he traveled out of the city. According to pro-ʿAlid transmitters, during the Tabūk expedition of 8/630, the selected deputy was ʿAlī.

[47] Al-Jāḥiẓ, "Risālat al-ʿUthmāniyya," 155. [48] Ibid., 157–158.
[49] Al-Ḥākim al-Naysābūrī, *al-Mustadrak*, 3:14; Ibn ʿAbd al-Barr, *al-Istīʿāb*, 3:1098–1099; al-Tirmidhī, *Sunan*, 5:300.
[50] Al-Jāḥiẓ, "Risālat al-ʿUthmāniyya," 239–241. [51] Ibid., 232–239.

However, on the basis of other reports al-Jāḥiẓ contends that the deputy was Muḥammad b. Maslama (d. 43/663) or another Companion.[52] According to these reports, the Prophet only charged ʿAlī with caring for the women and children of his household.[53]

Thus, for ʿUthmānīs, the following can be inferred from the *ḥadīth al-manzila*: When Moses left the Israelites under Aaron's care, the family of Moses became wards of Aaron in Moses's stead. The Prophet similarly entrusted ʿAlī with the affairs of his household on this occasion. When ʿAlī complained that all of the men in the city were joining the Prophet in his expedition, while he remained behind with women and children, the Prophet likened him to Aaron to cheer him up.

For al-Jāḥiẓ, ʿAlī resembled Aaron only in having kinship ties to a scripture-bearing prophet and bearing the responsibility of caring for his relatives in that prophet's absence. Against the claims of Shīʿīs, ʿUthmānīs would retort that such responsibility is irrelevant to debates about ʿAlī's candidacy for the caliphate: neither kinship to a prophet nor one's ability to care for women and children can determine one's eligibility for leadership of a religious community or salvation on the Day of Judgment. A prophet's cousin or descendant has no right to be conceited about his ancestry, nor should others consider such ancestry to confer merit in religious matters.[54] Shīʿīs have thus misinterpreted the *ḥadīth al-manzila* to support their belief in ʿAlī's superiority to Abū Bakr.

One of the most famous *ḥadīth* regarding ʿAlī is the *ḥadīth al-ghadīr*, in which the Prophet proclaims that "ʿAlī is the *mawlā* of whosoever considers me his *mawlā*."[55] Shīʿīs and Sunnīs who accept the authenticity of the report agree that the Prophet made this declaration in front of a large crowd in 10/632 after completing his final pilgrimage when he was on his way back to Medina. Shīʿīs have argued that the statement confirms ʿAlī as the Prophet's successor in religious and political authority, whereas Sunnīs have dealt with the *ḥadīth* in different ways. Some pro-ʿAlids consider it indicative of ʿAlī's succession to the Prophet in spiritual authority, but not

52 Ibid., 234.

53 Ibn ʿAsākir, *Taʾrīkh*, 2:31; Ibn Hishām, *Sīrat al-Nabī*, 4:946–947; Ibn Kathīr, *al-Bidāya wa ʾl-nihāya*, 5:11; al-Ṭabarī, *Tārīkh*, 2:368.

54 Al-Jāḥiẓ makes veiled references to ʿAlī by mentioning "a cousin of a prophet." See al-Jāḥiẓ, "Risālat al-ʿUthmāniyya," 273–277.

55 ʿAbd al-Razzāq al-Ṣanʿānī, *al-Muṣannaf*, 11:225; Aḥmad b. Ḥanbal, *al-Musnad*, 1:84, 118, 152; al-Ḥākim al-Naysābūrī, *al-Mustadrak*, 3:109–110; Ibn Abī Shayba, *al-Muṣannaf*, 7:495, 496, 499, 503, 506; Ibn Māja, *Sunan*, 1:45, al-Tirmidhī, *Sunan*, 5:297. For an encyclopedic examination of relevant literature, see al-Amīnī, *al-Ghadīr*.

in the realm of the caliphate.[56] Others have argued that the statement reflects a communal duty to respect ʿAlī as an ally and to refrain from ever treating him with hostility.[57] Others have rejected the *ḥadīth* as a fabrication.[58] Al-Jāḥiẓ offers two responses: First, he doubts the authenticity of the *ḥadīth*. Second, he argues that even if it is authentic, it is addressed only to Zayd b. Ḥāritha (d. 8/629), the client and former slave of the Prophet, who was ordered to recognize that his tribal loyalties and clientage extended to ʿAlī as well, since the latter was a Hāshimid like Muḥammad.[59] It appears that other ʿUthmānīs contemporaneous with al-Jāḥiẓ and al-Maʾmūn similarly argued that the *ḥadīth al-ghadīr* was a statement that the Prophet made to resolve a personal dispute between ʿAlī and Zayd.[60] The chronological problem with this argument is that Zayd had famously died with two other commanders, Jaʿfar b. Abī Ṭālib and ʿAbd Allāh b. Rawāḥa, in the battle of Muʾta a few years earlier in 8/629. In a number of sources, *ḥadīth* transmitters offer a similar story but replace Zayd with his son Usāma b. Zayd.[61] Their implicit argument was that since clientage and family alliances were passed on to descendants, it made no difference whether the person in question was Zayd or his son: the Prophet's clients were clients of the Hāshimid clan. The Prophet thus made his statement about ʿAlī to affirm a truism that no one contests.

Prominent ninth-century scholars of *ḥadīth* who were actively engaged in defining orthodoxy for the nascent Sunnī community formulated doctrines that sometimes agreed with Umayyad, ʿUthmānī, or pro-ʿAlid positions. In other cases, the orthodox position that developed appeared to be milder and more compromising than the views espoused by the more radical partisans of these groups. For example, it appears that Umayyads, ʿUthmānīs, and pro-ʿAlids collectively agreed that ʿAlī considered himself a candidate for the caliphate upon the Prophet's death.[62] ʿAlī also defended his candidacy years later during the electoral council convened after the death of ʿUmar.[63] In addition, both Sunnī and Shīʿī sources

[56] See al Ghumārī, *ʿAlī ibn Abī Ṭālib imām al-ʿārifīn*, 66–69; Muḥammad b. Ṭalḥa al-Naṣībī, *Maṭālib al-saʾūl*, 28–31. See also Nasr, "Shiʿism and Sufism," 231–236; Tahir-ul-Qadri, *The Ghadīr Declaration*, 5–16.

[57] Ibn Taymiyya, *Minhāj*, 5:36, 7:322–323.

[58] Ibn Ḥazm, *al-Fiṣal*, 4:116; Ibn Taymiyya, *Minhāj*, 7:319–320.

[59] Al-Jāḥiẓ, "Risālat al-ʿUthmāniyya," 227–228.

[60] Ibn ʿAbd Rabbih, *al-ʿIqd*, 5:357; al-Iskāfī, *al-Miʿyār*, 210–211.

[61] Abū Nuʿaym al-Iṣbahānī, *Tathbīt al-imāma*, 220; al-Munāwī, *Fayḍ al-qadīr*, 6:282.

[62] Jafri, *Origins*, 58–79; Madelung, *Succession*, 28–44.

[63] Al-Kanjī, *Kifāyat al-ṭālib*, 386; al-Khuwārizmī, *al-Manāqib*, 313; al-Ṭabarī, *Tārīkh*, 3:297–298, 301–302. See also Madelung, *Succession*, 70–73.

indicate that a number of Companions supported his early bids for office and upheld *tafḍīl 'Alī*.[64] However, the mainstream, orthodox position in Sunnism, and that which al-Jāḥiẓ upholds, is that none of the Companions that Shī'īs venerate as partisans of 'Alī ever contested the election of the first three caliphs or supported the candidacy of 'Alī against them.[65] Although early Shī'īs, 'Uthmānīs, and Umayyads viewed 'Alī as someone who sometimes disagreed with his predecessors, the orthodox Sunnī position depicted him as an 'Uthmānī who revered them. From the latter perspective, it was unthinkable for 'Alī or any Companion to have contested the legitimacy of the early caliphs. Thus, al-Jāḥiẓ and many Sunnīs frequently rejected the authenticity of texts that portrayed 'Alī or other Companions in ways that supported Shī'ism. By contrast, reports in which 'Alī supported 'Uthmānī doctrines were included in canonical *ḥadīth* collections, and this image of 'Alī became normative.[66] Sunnīs would generally also agree with al-Jāḥiẓ's contention that neither 'Alī nor his disciples ever claimed that the Prophet explicitly designated him as his successor.[67] The canonical *ḥadīth* collections contain reports according to which, during his final illness, the Prophet requested Abū Bakr to lead the community in daily worship.[68] Sunnīs have interpreted this request by the Prophet as an indication of his support for Abū Bakr's succession. Nonetheless, they have generally stopped short of claiming that the Prophet officially named Abū Bakr as his successor. Some early *ḥadīth* transmitters endorsed the more radical 'Uthmānī position that the Prophet invested Abū Bakr (and 'Umar) with political authority either in word or in deed.[69] Al-Jāḥiẓ affirms the validity of this position by describing as sound the argument that the Prophet effectively designated Abū Bakr as his successor by appointing him to lead communal worship.[70]

64 Al-Bāqillānī, *Manāqib al-a'immat al-arba'a*, 294, 306, 480–481; Ibn 'Abd al-Barr, *al-Istī'āb*, 2:799, 3:1090, 1116; Ibn Ḥazm, *al-Fiṣal*, 4:90, 106; Ibn Khaldūn, *Tārīkh,* 3:170–171.

65 Al-Jāḥiẓ, "Risālat al-'Uthmāniyya," 251–263. These Companions include 'Ammār b. Yāsir, Abū Dharr, Miqdād, Salmān, and others.

66 According to some sources, 'Alī eagerly pledged allegiance to Abū Bakr: see al-Bayhaqī, *al-Sunan al-kubrā*, 8:143; al-Ḥākim al-Naysābūrī, *al-Mustadrak*, 3:76; al-Ṭabarī, *Tārīkh*, 2:447. For quotes from 'Alī and his progeny in which they support the preeminence of the first three caliphs, see al-Bukhārī, *Ṣaḥīḥ*, 4:195; Ibn Abī 'Āṣim, *Kitāb al-sunna*, 555–561; Ibn Ḥajar al-Haytamī, *al-Ṣawā'iq al-muḥriqa*, 60–65; Ibn Taymiyya, *Majmū' fatāwā*, 7:511–512; al-Samhūdī, *Jawāhir al-'aqdayn*, 248–250, 451–460.

67 Al-Jāḥiẓ, "Risālat al-'Uthmāniyya," 324. See also Afsaruddin, *Excellence*, 217–225.

68 Aḥmad b. Ḥanbal, *al-Musnad*, 6:249; al-Bukhārī, *Ṣaḥīḥ*, 1:166; Ibn Māja, *Sunan*, 1:389; Muslim, *Ṣaḥīḥ*, 2:24.

69 Afsaruddin, *Excellence*, 157, 165–170, 220–225.

70 Al-Jāḥiẓ, "Risālat al-'Uthmāniyya," 326.

THE KHAWĀRIJ

The protracted war between ʿAlī and Muʿāwiya culminated in the battle of Ṣiffīn in 37/657. The war was fought over many months, and ended soon after Muʿāwiya's Syrian soldiers raised parchments of the Qurʾān onto their spears and called for a negotiated settlement. According to pro-ʿAlid sources, ʿAlī had considered the request to be a ruse and ordered his soldiers to press on.[71] Shīʿīs portray ʿAlī as having been on the brink of victory and Muʿāwiya as making this request only when a total defeat and his own death appeared imminent. However, soon after ʿAlī's soldiers learned of Muʿāwiya's request, his army seemed to disintegrate into chaos. Some soldiers stopped fighting, believing that it would be unconscionable to ignore anyone's request to turn to the Qurʾān as a means to resolving a conflict. When others in ʿAlī's army continued fighting, ʿAlī ordered them to stop and return to camp. The war ended with ʿAli's acceptance of Muʿāwiya's call for arbitration to settle their dispute. ʿAlī's arbitrator, Abū Mūsā al-Ashʿarī, was the former governor of Kūfa and a revered Companion who had sat out ʿAlī's civil wars. Since he had supported neither ʿAlī nor those who fought him, the Kūfans likely considered him capable of judging impartially between the two sides. Muʿāwiya's representative, ʿAmr b. al-ʿĀṣ, was far less neutral. ʿAmr was Muʿāwiya's close confidant and a key military strategist, and later served as his governor to Egypt. After many months, the arbitration ended with Abū Mūsā and ʿAmr jointly deposing ʿAlī and ʿAmr publicly proclaiming Muʿāwiya the new caliph of the community. ʿAlī disavowed the outcome reached by the two arbitrators, but the entire episode dealt a deadly blow to his political career. A number of mutineers seceded from his army and proclaimed that the initial decision to accept arbitration had been a grave sin and error. The views of these men were championed by the Khawārij and, later, the Ibāḍīs. According to these groups, arbitration with Muʿāwiya had entailed unbelief, since the qurʾānic verse 49:9 commands the faithful to fight rebels until they are eliminated or accept a full surrender. ʿAlī's decision to negotiate with wicked rebels and enemies of God thus violated this commandment. Furthermore, the Qurʾān calls on the faithful to abide by the laws of God and not the judgments of men.[72]

[71] Ibn Aʿtham al-Kūfī, *al-Futūḥ*, 3:189; al-Iskāfī, *al-Miʿyār*, 162; Naṣr ibn Muzāḥim, *Waqʿat Ṣiffīn*, 489; al-Ṭabarī, *Tārīkh*, 4:34.

[72] See Q5:44, 5:45, 5:47. Khārijī–Ibāḍī views on the arbitration are discussed further in Chapter 4.

Relying on two arbitrators to provide a solution to the dispute instead of following the relevant laws of God was thus an act of unbelief as well.

In his treatise on the events of the arbitration, entitled *Risālat al-Ḥakamayn* ("On the Two Arbitrators"), al-Jāḥiẓ describes the views of the Khawārij as he understood them. According to al-Jāḥiẓ, they believed that ʿAlī became misguided when he put an end to the battle of Ṣiffīn and sought to negotiate with Muʿāwiya. Just as no one has the right to ignore *ḥudūd* punishments or to replace them with an alternative, ʿAlī had no right to cease fighting or to honor a peace treaty with Muʿāwiya.[73] The command of God is to fight rebels until they surrender rather than enter into arbitration with them. ʿAlī mistakenly stopped the battle of Ṣiffīn, motivated by doubt in his own cause, stupidity, cowardice (in the face of the mutineers), regret at engaging in a war that had led to a massive loss of life, or a desire for Muʿāwiya's repentance.[74] ʿAlī also erred in selecting Abū Mūsā al-Ashʿarī as his arbitrator, when there were others who were better suited to represent him.[75]

After mentioning these Khārijī critiques of ʿAlī, al-Jāḥiẓ then uses the ingenuity he previously used to deprecate ʿAlī (in the *Risālat al-ʿUthmāniyya*) to creatively defend ʿAlī's actions as a caliph. In the *Risālat al-Ḥakamayn*, al-Jāḥiẓ offers rebuttals to Khārijī and Umayyad critiques of ʿAlī's integrity and political acumen. He depicts ʿAlī as a clever and cunning personality who perceived the deficiencies of his followers and the faithlessness of his enemies. According to al-Jāḥiẓ, ʿAlī never believed that arbitration would resolve his conflict with Muʿāwiya. He agreed to it only because it provided an opportune pretext to delay continued warfare with Muʿāwiya and grant his army a much-needed respite.[76] ʿAlī had lost many key allies and soldiers in the war, and he needed to deal with the mutinous soldiers who remained. To Shīʿī narratives that depict ʿAlī as agreeing to arbitration moments before victory, al-Jāḥiẓ provides an ingenious rebuttal: ʿAlī accepted arbitration because he was on the brink of defeat. In this way and in others, al-Jāḥiẓ reveals a willingness to use his intellect to defend ʿAlī's deeds as a ruler. His ability to accurately document and present the anti-ʿAlid critiques of others is evident in his discussion of the Khawārij. The arguments that he attributes

73 Al-Jāḥiẓ, "Risālat al-Ḥakamayn," 358. After the mutineers realized their mistake in ceasing the war with Muʿāwiya, ʿAlī allegedly refused to follow their proposals to break his peace treaty and preempt war before arbitration. Al-Jāḥiẓ alludes to this point: see ibid., 365.

74 Al-Jāḥiẓ recognizes that some of these hypothetical reasons are implausible: see ibid., 360.

75 Ibid., 358.

76 Ibid., 357–359, 361–365. See also El-ʿAṭṭār, "al-Jāḥiẓ," 2:272–274, 278–280.

to them are corroborated by Ibāḍīs, who advocated the same positions and described early seceders as articulating identical arguments. The Khārijī–Ibāḍī tradition is examined in greater detail in Chapter 4.

THE UMAYYADS

In the same treatise, al-Jāḥiẓ also presents Umayyad critiques of 'Alī. According to al-Jāḥiẓ, the Umayyads considered 'Alī culpable in the death of 'Uthmān.[77] They claimed that 'Alī either ordered his killing or had foreknowledge of the conspiracy. The Umayyads may have also blamed him because those who had engaged in the protests that precipitated 'Uthmān's murder had selected 'Alī to listen to their grievances and share them with the caliph.[78] For the Umayyads, anyone who had criticized 'Uthmān, participated in the protests, or failed to come to his aid could be accused of betraying him and contributing to the chain of events that culminated in his death. It is on this basis that Marwān b. al-Ḥakam, 'Uthmān's son-in-law and future caliph, justified his treacherous killing of Ṭalḥa, who was leading an army composed of 'Uthmānīs and Umayyads in the battle of the Camel, as retribution for Ṭalḥa's earlier role in siding with the protestors.[79] In another example, when the army of Yazīd b. Mu'āwiya defeated an army composed of the children of the Medinese Anṣār in 63/683, the army reportedly pillaged the city of Medina for three days. Survivors of the event and later scholars explained that the pillaging was retaliation for the collective role that the residents of Medina had played decades earlier in the events that precipitated 'Uthmān's death.[80] The Medinese had allowed the protests to occur in their city and refrained from defending the caliph against the accusations made against him and his Umayyad governors. Given such a broad concept of blame, it comes as no surprise that the Umayyads would accuse 'Alī of culpability in 'Uthmān's murder since his own stepson, Muḥammad b. Abī Bakr, had led an Egyptian delegation of protestors, and since those who had opposed 'Uthmān subsequently approved of 'Alī's political ascendancy. The Umayyads believed that 'Alī had benefited from 'Uthmān's murder by agreeing to serve as the leader of his enemies.

77 Al-Jāḥiẓ, "Risālat al-Ḥakamayn," 346, 379.

78 Al-Balādhurī, *Ansāb al-ashrāf*, 5:549–556; Ibn A'tham al-Kūfī, *al-Futūḥ*, 2:404; al-Ṭabarī, *Tārīkh*, 3:402–404.

79 Al-Ḥākim al-Naysābūrī, *al-Mustadrak*, 3:371; Ibn 'Abd al-Barr, *al-Istī'āb*, 2:768–769; Ibn Abī Shayba, *al-Muṣannaf*, 3:262, 8:708, Ibn Sa'd, *al-Ṭabaqāt al-kubrā*, 3:223.

80 Ibn Kathīr, *al-Bidāya wa 'l-nihāya*, 8:242; al-Khallāl, *al-Sunna*, 3:520.

They also believed that ʿAlī offered amnesty and protection to ʿUthmān's killers. There are a number of conflicting theories about the events that led to the murder of ʿUthmān, the identities of his assassins, ʿAlī's treatment of those accused of the crime, and his opinion about the entire affair. The first theory concerning ʿUthmān's death, held by early ʿUthmānīs and Umayyads, was that ʿAlī and a few of his well-known associates were responsible. The second theory, associated with mild ʿUthmānīs and later adopted by Sunnīs, was that Ibn Sabaʾ and his co-conspirators carried out the crime secretly and then took cover in ʿAlī's army. This second theory affirms that the killers belonged to ʿAlī's army but exonerates him personally of blame: had ʿAlī had the ability to apprehend and execute them, he would have done so.

It appears that no one ever confessed to murdering ʿUthmān or was positively identified as his assassin. Some people were accused of the crime, including men close to ʿAlī, but ʿAlī may have viewed these accusations, like that leveled against himself, as mere slanders and as ʿUthmānī and Umayyad pretexts to arouse citizens against him and his governors. Two of the accused men, Muḥammad b. Abī Bakr and Mālik b. Ibrāhīm al-Ashtar (d. 37/658), had played a key role in leading the protests against ʿUthmān. ʿAlī's appointment of them both as governors afterward plainly demonstrates his approval of their characters and of their rebellion against the excesses of Umayyad governors during ʿUthmān's reign. In sermons and letters attributed to ʿAlī, he praises them as pious and just men.[81] Assuming their innocence, it could be argued that ʿAlī knew that neither of the two had plotted or participated in ʿUthmān's murder. For this reason, he ignored ʿUthmānī and Umayyad accusations about the two. Since the assailants were unknown, ʿAlī could not do anything with regard to the case unless someone came forward with a confession. If he interpreted the intentions of his rivals charitably, ʿAlī would have considered the revolts launched against him in ʿUthmān's name as misdirected and unlawful rebellions. An uncharitable interpretation would have cast them as political insurrections seeking regime change by means of a pretext that would appeal to many citizens.

Another possibility is that ʿAlī was aware that some of his partisans, such as Muḥammad b. Abī Bakr, had indeed participated in killing ʿUthmān, but he rejected the legality of vengeance for the murder because of extenuating circumstances or ambiguities in the case. For example,

[81] Ibn Abī ʾl-Ḥadīd, *Sharḥ*, 6:77, 93–94, 15:98; al-Sharīf al-Raḍī, *Nahj al-balāgha*, 3:14, 60, 63; al-Ṭabarī, *Tārīkh*, 3:565.

the day before ʿUthmān's murder, one of ʿUthmān's guards reportedly killed a Companion of the Prophet who had joined the protests outside the caliph's home.[82] The assassins may have considered ʿUthmān's murder just retribution for this person's death. The Egyptian delegation of protestors led by Muḥammad b. Abī Bakr had also intercepted a letter purportedly from the caliph ordering their executions upon their return to Egypt.[83] The members of this delegation may have assassinated the caliph in retribution for this attempt on their lives. In these scenarios, a judge would have to first consider the culpability of ʿUthmān himself in the series of events that culminated in his murder before deciding on the appropriate punishment for his murderers. In the presence of doubts, a judge may use his discretion to commute a death sentence, instead ordering that the responsible party offer financial compensation to the victim's family. In either of these scenarios, ʿAlī could have believed that the circumstances of the case did not warrant execution of ʿUthmān's assassins. Although he did not consider ʿUthmān's murder justified, previous provocations and deaths perhaps complicated the case for executing the perpetrators. By contrast, the Khawārij and the Ibāḍīs upheld a more radical interpretation of ʿAlī's stance: in their eyes, ʿAlī and other Companions collectively disavowed ʿUthmān and deemed his assassination warranted. This theory agreed with Umayyad and early ʿUthmānī perceptions of ʿAlī and his supporters.

It is ʿAlī's perceived opposition to or inadequacy in heeding public calls for vengeance for ʿUthmān's murder that led some to claim that Muʿāwiya was completely justified in waging war against ʿAlī.[84] As an Umayyad chieftain, they contended, Muʿāwiya had every right to seek vengeance for ʿUthmān's death independently if ʿAlī could not or would not do so. Al-Jāḥiẓ explains that an imām who does not punish murderers or help a victim's family seek retribution is unjust. Al-Jāḥiẓ rationalizes that on this basis the Umayyads could have argued that ʿAlī was unsuited for any leadership position.[85]

[82] Ibn Ḥajar al-ʿAsqalānī, *al-Iṣāba*, 6:381; al-Ṭabarī, *Tārīkh*, 3:413–414. See also Madelung, *Succession*, 135–136.

[83] Al-Balādhurī, *Ansāb al-ashrāf*, 5:556–558; Ibn Aʿtham al-Kūfī, *al-Futūḥ*, 2:411–413; al-Ṭabarī, *Tārīkh*, 3:406–408. See also Keaney, *Medieval Islamic Historiography*, 40; Madelung, *Succession*, 124–127.

[84] For example, Abū Bakr al-Aṣamm argued along these lines: see al-Nāshiʾ al-Akbar (attrib.), "Masāʾil al-imāma," 59–60. Those who hesitated in unequivocally justifying his actions argued that Muʿāwiya, at the very least, had a greater right in going to war (by rights of kinship) than the leaders of the battle of the Camel: see al-Jāḥiẓ, "Risālat al-Ḥakamayn," 383.

[85] Al-Jāḥiẓ, "Risālat al-Ḥakamayn," 387.

According to al-Jāḥiẓ, the Umayyads considered ʿAlī a pretender to the caliphate because they believed that only a small band of his followers recognized him as caliph. A rightful caliph must have other indications of his legitimacy. ʿAlī claimed the caliphate despite failing to obtain either a clear designation from ʿUthmān, the consensus of constituents supporting his candidacy, or the support of the surviving members of the electoral council convened after the death of ʿUmar.[86] Of the three other surviving members, two, Ṭalḥa and al-Zubayr, openly rebelled against ʿAlī. The last member, Saʿd b. Abī Waqqāṣ, maintained a neutral stance throughout ʿAlī's reign as caliph and did not participate in any of his wars. According to some sources, ʿAlī exempted Saʿd from participating in his civil wars because of the latter's concerns about fighting other Muslims.[87] ʿAlī explained that Saʿd and other Companions who asked him for permission to stay at home nonetheless helped his cause by remaining law-abiding citizens and refraining from rebellion. For al-Jāḥiẓ, however, Saʿd's quietism signaled his nonalignment with ʿAlī and his reservations about ʿAlī's legitimacy as caliph. Umayyad polemicists could argue the following: Since each of them had been equal members of the electoral council that elected the third caliph, ʿAlī had no right to the caliphate over Saʿd after the deaths of Ṭalha and al-Zubayr. Furthermore, had Saʿd fully supported ʿAlī, or had the two agreed with one another on the issue of the caliphate, Muʿāwiya would have piously obeyed them.[88]

Al-Jāḥiẓ reports that the Umayyads may have argued that Muʿāwiya had been a better candidate to succeed ʿUthmān thanks to his political acumen. Muʿāwiya is highly regarded in Islamic literature for his shrewdness as a leader.[89] His partisans may have believed that he possessed better judgment and was more effective as a ruler when comparing him to ʿAlī.[90] In addition, Muʿāwiya is often portrayed as securing and rewarding the loyalty of powerful men by granting them great wealth. By contrast, al-Jāḥiẓ explains, many people were averse to ʿAlī's stringent fiscal policies, particularly his refusal to use public funds for personal expenses or to reward his allies.[91] According to al-Jāḥiẓ, the Umayyads could have also

[86] Ibid., 346, 386. The three previous caliphs allegedly gained power through the following three methods: a consensus of the community; designation by the previous caliph; or winning the election of a council of leaders. Many sources mention Companions who in fact contested Abū Bakr's election: see al-ʿAskarī, *Maʿālim*, 1:124–135.

[87] Al-Dīnawarī, *al-Akhbār al-ṭiwāl*, 142–143; Ibn Abī 'l-Ḥadīd, *Sharḥ*, 18:119; al-Iskāfī, *al-Miʿyār*, 105–106; ʿAbd al-Jabbār, *al-Mughnī*, 20.II:66–68.

[88] Al-Jāḥiẓ, "Risālat al-Ḥakamayn," 386.

[89] Ibn ʿAbd al-Barr, *al-Istīʿāb*, 4:1446; Ibn ʿAsākir, *Taʾrīkh*, 19:182–183, 59:172–179, 185.

[90] Al-Jāḥiẓ, "Risālat al-Ḥakamayn," 365. [91] Ibid., 350.

argued that ʿAlī was assassinated because of his own negligence, whereas Muʿāwiya and ʿAmr b. al-ʿĀṣ escaped assassination attempts through their own prudence.[92]

Early proto-Sunnī and Shīʿī sources occasionally portray ʿAlī and other Hāshimids as nonconformists who disagreed with the legal opinions of the early caliphs or upheld doctrines that diverged from certain social and legal norms.[93] Al-Jāḥiẓ accepts the authenticity of some of these reports and argues that the Umayyads' critiques of ʿAlī as misguided and sinful could reflect his departures from the opinions of ʿUmar and other respected jurists in the community.[94] An example of an issue on which ʿAlī and his family reportedly differed with ʿUmar is the legality of temporary marriages. Finding members of the community still practicing this type of marriage, ʿUmar is said to have issued an edict prohibiting it a few years into his reign.[95] The canonical Sunnī *ḥadīth* collections preserve reports in which ʿAlī and others explain that temporary marriages were once valid and then abrogated in the lifetime of the Prophet.[96] However, there are also contrary reports from ʿAlī, Ibn ʿAbbās, Jābir b. ʿAbd Allāh al-Anṣārī (d. 78/697), and Ibn Jurayj (d. 150/767) that indicate their belief in the continued legality of the practice.[97] The ʿAlid imāms of Twelver Shīʿism reportedly supported the institution.[98] ʿAlī's son al-Ḥasan is accused of marrying and divorcing hundreds of women; the criticism is perhaps a way of defaming him and of maligning Hāshimid marriage practices.[99] According to al-Jāḥiẓ, the Umayyads directed the same criticism at ʿAlī.[100] There are reports that ʿAlī left a large number of widows and concubines at his death.[101] It is clear that anti-ʿAlids believed members of the ʿAlid house to be self-indulgent and unfaithful husbands. ʿAlī is depicted as a bad husband to Fāṭima in a number of *ḥadīth*, and his son

92 Ibid., 368. 93 See the Introduction, nn. 17–20.

94 Al-Jāḥiẓ, "Risālat al-Ḥakamayn," 389; al-Jāḥiẓ, "Risālat al-ʿUthmāniyya," 186–188.

95 Al-Jaṣṣāṣ, *Aḥkām al-Qurʾān*, 1:352. For additional references, see n. 97 in this chapter.

96 Al-Bukhārī, *Ṣaḥīḥ*, 6:129, 230; Ibn Māja, *Sunan*, 6:130; Muslim, *Ṣaḥīḥ*, 4:134–135; al-Nasāʾī, *Sunan al-al-Nasāʾī*, 6:125–126; al-Shāfiʿī, *al-Umm*, 7:183; al-Shawkānī, *Nayl al-awṭār*, 6:269; al-Tirmidhī, *Sunan*, 2:295.

97 Aḥmad b. Ḥanbal, *al-Musnad*, 3:363, 380; Ibn Ḥazm, *al-Muḥallā*, 9:519–520; Ibn ʿAbd al-Barr, *al-Istidhkār*, 5:506; Ibn ʿAbd al-Barr, *al-Tamhīd*, 10:111–115; Ibn ʿAsākir, *Taʾrīkh*, 42:419; Muslim, *Ṣaḥīḥ*, 4:130–131; al-Ṭabarī, *Tafsīr*, 5:19.

98 Ibn Bābawayh, *Man lā yaḥḍuruhu al-faqīh*, 3:458–460; al-Kulaynī, *al-Kāfī*, 5:448–450.

99 Al-Makkī, *Qūt al-qulūb*, 3:1621. See also Madelung, *Succession*, 380–387.

100 Al-Jāḥiẓ cites an alleged statement by Muʿāwiya, "I am one who neither marries nor divorces frequently," as a criticism of ʿAlī: see al-Jāḥiẓ, "Risālat al-ʿUthmāniyya," 193; al-Makkī, *Qūt al-qulūb*, 3:1621.

101 Al-Makkī, *Qūt al-qulūb*, 3:1621.

al-Ḥasan earns the same reputation. The Prophet reportedly described divorce as greatly detested in the sight of God.[102] According to canonical *ḥadīth*, he also ended the practice of temporary marriage. It is possible, however, that Hāshimids did not view divorce or temporary marriage in a negative light. In any case, anti-ʿAlids evidently sought to undermine the reputations of ʿAlī and al-Ḥasan for piety by depicting them as abusing these institutions to marry a great number of women.

As al-Jāḥiẓ admits, he sometimes supplies arguments in support of Umayyad doctrines for the sake of the discussion because he knows that their positions are ultimately flawed.[103] Thus, it is unclear whether the arguments he cites are original to him or taken from pro-Umayyad theologians. Nonetheless, his survey of pro-Umayyad doctrines about ʿAlī offers an insight into the ways in which Muslims could have theoretically rejected faith in ʿAlī's piety and legitimacy as caliph.

True to form, in a treatise on Zaydism, al-Jāḥiẓ zealously defends ʿAlī as a wise leader and presents eloquent arguments in favor of ʿAlī's superiority over all other Companions.[104] His extant works make clear that al-Jāḥiẓ considered ʿAlī a pious, wise, and legitimate caliph. As a Baṣran Muʿtazilī, however, he upheld a doctrine that became orthodoxy in Sunnism: upon the Prophet's death, the person with the most merit became the caliph. Consequently, al-Jāḥiẓ feels compelled to deny stridently any basis to claims of ʿAlī's superiority to Abū Bakr. He admits, however, that the complete rejection of pro-ʿAlid *ḥadīth* is unnecessary and extreme. In al-Jāḥiẓ's view, the significance of pro-ʿAlid reports must be undermined only when Shīʿīs characterize them as unassailable and relevant to the caliphate. So, on the one hand, no one should doubt ʿAlī's valor and the important role he played in the battles of Badr and Khaybar.[105] For al-Jāḥiẓ, these are undeniable truths, and ʿAlī should properly be revered for his contributions on the battlefield. The *ḥadīth al-manzila*, on the other hand, does not possess the same epistemic value as knowledge about the valor of ʿAlī. According to al-Jāḥiẓ, the authenticity of many of the *ḥadīth* that the partisans of both Abū Bakr and ʿAlī circulate about their heroes merits the same skepticism.[106]

More relevant to al-Jāḥiẓ is the second condition regarding a *ḥadīth*'s relevance to the caliphate. He explains that reports in which the Prophet praises Abū Bakr or ʿAlī are frequently taken as evidence of that person's

[102] Abū Dāwūd al-Sijistānī, *Sunan*, 1:484; Ibn Māja, *Sunan*, 1:650.
[103] Al-Jāḥiẓ, "Risālat al-Ḥakamayn," 393. [104] Al-Jāḥiẓ, "Istiḥqāq al-imāma," 179–183.
[105] Al-Jāḥiẓ, "Risālat al-ʿUthmāniyya," 226. [106] Ibid., 223, 226.

superior right to the caliphate, but drawing such conclusions is misleading, since *ḥadīth* can be used to support the candidacy of practically any Companion.[107] The Prophet always praised people in a way that seemed to exalt them above others. Al-Jāḥiẓ theorizes that when the Prophet spoke such words of praise, his contemporaries understood his intention – to laud the praised individual without necessarily ranking that individual vis-à-vis others. By contrast, Muslims of later generations have transmitted his words but have failed to grasp their appropriate meaning and context. This failure has led partisans to take innocuous statements of the Prophet and to confer on them great significance in debates about the caliphate. Although al-Jāḥiẓ appears to diminish the significance of reports about ʿAlī's merits and achievements in his *Risālat al-ʿUthmāniyya*, his actual position is that neither pro-ʿAlids nor ʿUthmānīs should appeal to such *ḥadīth* to substantiate their views. Once it is agreed that the Prophet did not officially name anyone as caliph and that he praised many of his Companions on countless occasions, partisan attempts to imbue some of these statements with special meaning and authority can be recognized as arbitrary and futile. No one can truly know the Prophet's actual intent when he made these statements. Al-Jāḥiẓ's point is thus not that one *should* employ anti-ʿAlid arguments to deprecate ʿAlī, but rather that one *can*.

Al-Jāḥiẓ most likely considered arguments about Abū Bakr's and ʿAlī's respective conversions irrelevant to the debate about each person's capacity to lead the community as a caliph. For him, such details did not really matter, and it is only the insistence of pro-ʿAlids and Shīʿīs that ʿAlī's conversion demonstrated his superiority that prompted al-Jāḥiẓ to provide an ʿUthmānī response to establish the claim's irrelevance. In al-Jāḥiẓ's eyes, a caliph should be just and wise, and he trusted that each time a caliph acceded to power, the community pledged allegiance to the candidate who best represented those ideals. Any arguments to the contrary he dismissed as radical Shīʿī attempts to retell history with misleading arguments or fabricated accounts.

[107] Ibid., 222–226.

4

The Ibāḍī: al-Wārjalānī

When ʿAlī became caliph, he left the city of Medina for Kūfa in Iraq, where he must have believed that he would find strong political and military support. Kūfa had been established as a garrison town in 17/638 and, indeed, as ʿAlī fought the civil wars that plagued his reign as caliph, most of his soldiers came from Kūfa. In terms of politics, many of its residents had publicly protested ʿUthmān's governor there and collectively pressured the caliph to remove him from power after a number of scandals. After ʿAlī's death, Kūfa became an important center of pro-ʿAlid sentiment. *Ḥadīth* transmitters circulated numerous reports about the virtues of ʿAlī and his progeny. Kūfans also repeatedly supported ʿAlids and Shīʿīs who launched insurrections in the city. Although pro-ʿAlids made up an important segment of the city's population, many who were hostile to ʿAlī also lived there. For example, many ʿUthmānīs lived in the city and established mosques there.[1] There were also soldiers who had once served ʿAlī, but became disillusioned with him. Those disillusioned soldiers, known as the Muḥakkima, eventually fought ʿAlī and lost to him in the battle of Nahrawān in 38/658. For reasons discussed further below, two closely related sects in Islamic history, the Khawārij ("seceders") and Ibāḍīs, came to revere the Muḥakkima and considered them their predecessors. The Khārijī–Ibāḍī tradition diverged sharply from pro-ʿAlids in their assessment of ʿAlī's character and legacy.

Sunnī, Shīʿī, and Ibāḍī sources agree that the Muḥakkima parted ways with ʿAlī after the battle of Ṣiffīn in 37/657. This battle between the armies of ʿAlī and Muʿāwiya ended with no clear victory for either side. Instead,

[1] Haider, *Origins*, 231–242.

the two commanders agreed to halt hostilities and pursue arbitration. In pro-ʿAlid narratives, ʿAlī is skeptical of Muʿāwiya's sincerity and doubts that the arbitration will lead to any substantive resolution. In Ibāḍī narratives, by contrast, ʿAlī is eager to negotiate with Muʿāwiya and to accept any terms that will ensure his ability to continue ruling over Iraq. According to Ibāḍīs, ʿAlī was betraying the faithful and violating commandments of the Qurʾān by agreeing to negotiate with rebels such as Muʿāwiya and ʿAmr b. al-ʿĀṣ, whom they cast as enemies of God. According to some narratives sympathetic to early Khawārij, ʿAlī further agrees to grant immunity to those who commit a crime, but then identify themselves as partisans of Muʿāwiya or flee to the Levant.[2] Likewise, Muʿāwiya was to refrain from punishing partisans of ʿAlī who appeared to commit crimes within his jurisdiction. They would respect each other's right to govern their respective partisans. For the Ibāḍīs, this was another indication of ʿAlī's misguidance. In his desire to ensure his continued hegemony over his own followers, ʿAlī had unlawfully acknowledged the sovereignty of a usurper.

Some time after the battle of Ṣiffīn, thousands of ʿAlī's soldiers withdrew from his army and encamped near a region known as Ḥarūrāʾ. They also encamped in other regions such as Nukhayla and Nahrawān. This faction became known as the Muḥakkima, for their belief that arbitration (*taḥkīm*) in matters already adjudicated by God in the Qurʾān was unlawful. They claimed that ʿAlī was doing just that by negotiating with the rebels when Q49:9 obliged him to fight them.

After a few months, ʿAlī fought the Muḥakkima at the battle of Nahrawān, which ended in his favor. In the decades that followed, those who were sympathetic to the Muḥakkima became known as Khawārij in reference to the soldiers who had famously seceded from ʿAlī's army. The Khawārij mounted several insurrections against the Umayyads and the ʿAbbāsids. They gained a reputation for holding radically puritan views of piety and sin. They held that a Muslim who committed a major sin was guilty of unbelief. Such a person needed to renew his or her faith to be a Muslim. Muslims who refused to acknowledge their misdeeds were considered nonbelievers. Radical Khārijī factions such as the Azāriqa became infamous for killing anyone who did not belong to the sect (including women and children) in the course of their insurrections. It appears that by the end of the formative period, every Khārijī sect mentioned in

[2] Al-Izkawī, *Kashf al-ghumma*, 1:537; al-Siyar al-Ibāḍiyya, 28. See also Gaiser, "Ibādī Accounts," 67.

heresiographical works had disappeared. The only exception was the Ibāḍī community, which claimed the early Muḥakkima as their predecessors, but condemned members of other Khārijī sects as extremists.

The Ibāḍīs were named after a certain ʿAbd Allāh b. Ibāḍ, a figure active in the second/eighth century; however, biographical details about this person are speculative.[3] In treatises attributed to him, he appears to support key Khārijī assumptions and values such as rejecting the rule of tyrants. Khawārij and Ibāḍīs considered Abū Bakr and ʿUmar ideal caliphs and imāms. Ibāḍīs followed Khawārij in disassociating themselves from ʿUthmān and ʿAlī, whom they believed acceded to the caliphate legitimately, but went astray as rulers.

Whereas the Khawārij rejected the faith of other Muslims, the Ibāḍīs were willing to accept non-Ibāḍīs as Muslims. Khārijī groups argued about the legitimacy of sharing allegiance (*walāʾ*) with Muslims of other sects, with many arguing that disassociation from other Muslims and war against illegitimate caliphs was a religious obligation. The Ibāḍīs were more inclined toward compromise. They disassociated from non-Ibāḍīs, but considered it lawful to coexist peacefully with them and to live under tyrannical rulers. This allowed the Ibāḍīs to flourish while other Khārijī factions were driven to extinction by their aggressive and intolerant stance even toward other Khawārij.

Ibāḍism flourished in two places: Oman and parts of North Africa. Save for a few scholars who traveled between them, the two Ibāḍī communities largely developed independently of one another. In theology and law, the scholars of the two regions agreed on some matters but differed in many others. Wargla (Arab. Wārjalān) was an important city of Ibāḍī learning located in southern Algeria. It produced scholars who penned many influential, still extant books. The three most famous scholars of the region were all contemporaries of one another: Abū ʿAmr ʿUthmān b. Khalīfa al-Sūfī al-Marghīnī (active sixth/twelfth century), followed by Abū ʿAmmār ʿAbd al-Kāfī b. Yūsuf al-Tanāwatī al-Wārjalānī (d. before 570/1175) and Abū Yaʿqūb Yūsuf b. Ibrāhīm al-Wārjalānī (d. 570/1175).[4] Each scholar composed theological and juridical treatises that expounded on diverse topics relating to Ibāḍī orthodoxy, political theory, history, and law. Abū Yaʿqūb al-Wārjalānī was born in Sedrata, a village in the area of Wārjalān, some time in the early sixth/twelfth century. Abū Yaʿqūb outlived his two

[3] For more on the rise of the Ibāḍī tradition, see Gaiser, *Muslims, Scholars, Soldiers*, 19–48; Hoffman, *Essentials*, 3–53.

[4] For more on these three scholars, see Hoffman, *Essentials*, 22.

peers and when he composed his magnum opus, *Kitāb al-Dalīl li-ahl 'l-ʿuqūl li-bāghy 'l-sabīl* (The Book of Proofs for Men of Reason Seeking the Right Path), he mentions the death of Abū ʿAmmār and al-Marghīnī's poor health at the time of his writing.[5]

The *Kitāb al-Dalīl* is a comprehensive theological work consisting of three volumes. Abū Yaʿqūb discusses the fragmentation of the Muslim community into sects and defends Ibāḍī doctrines against the views of Sunnīs (specifically Ashʿarīs) and Shīʿīs in matters relating to monotheism, legal theory, epistemology, Islamic political theory, and many other issues. Abū Yaʿqūb does not appear to set out to write a book with one topic in mind or limit himself to a particular discipline of knowledge. In some places, he discusses a subject without referring to any outside inquiries he had received. At other times, he provides what he considers to be the correct answer among Ibāḍīs to a religious question posed to him. Consequently, as the *Kitāb al-Dalīl* progresses, it becomes a type of anthology of *responsa*.

In this chapter, I aim to document Ibāḍī grievances regarding ʿAlī, and thereby the Muḥakkima and extinct Khārijī factions that also condemned him. I draw on Ibāḍī literature about ʿAlī and some non-Ibāḍī literature that allegedly drew on Khārijī informants. First, I pay particular attention to Abū Yaʿqūb's *Kitāb al-Dalīl* due to its long treatment of questions relating ʿAlī, Muʿāwiya, and the theological significance of their political careers. Second, following the work of Adam Gaiser,[6] I also examine Ibāḍī literature, published and unpublished, that depicts the debates that allegedly occurred between ʿAlī and the Muḥakkima before the two parties met at the battle of Nahrawān. Finally, I compare portrayals of the Muḥakkima in Ibāḍī literature to those in non-Ibāḍī sources, and consider key divergences between the two.

ON THE ASSASSINATION OF ʿUTHMĀN

In Sunnī and Shīʿī literature, no individual or group confesses to murdering the third caliph, ʿUthmān b. ʿAffān. Many leading Companions and later converts are portrayed as participating in the protests that precipitated his murder. ʿUthmānīs and Umayyads accused prominent individuals such as ʿAlī b. Abī Ṭālib and Muḥammad b. Abī Bakr of either participating in or approving of a conspiracy to assassinate the caliph. For these factions,

[5] Al-Wārjalānī, *Kitāb al-Dalīl*, 1:54, 3:100.
[6] Gaiser, "Ibādī Accounts"; Gaiser, *Shurāt Legends*, 92–94, 98.

ʿAlī's succession to the caliphate after ʿUthmān and interactions with protestors served as evidence of motive and fueled suspicions of his culpability. Despite ʿUthmān's condemnation in pro-ʿAlid and Shīʿī literature, ʿAlī and his associates do not participate in his murder, praise his assassins, or claim to know their identities in such sources. Umayyad and ʿUthmānī suspicions about ʿAlī and his followers largely remain unfounded until one considers Ibāḍī historiography.

Ibāḍī authors generally cited the same sets of arguments and historical events to substantiate their negative assessments of ʿUthmān and ʿAlī. Ibāḍīs condemned ʿUthmān and disavowed themselves of him on account of a number of grievances. They blamed him for prohibiting the recitation of Ibn Masʿūd's recension of the Qurʾān, removing ʿUmar's governors from office and replacing them with his unqualified Umayyad relatives, waiving *ḥadd* punishments in high-profile cases involving ʿUbayd Allāh b. ʿUmar b. al-Khaṭṭāb, the Umayyad Walīd b. ʿUqba, and other notables, and providing the Umayyads with rights to conquered lands and the spoils of war at the expense of disenfranchised, late converts.[7] According to Ibāḍīs, the Companions of the Prophet collectively and publicly criticized ʿUthmān for these excesses. Pro-ʿAlid and Ibāḍī narratives appear to draw on the same sources and examples in listing their grievances against ʿUthmān. Readers familiar with the reports that appear in al-Balādhurī and al-Ṭabarī about Abū Dharr (d. 32/652), Ibn Masʿūd (d. 32/652–3), ʿAmmār b. Yāsir (d. 37/657), Muḥammad b. Abī Bakr, and others confronting ʿUthmān or parting ways with him before the siege on his palace and murder will find many of the same narratives in Ibāḍī sources.[8] The key divergence from Sunnī and Shīʿī narratives was that Ibāḍīs further claimed that the same group of venerable Companions who publicly criticized ʿUthmān collectively carried out his execution. Echoing the sentiments expressed by Umayyads who blamed everyone who ever criticized ʿUthmān for his murder, Ibāḍīs do not differentiate between ʿUthmān's critics and his killers. They are one and the same.

Al-Wārjalānī and other Ibāḍīs describe the Muhājirūn and Anṣār as protesting against ʿUthmān's policies and then members of this group collectively agreeing to kill him for his misdeeds.[9] ʿAlī, ʿAmmār b. Yāsir, Ṭalḥa, and al-Zubayr are named as leading this faction of Companions who

[7] Hinds Xerox, 106–127, 137, 139–154; al-Izkawī, *Kashf al-ghumma*, 1:480–485; al-Siyar al-Ibāḍiyya, 1:95–97, 2:330–335; al-Wārjalānī, *Kitāb al-Dalīl*, 1:14, 27, 3:188.

[8] For references to the revolt against ʿUthmān in Sunnī historiography, see al-Ṭabarī, *Tārīkh*, 3:399–426. See also Madelung, *Succession*, 81–140.

[9] Al-Wārjalānī, *Kitāb al-Dalīl*, 1:36, 3:41–43, 130, 188; al-Kāshif, ed., *al-Siyar*, 2:81.

deemed it lawful to kill ʿUthmān. According to Ibāḍīs, the Companions disagreed with one another on the lawfulness of ʿUthmān's execution and split into three groups. The Ibāḍīs praised the first group of Companions who approved of and carried out the murder as the one that followed the right path.[10] A second group, led by Ṭalḥa and al-Zubayr, also believed that ʿUthmān had committed misdeeds. In both Ibāḍī and non-Ibāḍī sources, Ṭalḥa and al-Zubayr lend their support to protestors. Nonetheless, members of this second faction maintained that ʿUthmān repented of his misdeeds and did not deserve to be executed. Since they believed he was wrongfully killed, they believed his assassins deserved to be punished. According to Ibāḍīs, since ʿAlī and his faction disagreed with this assessment, they ignored the demands of Ṭalḥa and al-Zubayr and considered their rebellion unlawful. A third group of Companions, led primarily by ʿAbd Allāh b. ʿUmar, Saʿd b. Abī Waqqāṣ, Muḥammad b. Maslama, and others, abstained from judging the lawfulness of ʿUthmān's murder. Ambiguities in the case of ʿUthmān led them to refrain from lending support to either ʿAlī or his adversaries.

Al-Wārjalānī explains that the Ibāḍī position coincides with that of the first faction of Companions; however, he does not condemn the other two groups. He explains that as long as members of the other two factions do not claim that all Muslims must agree with them and that to disagree with them constitutes unbelief, they are to be respected as scholars who exercised their own discretion in judging the case of ʿUthmān.[11] Al-Wārjalānī argues that God will reward the first group for coming to the correct opinion and forgive the other two for their humble attempts to discern the truth. It should be noted that other Ibāḍī theologians were less forgiving. They condemned the party of Ṭalḥa and al-Zubayr as misguided and the party of ʿAbd Allāh b. ʿUmar and Saʿd b. Abī Waqqāṣ as men of doubt (*ahl al-shakk*).[12]

As with other *faḍāʾil* literature utilized in Sunnī–Shīʿī polemical disputes, the Ibāḍīs cited prophetic *ḥadīth* exalting the character of a particular Companion as evidence of the correctness of their doctrines. For Ibāḍīs, ʿAmmār b. Yāsir emerges as a key figure representing those on the right path against other Companions such as ʿUthmān, ʿAlī, Ṭalḥa, and al-Zubayr, who go astray. In all historiography (Sunnī, Shīʿī, and Ibāḍī)

[10] Al-Wārjalānī, *Kitāb al-Dalīl*, 3:188.
[11] Al-Wārjalānī, *Kitāb al-Dalīl*, 1:13–4, 3:188–189.
[12] Hinds Xerox, 396–413; al-Kāshif, ed., *al-Siyar*, 2:142–143, 309–310. See also Madelung and al-Salimi, eds., *Ibāḍī Texts*, 330–350; Crone and Zimmerman, *The Epistle of Sālim ibn Dhakwān*, 244–247, 331–332.

about the protests against ʿUthmān, the Muhājirūn and Anṣār are depicted as electing ʿAmmār to deliver a letter to ʿUthmān with their demands for reform.[13] One *ḥadīth* warns the community that a transgressing party (*fiʾat bāghiya*) doomed to hell will one day kill ʿAmmār.[14] When ʿAmmār died fighting the army of Muʿāwiya at the battle of Ṣiffīn, pro-ʿAlid, Shīʿī, and Ibāḍī authors utilized the *ḥadīth* as evidence of the wickedness of Muʿāwiya and the righteousness of ʿAlī's cause. ʿAmmār's central role in the protests against ʿUthmān and in the civil wars that followed appears to be the reason that Ibāḍīs selected him as the symbolic leader of their cause. Resembling Shīʿī attempts to do the same with ʿAlī, Ibāḍīs utilized hagiography praising ʿAmmār's character and implicitly validating his political career after the Prophet to characterize him as an imām.[15] Before ʿAmmār dies as a martyr, he furthermore warns ʿAlī against accepting Muʿāwiya's invitations to arbitration. According to Ibāḍīs, it is the issue of arbitration that leads the Muhājirūn and Anṣār to part ways with ʿAlī and encamp at Nahrawān. Those who secede from ʿAlī's army allegedly include seventy Companions who took part in the battle of Badr and many who converted to Islam early in the Prophet's career when the community still faced Jerusalem for worship. Desiring to honor the memory of ʿAmmār and those who died with him fighting Muʿāwiya, these Companions considered arbitration with Muʿāwiya and further obedience to ʿAlī unlawful. In the sections that follow, I consider Ibāḍī historiography about ʿAlī and the rationale that authors provided to explain his shift from a righteous leader to misguided military commander.

ʿALĪ BEFORE ARBITRATION

For many Umayyads and zealous ʿUthmānīs, ʿAlī was a total hypocrite. He deceived the Prophet and those around him into believing that he was a pious man, but in reality he was one who concealed his unbelief and ill will toward the faithful. As Chapter 1 noted, ʿUthmānīs circulated tales in which ʿAlī tried to injure or kill the Prophet, while Umayyads believed that ʿAlī had led other hypocrites in slandering a wife of the Prophet. If the

[13] Al-Amīnī, *al-Ghadīr*, 9:17–18; al-Balādhurī, *Ansāb al-ashrāf*, 5:539; Hinds Xerox, 143–144; Ibn ʿAbd Rabbih, *al-ʿIqd*, 5:57.

[14] Aḥmad b. Ḥanbal, *al-Musnad*, 3:91; al-Amīnī, *al-Ghadīr*, 9:21; al-Bukhārī, *Ṣaḥīḥ*, 3:207; al-Wārjalānī, *Kitāb al-Dalīl*, 1:36, 3:188.

[15] For Ibāḍī references to ʿAmmār as an imām, see al-Kāshif, ed., *al-Siyar*, 2:313; al-Wārjalānī, *Kitāb al-Dalīl*, 1:36. See also Gaiser, *Muslims, Scholars, Soldiers*, 96–98.

Khārijī–Ibāḍī tradition can also be characterized as anti-ʿAlid, it is of a different sort.

Ibāḍī authors do not deny that ʿUthmān and ʿAlī both had been pious members of the community who faithfully served the Prophet in his mission. They were men of merit who shared close kinship ties with the Prophet. Not only were they cousins of the Prophet, but also his sons-in-law. The Ibāḍīs argued that after the Prophet's death, the community possessed a collective duty to appoint the best among them to serve as imāms. Similar to Sunnīs, the Ibāḍīs are certain that the Muhājirūn and Anṣār successfully fulfilled this duty by selecting Abū Bakr, then ʿUmar, ʿUthmān, and ʿAlī. Each time, the senior members of the community consulted one another and selected the most qualified candidate to rule.

It appears that, as with Sunnīs, Ibāḍī authors acknowledged two different theories about ʿAlī's political views during the period of his predecessors. On one hand, Ibn ʿAbbās is depicted in a few reports as discussing his memories of each caliph's succession and how the Hāshimids had hoped for ʿAlī's election.[16] In these reports, ʿAlī and the Hāshimids are portrayed as collectively believing that ʿAlī had been a superior candidate to Abū Bakr, ʿUmar, and ʿUthmān. On the other hand, Ibāḍī authors composed many treatises in which they discussed succession after the Prophet and refuted Shīʿī claims about early Islamic history. In their defense of orthodoxy, these authors frequently deny that ʿAlī considered himself a better candidate than his predecessors or ever argued for the right to succeed the Prophet before he became caliph.[17] Like Sunnism, Ibāḍī orthodoxy understands ʿAlī to have been a member of a larger collective of Companions that actively supported the succession of the first three caliphs despite both traditions transmitting a few reports indicative of the contrary.

As noted above, when members of the Muslim community begin to protest the governors and policies of ʿUthmān, ʿAlī's role in Ibāḍī literature follows the one that appears in the well-known chronicles of al-Balādhurī and al-Ṭabarī. Both ʿUthmān and the protestors utilize ʿAlī as an envoy to deescalate the conflict and negotiate a resolution. When ʿUthmān requests that protestors give him a few days to implement reforms, he asks ʿAlī to meet with them on his behalf to ensure their assent.[18] However, when ʿUthmān reneges on his promises for reform and commands his governor

[16] Hinds Xerox, 225–226; Kitāb al-Siyar, 31.

[17] Al-Kāshif, ed., *al-Siyar*, 1:69, 2:133–134, 300–302; al-Siyar al-Ibāḍiyya, 8–15.

[18] Hinds Xerox, 150; al-Siyar al-Ibāḍiyya, 20–22; al-Ṭabarī, *Tārīkh*, 3:403–404.

in Egypt to execute some of the leaders of the protest, the protestors lay siege to his palace. For Ibāḍīs, an imām who is guilty of misconduct must be encouraged to repent and reform his ways. In Sunnī and Ibāḍī literature, the protestors successfully compel ʿUthmān to repent before the Muslim public and promise to make amends.[19] According to Ibāḍīs, when an imām refuses to repent or follow through with reforms, the community must remove him from office. If the imām refuses to leave office, then the faithful must wage war against him and rid themselves of him.[20]

In the case of ʿUthmān, his refusal to remove his Umayyad kin from office and replace them with respected Companions was a key indication that he was not going to implement the promised reforms. For Ibāḍīs, this meant that there was now an obligation to remove ʿUthmān from office. The siege on his palace is characterized as a strategy to compel ʿUthmān to either implement reforms or abdicate. Both Sunnī and Ibāḍī sources portray ʿUthmān as rejecting requests that he leave office by arguing that he would not relinquish a mantle bestowed upon him by God.[21] In hagiography about ʿUthmān, it is the Prophet himself who commands him to remain steadfast in holding on to power when others pressure him to renounce it.[22]

After a number of weeks under siege and out of sight, ʿUthmān finally confronts the protestors from a balcony on his palace. After ʿUthmān argues with a protestor who is described as a senior citizen and Companion of the Prophet named Dīnār or Nayyār b. ʿIyyāḍ, the latter is shot dead by a palace guard.[23] When the protestors demand that ʿUthmān surrender the guard to them, he refuses, arguing, "How can I surrender someone who is guarding my life while you desire to kill me and execute him as well?"[24] It is the following day that the siege erupts into violence and ʿUthmān is assassinated. When protestors attempt to force their way into the palace, Marwān b. al-Ḥakam, Saʿīd b. al-ʿĀṣ, and ʿAbd Allāh b. al-Zubayr all engage in skirmishes with them to push them back. According to one report, ʿUthmān's assassins are only able to enter the

19 Hinds Xerox, 147; al-Siyar al-Ibāḍiyya, 20; al-Ṭabarī, *Tārīkh*, 3:400.
20 Hinds Xerox, 20–21; al-Kāshif, ed., *al-Siyar*, 1:202–205. See also Gaiser, *Muslims, Scholars, Soldiers*, 46, 122–123, 126, 134–136.
21 Hinds Xerox, 151; al-Siyar al-Ibāḍiyya, 22; al-Ṭabarī, *Tārīkh*, 3:404.
22 Aḥmad b. Ḥanbal, *al-Musnad*, 6:87, 114; Ibn Abī Shayba, *al-Muṣannaf*, 7:490; Ibn Māja, *Sunan*, 1:41; al-Ṭabarānī, *al-Muʿjam al-awsaṭ*, 3:171; al-Tirmidhī, *Sunan*, 5:292.
23 Hinds Xerox, 153; Ibn Ḥajar al-ʿAsqalānī, *al-Iṣāba*, 6:381; al-Kāshif, ed., *al-Siyar*, 1:103; al-Siyar al-Ibāḍiyya, 23; al-Ṭabarī, *Tārīkh*, 3:413–414. See also Madelung, *Succession*, 135–136.
24 Hinds Xerox, 153; al-Siyar al-Ibāḍiyya, 23; al-Ṭabarī, *Tārīkh*, 3:414.

palace through a back entrance, when a neighbor of ʿUthmān, ʿAmr b. Ḥazm al-Anṣārī, agrees to open his home to the protestors and grant them access to this entrance.[25]

Ibāḍī sources diverge from Sunnī historiography in identifying ʿAlī and ʿAmmār as leading a faction of Companions who considered ʿUthmān's murder lawful. ʿAlī is even described as one of the killers of ʿUthmān (*qatalat ʿUthmān*).[26] Like those zealous ʿUthmānīs and Umayyads who blamed ʿAlī for ʿUthmān's murder, it is unlikely that Ibāḍīs meant by this that ʿAlī actually entered the palace and killed ʿUthmān. In Ibāḍī sources, it is explicitly mentioned that ʿAlī sat at the Prophet's mosque armed and ready for war with ʿUthmān's partisans.[27] ʿAlī is portrayed as directing the protestors and assassins on that day from inside the mosque. Thus, he is depicted as the head of a conspiracy to kill ʿUthmān, but not as actually taking part in the killing. While Ibāḍī historiography does not provide any more detail on the identities of ʿUthmān's assassins, the unique aspect about it is the strong conviction that ʿUthmān was rightfully killed and that leading Companions planned and approved of the murder. In the civil wars that followed, the same Companions remained steadfast in their position and fought against insurgents who believed that ʿUthmān was wrongfully killed or demanded punishment for his killers.

IBĀḌĪ VIEWS ON THE BATTLE OF THE CAMEL

In Ibāḍī historiography, the Muhājirūn, Anṣār, and the majority of the Muslim community are portrayed as individuals who rebelled against ʿUthmān. This majority elects ʿAlī as the fourth caliph and backs him and ʿAmmār in their wars against insurgents. For Ibāḍīs, the battle of the Camel and the battle of Ṣiffīn were the results of two rebellions with the same cause. In each case the insurgents held that (1) ʿUthmān had been wrongfully killed and (2) his killers warranted punishment. ʿAlī waged war against these insurgents because he wholly disagreed with both of their assessments. According to Ibāḍīs, ʿAlī and the majority of the community that backed him contended that ʿUthmān had been rightfully killed after committing misdeeds, refusing to reform, and refusing to leave office. It had become incumbent upon members of the community to wage war against ʿUthmān, who had become a tyrant. Those insurgents who sought

[25] Hinds Xerox, 154; al-Siyar al-Ibāḍiyya, 23; al-Ṭabarī, *Tārīkh*, 3:414.
[26] Al-Wārjalānī, *Kitāb al-Dalīl*, 3:41, 130, 188.
[27] Hinds Xerox, 153; al-Siyar al-Ibāḍiyya, 23.

to punish ʿUthmān's killers were mistaken in accusing them of any wrongdoing.

In pro-ʿAlid and Shīʿī sources, the grave sin of those who fight against ʿAlī in the battle of the Camel and the battle of Ṣiffīn is their rebellion against a pious and just imām. In Ibāḍī sources, their rebellion is less of a sin against the person of ʿAlī. The insurgents in these two battles are viewed as treacherously waging war against the Muhājirūn, Anṣār, and, more broadly, the entire Muslim community. Ibāḍī sources consistently cite one key argument and two verses of the Qurʾān to make their case. They argue that the Qurʾān condemns insurgency as a high crime against God that requires a *ḥadd* punishment. Other crimes delineated in the Qurʾān that carry a *ḥadd* punishment include theft, slander, and fornication. If one is found guilty of committing one of these offenses, then, barring certain ambiguities or extenuating circumstances, the relevant *ḥadd* punishment delineated in the Qurʾān would be the appropriate sentence. Any community or ruling authority that fails to implement *ḥadd* punishments would be considered delinquent in their duties to God.

Ibāḍī authors contended that the Muslim community possessed a duty to wage war against such insurgents until they were completely destroyed or they surrendered and repented of their actions. As evidence of their duties, Ibāḍīs cited Q2:193, "And fight them until there is no more civil strife and the religion of God prevails. But if they cease, let there be no hostility except to the wicked." More frequently, they cited Q49:9, "And if among the faithful two parties should begin to fight, then make peace between them. And if one party should wrong the other, then fight the transgressing party until it complies with the command of God. But if it complies, then make peace between them with justice and fairness. Indeed, God loves the equitable."[28]

To fulfill their duties to God, the faithful were obliged to fight the insurgents at the battle of the Camel and the battle of Ṣiffīn. Similar to the pro-ʿAlids and Sunnīs discussed in the previous chapter, Ibāḍīs did not want to condemn ʿĀʾisha to hell, so they argued that she repented of her actions.[29] By contrast, Ṭalḥa and al-Zubayr are portrayed as deceiving ʿĀʾisha into joining their army, dying before any repentance, and, thus, considered doomed. Muʿāwiya and ʿAmr b. al-ʿĀṣ are portrayed as lifelong enemies of God and the faithful. They deliberately shed the blood of the

[28] Al-Barrādī, *al-Jawāhir*, 121, 123; Hinds Xerox, 228; al-Kāshif, ed., *al-Siyar*, 1:106, 2:306; Kitāb al-Siyar, 307–308; al-Siyar al-Ibāḍiyya, 28, 32. See also Gaiser, *Muslims, Scholars, Soldiers*, 46.

[29] Al-Kāshif, ed., *al-Siyar*, 1:107–108; al-Wārjalānī, *Kitāb al-Dalīl*, 1:28.

innocent and remained steadfast in their wickedness until their deaths. It is this perceived recalcitrance of Muʿāwiya and ʿAmr that serves as proof to Ibāḍīs that arbitration with them had been unlawful. Warfare with them was obligatory until they surrendered to the will of the greater Muslim community.

ARBITRATION WITH MUʿĀWIYA AND ʿAMR

According to Ibāḍīs, the battle of the Camel ended in a victory for the "Muslims." Ibāḍī historiography refers to both proto-Ibāḍī predecessors and the Ibāḍīs of subsequent centuries as the "Muslims" more frequently than with any other moniker. Thus, the insurgents at the battle of the Camel and the battle of Ṣiffīn and non-Ibāḍī Muslims of subsequent generations were excluded from this sub-community of "Muslims." Unlike their Khārijī peers, Ibāḍīs refrained from outright condemnation of non-Ibāḍīs as non-Muslims. Nonetheless, similar to Sunnī and Shīʿī views of Muslims who followed other sects, Ibāḍīs considered non-Ibāḍīs guilty of harboring certain heretical doctrines that constituted a type of unbelief (*kufr*).[30] Regardless of the terms that were deployed to refer to themselves or to their opponents, it is clear that Ibāḍīs viewed themselves as representing the party of God and their enemies in war as the enemies of God. While ʿĀʾisha repented of her transgressions against the faithful, Muʿāwiya and ʿAmr remained openly antagonistic.

Ibāḍīs argued that Muʿāwiya and ʿAmr disregarded the sanctity of the "Muslims" or the party representing God and proto-Ibāḍī predecessors. By waging war against ʿAlī and most of the Muslim community that had pledged allegiance to him, these two men had plainly showed their enmity to God, the Prophet Muḥammad, and his followers. There is a slight resemblance between Ibāḍī and Shīʿī views of Muʿāwiya and ʿAmr. The two become caricatures of evil and openly disdain God and religion in Twelver Shīʿī literature. In Shīʿī narratives, the motivation of all villains is hatred for ʿAlī and his family. In Ibāḍī historiography, however, this personal vendetta or tribal animus does not appear to be the source of the conflicts that erupt. The key disagreement between ʿAlī and his rivals was whether or not ʿUthmān had been wrongfully killed. Muʿāwiya and ʿAmr were wrong in remaining allies of ʿUthmān, when there had been

[30] Non-Ibāḍīs were guilty of *kufr al-niʿma* or *nifāq* whereas non-Muslims were associated with a different type of unbelief, *kufr al-shirk*: see Crone and Zimmerman, *The Epistle of Sālim ibn Dhakwān*, 198–202; Gaiser, *Shurāt Legends*, 161–168.

a religious duty to disassociate (*barāʾa*) from him. They compounded their misdeeds by seeking vengeance for ʿUthmān and leading an insurgency against the "Muslims." Shīʿī authors drew heavily on anti-Umayyad literature that sought to disgrace Muʿāwiya by listing vices (*mathālib*) in his character and depicting him as cursed.[31] For Ibāḍīs, however, the crime of insurgency sufficed. Muʿāwiya and ʿAmr were clearly enemies of God because of their support for ʿUthmān and the tyranny he represented in his final years as caliph and their willingness to wage war on his behalf. There does not seem to be a preoccupation with defaming their characters by means of other evidence.

According to pro-ʿAlid historiography, when Muʿāwiya and ʿAmr invited ʿAlī's army to settle their differences by means of arbitration, the group of soldiers that had coalesced to form the Muḥakkima initially supported the initiative with fervor. In their reverence for the Qurʾān, these soldiers feared that ignoring Muʿāwiya's calls to have the Qurʾān arbitrate between them constituted a form of unbelief. This group threatened to slay ʿAlī and those who followed him, if they continued fighting and did not heed such calls. ʿAlī, in turn, argued that Muʿāwiya's invitation was a ruse and that they should not be deceived by it. However, these soldiers eventually compelled ʿAlī and the rest of his army to discontinue fighting. In a few sources, ʿAlī explains that when he saw that his soldiers were willing to murder al-Ḥasan and al-Ḥusayn, the two grandsons of the Prophet, and other young Hāshimids in his ward, he relented.[32] He made an oath not to bring them again, were he to face Muʿāwiya's army once more. According to this narrative, the Muḥakkima only realize that Muʿāwiya and ʿAmr did not invite them to arbitration in good faith after ʿAlī is forced to agree to a temporary peace settlement with Muʿāwiya. The two agree to end all hostilities as they wait for the outcome of arbitration. During this time the Muḥakkima acknowledge their folly in accepting arbitration with Muʿāwiya and ask ʿAlī to resume hostilities with Muʿāwiya, but ʿAlī refuses to renege. Such unilateral action would have constituted treachery or encouraged onlookers to believe that ʿAlī feared arbitration because of the weakness of his cause and the strength of Muʿāwiya's. In this pro-ʿAlid narrative, it is the Muḥakkima who insist on arbitration and ʿAlī who is coerced into accepting it. Although one Ibāḍī historian cites a debate between ʿAlī and the Muḥakkima where they

[31] For example, see Yūnus, *Muʿāwiya*.
[32] Al-Ṭabarī, *Tārīkh*, 4:44. See also Madelung, *Succession*, 244.

acknowledge that they were initially deceived, this version of events is not normative in Ibāḍī sources.[33]

In Ibāḍī historiography, the Muḥakkima stridently oppose arbitration from the beginning. These soldiers are certain that arbitration is unlawful for a litany of reasons that are laid out in an Ibāḍī treatise entitled "Proofs that the 'Muslims' Presented Against ʿAlī b. Abī Ṭālib" and in chapters dedicated to the subject in many larger theological works.[34] The mutinous soldiers cite verses of the Qurʾān such as Q49:9 to argue that the command to fight insurgents is clear. Furthermore, other verses such as Q33:36 indicate that humans have no choice in a matter when the command of God is evident. The faithful are obliged to carry out such commands rather than defer to some alternative.

After the Muḥakkima leave ʿAlī's army, they encamp in a place known as Ḥarūrāʾ and, according to both Ibāḍī and non-Ibāḍī literature, ʿAlī sends Ibn ʿAbbās to their camp in order to debate with them and convince them to renew their allegiance to ʿAlī.[35]

When Ibn ʿAbbās initially arrives at their camp, he cites Q4:35 and Q5:95 as evidence of the legality of deferring to arbitration in disputes. The Muḥakkima respond that God has ordained arbitration in those particular cases (involving pilgrims or two spouses), but has not provided such an option in settling disputes with insurgents. Furthermore, even if arbitration was lawful in such cases, the selected arbitrators must be faithful and upright Muslims. It would be unlawful to appoint the likes of ʿAmr b. al-ʿĀṣ and Abū Mūsā al-Ashʿarī to serve in such a capacity. ʿAmr, like Muʿāwiya, disqualified himself by waging war against faithful Muslims and deeming it lawful to take their lives. Abū Mūsā disqualified himself when he publicly urged Kūfans to ignore ʿAlī's repeated requests to mobilize for war before the battle of the Camel. Abū Mūsā deemed warfare with other Muslims unlawful and believed that it was better to remain at home during times of civil strife. However, in arguing this, Abū Mūsā misled Kūfans from fulfilling their duty to fight insurgents, urged disobedience to God, and made unlawful what God had made lawful.

[33] Al-Barrādī, *al-Jawāhir*, 124. See also Gaiser, "Ibādī Accounts," 68.

[34] Al-Barrādī, *al-Jawāhir*, 117–127; Hinds Xerox, 224–237; Kitāb al-Siyar, 307–311; al-Izkawī, *Kashf al-ghumma*, 1:510–517, 538–539; al-Siyar al-Ibāḍiyya, 23–34; Majmūʿ al-siyar, 398–401.

[35] Al-Ḥākim al-Naysābūrī, *al-Mustadrak*, 2:150–152; al-Nasāʾī, *al-Sunan al-kubrā*, 5:165–167. For Ibāḍī references, see the previous footnote and Gaiser, "Ibādī Accounts."

In Ibāḍī sources, the Muḥakkima cite a number of *ḥadīth* to substantiate their rejection of arbitration.[36] For example, they narrate a *ḥadīth* in which the Prophet warns Muslims of the misguidance of two wicked arbitrators. In another *ḥadīth*, the Prophet condemns an unnamed close relative as someone who will claim to represent the Prophet, but will not truly represent his character or mission. Instead, this man will be a warmonger who causes great tumult.[37] This *ḥadīth* clearly aims to condemn 'Alī. In other *ḥadīth*, the Prophet advises the community to follow the path of 'Ammār b. Yāsir and explains that he will die on the right path. *Ḥadīth* praising 'Ammār in this way are particularly important for the Ibāḍīs since they revered him as a key figure who exemplified Ibāḍī conceptions of righteousness and justice. Unlike 'Alī, 'Ammār remains steadfast in fighting insurgents until his death. In Ibāḍī sources, before 'Ammār dies he even warns 'Alī not to accept Mu'āwiya's calls for arbitration since it would constitute misguidance.[38] Thus, when Ibn 'Abbās visits the Muḥakkima, they cite the memory of 'Ammār and their desire to remain true to his example. In Ibāḍī literature, the Muḥakkima ultimately convince Ibn 'Abbās of their arguments and he loses faith in 'Alī's authority before parting ways with him and vowing not to fight the Muḥakkima.

In Ibāḍī historiography, 'Alī enthusiastically supports Mu'āwiya's calls for arbitration. 'Alī appears to be tired of warfare with Mu'āwiya and content with the idea of making peace with him by restricting his own realm of authority to Iraq and leaving the Levant to Mu'āwiya. Ibāḍīs also portray 'Alī as relying on the advice of Ash'ath b. Qays al-Kindī (d. 40/661), a Kūfan notable who may have become a proponent of peace settlements with Mu'āwiya after the latter secretly promised to reward him financially for his support.[39] Ibāḍī authors criticized 'Alī as someone who accepted arbitration as a result of a worldly desire for power. They argued that this one misdeed destroyed 'Alī's character since deferring to arbitration at this juncture constituted unbelief. Had 'Alī remained faithful, he would have continued fighting insurgents and remained obedient to the command of God. Since the decision to defer to the two arbitrators entailed supplanting the ruling of God with the rulings of

[36] Al-Barrādī, *al-Jawāhir*, 142–143; al-Izkawī, *Kashf al-ghumma*, 1:507; al-Kāshif, ed., *al-Siyar*, 1:110.

[37] Al-Wārjalānī, *Kitāb al-Dalīl*, 3:42.

[38] Al-Barrādī, *al-Jawāhir*, 150; al-Izkawī, *Kashf al-ghumma*, 1:501–502. See also Gaiser, *Shurāt*, 127–128.

[39] Al-Barrādī, *al-Jawāhir*, 124, 126. See also Gaiser, "Ibādī Accounts," 67. For reports about Mu'āwiya persuading Ash'ath to support him, see al-Balādhurī, *Ansāb al-ashrāf*, 2:383; al-Ya'qūbī, *Tārīkh*, 2:188–189.

men, ʿAlī was guilty of a major blasphemy: ruling by something other than the revelation of God. The Muḥakkima and later Ibāḍīs argued that this meant ʿAlī had followed the path of the wicked who are condemned in the Qurʾān (5:44–47) for this sin.

The mutinous soldiers were memorialized in Muslim historiography for shouting their demand that one turn to God for all judgments (*lā ḥukm illā li-llāh*) as a type of slogan.[40] Their condemnation of arbitration (*taḥkīm*) and insistence that Muslims abide by the ruling (*ḥukm*) of God are the reasons for which historians referred to them occasionally as the *muḥakkima*, those who would chant the slogan *lā ḥukm illā li-llāh*.

IBĀḌĪ NARRATIVES OF NAHRAWĀN

In pro-ʿAlid reports, the Muḥakkima are described as killing civilians they encountered who did not support their ideology.[41] When ʿAlī sends messengers to investigate and arrest the persons responsible, the Muḥakkima kill his messengers and send him word that they were collectively responsible for the executions. It is after these killings that ʿAlī feels compelled to attack the group. In discussions with his soldiers, it becomes apparent that ʿAlī strongly desires to first wage war against Muʿāwiya. Such a move would possibly persuade the Muḥakkima to join the campaign and end their rebellion. His Kūfan soldiers, however, argue that they cannot risk leaving their families behind in Iraq with the Muḥakkima unchecked, fearing that they would all be massacred. ʿAlī capitulates and moves to confront the Muḥakkima. The day before the battle of Nahrawān begins, ʿAlī offers amnesty to any soldier who withdraws from the encampment or rejoins his army. The following day, ʿAlī's army annihilates the Muḥakkima. Few are able to flee. One survivor, ʿAbd al-Raḥmān b. Muljam, eventually exacts revenge on ʿAlī when he assassinates him two years later.

In Ibāḍī narratives, the Muḥakkima never kill any civilians or provoke ʿAlī to attack them. Those encamped at Nahrawān are described as pious scholars and early converts who had fought for the Prophet at the battle of Badr. They are all ascetics who desire nothing but to worship and obey God. They disassociated themselves from ʿAlī and peacefully parted ways with him when they saw him violate a sacred commandment of God.

40 Al-Ṭabarī, *Tārīkh*, 4:41, 53–54. See also Gaiser, *Muslims, Scholars, Soldiers*, 35.

41 Al-Dīnawarī, *al-Akhbār al-ṭiwāl*, 207; Ibn al-Athīr, *Usd al-ghāba*, 3:150. See also Gaiser, *Shurāt Legends*, 47–48.

When Ibn ʿAbbās and ʿAlī visit them to discuss their differences, neither of the two are able to refute their arguments. Thus, in Ibāḍī literature, ʿAlī is criticized for shedding the blood of 4,000 pious Muslims without cause.[42]

Ibāḍī authors depicted ʿAlī in one of two ways after the battle of Nahrawān. In some sources, ʿAlī is mournful and haunted by the battle.[43] ʿAlī affirms Ibāḍī conceptions of the men who died there: he regards them as innocent of any wrongdoing as well as righteous, faithful Muslims. He also regrets killing them, and prays for their forgiveness after their deaths. There is no clear explanation for why he attacked them. The reader surmises that he did so simply because they had disagreed with arbitration and parted ways with him. According to another set of Ibāḍī reports, ʿAlī is heedless of the gravity of his actions, and essentially allies himself with Muʿāwiya against the faithful. Muʿāwiya even offers to fight the Muḥakkima on ʿAlī's behalf.[44] In these narratives, ʿAlī and Muʿāwiya make peace with one another after Ṣiffīn and agree to rule their own realms. The Muḥakkima represent the righteous faction of Muslims who risk destroying this peace agreement between two tyrants who care only for power. In pro-ʿAlid reports, Muʿāwiya and the Umayyads are depicted as wantonly killing rivals and dissenters to attain and maintain political power. The Ibāḍīs describe ʿAlī in very similar terms. Power corrupts him, and thus Ibn ʿAbbās, a close confidant and cousin, feels obliged to part ways with him after the battle of Nahrawān. He cannot continue to serve ʿAlī after seeing him kill innocent believers – the Muḥakkima – without cause.

IBN MULJAM

Since it is a survivor of the battle of Nahrawān who eventually assassinates ʿAlī, one would expect Ibāḍī sources to commemorate the assassin. ʿAlī had become a tyrant who refused to admit to any wrongdoing or leave office. As with ʿUthmān, if pious Muslims attempted to forcibly remove him from office and he was killed after refusing to comply, this would be considered a lawful killing. However, it appears that most Ibāḍīs did not praise ʿAlī's assassin, Ibn Muljam, as a hero. He did not become a recurring symbol of justice like ʿAmmār or the leaders of the Muḥakkima in Ibāḍī

[42] Al-Barrādī, *al-Jawāhir*, 143; al-Kāshif, ed., *al-Siyar*, 1:114; al-Siyar al-Ibāḍiyya, 33; al-Wārjalānī, *Kitāb al-Dalīl*, 1:15, 28.

[43] Al-Barrādī, *al-Jawāhir*, 138–139, 143; al-Izkawī, *Kashf al-ghumma*, 1:518, 539.

[44] Al-Izkawī, *Kashf al-ghumma*, 1:508; al-Kāshif, ed., *al-Siyar*, 1:114.

literature. Furthermore, contemporary Ibāḍī authors have sought to distance themselves from Ibn Muljam by arguing that the assassin did not represent the Muḥakkima or the Ibāḍī tradition in killing ʿAlī.[45] A medieval Ibāḍī historian, Faḍl b. Ibrāhīm al-Barrādī (active eighth/fourteenth century), offers a similar assessment. Al-Barrādī cites a respected authority, Abū Sufyān Maḥbūb b. Raḥīl (active third/ninth century), who states that he has not found scholars praising or condemning Ibn Muljam.[46] Ibāḍīs may have refrained from passing judgment on Ibn Muljam because they were unsure whether he truly represented the values of the Muḥakkima and the Ibāḍīs or one of the more extreme Khārijī factions that rationalized the killing of civilians and considered all other Muslims nonbelievers. It is ambiguities about Ibn Muljam's own doctrines that likely encouraged Ibāḍīs to refrain from judging him. If he was a righteous person, then one should not disparage or disassociate from him. If he was an extremist or a murderer who killed ʿAlī for some unlawful reason, then he should not be praised. Ibāḍī scholars recommended abstaining from judgment (*wuqūf*) on the righteousness of a person in cases where there was doubt about his character.[47] It would make sense that some Ibāḍīs exercised the same caution in the case of Ibn Muljam.

Although many Ibāḍīs refrained from passing judgment on Ibn Muljam, some Khawārij and Ibāḍīs did venture to praise him. A Khārijī named ʿImrān b. Ḥiṭṭān wrote an elegy praising Ibn Muljam's blow to ʿAlī as one of the most pious deeds in human history.[48] Another Khārijī, Ibn Abī Mayyās al-Murādī, also praises Ibn Muljam's assassination of ʿAlī in poetry.[49]

ʿAbd al-Qāhir al-Baghdādī (d. 329/1037) noted that some Khawārij claimed that Q2:207, "And from among mankind is the one who willingly sells his soul to obtain the grace of God," was revealed about Ibn Muljam and his decision to martyr himself by assassinating ʿAlī.[50] In a few other Sunnī sources, Ibn Muljam is described as reciting this verse and the slogan of the Muḥakkima, *lā ḥukm illā li-llāh*, before striking ʿAlī.[51]

[45] Al-Sābiʿī, *al-Khawārij*, 157–168. See also Gaiser, *Shurāt Legends*, 97, 133; Hoffman, *Essentials*, 11.

[46] Al-Barrādī, *al-Jawāhir*, 145. [47] Ibid., 171. See also Gaiser, *Shurāt Legends*, 157.

[48] Al-Barrādī, *al-Jawāhir*, 146; al-Izkawī, *Kashf al-ghumma*, 519–520. For references in Sunnī literature, see al-Baghdādī, *al-Farq bayn al-firaq*, 95; al-Dhahabī, *Siyar*, 4:215; Ibn ʿAbd al-Barr, *al-Istīʿāb*, 3:1128; Ibn ʿAsākir, *Taʾrīkh*, 43:495; Ibn Ḥazm, *al-Muḥallā*, 10:484.

[49] Al-Ṭabarī, *Tārīkh*, 4:115–116. See also Gaiser, *Shurāt Legends*, 51.

[50] Al-Baghdādī, *al-Farq bayn al-firaq*, 104; al-Ījī, *al-Mawāqif*, 3:697.

[51] Ibn al-Jawzī, *al-Muntaẓam*, 5:176; Ibn Kathīr, *al-Bidāya wa 'l-nihāya*, 7:362.

Qur'ān 2:207 is important to both Ibāḍī and pro-ʿAlid authors. For Ibāḍīs, the verse provides scriptural basis for those who choose the path of martyrdom and war against tyrants even when there is no obligation to do so. In Ibāḍī political theory, when the faithful have the means and requisite numbers to revolt against a tyrant and appoint a righteous imām, then they have a duty to do just that.[52] However, if the faithful do not have the means, then Ibāḍīs are allowed to dissemble and live peacefully until circumstances change. Those who wish to sacrifice themselves to God and are overwhelmed by the desire to command justice and forbid evil in their society may revolt independently. These martyrs are referred to as *shurāt* (sing. *shārī*) or those who sell their own selves, in reference to Q2:207. Khawārij referred to themselves as *shurāt* and differed from Ibāḍīs in considering the obligation to oppose tyrants perpetual.[53] The fact that Ibn Muljam is described as reciting this verse while appearing to choose the path of the *shurāt* plainly indicates why some Khawārij and Ibāḍīs revered him.

In pro-ʿAlid Sunnī and Shīʿī exegesis, the revelation of Q2:207 is tied to an act of valor performed by ʿAlī. To safeguard the life of the Prophet, ʿAlī agrees to help him flee from Mecca to Medina by wearing the Prophet's mantle and staying in his home on an evening which assassins had planned to kill him. By agreeing to serve as a decoy and possible martyr, ʿAlī proved on that night that he was among those who would sell their own souls "to obtain the grace of God."[54] Thus, in polemics between pro-ʿAlids and anti-ʿAlids, interpretations of Q2:207 becomes an important subject of dispute.

Anti-ʿAlids such as Samura b. Jundab (d. 60/680) celebrated ʿAlī's assassination by proclaiming that the verse was revealed about Ibn Muljam. The Muʿtazilī Ibn Abī 'l-Ḥadīd notes that Samura also interpreted Q2:204, "And among mankind is the one whose speech you admire in this life. Though he cites God as a witness to that which is in his heart, he is the most obstinate of adversaries," as a reference to ʿAlī.[55] ʿAbd al-Qāhir al-Baghdādī also cites Khawārij as interpreting the verse in the same way.[56]

52 ʿAbd al-Kāfī, *al-Mūjaz*, 2:236–238. For an in-depth study of Ibāḍī conceptions of the imāmate, see Gaiser, *Muslims, Scholars, Soldiers*.

53 Gaiser, *Muslims, Scholars, Soldiers*, 39, 80–82, 86–89, 104–109, 126.

54 Al-Ḥākim al-Ḥaskānī, *Shawāhid al-tanzīl*, 1:123–131; Ibn ʿAsākir, *Taʾrīkh*, 42:67–68; Ibn al-Athīr, *Usd al-ghāba*, 4:25; al-Thaʿlabī, *Tafsīr*, 2:126.

55 Ibn Abī 'l-Ḥadīd, *Sharḥ*, 4:73.

56 Al-Baghdādī, *al-Farq bayn al-firaq*, 104; al-Ījī, *al-Mawāqif*, 3:697.

In describing ʿAlī's assassination, a few Ibāḍīs state that God sent Ibn Muljam to kill ʿAlī.[57] On one hand, one could read such statements as simply reflecting a fatalistic attitude that God preordains all events in the world, good or bad. On the other hand, they may reflect an author's subtle approval of Ibn Muljam's deed. The Ibāḍī heresiographer Muḥammad b. Saʿīd al-Qalhatī (sixth/twelfth century), for example, states that after ʿAlī killed the innocent Muḥakkima at Nahrawān, he lost most of his support in the community. He spent his last years disgraced, powerless, and estranged from the public until God sent Ibn Muljam to finally end his life.[58] The sense one has from the narrative is that God selects Ibn Muljam to rid the world of a tyrant. It is in approval of Ibn Muljam's deed that al-Qalḥaṭī then cites ʿImrān b. Ḥiṭṭān's ode to the assassin. In an epistle attributed to Khālid b. Qaḥṭān (active third/ninth century), he describes ʿAlī as treacherously killing the pious Muḥakkima to ensure peace with Muʿāwiya. He similarly states that it was God who sent Ibn Muljam. The latter killed ʿAlī in vengeance for those innocent lives that were lost at Nahrawān.[59] The author or a copyist respectfully wishes God's mercy on Ibn Muljam, an utterance that is made to dignify deceased Muslims.

Abū 'l-Ḥasan ʿAlī b. Muḥammad al-Bansāwī (fifth/eleventh century) states in an epistle that it is a religious duty to disassociate from ʿAlī and regard Ibn Muljam as a faithful Muslim. Al-Bansāwī also respectfully wishes God's mercy on Ibn Muljam.[60] One would not offer such a prayer for someone considered an enemy of God. Other Ibāḍī authors similarly pray for Ibn Muljam and condemn the Prophet's grandsons, al-Ḥasan and al-Ḥusayn, for executing him.[61] Ṣalt b. Khamīs (active second/eighth century) prays that God will have mercy on Ibn Muljam and defends the assassination of ʿAlī as lawful retaliation for those killed at Nahrawān.[62] Ṣalt b. Khamīs also includes Ibn Muljam in his summary list of imāms and leading personalities in the community whom the faithful should strive to emulate.[63] From these references it is clear that some Ibāḍī authors accepted Ibn Muljam as one of their predecessors and considered him a pious Muslim who carried out a lawful killing. Nevertheless, ʿAlī's assassination was neither justified nor discussed to the same extent as ʿUthmān's murder. Ibāḍīs transmitted many accounts of *shurāt*, martyrs who rebelled against tyrants, and developed a genre of literature dedicated

[57] Al-Izkawī, *Kashf al-ghumma*, 1:519; al-Qalhātī, *al-Kashf wa 'l-bayān*, 2:253.
[58] Al-Qalhātī, *al-Kashf wa 'l-bayān*, 2:252–253. [59] Al-Kāshif, ed., *al-Siyar*, 1:115.
[60] Al-Barrādī, *al-Jawāhir*, 145.
[61] Al-Izkawī, *Kashf al-ghumma*, 1:545; al-Kāshif, ed., *al-Siyar*, 1:116.
[62] Al-Kāshif, ed., *al-Siyar*, 2:307. [63] Ibid., 2:314.

to the subject.[64] However, the Ibāḍīs appear not to have transmitted or preserved any tales valorizing Ibn Muljam's exploits or execution. Perhaps the same group of early Khawārij who believed that Q2:207 was revealed about Ibn Muljam once circulated martyrdom stories about him, but the circulation of these narratives ceased with their extinction.

CRITIQUES OF AL-ḤASAN AND AL-ḤUSAYN

In a number of sources, Ibāḍī authors condemn the two grandsons of the Prophet, al-Ḥasan and al-Ḥusayn.[65] The two men supported their father ʿAlī's political career and participated in his civil wars. They presumably remained loyal to him when he accepted the opportunity for arbitration with Muʿāwiya. The two would also have either supported ʿAlī's decision to attack the Muḥakkima or directly participated in the battle of Nahrawān. For Ibāḍīs, their support for ʿAlī in either of these two matters would suffice to incriminate them as enemies of God. However, al-Ḥasan and al-Ḥusayn are also criticized for their conduct after ʿAlī's assassination.

Al-Ḥasan b. ʿAlī succeeds ʿAlī as caliph, but abdicates from power once his fragile coalition of Iraqi supporters begins to disintegrate and it is clear that Muʿāwiya would crush them in any military conflict. Al-Ḥasan is depicted as betraying the Muslim community by making peace with a tyrant who lavishly rewards him with money. One Ibāḍī author writes that when al-Ḥasan surrendered to Muʿāwiya and instructed his followers to do the same, "he traded his salvation in the Hereafter" for some wealth in this world.[66] The Muḥakkima gather at a place called Nukhayla, and as Muʿāwiya approaches Iraq, they wage war against his forces. They are initially victorious in their attacks, so Muʿāwiya is compelled to write to al-Ḥasan and ask for his help. Muʿāwiya also threatens to punish the residents of Kūfa and give them no amnesty if they fail to aid him in suppressing this rebellion. It is at this juncture that Ibadis describe al-Ḥasan, and occasionally, al-Ḥusayn, as coming to the aid of Muʿāwiya and fighting the Muḥakkima at the battle of Nukhayla.[67] Consequently,

[64] See Gaiser, *Shurāt Legends*.
[65] Al-Izkawī, *Kashf al-ghumma*, 1:545; al-Kāshif, ed., *al-Siyar*, 1:115–116, 374.
[66] Al-Izkawī, *Kashf al-ghumma*, 1:521, 540.
[67] Al-Barrādī, *al-Jawāhir*, 146–147; al-Izkawī, *Kashf al-ghumma*, 1:520; al-Kāshif, ed., *al-Siyar*, 1:116, 2:314. See also Gaiser, *Muslims, Scholars, Soldiers*, 99; Gaiser, *Shurāt Legends*, 133.

the two are viewed as unlawfully killing the pious Muḥakkima who are defeated in this battle.

In non-Ibāḍī sources, neither al-Ḥasan nor al-Ḥusayn participates in the battle. When Muʿāwiya asks al-Ḥasan to join him in fighting the Muḥakkima, al-Ḥasan caustically responds that were he to wage war against anyone in the Muslim community, that he would begin with Muʿāwiya himself.[68] In these accounts, Muʿāwiya also threatens to punish the residents of Kūfa if they do not aid in suppressing the Muḥakkima revolt. Since it is with the support of Kūfan soldiers that the Muḥakkima are defeated, Ibāḍī historians attributed this loss to al-Ḥasan. Even if he did not directly join Muʿāwiya's army, the residents of Kūfa had previously pledged allegiance to him and it was his peace settlement with Muʿāwiya and abdication that led these soldiers to join Muʿāwiya's army. By instructing his followers to peacefully submit to the new ruler and to refrain from aiding Khārijī revolts, al-Ḥasan essentially helped Muʿāwiya secure his ascendency in Iraq. For these reasons, it is likely that Ibāḍī historians described al-Ḥasan as aiding Muʿāwiya in the battle of Nukhayla, although it appears al-Ḥasan had already withdrawn from politics.

In abdicating his authority and commanding his followers to pledge oaths of fealty to Muʿāwiya, al-Ḥasan has been accused by Ibāḍīs of violating Q11:113, which states, "And do not incline towards those who transgress, lest the fire [of the Hereafter] touch you."[69]

Thus, it is for their support of their father's political career, execution of Ibn Muljam, surrender to Muʿāwiya, and direct or indirect aid to his army at the battle of Nukhayla that al-Ḥasan and al-Ḥusayn are condemned among Ibāḍīs. Like ʿUthmān and ʿAlī, they are considered to be individuals who betrayed the faithful and are deemed enemies of God.

CONCLUSION

From this survey of Ibāḍī literature, it is apparent that condemnation of ʿAlī was not at all tied to his identity or political aspirations as a Hāshimid. Ibāḍīs criticized ʿAlī's conduct as a ruler and, in particular, his handling of arbitration and the Muḥakkima without regard for his status as a close relative or Companion of the Prophet. It is clear that the Khārijī–Ibāḍī tradition considered all Muslims equal before God. Those who piously represented their strict sense of justice included notable Companions and

[68] Al-Balādhurī, *Ansāb al-ashrāf*, 5:163–164; Ibn al-Athīr, *Usd al-ghāba*, 3:409.
[69] Al-Izkawī, *Kashf al-ghumma*, 1:540.

kinsmen of the Prophet from the tribe of Quraysh. They also included non-Arabs and late converts who had not been among the Muhājirūn and the Anṣār.

To best understand the animus between ʿUthmānīs, Umayyads and pro-ʿAlids one must tie claims to religious and political authority to the powerful clans that made them. Abū Bakr, ʿAlī, and Muʿāwiya were not simply charismatic leaders. They were the heads of families and political factions that continued to make claims to authority long after their deaths. Members of these factions transmitted narratives about the past that sought to exalt their own leaders and deprecate their rivals. While the Ibāḍīs certainly did the same in their tales, there was less of a tendency to exalt characters by means of long hagiographical backstories. What would be the point of dwelling on the many years that a person served as the Prophet's Companion if it was possible for such a person to die as an enemy of God and the community? The Khārijī–Ibāḍī tradition was chillingly pragmatic. Individuals were lauded only for their deeds and their commitment to justice. Nothing else guaranteed a person's righteousness. Ibāḍīs greatly differed from their Sunnī and Shīʿī interlocutors who reasoned the necessity of believing that so-and-so *must have been* a legitimate caliph because of his many years of service to the Prophet and kinship with him. For Ibāḍīs anything was possible. Had it not been for the events that unfolded after arbitration, ʿAlī and the Prophet's two grandsons could have remained symbols of righteousness among Ibāḍīs. Moreover, despite their condemnation of ʿAlī's final years as a ruler, Ibāḍī scholars over the centuries still cited him as an authority in matters of law and as a transmitter of *ḥadīth*.[70] Since ʿAlī would have shared such knowledge and given such rulings during his many years as a righteous Muslim, it made perfect sense to Ibāḍīs to occasionally cite this material. This is yet another indication of their pragmatism.

[70] For example, see al-Wārjalānī, *Kitāb al-Dalīl*, 2:2, 8, 3:118. See also Hoffman, *Essentials*, 83, 119; Madelung and al-Salimi, eds., *Ibāḍī Texts*, 121.

5

The Sunnī: Ibn Taymiyya

The most infamous of all Umayyad military commanders was the ruthless al-Ḥajjāj b. Yūsuf (in office 75–95/694–714). This widely feared governor of Iraq executed thousands and successfully crushed numerous anti-Umayyad insurrections. Al-Ḥajjāj was so certain of the Umayyads' right to the caliphate that he even killed notable Companions of the Prophet and their disciples who rebelled against the state, including ʿAbd Allāh b. al-Zubayr, Muṣʿab b. al-Zubayr, Kumayl b. Ziyād, and Saʿīd b. Jubayr. No one was safe from al-Ḥajjāj if he or she was identified as an enemy of the Umayyads.

A little more than three centuries later, the fiercely independent-minded jurist Ibn Ḥazm studied and lived in Andalusia. Ibn Ḥazm rejected the four Sunnī schools of law for the text-based Ẓāhirī school. He condemned his Sunnī peers for excessively venerating the eponyms of their schools and for relying on legal opinions that he considered speculative and arbitrary. His critiques of Ashʿarī theologians, Mālikī jurists, and other scholars were so virulent that he was driven into exile on multiple occasions and his books were burned. A number of scholars felt that Ibn Ḥazm was too harsh in his rebukes of other Sunnīs. Al-Dhahabī complained that Ibn Ḥazm denigrated pious men with his words and his pen.[1]

After another three centuries, the ruthlessness of al-Ḥajjāj and the vehemence of Ibn Ḥazm were linked to a Damascene scholar who alienated countless contemporaries with his iconoclasm and his diatribes against them. A former friend and student finally dared to reproach him in a letter, writing, "The sword of al-Ḥajjāj and the tongue of Ibn Ḥazm

[1] Al-Dhahabī, *Siyar*, 18:186; Ibn Taghrībirdī, *al-Nujūm al-zāhira*, 5:75.

were siblings of one another, and you have now joined them as a brother."[2] The recipient of the letter was Taqī al-Dīn Aḥmad b. Taymiyya, whose views about ʿAlī we consider in this chapter.

This claim that Ibn Taymiyya bore a resemblance to al-Ḥajjāj and Ibn Ḥazm in his absolutist sensibilities and abrasiveness toward others is not altogether unfair. The scorn that the three heaped on their respective adversaries made them infamous, but Ibn Taymiyya also resembled his two predecessors in his peculiar and avid support for a particular dynasty. Al-Ḥajjāj was a Marwānid military commander and governor; Ibn Ḥazm served multiple Umayyad caliphs in Andalusia as a loyal vizier; and Ibn Taymiyya was a talented polemicist who defended the honor of the first Umayyad caliphs, Muʿāwiya and Yazīd, against their critics. Instead of justifying the actions of ʿAlī and al-Ḥusayn, Ibn Taymiyya criticized their political careers, particularly their decision to wage war against the Umayyads. A reading of Ibn Taymiyya's reflections on early Islamic history makes it clear that he also resembled al-Ḥajjāj and Ibn Ḥazm in holding the Umayyad caliphs in very high esteem.

When Ibn Taymiyya believed something to be false, he was unrelenting in arguing against it. Even if those who supported such false doctrines included pious men respected in the Muslim community, he would not hesitate to point out their error. His former student's letter is not the only evidence we have of his peers' exasperation with his tendency to denigrate and condemn respected figures of previous generations. In the pages that follow, we examine the criticisms of Ibn Taymiyya's interlocutors, particularly those who believed that he denigrated ʿAlī and the family of the Prophet in his writings against Shīʿism. In his efforts to refute Shīʿism, Ibn Taymiyya showed no compunction in discrediting nearly all pro-ʿAlid doctrines and texts that appeared in Sunnī literature. In his view, most texts exalting ʿAlī or justifying his actions as caliph served to bolster the claims of heretics, and thus could not be true. Ibn Taymiyya wrote with great urgency about Shīʿī heretics who intentionally sought to lead the entire community astray. In the tradition of his Ḥanbalī forebears, he considered it his duty to safeguard the community against such threats to orthodoxy.[3] By exposing the weakness of their arguments and their tendency to engage in mendacity, and by countering their claims with evidence from the Qurʾān and authentic *ḥadīth*, Ibn Taymiyya was certain

[2] Subkī, *al-Sayf*, 218.

[3] For the Ḥanbalī tradition of commanding justice and forbidding immorality, which included heresy, see Cook, *Commanding Right*, 114–122, 128–136.

that all rightly guided Muslims would find his critiques compelling. He relied on the same set of assumptions when engaging with Sunnī scholarship that he judged to have deviated from divine guidance. These preoccupations shed light on his motivations for composing a multivolume refutation of Shīʿism that laid out his understanding of early Islamic history and the caliphate, and they form the basis for our subsequent discussion of his views on ʿAlī and the family of the Prophet.

THE AUTHOR

Ibn Taymiyya was born in 661/1263 in the ancient Mesopotamian city of Ḥarrān, today located near Turkey's border with Syria. Under the impact of Mongol advances and instability in the region, his family moved to Damascus in 667/1269.[4] Ibn Taymiyya hailed from a respected Ḥanbalī family: his grandfather Majd al-Dīn b. Taymiyya (d. 653/1255) published many scholarly works, and his father, ʿAbd al-Ḥalīm b. Taymiyya (d. 682/1284), became the director of an important Ḥanbalī center of study in Damascus, Dār al-Ḥadīth al-Sukkariyya. It is at the Sukkariyya that Ibn Taymiyya trained as a jurist and a scholar of *ḥadīth*. As a testament to his scholarly talent as a young man, by the age of twenty he had received a license to issue legal opinions (*fatāwā*, sing. *fatwā*) from Sharaf al-Dīn Aḥmad al-Maqdisī (d. 694/1295).[5] Sharaf al-Dīn had been a sermonist for Friday congregational services at the Umayyad mosque, a prominent position in the city, and by the time of his death he was the leading Shāfiʿī jurist in Damascus.[6] Although many Shāfiʿīs identified as Ashʿarīs in theology and engaged in figurative readings of verses of the Qurʾān that appeared to describe God in anthropomorphic terms, Sharaf al-Dīn likely represented the more conservative wing of the Shāfiʿīs, who claimed to follow previous generations of Muslims, the *salaf*, by refraining from such speculation.[7] Ibn Taymiyya shared these *salafī* sensibilities, and their common convictions probably strengthened their admiration for one another. Given Sharaf al-Dīn's stature, the endorsement that Ibn

[4] Murad, "Ibn Taymiya on Trial," 1. See also *EI*^{2}, s.v. "Ibn Taymiyya" (H. Laoust).

[5] Ibn Kathīr, *al-Bidāya wa 'l-nihāya*, 13:403. See also Adem, "Intellectual Genealogy," 466. For reports that he began issuing legal opinions before the age of twenty, see Ibn ʿAbd al-Hādī, *Manāqib*, 8, 21–22; Murad, "Ibn Taymiya on Trial," 1. These reports depicting Ibn Taymiyya as a famous prodigy appear to have a hagiographical quality.

[6] Al-Ṣafadī, *al-Wāfī*, 6:145.

[7] For reports in which he is described as a *salafī* and Ḥanbalī in matters of theology, see al-Dhahabī, *Taʾrīkh*, 52:205–206.

Taymiyya received from him likely provided the young scholar with some prestige in Damascus, whose scholarly community consisted predominantly of Shāfiʿīs.

In 683/1284, Ibn Taymiyya succeeded his father as the director of the Sukkariyya, shortly after the latter's death. He taught *ḥadīth* at the institution and also began delivering lectures on qurʾānic exegesis each Friday at the Umayyad mosque. It was in the course of his Friday lectures at the mosque, some time in 690/1291, that he made comments about the nature of God that angered leading jurists in the city. They accused him of anthropomorphism, a heresy for which he was taken to court on multiple occasions.[8] To this day, his Ashʿarī and Shīʿī critics consider his views about God anthropomorphic and point to them as evidence of his misguidedness. However, the controversy over this issue was only one of a number of hostile doctrinal and legal debates that made Ibn Taymiyya infamous. His censure of standard Ashʿarī creeds, his condemnation of the mystic Ibn ʿArabī (d. 638/1240), his denunciation of the practice of tomb visitation, his rejection of the power of legal oaths pertaining to divorce, and his opinions about ʿAlī alienated him from many of his contemporaries. Nonetheless, he gained a following among *salafī*-minded scholars who considered him a brave reformer and reviver of the Islamic tradition.

Following the precedent of his Ḥanbalī predecessors, Ibn Taymiyya earned a reputation for publicly opposing what he deemed heretical innovations and sinful practices in the Muslim community. With a group of loyal supporters, he attacked wine shops in Damascus, breaking containers, pouring out their liquids, and censuring the shop owners.[9] On another occasion, he and his men destroyed a large rock popularly believed to contain a footprint of the Prophet.[10] His actions evoked discontent among the residents of Damascus, who had considered the rock sacred. But Ibn Taymiyya felt he had had no choice in the matter: the rock had become a site of idolatrous visitation, and he could not stand by and watch such heresy and superstition fester.

One of the most important aspects of Ibn Taymiyya's public life was his relationship to the Mamluk state and its military. Although he did not join the bureaucracy as a state official, he met and communicated with various rulers and military commanders on multiple occasions. Ibn Taymiyya appears to have played an important role in legitimizing the

[8] Jackson, "Ibn Taymiyyah on Trial"; Murad, "Ibn Taymiya on Trial," 1–10.
[9] Bori, "Ibn Taymiyya wa Jamāʿatuhu," 30.
[10] Al-Mizzī, *Tahdhīb al-Kamāl*, 1:19. See also Bori, "Ibn Taymiyya wa Jamāʿatuhu," 30; Murad, "Ibn Taymiya on Trial," 5.

state's military expeditions and fostering popular support for them. Another indication of his prominence is that at a time of great crisis, the Mongol siege of Damascus in 699/1299–1300, he was one of the delegates selected to leave the city to meet the Ilkhānid sultan, Ghāzān Khān (r. 694–703/1295–1304).[11]

Ibn Taymiyya took his role as a defender of orthodoxy and the Muslim community, as he conceived of it, seriously. On multiple occasions, he used his platform as a scholar and a preacher to exhort civilians to join the military and to encourage soldiers to participate in expeditions. In conjunction with key Mamluk military victories in neighboring Armenian territories in 697/1298, he gave a rousing speech celebrating the merits of holy war and God's reward for soldiers.[12] During the Mongol siege of Damascus, he met with Mongol authorities several times to request the restoration of order to the city, the release of prisoners, an end to looting, and a guarantee of amnesty for the city's residents. According to one source, at the same time he secretly encouraged Mamluk defenders of the citadel of Damascus to remain steadfast against Mongol attacks and offers of amnesty.[13] When the Mongol army finally left Damascus, Ibn Taymiyya led efforts to prepare residents for another invasion. He ensured that students and teachers in schools around the city were trained in archery. He would also visit the watchmen along the city's walls to raise their morale and recite qurʾānic verses about war to them.[14]

After the people of Kasrawān (located on Mount Lebanon) joined the Mongols and other rival communities in attacking the Mamluk army during its retreat to Palestine and Egypt, Ibn Taymiyya participated in the subsequent military expeditions to Mount Lebanon.[15] In legal opinions he issued to Mamluk rulers and soldiers who worried about the sinfulness of attacking the region's inhabitants, composed of Christians, Druze, Nuṣayrīs, and Twelver Shīʿīs, he argued that fighting these communities was a religious duty.[16] For him, the residents of Mount Lebanon not only represented an existential security threat but also endangered the integrity of the Islamic faith by influencing neighboring Sunnīs with their false doctrines and practices. Those residents who claimed to be Muslims

[11] Ibn Kathīr, *al-Bidāya wa 'l-nihāya*, 14:12–13. See also Aigle, "Mongol Invasions," 100, 103, 106; Amitai, "Mongol Occupation," 28–31.
[12] Ibn Kathīr, *al-Bidāya wa 'l-nihāya*, 13:416. See also Murad, "Ibn Taymiya on Trial," 3.
[13] Ibn Kathīr, *al-Bidāya wa 'l-nihāya*, 14:10. See also Amitai, "Mongol Occupation," 34 n. 56; Murad, "Ibn Taymiya on Trial," 4.
[14] Al-Mizzī, *Tahdhīb al-Kamāl*, 1:20.
[15] Mourad, "Ibn Taymiyya"; Murad, "Ibn Taymiya on Trial," 4.
[16] Friedman, "Ibn Taymiyya's Fatāwā"; Mourad, "Ibn Taymiyya."

did not truly qualify as believers either. Under the circumstances, Ibn Taymiyya argued that the Mamluks had a duty to destroy the towns of Mount Lebanon. The Mamluks attacked the region in 691/1292, 699/1300, and 704/1305, with Ibn Taymiyya participating in the latter two campaigns.[17] A letter that he wrote to the Mamluk sultan after the expedition of 699/1300 remains extant.[18] In it, he justifies waging war against the area's inhabitants because of their open enmity for early caliphs, Companions, and scholars venerated in Sunnism. Shīʿism, in its many manifestations, was the source of Ibn Taymiyya's anxieties.

SHĪʿISM AS BAD RELIGION

The Umayyads and ʿUthmānīs of the seventh and eighth centuries who cursed ʿAlī would have considered love for and allegiance to ʿAlī and his family a key objectionable aspect of Shīʿism. A later Sunnī polemicist such as Ibn Taymiyya, by contrast, embraced love for the Prophet's kinsmen as orthodoxy and subsumed it under love for the Prophet's Companions. For him, the issue was that the Shīʿīs engaged in an extreme type of partisanship. This extremism resulted in heresies such as the public condemnation of other Companions and the transmission of fabricated *ḥadīth* about ʿAlī. As an anti-Shīʿī polemicist, Ibn Taymiyya was careful to criticize only *radical* partisanship to ʿAlī, whereas anti-ʿAlids disapproved of partisanship to ʿAlī altogether. However, whether in the formative period or in later centuries, Shīʿīs were always accused of advocating "bad religion." This included any heresy that contradicted the views of those who considered themselves representatives of orthodoxy and the majority of Muslims. Those who identified with a sect other than Sunnism manifestly practiced heresy or bad religion.

The crystallization of Shīʿism entailed the establishment of *rafḍ*, the rejection of non-ʿAlids as imāms, as a core doctrine of both Imāmī and Zaydī Shīʿism by the tenth century. Thenceforth, only ʿAlī and the Prophet's descendants were considered legitimate imāms in these communities. Understandably, this position offended Sunnīs. *Rafḍ* delegitimized the first three caliphs as well as all Companions, jurists, and political figures who disagreed with or opposed ʿAlī and his family. At times, Sunnīs have identified *rafḍ* as the most subversive heresy to affect the

[17] Al-Jamil, "Ibn Taymiyya," 233–234; Harris, *Lebanon*, 69–71; Laoust, "Remarques"; Mourad, "Ibn Taymiyya," 374.

[18] Ibn Taymiyya, *Majmūʿ fatāwā*, 28:398–409. See also Mourad, "Ibn Taymiyya," 374.

Muslim community.[19] It undermined the basis for faith in the authority of the Prophet's Companions and the decisions they made after him in matters of law, religion, and politics.

Over the centuries, Shīʿī armies conquered major cities with predominantly Sunnī populations. The accession of rulers who professed *rafḍ* and supported the public practice of Shīʿism often aroused great fear and loathing among Sunnīs. For example, when the Būyids and the Fāṭimids took control of Baghdad and Cairo, respectively, the Shīʿī *adhān* could be heard from minarets, and Shīʿī holidays, such as the commemoration of al-Ḥusayn's death on ʿĀshūrāʾ and ʿĪd al-Ghadīr, were observed publicly.[20] The Fāṭimid caliph al-Ḥākim (r. 386–411/996–1021) endorsed the ritual cursing of Abū Bakr, ʿUmar, and other revered Companions in mosques and ordered that inscriptions of these curses be painted on mosque walls.[21] In such circumstances, many Sunnīs considered Būyid and Fāṭimid ascendancy to represent a rebellion against God and the triumph of bad religion. Heresy was to be challenged, defeated, and relegated to the margins – not brought to the center of public life or ever accepted as valid.

The Mongol Conversion to Shīʿism

Given his antipathy to Shīʿism, Ibn Taymiyya must have been extremely dismayed by the news that the Ilkhānid Öljeitü (r. 704–716/1304–1316) had converted to Twelver Shīʿism sometime in 708–9/1308–9. Furthermore, Öljeitü made Shīʿism the Ilkhānate state religion. In support of their ruler, military commanders and members of his court converted along with him.[22] It was a Sunnī custom to mention the names of the first four caliphs at the end of every Friday sermon, but Öljeitü ordered mosques to replace this custom with the Shīʿī practice of reciting the names of the twelve ʿAlid imāms. To demonstrate his devotion to them, he began minting coins with the names of ʿAlī, al-Ḥasan, al-Ḥusayn, and other imāms. He also generously funded hostels across his empire that exclusively served the needs of descendants of the Prophet.[23]

Öljeitü appears to have been someone whose curiosity about religion and search for God led him to have multiple conversion experiences.

19 Al-Bayhaqī, *al-Sunan al-kubrā*, 10:208–209; Ibn Ḥajar al-Haytamī, *al-Ṣawāʿiq al-muḥriqa*, 46; Ibn Taymiyya, *Majmūʿ fatāwā*, 13:209; Ibn Taymiyya, *Minhāj*, 1:59–63.

20 Daftary, *The Ismāʿīlīs*, 177–178; Momen, *Introduction*, 82; Stewart, "Popular Shiism," 53–55.

21 Stewart, "Popular Shiism," 54.

22 Pfeiffer, "Conversion Versions," 41.

23 Pfeiffer, "Confessional Ambiguity," 151; Pfeiffer, "Conversion Versions," 37.

He converted to Shīʿism after previously identifying as a Christian, a Buddhist, and a Shāfiʿī at various phases of his life.[24] Both before and after his conversion to Shīʿism, he reportedly held doctrinal and legal debates in his court in which Muslim scholars representing a variety of schools were invited to participate. Of the many views he heard, he found the arguments of the Twelver Shīʿī scholars of Iraq most convincing. He eventually summoned to his court the most prominent scholar among them, al-ʿAllāma Ḥasan b. Yūsuf al-Ḥillī.[25] Öljeitü must have been impressed with al-Ḥillī, whom he appointed as his personal advisor and teacher in the mobile camp that moved with the ruler.[26] It was al-Ḥillī whom Öljeitü officially appointed to write a number of works elaborating the theological and legal doctrines of Shīʿism.[27] The key aim of three of these texts was to establish the legitimacy of Shīʿī doctrines about ʿAlī and the imāmate against normative Sunnī assumptions.[28] Al-Ḥillī composed these works very soon after Öljeitü's conversion to Shīʿism, and they reflect the second moment in Twelver Shīʿī history, after the era of the Būyids, in which Shīʿī scholars benefited from state patronage and freely wrote works explicating their views. Shīʿīs were once again empowered to occupy the public space and to contribute to public discourses on religion.

One of Öljeitü's most trusted advisors was his chief justice (*qāḍī al-quḍāt*) in Iran and his minister of religious affairs, Niẓām al-Dīn ʿAbd al-Malik al-Marāghī (d. 716/1316). Despite Öljeitü's shifting sensibilities, he maintained al-Marāghī, a devout Shāfiʿī, in these positions until the end of his reign. Öljeitü reportedly hosted debates between al-Ḥillī and al-Marāghī in which each endeavored to demonstrate the superiority of his respective school.[29] Al-Ḥillī's works from this period may be viewed as a concerted effort on his part to convince not only the ruler but also his Sunnī interlocutors at the royal court of the validity of his religious claims.

In Jumāda I 709/October 1309, al-Ḥillī completed the shortest of the three abovementioned works, *Minhāj al-karāma fī maʿrifat al-imāma* (The Way of God's Favor is in Knowledge of the Imāmate), which is a synopsis of key proofs for Twelver doctrines about the imāmate.[30] Ibn Taymiyya sought to refute this work in one of the most comprehensive

24 Pfeiffer, "Conversion Versions," 37.
25 For a brief biography of al-Ḥillī, see Stewart, *Islamic Legal Orthodoxy*, 72–77.
26 Al-Jamil, "Cooperation and Contestation," 87; Stewart, *Islamic Legal Orthodoxy*, 76–77.
27 Al-Jamil, "Ibn Taymiyya," 231–232.
28 See al-Ḥillī, *Kashf al-yaqīn*; al-Ḥillī, *Minhāj al-karāma*; al-Ḥillī, *Nahj al-ḥaqq*, 164–375.
29 Al-Ḥillī, *Nahj al-ḥaqq*, 32; Pfeiffer, "Conversion Versions," 42.
30 For the author's note regarding the date of the book's composition, see al-Ḥillī, *Minhāj al-karāma*, 188.

Sunnī critiques of Shīʿism to be written in Islamic history, entitled *Minhāj al-sunna al-nabawiyya fī naqḍ kalām al-Shīʿa al-Qadariyya* (The Way of the Prophetic Sunna in Discrediting the Teachings of Qadarī Shīʿīs). The comments that Ibn Taymiyya makes in this work about ʿAlī and his family constitute the focus of the present chapter.

Many people did not welcome the return of Shīʿism to power. Widespread discontent with Öljeitü's order concerning Friday sermons eventually led him to reverse his policy so that Sunnīs could recite the names of the early caliphs as they pleased.[31] During the reigns of Öljeitü and his predecessors, Ibn Taymiyya believed that his own life and the lives of other Muslims in the Mamluk world were not secure from Mongol conquest and death. It had been only decades earlier, in 656/1258, that the Mongols had sacked Baghdad. The Mamluks had successfully withstood the Mongol attempt to take Syria two years later, but Ibn Taymiyya witnessed the Mongols return and occupy Damascus in 699/1300. He feared that another occupation might cause Damascus to suffer the same fate that had befallen Baghdad. Given the circumstances in which he wrote about the errors of Shīʿism and the merits of waging war against the Mongols and the inhabitants of Mount Lebanon, his writings inform us not only of his views on these subjects but also of his resolve in the face of a possible Mongol sack of Damascus. Ibn Taymiyya did not waver in his condemnation of the Mongols even after their rulers and military commanders began to convert to Islam. However, the Mamluks faced some difficulty in drumming up the necessary enthusiasm among their subjects for fighting the Ilkhānids. Ibn Taymiyya issued at least three legal opinions in which he sought to remove any doubts about the legality of fighting the newly converted Mongols.[32] Öljeitü's public conversion to Shīʿism only confirmed Ibn Taymiyya's belief that the Mongols remained misguided and enemies of Islam (as he understood it).

Ghāzān Khān, who became a Muslim shortly before taking power, was not the first Ilkhānid convert to Islam, but he was the first to launch a military campaign to Syria and provide religious justifications as a Muslim for doing so. During his reign, prominent Mamluk military commanders defected to the Mongols.[33] Ibn Taymiyya likely encountered Syrians who were apathetic regarding the conflict between the two powers. Which of the two would gain the upper hand did not appear to matter

[31] Pfeiffer, "Conversion Versions," 42–43.

[32] Ibn Taymiyya, *Majmūʿ fatāwā*, 28:501–553. See also Aigle, "Mongol Invasions."

[33] Amitai, "Mongol Occupation," 22–23.

significantly to some civilians. Ibn Taymiyya thus wrote with some urgency to differentiate the Mamluks from their enemies and to counteract his audience's impulse to remain aloof.

Just before Ghāzān Khān's third attempt to conquer Syria in 702/1303, Ibn Taymiyya issued a legal opinion in which he argued that the Ilkhānid and his followers were not truly Muslim because they upheld Mongol customs and observed the laws associated with Ghengiz Khan, known as the *Yāsā*.[34] Ibn Taymiyya accused the Mongols of insincere conversion and of flouting the duties of daily worship, fasting, and pilgrimage. For Ibn Taymiyya, Ghāzān Khān's continued attempts to conquer the region and demands that the Mamluks surrender to him served as further evidence that he remained a threat to the Muslim community.

Previously, when a non-Muslim force had sought domination over Mamluk lands, it had been easy to argue that fighting them qualified as *jihād*. But now that the Ilkhānids identified as Muslims, some residents of Damascus feared that God found armed conflict with them reprehensible. When Öljeitü succeeded Ghāzān Khān and then converted to Shīʿism, his conversion helped Ibn Taymiyya persuade the public that fighting the Mongols remained a duty. His unequivocal condemnation of Shīʿism as dangerous and foreign to the "real" Islam that the Prophet had preached was a consistent theme in his writings. To him, combating Shīʿī communities in the Levant and Öljeitü's Mongol forces was a holy endeavor in service of religion – not a political contest. It seems that Ibn Taymiyya saw the fruits of his labor: when Öljeitü attempted to take Syria in 712/1312, the Mamluks successfully pushed back his forces at the town of al-Raḥba. Öljeitü died in 716/1316, and no Ilkhānid ever attempted conquest of Syria again.

THE *MINHĀJ AL-SUNNA*

A careful examination of Ibn Taymiyya's *Minhāj al-sunna* reveals his alarm and dismay at the "rise in Shīʿī production of scholarly works in legal theory, theology, and philosophy" and what he perceived as Shīʿīs' increasing influence in Sunnī circles.[35] A key theme in Ibn Taymiyya's works is his desire to diagnose the phenomenon of error.[36] His writings reveal his

[34] Ibn Taymiyya, *Majmūʿ fatāwā*, 28:530. See also Aigle, "Mongol Invasions," 95–96; al-Jamil, "Cooperation and Contestation," 119.
[35] Al-Jamil, "Cooperation and Contestation," 150.
[36] Michel, ed., *A Muslim Theologian's Response*, 2, 4, 14.

conviction that his opponents are always falling victim to error, and that it is up to him to correct the errors in their thought. In his view, people make mistakes when they deviate from the teachings of the Qurʾān and the Prophet Muḥammad, whether they are Companions or theologians of later generations. But the errors of the pious constitute only one perilous avenue to misguidance: heretics who intend to mislead other Muslims are another danger. For Ibn Taymiyya, Shīʿism at its core represented this second threat. He believed that the legendary Ibn Sabaʾ who conspired to kill ʿUthmān, launched the first civil war, and believed in *tafḍīl ʿAlī* did all of these things purposely to mislead the faithful and cause havoc within the community. In other words, he acted in bad faith. In Sunnī historiography, Ibn Sabaʾ was depicted as an outsider and utilized as a scapegoat to explain the conflicts that occurred after the Prophet's death. Ibn Sabaʾ also served to illustrate and discredit the phenomenon of Shīʿism. After all, there could be no reason to doubt the illegitimacy of Shīʿism if its founder was a Jewish man who pretended to be Muslim in order to mislead and harm the community of Muḥammad.[37] Ibn Taymiyya subscribed to this view and made his prejudice against Shīʿism plain. For him, all of Shīʿism was a lie because Shīʿīs were liars.[38] This mendacity went back to the sect's founder, Ibn Sabaʾ.

The increased visibility of Shīʿism thus forced Sunnīs such as Ibn Taymiyya to acknowledge its existence and diagnose its errors in greater depth. Ibn Taymiyya relied on origin myths about Shīʿism to discredit the tradition. This was a common method among heresiographers, who rarely consulted the literature produced by members of other sects when discussing their doctrines. The hazards of this method are quite obvious; frequently, information circulated about various sects was false, exaggerated, and hostile.[39] Following the tradition of al-Jāḥiẓ and Ibn Ḥazm, Ibn Taymiyya did not shy away from repudiating pro-ʿAlid *ḥadīth* in Sunnī literature in his effort to refute Shīʿism. In reading al-Ḥillī's *Minhāj al-karāma*, Ibn Taymiyya realized that his Shīʿī rival was relying on this pro-ʿAlid tradition within Sunnism to substantiate Shīʿism. Rather than defend the former and limit his attacks to the latter, Ibn Taymiyya followed other anti-Shīʿī polemicists in undermining both.

[37] Anthony, *The Caliph and the Heretic*, 58–103, 111–116, 122, 126–130; Barzegar, "Remembering Community," 98–125.

[38] Ibn Taymiyya, *Majmūʿ fatāwā*, 13:209; Ibn Taymiyya, *Minhāj*, 1:59–63.

[39] For example, see Daftary, *The Ismāʿīlīs*, xvi, 7–19.

The Pro-ʿAlid Sunnī Response

In his *Minhāj al-sunna*, Ibn Taymiyya rejects the authenticity of nearly every report about ʿAlī's merits and expresses disapproval of ʿAlī's actions as caliph. He criticizes ʿAlī for allegedly angering the Prophet and Fāṭima by seeking a second wife, refusing to pray with the Prophet, giving many erroneous legal opinions, supporting Fāṭima's claims against Abū Bakr, and fighting at Ṣiffīn. Although he evinces skepticism regarding the historicity of the dispute, Ibn Taymiyya criticizes Fāṭima for seeking ownership of the estate of Fadak and becoming upset with Abū Bakr's judgment against her. He also disapproves of al-Ḥusayn's rebellion against Yazīd.[40] Ibn Ḥajar al-Haytamī later called Ibn Taymiyya heretical for his censure (*iʿtaraḍa*) of the conduct of caliphs such as ʿUmar and ʿAlī as well as various Sufi authorities of later generations.[41] He wrote that Ibn Taymiyya "mentioned ʿAlī b. Abī Ṭālib in a gathering and said, 'Indeed ʿAlī erred in more than three hundred places.'"[42]

In his biographical entry on Ibn Taymiyya, Ibn Ḥajar al-ʿAsqalānī quotes Najm al-Dīn al-Ṭūfī (d. 716/1316), who reported that some of Ibn Taymiyya's contemporaries considered him a hypocrite (*munāfiq*) because they perceived anti-ʿAlid sentiment in his views. According to al-Ṭūfī, Ibn Taymiyya said: "'ʿAlī was wrong on seventeen matters in which he violated a clear proof-text from scripture.[43] For example, ʿAlī held the legal opinion that a widow should wait the longer of the two terms [before contracting another marriage]."[44] Al-Ṭūfī further explained:

> Some [of Ibn Taymiyya's detractors] attributed hypocrisy (*nifāq*) to him because of the aforementioned statement about ʿAlī and his arguments that "ʿAlī was forsaken (*makhdhūl*) wherever he turned,"[45] "He attempted to become caliph multiple times but never truly obtained [the position],"[46] and "He fought for the sake of

[40] Ibn Taymiyya, *Minhāj*, 4:243, 247, 248, 256, 257, 264, 389, 392, 530, 559. For more on these topics, see the relevant sections later in this chapter.

[41] For Ibn Taymiyya's criticism of the legal opinions of ʿUmar and ʿAlī, see Ibn Taymiyya, *Minhāj*, 7:502.

[42] Ibn Ḥajar al-Haytamī, *Kitāb al-fatāwā al-ḥadīthiyya*, 84–85.

[43] This indirect source states that Ibn Taymiyya claimed ʿAlī violated verses of the Qurʾān. Ibn Taymiyya, in fact, claimed that ʿAlī violated *nuṣūṣ* (proof-texts) which may equally refer to *ḥadīth*: see Ibn Taymiyya, *Minhāj*, 7:505–507.

[44] In his *Minhāj*, Ibn Taymiyya does not count the number of edicts in which ʿAlī erred; rather, he says, "examples of this are abundant": see ibid., 4:242–243.

[45] Ibid., 7:20–21, 57–59.

[46] Ibn Taymiyya notes the existence of *ḥadīth* transmitters in the Levant and Baṣra as well as Sunnīs of Andalusia who held that ʿAlī's caliphate was never established: see ibid., 1:537, 4:388–389, 401–404, 6:191. Ibn Taymiyya generally wished to depict ʿAlī as someone

worldly power (*riyāsa*) rather than religion (*diyāna*)."[47] [Ibn Taymiyya claimed that ʿAlī] "loved worldly power and ʿUthmān loved wealth"[48] and that "Abū Bakr converted as an adult with full mental faculties and ʿAlī converted as a child, but the conversion of a child is not valid according to some scholars."[49] He also maligned (*shannaʿa*) [ʿAlī] in his comments regarding the report about Abū Jahl's daughter ... and the lesson he derived from it.[50] So they [Ibn Taymiyya's detractors] were certain of his hypocrisy because of the Prophet's statement [to ʿAlī], "None but a hypocrite shall bear malice against you."[51]

Since ʿAlī never defeated Muʿāwiya, Ibn Taymiyya considers ʿAlī to have been forsaken (*makhdhūl*) by God and the most respected members of the Muslim community. Since Muʿāwiya went on to establish a dynasty with an army that led successful conquests against non-Muslims, it is clear to Ibn Taymiyya that God gave victory to those who forsook ʿAlī and waged war against him.[52] Ibn Taymiyya argues this point to reject the authenticity of a portion of the *ḥadīth al-ghadīr*, discussed further in this chapter, in which the Prophet prays that God forsake those who forsake ʿAlī and aid those who come to ʿAlī's aid.[53] For Ibn Taymiyya, however, the political career of Muʿāwiya confirms that he and his army were ultimately victorious and aided (*manṣūrūn*) by God. According to Ibn Taymiyya, one cannot say the same about the political career of ʿAlī.

Ibn Ḥajar referenced a *ḥadīth* that appears in the canonical collections wherein the Prophet tells ʿAlī, "None but a believer shall love you and none but a hypocrite shall bear malice against you."[54] Some of Ibn Taymiyya's pro-ʿAlid peers viewed him as the type of person whose faith was negated by this dictum of the Prophet. Ibn Ḥajar al-ʿAsqalānī also read the *Minhāj al-sunna* for himself and was unhappy with its contents. Ibn Ḥajar was a respected *ḥadīth* scholar who was more nonpartisan than pro-ʿAlid in his understanding of history. He was affronted that Ibn Taymiyya

who supported the succession of his predecessors. In a few cases, however, he alludes to evidence that suggested the contrary and agreed with early ʿUthmānī and Shīʿī contentions that ʿAlī had been dissatisfied with the succession of the first three caliphs: see ibid., 4:388, 6:156, 162, 176, 8:270, 8:330–331, 333–335.

47 Ibid., 6:191, 8:329–330. Elsewhere, Ibn Taymiyya presented this opinion as a hypothetical argument of *nawāṣib*: see ibid., 4:499–500.

48 Ibn Taymiyya implicitly argued this by praising ʿAlī as more austere with wealth and ʿUthmān with worldly power: see ibid., 8:229, 231.

49 Ibid., 7:155, 8:424. See Chapter 3 for similar arguments from al-Jāḥiẓ.

50 Ibid., 4:255.

51 Ibn Ḥajar al-ʿAsqalānī, *al-Durar al-kāmina*, 1:179, 181–182.

52 Ibn Taymiyya, *Minhāj*, 4:504, 7:21.

53 Ibid., 7:20–21, 55–59.

54 Aḥmad b. Ḥanbal, *al-Musnad*, 1:95, 128; Ibn Māja, *Sunan*, 1:42; Muslim, *Ṣaḥīḥ,* 1:61; al-Nasāʾī, *Sunan al-Nasāʾī*, 8:116; al-Tirmidhī, *Sunan*, 5:306.

could readily reject the authenticity of so many acceptable reports about ʿAlī and even disparage him in some sections of his work.[55]

Muḥammad ʿAbd al-Ḥalīm b. Muḥammad Amīn al-Laknawī (d. 1285/1868) agreed with Ibn Ḥajar's assessment.[56] Al-Laknawī also found Ibn Taymiyya's allusions to ʿAlī's love of worldly power and the insignificance of his conversion as a child to be offensive. Al-Laknawī concluded, "He spoke words about the Household of the Prophet that a faithful person would never say."[57]

Pro-ʿAlid Sunnīs of the twentieth century, such as Abū Bakr b. Shihāb al-Dīn al-ʿAlawī al-Ḥadramī (d. 1341/1922), Muḥammad b. ʿAqīl al-ʿAlawī (d. 1350/1931), Aḥmad al-Ghumārī, his brother ʿAbd Allāh al-Ghumārī (d. 1413/1993), ʿAlawī b. Ṭāhir al-Ḥaddād (d. 1382/1962), ʿAbd Allāh al-Hararī (d. 1429/2008), Ḥasan b. ʿAlī al-Saqqāf (b. 1380/1961), and Ḥasan b. Farḥān al-Mālikī (b. 1390/1970), have all likewise criticized Ibn Taymiyya for his anti-ʿAlidism.[58] They contend that his views insult the *ahl al-bayt* and betray insufficient reverence for the Prophet's family.

In Chapter 1, I identified a spectrum of attitudes toward ʿAlī, dividing Muslims into six groups according to their views about him. Group 1 consisted of anti-ʿAlids who openly condemned ʿAlī, whereas members of Group 2 merely opposed any special veneration of him. It is quite possible that some members of Group 2 also despised ʿAlī in private, but some explicitly claimed that they did not. Ibn Taymiyya appears to fall into Group 2, notwithstanding his detractors' arguments that he was in fact an anti-ʿAlid of the type represented by Group 1. In spite of his objections to the political careers of ʿAlī and al-Ḥusayn, Ibn Taymiyya himself claimed to belong to Group 3, which consisted of Sunnīs who revered ʿAlī as the most meritorious Muslim after the first three caliphs.[59] Thus, a distinct tension exists between Ibn Taymiyya's own stated identity in

[55] Ibn Ḥajar al-ʿAsqalānī, *Lisān al-Mīzān*, 1:319–320.

[56] See al-Laknawī, *Ḥall al-maʿāqid fī sharḥ al-ʿAqāʾid*, 28 (read *wa qad radda al-aḥādīth al-ṣiḥāḥ* for *wa qad warada al-aḥādīth al-ṣiḥāḥ*).

[57] Ibid.

[58] ʿAbd Allāh al-Hararī, *Ḍalālāt Aḥmad ibn Taymiyya*, 353–374 (for al-Ḥaddād's statements, see 353); Abū Bakr ibn Shihāb, *Wujūb al-ḥamiyya*, 10; Muḥammad b. ʿAqīl al-ʿAlawī, *Taqwiyat al-īmān*, 71; al-ʿAwwād, *al-Naṣb*, 512; al-Ghumārī, *al-Radd ʿalā al-Albānī*, 6–9; al-Ghumārī, *ʿAlī ibn Abī Ṭālib Imām al-ʿārifīn*, 51–56; al-Ghumārī, *Fatḥ al-Malik al-ʿAlī*, 108–109; al-Mālikī, *al-Ṣuḥba wa ʾl-ṣaḥaba*, 238–239; al-Mālikī, *Sulaymān al-ʿAlwān fī Muʿāwiya*, 18 n. 5; al-Saqqāf, *al-Salafiyya al-wahhābiyya*, 72–73; al-Saqqāf, *Majmūʿ rasāʾil al-Saqqāf*, 1:96 n. 51 (for ʿAbd Allāh al-Ghumārī's comments); al-Saqqāf, *Sharḥ al-ʿAqīda al-Ṭaḥāwiyya*, 651 n. 383.

[59] He states that no one was more meritorious than ʿAlī except for the three caliphs who preceded him: see Ibn Taymiyya, *Minhāj*, 4:396.

terms of his position on ʿAlī and communal perceptions of the boundaries of this identity. For Ibn Taymiyya, accepting ʿAlī as Islam's fourth caliph did not entail special reverence for him. Ibn Taymiyya was not the only Sunnī to hold this view. Other anti-Shīʿī polemicists also argued that ʿAlī possessed no merits that would have made him unique while accepting him as a legitimate caliph.[60]

Ibn Ḥajar al-ʿAsqalānī's comment that Ibn Taymiyya rejected a multitude of sound *ḥadīth* favorable to ʿAlī further reflects the divergences that existed among Sunnīs. The acceptance or rejection of *ḥadīth* about ʿAlī's merits was more an indication of one's views about ʿAlī than it was of one's methodology in the authentication of *ḥadīth*. Anti-Shīʿī polemicists such as Ibn Taymiyya would have been offended by the accusation that they were anti-ʿAlid, since they were sure that ʿAlī himself would also have denied the claims made in pro-ʿAlid literature that exalts him.

As noted in Chapter 1, the characterization of a statement as anti-ʿAlid or irreverent rather than simply as anti-Shīʿī was contentious. Sunnīs held a range of pro-ʿAlid beliefs, with the proponents of each position criticizing the others. Although pro-ʿAlids considered Ibn Taymiyya anti-ʿAlid, Sunnīs influenced by him viewed him as an exemplary scholar. From the pro-ʿAlid perspective, one could endorse pro-ʿAlid doctrines and the authenticity of hundreds of *ḥadīth* praising ʿAlī and oppose Shīʿism at the same time. For example, Ibn Taymiyya's contemporary ʿAlāʾ al-Dawla al-Simnānī (d. 736/1336) condemned Muʿāwiya as a corrupt enemy of ʿAlī and was a proponent of *tafḍīl ʿAlī*. He also accepted historical reports about ʿAlī's objections to the accession of his predecessors to the caliphate. Nonetheless, al-Simnānī was a Sunnī who criticized Twelver Shīʿīs for their custom of cursing revered Companions and combining the daily prayers.[61] Al-Simnānī rejected ʿUthmānī attempts to depict ʿAlī as faithfully supporting the accession of his predecessors. By contrast, Ibn Taymiyya drew on the views of ʿUthmānīs and Umayyads to inform his views on ʿAlī and early Islamic history.

The difficulty in categorizing the thought of Ibn Taymiyya and other anti-Shīʿī polemicists who shared his sensibilities lies in their appeal to arguments characteristic of Groups 1 and 2. Although Sunnī polemicists were proponents of the four-caliph theory, their reliance on such arguments reflected the ever-present option among Sunnīs to utilize the legacy of outright anti-ʿAlids and of those who opposed the veneration of ʿAlī in

[60] See Chapter 1 nn. 24–32. [61] Al-Simnānī, *Manāẓir al-maḥāḍir*, 14–19.

particular. As a result, this legacy remains simultaneously suppressed and partially assimilated in Sunnism.

IBN TAYMIYYA'S OWN WORDS

In the sections that follow I discuss the arguments of Ibn Taymiyya that some characterized as irreverent toward ʿAlī and his family and consider the polemical issues at stake. Some Sunnī authors judged Ibn Taymiyya's arguments to be excellent responses to Shīʿi doctrine, whereas others were ambivalent. Sunnīs variously expressed contradictory opinions on these historiographical and doctrinal topics or showed indifference to them because Sunnism encompassed a myriad of divergent views – not unlike the diversity of opinions that existed in matters of law.

Discrediting Pro-ʿAlid Exegesis

Many years before Ibn Taymiyya began writing his polemic against al-Ḥillī, he had been a respected lecturer who taught exegesis of the Qurʾān every Friday at the Umayyad mosque. This experience gave him ample opportunity to evaluate the work of exegetes and the different methods of interpretation found in the Sunnī tradition. Ultimately, his exposure to this literature led him to reject most pro-ʿAlid exegetical reports as false.[62] He was dismayed to find Shīʿīs carefully searching the Sunnī exegetical tradition for cases in which exegetes identified a particular verse as having been revealed about ʿAlī. Frequently, Sunnī exegetes would mention the views of multiple authorities on each verse, with each scholar propounding a different opinion. Among these interpretations were some that identified a verse as praising ʿAlī. Shīʿīs would mine Sunnī exegetical works for such references and then cite their authors as authorities confirming the pro-ʿAlid interpretation of the verses in question. The first problem in such polemical citations is that the exegete may have simply related this interpretation as one of many, without necessarily believing it to be true or endorsing it as his own opinion. Second, reading only the Shīʿī polemical literature without consulting the Sunnī exegetical works directly resulted in the misleading impression that no other interpretations about the verse existed; such a reader might have concluded wrongly that the Sunnī

62 ʿAbd-al-Ḥamīd, *Ibn Taymiyya*, 73–74; Saleh, *Formation*, 218–221.

exegetes concurred with the Shīʿīs on this particular interpretation. Ibn Taymiyya desired to put a stop to such misleading tactics by discrediting such reports altogether. He was sure that the reports exalting ʿAlī could not be authentic for two reasons: they mostly appeared in noncanonical works, and they supported Shīʿism, which was a heresy.

With regard to his first justification, it was clear to Ibn Taymiyya that only the reports that leading *ḥadīth* scholars documented in canonical compilations counted as authentically transmitted. For him, the collections of al-Bukhārī and Muslim, known as the "two authentic collections" (*Ṣaḥīḥayn*), were the gold standard; by contrast, *ḥadīth* that appeared only in the other four *sunan* collections or in the *Musnad* of Aḥmad could potentially be criticized and rejected. But since the authors of these other works incorporated the contents of authentic *ḥadīth* into their views of the Qurʾān, orthodoxy, and history, they were nonetheless respected as authorities. Ibn Taymiyya believed that most exegetes, historians, and authors of works about the merits of ʿAlī were circulating reports about ʿAlī that did not agree with the tenor or content of the *Ṣaḥīḥayn* or with other authentically transmitted *ḥadīth*. Since he was certain that the canonical body of literature represented the truth, the contradictory reports about ʿAlī that were transmitted by only a few transmitters who were either pro-Alid or, worse, heretical Shīʿīs could not also be true. The pro-ʿAlid reports could not be considered authentic when the authors of the *Ṣaḥīḥayn* and their teachers had refrained from narrating most of them. The polemical value that such reports possessed for Shīʿīs such as al-Ḥillī who were engaged in polemics only strengthened Ibn Taymiyya's resolve to reject them as false. For him, these reports only encouraged Muslims to believe in heresy.

From the pro-ʿAlid perspective, Ibn Taymiyya appeared unfairly prejudicial in his blanket rejection of reports exalting ʿAlī. He insisted on dismissing such reports as fabricated even in cases in which other Sunnīs accepted a particular report's authenticity and considered the transmitters of the report to have been trustworthy. For example, Ibn Taymiyya rejected reports claiming that Q5:55 was revealed about ʿAlī after he donated a ring while bowing in prayer. Ibn Taymiyya states, "The consensus among people of knowledge is that this story is a fabrication."[63] However, Ibn Taymiyya's statement is misleading, since several individuals whom he otherwise deemed respectable scholars of *ḥadīth* narrated exegetical

[63] Ibn Taymiyya, *Minhāj*, 2:30. See also ʿAbd al-Ḥamīd, *Ibn Taymiyya*, 74.

reports about the verse's connection to ʿAlī.[64] These individuals included al-Ṭabarī, whom Ibn Taymiyya praised as the best source for learning about the views of the early community (*salaf*) on matters of exegesis,[65] as well as ʿAbd al-Razzāq al-Ṣanʿānī (d. 211/827), Ibn Mardawayh (d. 410/1019), al-Khaṭīb al-Baghdādī (d. 463/1071), and others. Ibn Taymiyya's claim that a scholarly consensus supported his dismissal of the reports is also belied by the analysis of al-Ālūsī, who states that most transmitters of reports (*akhbār*) are of the opinion that the verse was revealed as a consequence of ʿAlī's actions.[66] Nonetheless, Ibn Taymiyya reiterates in his *Minhāj al-sunna*: "All scholars of *ḥadīth* concur that this verse was not revealed about ʿAlī in particular and that ʿAlī never donated a ring of his in prayer. Scholars of *ḥadīth* have agreed as a matter of consensus that the stories narrated about such an event are fabricated and false."[67]

Ibn Taymiyya also claims that it is a matter of consensus among scholars of *ḥadīth* that al-Thaʿlabī (d. 427/1035), in particular, tended to include fabricated reports in his exegesis.[68] According to Ibn Taymiyya, al-Thaʿlabī and his student al-Wāḥidī (d. 468/1075) were undiscerning authors who narrated weak reports alongside authentic ones. To prove his point, Ibn Taymiyya contrasts their exegetical works with those of al-Baghawī (d. 516/1122), arguing that the latter was much more judicious in his evaluation of *ḥadīth*. He describes al-Baghawī's exegesis as an abridgment of al-Thaʿlabī's without all of the fabricated material that al-Thaʿlabī had regrettably transmitted. Yet Ibn Taymiyya's argument is contradicted by the fact that al-Baghawī also transmitted pro-ʿAlid reports in his exegesis, including some tying Q5:55 to ʿAlī.[69] So even the person whom Ibn Taymiyya lauds for refraining from transmitting "fabricated" reports about Q5:55 in fact narrates such reports.

Against many other exegetes, Ibn Taymiyya denies that Q76 was revealed after ʿAlī and his family had patiently fasted for three days without food.[70]

[64] ʿAbd al-Razzāq al-Ṣanʿānī, *Tafsīr al-Qurʾān*, 4:1162; al-Balādhurī, *Ansāb al-ashrāf*, 2:150; Ibn ʿAsākir, *Taʾrīkh*, 42:357; Ibn Mardawayh, *Manāqib ʿAlī*, 233–238; al-Khaṭīb al-Baghdādī, *al-Muttafiq wa ʾl-muftariq*, 1:258–259; al-Samʿānī, *Tafsīr al-Qurʾān*, 2:47–48; al-Ṭabarānī, *al-Muʿjam al-awsaṭ*, 6:218; al-Ṭabarī, *Tafsīr*, 6:389–390; al-Thaʿlabī, *Tafsīr*, 4:80–81; al-Wāḥidī, *Asbāb al-nuzūl*, 133–134.

[65] Ibn Taymiyya, *Majmūʿ fatāwā*, 13:385. [66] Al-Ālūsī, *Rūḥ al-maʿānī*, 6:167.

[67] Ibn Taymiyya, *Minhāj*, 7:11.

[68] Ibid., 7:12. See also Saleh, "Radical Hermeneutics," 138–139.

[69] Al-Baghawī, *Tafsīr*, 2:47.

[70] Ibn Taymiyya, *Minhāj*, 2:117; cf. ibid., 4:428; al-Ḥākim al-Ḥaskānī, *Shawāhid al-tanzīl*, 2:394–408; Ibn al-Athīr, *Usd al-ghāba*, 5:530–531; Thaʿlabī, *Tafsīr*, 10:98–101; al-Wāḥ idī, *Asbāb al-nuzūl*, 296.

Instead, he argues that the chapter was revealed in Mecca, so reports that purport to connect it to the deeds of ʿAlī, Fāṭima, and their two sons are clearly anachronistic, since this household formed only in Medina. A modern interlocutor deems Ibn Taymiyya's reasoning to be flawed: the chapter's verses reference prisoners of war, whom Muslims began to capture only in the Medinese period.[71]

Exegetes offer differing interpretations of a portion of Q13:7 that reads, "You are only a warner, and for every people is a guide." When the verse was revealed, the Prophet allegedly addressed ʿAlī and identified him as a guide for the Muslims.[72] The implication of the reports describing this event is that God selected ʿAlī to serve the community as its *designated guide*, and the Muslims were thus obliged to follow ʿAlī after the Prophet's death. Pro-ʿAlid Sufis claimed precisely this by arguing that ʿAlī directly inherited the Prophet's spiritual authority.[73] According to pro-ʿAlids, Q69:12 was also revealed about ʿAlī.[74] The verse reads, "so that We might make all this a [lasting] reminder to you all, and that every attentive ear should bear its remembrance." Pro-ʿAlid exegetical *ḥadīth* on this verse depicted ʿAlī as a student who, uniquely and miraculously, never forgot anything that the Prophet uttered. However, Ibn Taymiyya flatly denies the authenticity of pro-ʿAlid reports about Q13:7 and Q69:12.[75]

In a couple of cases, Ibn Taymiyya is unable to reject the authenticity of a pro-ʿAlid exegetical report either because the report appears in canonical collections or the events it describes are so widely reported that it would make little sense to argue that the report is fabricated. One such case is the revelation of the final phrase of Q33:33, "God desires to keep all abominations from you, O *ahl al-bayt*! And purify you with a thorough purification." Both Sunnī and Shīʿī exegetes reported that when this verse was revealed, the Prophet gathered ʿAlī, Fāṭima, and their two sons under his cloak and identified them as the addressees of the verse.[76] The exegetes also explained that the word "abominations" (*rijs*)

71 ʿAbd al-Ḥamīd, *Ibn Taymiyya*, 308.

72 Al-Ḥākim al-Naysābūrī, *al-Mustadrak*, 3:130; Ibn Abī Ḥātim al-Rāzī, *Tafsīr*, 7:2225; Ibn ʿAsākir, *Taʾrīkh*, 42:359–360; al-Ṭabarānī, *al-Muʿjam al-awsaṭ*, 2:94; al-Ṭabarī, *Tafsīr*, 13:142; al-Thaʿlabī, *Tafsīr*, 5:272.

73 See Chapter 3 n. 56.

74 Ibn Abī Ḥātim al-Rāzī, *Tafsīr*, 10:3369–370; Ibn ʿAsākir, *Taʾrīkh*, 38:349, 42:361; al-Ṭabarī, *Tafsīr*, 29:69.

75 Ibn Taymiyya, *Minhāj*, 7:139–143, 171.

76 Aḥmad b. Ḥanbal, *al-Musnad*, 1:331, 3:285, 4:107, 6:292, 298; al-Ḥākim al-Ḥaskānī, *Shawāhid al-tanzīl*, 2:18–139; al-Ḥākim al-Naysābūrī, *al-Mustadrak*, 2:416, 3:146–148; al-Haythamī, *Majmaʿ al-zawāʾid*, 9:167–169; Ibn Abī Shayba, *al-Muṣannaf*, 7:501; Muslim,

referred to evil, sin, doubt, and unbelief.[77] As a consequence, pro-ʿAlid reports about this verse bolstered the popular belief that ʿAlī and the Prophet's kin possessed a unique spiritual purity and grace. Ibn Taymiyya concedes the authenticity of the reports, but he argues that no guarantee exists that those whom God desired to purify were in fact purified or remained pure afterward.[78] The verse speaks only of God's desire to purify them and their responsibility to conduct themselves as people of purity; their actual state could resemble that of the rest of humanity, whom God has commanded to follow the path of guidance and do good deeds. God's desire for an outcome does not necessarily entail its occurrence. In both cases, the outcome is wholly dependent on humans' fulfilling certain duties to God.

Ibn Taymiyya is similarly compelled to explain away the significance of pro-ʿAlid reports about Q3:61. After the Prophet had engaged in a theological debate with a delegation of Christians visiting him in Medina, the verse was revealed, instructing the Prophet to challenge the Christians to a mutual imprecation (*mubāhila*), in which each side would call on God to strike down any of its members speaking lies. When the verse commanded the gathering of "our sons and your sons, our women and your women, our selves and your selves" to offer this special prayer, the Prophet gathered the same members of his family who had been previously addressed in Q33:33.[79] Pro-ʿAlids considered the occasion a testament to the grandeur of the Prophet's *ahl al-bayt*: Fāṭima was selected out of all of the women in the Prophet's household and community to represent them, and the participation of ʿAlī, al-Ḥasan, and al-Ḥusayn likewise reflected their elevated status. But Ibn Taymiyya rejects such pro-ʿAlid interpretations of their participation.[80] He argues instead

Ṣaḥīḥ, 7:130; al-Nasāʾī, *al-Sunan al-kubrā*, 5:108; al-Ṭabarānī, *al-Muʿjam al-kabīr*, 3:52–57, 22:66–67; al-Ṭabarī, *Tafsīr*, 22:9–13; al-Tirmidhī, *Sunan*, 5:30–31; al-Zarandī, *Naẓm durar al-simṭayn*, 238–239. See also al-Fīrūzābādī, *Faḍāʾil al-khamsa*, 1:221–243. For Shīʿī sources, see Ibn Bābawayh, *al-Amālī*, 559; Ibn Ṭāwūs, *al-Ṭarāʾif*, 122–130; al-Kulaynī, *al-Kāfī*, 1:287; al-Qāḍī al-Nuʿmān, *Sharḥ al-akhbār*, 1:203–204, 2:337–339, 515.

77 Al-ʿAynī, *ʿUmdat al-qārī*, 2:303–304; Ibn al-ʿArabī, *Aḥkām al-Qurʾān*, 3:571; Ibn Ḥajar al-ʿAsqalānī, *Hady al-sārī*, 118; al-Nawawī, *al-Majmūʿ*, 20:117–118; al-Ṭabarī, *Tafsīr*, 22:9; Ibn Rustam al-Ṭabarī, *al-Mustarshid*, 400; *Kitāb Sulaym*, 428–429; al-Mufīd, *al-Fuṣūl al-mukhtāra*, 54.

78 Ibn Taymiyya, *Minhāj*, 7:70–73.

79 Aḥmad b. Ḥanbal, *al-Musnad*, 1:185; al-Baghawī, *Tafsīr*, 1:310; al-Ḥākim al-Naysābūrī, *al-Mustadrak*, 3:150; Ibn Mardawayh, *Manāqib ʿAlī*, 226–228; Muslim, *Ṣaḥīḥ*, 7:121; al-Thaʿlabī, *Tafsīr*, 3:85; al-Tirmidhī, *Sunan*, 5:302.

80 Ibn Taymiyya, *Minhāj*, 4:27–28, 5:45–46, 7:123–128. See also ʿAbd al-Ḥamīd, *Ibn Taymiyya*, 313.

that the Prophet brought his progeny with him on that day only because prevailing social conventions required it. When two individuals engaged in a mutual imprecation, the custom was for both to bring along their closest kin – those whom they would never willfully subject to God's wrath. On the one hand, the practice served as a deterrent to discourage people from engaging in the ritual under false pretenses; on the other hand, when undertaken, it was evidence that the parties were willing to stake the lives and salvation of their closest loved ones on the truth of their claims.

In the *Minhāj al-sunna*, Ibn Taymiyya argues that those who consider the participation of the Prophet's kin in this customary practice to amount to evidence of their spiritual precedence over others are simply misleading themselves. His certainty in the superiority of Abū Bakr and ʿUmar to ʿAlī leads him to argue further that had the two men appeared in lieu of the Prophet's kin, their collective supplications would have been more powerful and sooner answered by God.[81] The Prophet's kin, he concludes, can never surpass the first two caliphs in terms of spirituality and proximity to God.

Discrediting Pro-ʿAlid Ḥadīth

Like al-Jāḥiẓ before him, Ibn Taymiyya sought to discredit the authenticity and significance of most reports that were circulated in praise of ʿAlī and his family. For example, he rejects the authenticity of reports claiming that Fāṭima's children were protected from the punishments of hell,[82] that ʿAlī would worship God daily in one thousand cycles (*rakaʿāt*) of prayer,[83] and that the Prophet once selected ʿAlī as his spiritual brother.[84] Ibn Taymiyya dismisses belief in such claims as baseless (*bāṭil*) and describes the reports promoting them as a lie (*kidhb*) or fabricated (*mawḍūʿ*). This is Ibn Taymiyya's assessment of a famous *ḥadīth* in which the Prophet states, "I am the city of wisdom (*ḥikma*) [or of knowledge (*ʿilm*)] and ʿAlī is its gate,"[85] and of another in which the Prophet proclaims, "ʿAlī stands by the

81 Ibn Taymiyya, *Minhāj*, 7:128.

82 Ibid., 4:59, 62; cf. al-Ḥākim al-Naysābūrī, *al-Mustadrak*, 3:150; Ibn ʿAsākir, *Taʾrīkh*, 14:174, 63:30; al-Khaṭīb al-Baghdādī, *Taʾrīkh Baghdād*, 3:266.

83 Ibn Taymiyya, *Minhāj*, 4:42; cf. Ibn Bābawayh, *al-Amālī*, 356; Ibn Bābawayh, *al-Khiṣāl*, 517.

84 Ibn Taymiyya, *Minhāj*, 7:117, 279; cf. al-Ḥākim al-Naysābūrī, *al-Mustadrak*, 3:14; Ibn ʿAbd al-Barr, *al-Istīʿāb*, 3:1098–1099; al-Tirmidhī, *Sunan*, 5:300.

85 Ibn Taymiyya, *Minhāj*, 7:515; cf. Aḥmad b. Ḥanbal, *Faḍāʾil al-ṣaḥāba*, 2:634; al-Ḥākim al-Naysābūrī, *al-Mustadrak*, 3:126–127; al-Ṭabarānī, *al-Muʿjam al-kabīr*, 11:55; al-Tirmidhī, *Sunan*, 5:301.

ḥaqq (truth and that which is right) and the *ḥaqq* is with ʿAlī."[86] As a scholar of *ḥadīth*, Ibn Taymiyya does not find the presence of such reports in the works of al-Tirmidhī, Aḥmad b. Ḥanbal, or al-Nasāʾī sufficient evidence of their veracity. Although he certainly respected these men, he insists that when one cites a *ḥadīth* from their respective collections, one must still prove that the *ḥadīth* in question is authentic by substantiating the reliability of its transmitters.[87] Ibn Taymiyya argues that al-Ḥillī has ignored the fact that such reports are open to criticism.

Al-Ḥillī, by contrast, considered the inclusion of such *ḥadīth* in Sunnī collections sufficient proof of their authenticity or admissibility as proofs in doctrinal debates. Since identical reports about the merits of ʿAlī and his family were documented in Shīʿī collections, the Sunnī attestations were, for him, merely external, corroborating evidence, useful for persuading his Sunnī interlocutors. This approach left al-Ḥillī open to Ibn Taymiyya's criticism that he had ignored the contingent status of such *ḥadīth* and failed to prove anything of substance.

Blunting Shīʿī Dialectical Tools

As in the case of some of the pro-ʿAlid exegetical reports discussed earlier, a few of the *ḥadīth* on ʿAlī's merits are likewise included in the famous *ḥadīth* compilations of al-Bukhārī and Muslim. Ibn Taymiyya does not reject these reports as fabrications, since such a position would challenge the canonical status of the *Ṣaḥīḥayn*. Instead, he chooses to interpret them in a way that precludes their polemical use by Shīʿīs. Like al-Jāḥiẓ, he is compelled to engage in a type of hermeneutical blunting of pro-ʿAlid *ḥadīth*. To accomplish this goal, he first dismisses most versions of a pro-ʿAlid *ḥadīth* as containing Shīʿī accretions and partially accepts only the most concise version of it as true. He then interprets the *ḥadīth* so that the Prophet no longer seems to describe ʿAlī as possessing any unique merit. Rather, in each case, the Prophet praises ʿAlī only in ways in which he has previously praised others. In this way, pro-ʿAlid *ḥadīth* merely confirm that ʿAlī was a member of a larger community of faithful Muslims, nothing more.

[86] Ibn Taymiyya, *Minhāj*, 4:238–239; cf. al-Haythamī, *Majmaʿ al-zawāʾid*, 7:235; Ibn ʿAsākir, *Taʾrīkh*, 20:361, 42:419, 449; al-Iskāfī, *al-Miʿyār*, 35, 119; al-Khaṭīb al-Baghdādī, *Taʾrīkh Baghdād*, 14:322.

[87] Ibn Taymiyya, *Minhāj*, 5:41–42, 73, 512, 7:10–11, 33–42, 52–53.

Ḥadīth al-Ghadīr

Ibn Taymiyya draws on an arsenal of tools to discredit the famous *ḥadīth al-ghadīr*, discussed in Chapter 3. He does not attempt to reject the entire event as a fabrication, although he notes Ibn Ḥazm's comment that no authentic chain of transmission existed for the *ḥadīth*.[88] In many versions of the *ḥadīth*, Muḥammad follows his statement "ʿAlī is the *mawlā* of whosoever considers me his *mawlā*" with the invocation, "O God! Be the ally of the one who allies with him and the enemy of the one who shows enmity to him." Al-Ḥākim al-Naysabūrī judged reports containing the added invocation to be authentic.[89] Aḥmad b. Ḥanbal and al-Nasāʾī each transmitted the version with the invocation with more than a dozen different chains of transmission.[90] Nonetheless, Ibn Taymiyya argues that all reports about such an invocation are false.[91] It is unlikely that Ibn Taymiyya in fact studied each chain of transmission for this version of the *ḥadīth* before issuing his judgment. A brief appraisal of the transmitters involved indicates that they were men of good repute; they are praised as trustworthy (*thiqa*) in their biographical entries, and many of them transmitted *ḥadīth* that are preserved in the canonical collections of al-Bukhārī and Muslim. Instead, Ibn Taymiyya appears to know intuitively that any pro-ʿAlid text that exalts ʿAlī above others or depicts him in ways that challenge ʿUthmānī doctrines and portrayals of him must be a fabrication. Given this assumption, Ibn Taymiyya's thinking is quite consistent: if Shīʿī doctrines are false, then anything that appears to support Shīʿī doctrines must also be false. This ideological commitment, rather than any sustained examination of the trustworthiness of the *ḥadīth* narrators, is the basis of his rejection of many pro-ʿAlid *ḥadīth*. It is the source of the certainty with which Ibn Taymiyya can reject outright another *ḥadīth* corroborating the *ḥadīth al-ghadīr* in which the Prophet says to ʿAlī, "You are the *walī* of the faithful after me."[92]

Ibn Taymiyya's strategy for the hermeneutical blunting of the *ḥadīth al-ghadīr* hinges on the meaning of the term *mawlā*. This ambiguous word can

88 Ibn Ḥazm, *al-Fiṣal*, 4:116; Ibn Taymiyya, *Minhāj*, 7:320.

89 Al-Ḥākim al-Naysābūrī, *al-Mustadrak*, 3:109.

90 Aḥmad b. Ḥanbal, *al-Musnad*, 1:118–119, 152, 4:281, 368, 370, 373, 5:370; Aḥmad b. Ḥanbal, *Faḍāʾil al-ṣaḥāba*, 2:585–586, 596, 599, 610, 682, 705; al-Nasāʾī, *Khaṣāʾiṣ*, 93, 96, 100–104, 132; al-Nasāʾī, *al-Sunan al-kubrā*, 45, 130–136, 155.

91 Ibn Taymiyya, *Minhāj*, 7:55.

92 Ibn Taymiyya, *Minhāj*, 5:36; cf. Aḥmad b. Ḥanbal, *al-Musnad*, 4:438; al-Ḥākim al-Naysābūrī, *al-Mustadrak*, 3:134; Ibn Abī Shayba, *al-Muṣannaf*, 7:504; al-Nasāʾī, *Khaṣāʾiṣ*, 64.

refer, among others, to a master, the client of a master, a leader, a follower, and an ally. In the context of the *ḥadīth al-ghadīr*, Shīʿīs interpret it as denoting a position of authority that the Prophet bestowed on ʿAlī. To prove this interpretation, they point to the fact that the Prophet stopped a caravan of thousands of people returning from his final pilgrimage to make his statement. They also appeal to pro-ʿAlid exegetical reports according to which Q5:67 commanded the Prophet to proclaim ʿAlī's role as the *mawlā* of the faithful.[93] And they cite versions of the *ḥadīth al-ghadīr* in which the Prophet first introduces himself as having authority (*awlā*) over members of the community and then, having received the crowd's affirmation, turns to ʿAlī and proclaims that the faithful should recognize ʿAlī's authority over them as they recognize his own. Ibn Taymiyya, by contrast, takes *mawlā* to mean a mere ally in this *ḥadīth*. He thus concludes that the Prophet did not single ʿAlī out for any distinctive honor in his statement, since every faithful Muslim is an ally of the Prophet and of other believers.[94] Every Muslim should also refrain from treating the Prophet or another Muslim as an enemy. The various reports that Shīʿīs cite to support their interpretation of the term Ibn Taymiyya dismisses as mere fabrications.[95] According to him, any instances in which the Prophet appears to tie the term *mawlā* to authority must reflect Shīʿī accretions.

Ḥadīth al-manzila

In the *ḥadīth al-manzila*, the Prophet says to ʿAlī, "You are unto me like Aaron unto Moses." The report is considered canonical and is widely reported in Sunnī *ḥadīth* collections.[96] The Sunnīs were split as to how to interpret the significance of this statement. Pro-ʿAlids referred to Q20:29, Q25:35, and other verses of the Qurʾān to argue that just as Aaron served as the vizier and close confidant of Moses, ʿAlī served the Prophet in the same capacity. Whereas anti-Shīʿī polemicists generally sought to limit the scope

[93] Al-Ḥākim al-Ḥaskānī, *Shawāhid al-tanzīl*, 1:239, 249–257, 2:391–392; Ibn Abī Ḥātim al-Rāzī, *Tafsīr*, 4:1172; Ibn ʿAsākir, *Taʾrīkh*, 42:237; Ibn Mardawayh, *Manāqib ʿAlī*, 239–240; al-Thaʿlabī, *Tafsīr*, 4:92; al-Wāḥidī, *Asbāb al-nuzūl*, 135.

[94] Ibn Taymiyya, *Minhāj*, 5:36, 7:319–325. [95] Ibid., 7:31–34.

[96] ʿAbd al-Razzāq al-Ṣanʿānī, *al-Muṣannaf*, 5:406, 11:206; Aḥmad b. Ḥanbal, *al-Musnad*, 1:170, 173, 175, 177, 179; al-Bukhārī, *Ṣaḥīḥ*, 4:28, 5:129; Ibn Abī Shayba, *al-Muṣannaf*, 7:496, 8:562; Ibn Māja, *Sunan*, 1:43, 45; Muslim, *Ṣaḥīḥ*, 7:120–121; al-Tirmidhī, *Sunan*, 5:302, 304.

of the similarity between ʿAlī and Aaron,[97] pro-ʿAlids argued that the parallel was absolute: just as Moses and Aaron had distinguished themselves in guiding their people, the Israelites, the Prophet and ʿAlī had done the same for their community, deserving Muslims' reverence.[98]

Ibn Taymiyya is unmoved by such arguments.[99] He argues that the Prophet said those words only to comfort ʿAlī, whom he was about to leave in charge of his affairs in Medina while he himself embarked on the expedition to Tabūk. He explains that a few residents of Medina had begun to mock ʿAlī, jeering that the Prophet thought so little of ʿAlī that he preferred to leave him behind with women and children rather than have him accompany himself and the other men on the expedition. According to Ibn Taymiyya, the Shīʿīs have misconstrued the Prophet's intent and the significance of his words and actions in order to aggrandize ʿAlī. He further notes that the Prophet appointed many other Companions both before and after this incident to serve as his deputies in Medina.[100] It is for this reason that he deems some versions of the *ḥadīth al-manzila* false,[101] especially versions in which the Prophet adds, "It does not befit me to leave [Medina] unless you serve as my deputy (*khalīfa*)." Ibn Taymiyya points out that it was the Prophet's habit to always appoint a deputy to manage the city's affairs in his absence, but that in the two dozen times that he left Medina, ʿAlī served as his deputy only once. There was thus nothing significant about this occasion.

Ibn Taymiyya also attempts to downplay the parallel between ʿAlī and Aaron by claiming that the former resembled the latter only in sharing kinship ties with a prophet and shouldering the responsibility of managing the affairs of that prophet's family in the latter's absence. Moses depended on Aaron to take care of his wards while he was gone, and the Prophet appointed ʿAlī to do the same for his. However, Ibn Taymiyya warns, such duties, which are ordinarily tied to one's membership in a tribe or a family, should not be misunderstood to indicate ʿAlī's right to succeed the Prophet as caliph.[102] This is the error that Ibn Taymiyya sees the Shīʿīs as having committed with pro-ʿAlid *ḥadīth* such as the *ḥadīth al-manzila*. In another

[97] Al-Dihlawī and al-Ālūsī, *Mukhtaṣar al-Tuḥfa al-Ithnā ʿashariyya*, 163–164; Ibn Ḥajar al-Haytamī, *al-Ṣawāʿiq al-muḥriqa*, 49; Ibn Ḥazm, *al-Fiṣal*, 4:78; al-Taftāzānī, *Sharḥ al-Maqāṣid*, 2:291.

[98] Ibn Abī 'l-Ḥadīd, *Sharḥ*, 13:211; al-Iskāfī, *al-Miʿyār*, 219–221, 253; Muḥammad b. Ṭalḥa al-Naṣībī, *Maṭālib al-saʾūl*, 114–115, 129–132. Al-ʿAynī also notes that the parallel between ʿAlī and Aaron could be considered absolute: see al-ʿAynī, *ʿUmdat al-qārī*, 16:214.

[99] Ibn Taymiyya, *Minhāj*, 4:87–88, 5:34–36, 7:326–341. [100] Ibid., 5:67–69, 7:331.

[101] Ibid., 4:274, 5:34. [102] Ibid., 4:273–274, 5:34–35, 43.

ḥadīth appearing in the canonical collections, the Prophet says to ʿAlī, "You are of me and I am of you."[103] In this case, too, Ibn Taymiyya contends that the Prophet is affirming only that the two are members of the same family or that they follow the same religion.[104] There is nothing special about the statement, and pro-ʿAlids are mistaken in entertaining notions of some spiritual bond between the two.

Sūrat al-Tawba

In 9/630, the Prophet could not travel to Mecca, so he sent Abū Bakr at the head of a caravan of pilgrims and charged him with announcing the revelation of new laws regarding relations between the Muslims and their Meccan adversaries. Abū Bakr was en route to Mecca when the Prophet dispatched ʿAlī from Medina to stop him. ʿAlī informed Abū Bakr that the angel Gabriel had appeared to the Prophet with additional instructions: only the Prophet or someone belonging to his family could convey new revelation to the public.[105] Consequently, the Prophet had selected ʿAlī to announce the contents of *Sūrat al-Tawba* (Q9) to the Meccans in Abū Bakr's place. Al-Ḥillī and many other Shīʿīs cited this incident as evidence that only members of the *ahl al-bayt* could lawfully act as representatives of God or the Prophet.[106] However, Ibn Taymiyya and others argue that the event merely exemplified the importance of tribal customs.[107] Since the Prophet was a Hāshimid and the opening verses of Q9 discuss a treaty that had been brokered between the Prophet and the Meccans, either the Prophet himself or a Hāshimid delegate would need to proclaim any annulments or revisions of the treaty's terms. ʿAlī was given the responsibility only in deference to these norms. Further, any Hāshimid could have theoretically fulfilled this function.[108]

[103] ʿAbd al-Razzāq al-Ṣanʿānī, *al-Muṣannaf*, 11:227; Aḥmad b. Ḥanbal, *al-Musnad*, 4:164–165; al-Bukhārī, *Ṣaḥīḥ*, 3:168, 4:207; Ibn Abī Shayba, *al-Muṣannaf*, 7:495; Ibn Māja, *Sunan*, 1:44; al-Nasāʾī, *al-Sunan al-kubrā*, 5:126–128, 168–169.

[104] Ibn Taymiyya, *Minhāj*, 4:34–35, 5:28–30, 7:392.

[105] Aḥmad b. Ḥanbal, *al-Musnad*, 3:212; Ibn Hishām, *Sīrat al-Nabī*, 4:972–973; al-Nasāʾī, *Khaṣāʾiṣ*, 91–93; al-Ṭabarānī, *al-Muʿjam al-kabīr*, 11:316; al-Ṭabarī, *Tafsīr*, 10:83–85.

[106] Al-Ḥillī, *Minhāj al-karāma*, 88, 94, 100, 181; Ibn Ṭāwūs, *al-Ṭarāʾif*, 38–39; al-Majlisī, *Biḥār al-anwār*, 30:411–427, 35:284–315; al-Qāḍī al-Nuʿmān, *Sharḥ al-akhbār*, 1:94–95; al-Sharīf al-Murtaḍā, *al-Shāfī fī ʾl-imāma*, 4:153–157.

[107] Al-Fīrūzābādī, *al-Radd ʿalā ʾl-rāfiḍa*, 37–38; Ibn al-ʿArabī, *Aḥkām al-Qurʾān*, 2:454; Ibn Ḥajar al-ʿAsqalānī, *Fatḥ al-bārī*, 8:239, 241; Ibn Taymiyya, *Minhāj*, 7:335–336; al-Qurṭubī, *Tafsīr*, 8:68; al-Rāzī, *al-Tafsīr al-kabīr*, 15:523–524; al-Samʿānī, *Tafsīr al-Qurʾān*, 2:286.

[108] Ibn Taymiyya, *Minhāj*, 5:36.

The thrust of Ibn Taymiyya's arguments is that ʿAlī was a Muslim who also happened to be a relative of the Prophet. The Prophet turned to ʿAlī for responsibilities that required discharge by a relative and occasionally expressed his appreciation to ʿAlī by highlighting their kinship ties. Such praise affirmed that ʿAlī not only aided him in the cause of the religion but also honored his duties as a kinsman. However, in Ibn Taymiyya's view these statements were never indicative of any sort of authority or high rank that ʿAlī might have attained over other Muslims.

The Siege of Khaybar

In reports about the Muslim siege of the lands of Khaybar, an oasis north of Medina, ʿAlī plays a key role in securing this stronghold, which had held out against the Muslims for some time. ʿAlī had initially sat out the war, recuperating from an illness. When other commanders, over a number of days, were unsuccessful in their efforts to secure a victory, the Prophet proclaimed that he would appoint a commander who "loves God and His Prophet and whom God and His Prophet also love." ʿUmar b. al-Khaṭṭāb, Saʿd b. Abī Waqqāṣ, and various other Companions reportedly hoped to be named as this person.[109] However, on the following day the Prophet identified the new commander as ʿAlī, who then led the army to victory.

For pro-ʿAlids, the Prophet's description of ʿAlī was significant because it was evidence that ʿAlī was a saint, someone beloved by God. Many pious believers could assert that they loved God and the Prophet, but few could claim with certainty that they were beloved by God and the Prophet in turn. For Shīʿīs, the Prophet's statement was another sign of ʿAlī's precedence over others, especially Abū Bakr and ʿUmar, in terms of the imāmate.

Ibn Taymiyya considers this *ḥadīth* one of the most reliably transmitted reports of Muḥammad's praise for ʿAlī in Sunnī literature. However, he contends that it does not constitute evidence of ʿAlī's superiority to others or his right to succeed the Prophet as caliph.[110] In fact, he argues, God and His Prophet love every pious believer, just as every faithful person loves God and His Prophet. The *ḥadīth* confirms only that ʿAlī was a faithful

[109] Al-ʿAynī, *ʿUmdat al-qārī*, 16:239; al-Ḥākim al-Naysābūrī, *al-Mustadrak*, 3:267; Muslim, *Ṣaḥīḥ*, 7:120–121; al-Nasāʾī, *al-Sunan al-kubrā*, 5:57; al-Tirmidhī, *Sunan*, 5:302.

[110] Ibn Taymiyya, *Minhāj*, 5:44, 46.

Muslim in the sight of God. It manifestly discredits the claims of anti-ʿAlids and Khawārij who denounced ʿAlī for a lack of faith, but it confers on him no special status.

In the versions of the report narrated by al-Ḥillī, the Prophet's appointment of ʿAlī is preceded by his appointment of Abū Bakr and then ʿUmar as commanders, but both are unsuccessful in their attempts to conquer Khaybar.[111] For al-Ḥillī, the Prophet's statement implicitly contrasts ʿAlī with Abū Bakr and ʿUmar, whom he did not describe as the beloved of God and the Prophet. The difference proves ʿAlī's superiority and his stronger claim to authority after the Prophet.[112]

However, Ibn Taymiyya unequivocally denies that either Abū Bakr or ʿUmar preceded ʿAlī as a commander.[113] Reports that portray the two as failing to take Khaybar are lies (*min al-akādhīb*). They fall into a genre of Shīʿī *ḥadīth* in which ʿAlī is depicted as outshining the first three caliphs – a genre that Ibn Taymiyya rejects as fiction as a matter of principle. He then demonstrates his skill in dialectics in a series of rebuttals of al-Ḥillī's claims. First, he points out, nowhere in the statement does the Prophet claim that no one else is beloved by God and His Prophet. There is no indication that this characteristic was unique to ʿAlī. Consequently, this *ḥadīth* proves merely that ʿAlī was one of many individuals who could be described in such terms. Second, ʿAlī's appointment as a commander shows that the Prophet believed he could bring the Muslims to victory, but it cannot be considered proof of his absolute superiority over his peers in areas unrelated to warfare. Third, even if the *ḥadīth* did demonstrate ʿAlī's superiority, there was nothing to prevent someone else from surpassing him after that day. It is quite possible that someone else subsequently proved himself the most meritorious (*afḍal*). Finally, even if one were to concede that ʿAlī was the most meritorious of the Companions, one could still hold, as did many Zaydīs, a faction of the Muʿtazilīs, and others, that Abū Bakr was nonetheless a legitimate caliph.[114] These groups accepted the imāmate of individuals with less merit (*imāmat al-mafḍūl*) as legitimate. Thus, for Ibn Taymiyya, even if the events at Khaybar proved ʿAlī's superiority over his peers, they would not necessarily entail the illegitimacy of Abū Bakr's caliphate or ʿAlī's right to caliphal authority, as al-Ḥillī claimed.

[111] Aḥmad b. Ḥanbal, *Faḍāʾil al-ṣaḥāba*, 2:593; Ibn ʿAsākir, *Taʾrīkh*, 41:464; Ibn Ḥajar al-ʿAsqalānī, *Fatḥ al-bārī*, 7:365.
[112] Al-Ḥillī, *Minhāj al-karāma*, 152–153.
[113] Ibn Taymiyya, *Minhāj*, 7:366.
[114] Ibid., 7:367–368.

Ḥadīth al-thaqalayn

The Shīʿīs considered a particular *ḥadīth* preserved in *Ṣaḥīḥ Muslim* and in many other sources to constitute unequivocal evidence of the community's responsibility to defer to the Qurʾān and the Prophet's progeny for guidance after the Prophet's death.[115] In the *ḥadīth* in question, the Prophet explains that he is approaching death and leaving two weighty items (*thaqalayn*) in the care of his community. In some versions of the report, he adds that these two items will never contradict one another.[116] The Prophet explicitly identifies the items as the Qurʾān and his family (*ʿitra, ahl al-bayt*). Ibn Taymiyya accepts the version of the *ḥadīth* that appears in *Ṣaḥīḥ Muslim*, but he notes that it does not explicitly command Muslims to follow these two entities in matters requiring guidance. Rather, he interprets the *ḥadīth* as obliging Muslims to follow the guidance of the Qurʾān and to care for the Prophet's progeny after his death by respecting their rights and refraining from any injustice toward them.[117] Those versions of the report that explicitly command believers to follow the Prophet's family Ibn Taymiyya rejects as untrustworthy.

Love for ʿAlī

Ibn Taymiyya accepts the authenticity of a *ḥadīth*, mentioned earlier in connection with Ibn Ḥajar al-ʿAsqalānī's critique of Ibn Taymiyya, that appears in *Ṣaḥīḥ Muslim* and states that none but a believer would love ʿAlī and none but a hypocrite would bear malice against him.[118] To refute the Shīʿīs who claimed that this *ḥadīth* is evidence of ʿAlī's exceptional nature, Ibn Taymiyya argues that one cannot claim this merit to be truly unique to ʿAlī: there are canonical reports in which the Prophet makes the same statement about the Medinese Anṣār.[119]

Ibn Taymiyya also angrily dismisses the veracity of pro-ʿAlid reports claiming that hatred of ʿAlī was the sole criterion by which Companions

115 Aḥmad b. Ḥanbal, *al-Musnad*, 3:14, 17, 26, 59; Ibn Abī Shayba, *al-Muṣannaf*, 7:418; Muslim, *Ṣaḥīḥ*, 7:123; al-Nasāʾī, *al-Sunan al-kubrā*, 5:45, 130; al-Tirmidhī, *Sunan*, 5:-328–329. For Shīʿī references to the report, see al-Ḥillī, *Minhāj al-karāma*, 155–156; Ibn Bābawayh, *al-Amālī*, 616; al-Kulaynī, *al-Kāfī*, 1:294.

116 Aḥmad b. Ḥanbal, *al-Musnad*, 3:14, 17, 26, 59; Ibn Abī Shayba, *al-Muṣannaf*, 7:418; al-Nasāʾī, *al-Sunan al-kubrā*, 5:45, 130; al-Tirmidhī, *Sunan*, 5:329.

117 Ibn Taymiyya, *Minhāj*, 7:318, 394–395.

118 Aḥmad b. Ḥanbal, *al-Musnad*, 1:84; Ibn Māja, *Sunan*, 1:42; Ibn Taymiyya, *Minhāj*, 4:296; Muslim, *Ṣaḥīḥ*, 1:61; al-Nasāʾī, *Sunan al-Nasāʾī*, 8:116–117.

119 Ibn Taymiyya, *Minhāj*, 4:297–300.

identified hypocrites.[120] He argues that the Companions were aware of many other qualities characteristic of a hypocrite that were outlined in the Qur'ān and in other *ḥadīth*, so it would be absurd to believe that they were compelled to rely on animosity toward ʿAlī as the only indicator.[121] He further reasons that anyone who believes love for ʿAlī to be a criterion of true faith must also acknowledge the same about love for Abū Bakr and ʿUmar; after all, Abū Bakr was the Prophet's most beloved Companion.[122] Thus, animosity toward Abū Bakr must in fact be the most egregious sign of hypocrisy.

Ibn Taymiyya's contempt for Shīʿism leads him to defend anti-ʿAlids in ways that likely shocked his pro-ʿAlid critics. He argues that Shīʿīs cannot justify their condemnation of Abū Bakr by appealing to reports about his acting as an enemy of the Prophet and his family, as the same justification could be offered for hatred of ʿAlī. Anti-ʿAlids sincerely believe that ʿAlī wrongfully killed faithful Muslims, desired sovereignty over others, caused ruin (*fasād*), and acted like the Pharaoh of Moses.[123] Such people view ʿAlī as an unbeliever and an apostate, but they cannot be deemed hypocrites on that account. Ibn Taymiyya's point is that if Shīʿīs can be excused for their antipathy toward Abū Bakr and ʿUmar because of certain evidence, then anti-ʿAlids must likewise be excused for their sentiments, which are similarly rooted in historical data. Each group is ignorantly following mistaken interpretations (*taʾwīl*), but is not committing unbelief or hypocrisy.

It is in such instances that Ibn Taymiyya's dialectical arguments teeter between the anti-Shīʿī and the anti-ʿAlid. To condemn Shīʿism, he periodically defends anti-ʿAlid doctrines as reasonable alternatives. In his excurses on the history of the caliphate, he also shows sympathy for ʿUthmānī and Umayyad interpretations of history and hostility to pro-ʿAlid alternatives. The sections that follow examine the history of the early caliphate according to Ibn Taymiyya in greater depth.

ʿAlī and his Followers as Pious ʿUthmānīs

In Chapter 6 I outline a shift that occurred in the ninth century: mild ʿUthmānīs ceased to see ʿAlī as a key antagonist who conspired against ʿUthmān and instead appropriated him in one of two ways. First, some

120 Aḥmad b. Ḥanbal, *Faḍāʾil al-ṣaḥāba*, 2:579, 639, 671; al-Ṭabarānī, *al-Muʿjam al-awsaṭ*, 2:328, 4:264; al-Tirmidhī, *Sunan*, 5:298.
121 Ibn Taymiyya, *Minhāj*, 4:298–299. 122 Ibid., 4:299–300. 123 Ibid., 4:300–301.

ʿUthmānīs transmitted reports according to which ʿAlī committed objectionable deeds unwittingly. For example, he may have upset the Prophet unintentionally or surrounded himself with unsavory characters in his later years as caliph. Second, some ʿUthmānīs depicted ʿAlī, his sons, and some of his partisans as pious ʿUthmānīs. Both of these types of ʿUthmānī reports abound in Sunnī biographical literature and *ḥadīth* collections, and Ibn Taymiyya relies on them to discredit other reports, narrated by early (more zealous) ʿUthmānīs, Umayyads, and pro-ʿAlids, that show ʿAlī contesting the authority of his predecessors. Like al-Jāḥiẓ, Ibn Taymiyya stridently rejects the authenticity of any report about ʿAlī or other Companions that seems to confirm Shīʿī claims about history. His stance differs markedly from that of other Sunnī historians, who acknowledged that the genesis of pro-ʿAlid sentiments in the community can be tied to the Prophet's close kin (*ahl al-bayt*) who considered themselves most suited to succeed the Prophet as caliphs. Ibn Khaldūn, for example, notes that after the Prophet's death certain Companions, such as al-Zubayr, ʿAmmār b. Yāsir, and al-Miqdād b. al-Aswad, became partisans of ʿAlī and recognized him as the best candidate for such authority. When ʿAlī was bypassed in favor of others, these Companions expressed disappointment and sorrow at the outcome.[124] For historians such as al-Balādhurī, al-Ṭabarī, and Ibn Khaldūn, this early history of pro-ʿAlid sentiment is part of the story of the caliphate and the political career of ʿAlī.

Ibn Taymiyya, however, cannot bring himself to acknowledge the historicity of the disagreements that occurred between the Hāshimids and other Companions after the Prophet's death. He denies that any Companion, or ʿAlī himself, ever considered ʿAlī superior to Abū Bakr or ʿUmar.[125] ʿAlī's close circle of associates was no exception: Ibn Taymiyya claims that the earliest Shīʿīs never questioned the preeminence of Abū Bakr and ʿUmar.[126] No one among the generation of Muslims that succeeded the Companions, the Followers (*tābiʿūn*), ever held a different opinion either.

When Abū Bakr denied Fāṭima's claims to inheritance and ownership of some of the Prophet's estates, reports in the *Ṣaḥīḥ* collections of al-Bukhārī and Muslim record that she became angry and ceased speaking with him until her death.[127] However, Ibn Taymiyya rejects the possibility that

[124] Ibn Khaldūn, *Tārīkh*, 3:170–171.
[125] Ibn Taymiyya, *Minhāj*, 1:11–12, 2:11, 72, 5:59, 6:329, 445–446, 7:85–86, 8:223–224.
[126] Ibid., 2:72.
[127] ʿAbd al-Razzāq al-Ṣanʿānī, *al-Muṣannaf*, 5:472; Aḥmad b. Ḥanbal, *al-Musnad*, 1:6; al-Bayhaqī, *al-Sunan al-kubrā*, 6:300–301; al-Bukhārī, *Ṣaḥīḥ*, 4:42, 5:82, 8:3; Muslim, *Ṣaḥīḥ*, 5:153; al-Ṭabarānī, *Musnad al-Shāmīyīn*, 4:198.

Fāṭima could have reacted in this way to Abū Bakr's ruling. He argues that if reports about her bearing a grudge against Abū Bakr were true, Fāṭima would bear a resemblance to hypocrites (*munāfiqūn*), who become angry when public funds (*ṣadaqāt*) are withheld from them and are content when they are paid.[128] If it were true that ʿAlī and Fāṭima were dismayed with the succession of Abū Bakr or with his decision regarding the Prophet's estates, they would have been guilty of disobedience to God, His Prophet, and the Prophet's legitimate successor.[129] Therefore, Ibn Taymiyya reasons, these reports must be false.

The same reports in the *Ṣaḥīḥayn* that describe Fāṭima's dispute with Abū Bakr also note that ʿAlī withheld his oath of fealty from Abū Bakr for six months.[130] Ibn Taymiyya acknowledges that some Sunnīs agree with the Shīʿīs on the historicity of this claim, but he (incorrectly) denies that any evidence exists in the *Ṣaḥīḥayn* to support it.[131] Again, his polemical stance against Shīʿism forces him to dismiss any report that lends credence to Shīʿī positions. It is this ideological commitment to disproving Shīʿism that allows him to ignore reports in the *Ṣaḥīḥayn* that contradict his claims on this occasion but to cite the very same reports elsewhere when they suit his arguments.[132]

The Political Careers of ʿAlī and his Sons

Ibn Taymiyya greatly disapproves of the political careers of ʿAlī and his son al-Ḥusayn. Although he is aware that animosity for these two amounts to heresy, he cannot help but justify the sovereignty and political philosophy of the Umayyads who opposed them. For Ibn Taymiyya, those who opposed or ignored the claims of ʿAlī and al-Ḥusayn were fully justified and correct in doing so. The fact that a few extremists incurred the heresy of hatred for ʿAlī and his sons is an ancillary issue that is beside the point. Ibn Taymiyya does not defend the heresy of hating ʿAlī and his family, but he employs his most creative rhetorical and epistemological weapons to

128 Ibn Taymiyya, *Minhāj*, 4:245–246. Ibn Taymiyya cites Q9:58 as evidence that hypocrites are those who become angry when public funds are withheld from them.
129 Ibid., 4:256.
130 Al-Bayhaqī, *al-Sunan al-kubrā*, 6:300; al-Bukhārī, *Ṣaḥīḥ*, 5:82; Ibn Ḥibbān, *Ṣaḥīḥ*, 11:152–154; Muslim, *Ṣaḥīḥ*, 5:153–154; al-Ṭabarānī, *Musnad al-Shāmīyīn*, 4:198–199.
131 Ibn Taymiyya, *Minhāj*, 4:388.
132 Near the end of his *Minhāj*, Ibn Taymiyya cites those reports from the *Ṣaḥīḥayn* wherein Fāṭima dies angry with Abū Bakr and ʿAlī refuses to pledge allegiance to him for six months to discredit pseudo-epigraphy circulated by Abū Ḥayyān al-Tawḥīdī (d. 414/1023): see ibid., 8:333–335.

support the political objectives of their opponents, since he considers such objectives well reasoned.

Twice Ibn Taymiyya argues that ʿAlī fought his rivals to make them obedient to him as their sovereign, not to bring them into obedience to God.[133] Ibn Taymiyya unequivocally denies pro-ʿAlid claims that ʿAlī's campaigns were motivated or legitimized by verses of the Qurʾān or words of the Prophet. He argues that ʿAlī's motives were purely secular and that he acted in pursuit of power; there were no religious justifications for ʿAlī's decisions to fight at the battles of the Camel and of Ṣiffīn. Ibn Taymiyya considers these wars to be the results of ʿAlī's personal opinion (*raʾy*) regarding the need to fight rebels.[134] He considers this opinion to have been folly, and makes his case in two ways.

First, wearing a theologian's hat, Ibn Taymiyya criticizes ʿAlī with some reserve when explaining views that he considered representative of orthodoxy. In these sections of his *Minhāj*, he argues that although as caliph ʿAlī had the right to use his discretion, it would have been better had he chosen not to fight other Companions.[135] Furthermore, those who chose to refrain from joining in his civil wars had religious justifications for their decision that ʿAlī lacked for his.[136] Ibn Taymiyya also argues that those who sat out of ʿAlī's wars were more eminent than and superior to those who participated in them.[137] Pro-ʿAlids and Shīʿīs would contest these claims as false, but in making them Ibn Taymiyya is essentially legitimizing a well-known Sunnī opinion that the Companions who refrained from fighting other Muslims were justified in declining to help ʿAlī.

Second, writing as a polemicist, Ibn Taymiyya seeks to discredit Shīʿī doctrines by spitefully championing anti-ʿAlid and Umayyad responses to them and promoting the latter as representing the stronger and more reasoned position. He sympathetically explains and justifies their views while admitting that orthodoxy would consider them extreme and misguided. He criticizes ʿAlī for causing ruin (*fasād*) in the community and acting like a pharaoh.[138] In some instances he tries to maintain a modicum of deniability by calling certain anti-ʿAlid doctrines false or extreme, but these disclaimers are unconvincing. Throughout the *Minhāj*, Ibn Taymiyya is obliged to draw on anti-ʿAlid perceptions of ʿAlī to justify the political career of Muʿāwiya.

[133] Ibid., 6:191–192, 8:329–330.
[134] Ibid., 4:496. See also ʿAbd al-Ḥamīd, *Ibn Taymiyya*, 322–323.
[135] Ibn Taymiyya, *Minhāj*, 4:389. [136] Ibid., 1:540–542. [137] Ibid., 4:105, 7:57.
[138] Ibid., 4:300–301.

In response to pro-ʿAlid *ḥadīth* in which the Prophet condemns Muʿāwiya as a rebel and curses him,[139] Ibn Taymiyya retorts that if Muʿāwiya can be slandered as an unjust rebel (*bāghī*), then an anti-ʿAlid (*nāṣibī*) can accuse ʿAlī of injustice and of waging war against innocent Muslims. Like al-Jāḥiẓ, Ibn Taymiyya then goes further by creatively bolstering the anti-ʿAlid position with his own arguments. He claims that since ʿAlī fought his rivals to establish his sovereignty over the Muslims rather than to ensure their obedience to God, he can be compared to tyrants who violated Q28:83 in pursuit of the same objectives.[140] ʿAlī's motives thus differed from those of Abū Bakr, who fought people who denied the sacred duty to offer the annual alms and whose goal was to ensure that the commandments of God were obeyed.[141] This argument appears original to Ibn Taymiyya himself: no evidence suggests that he is drawing on any previous articulation of this argument by Umayyad dialecticians.

Overall, then, Ibn Taymiyya argues that ʿAlī's wars with other Companions were not truly undertaken in the path of God. He dismisses pro-ʿAlid *ḥadīth* in which the Prophet likens war against ʿAlī to war against himself as absolutely false.[142] He insists that ʿAlī's war with Muʿāwiya, for example, falls short of these standards for two reasons. First, ʿAlī would not have agreed to arbitration with Muʿāwiya and sought peace with him had he truly considered Muʿāwiya an enemy of God. And second, God promised victory to prophets and the faithful when they wage war in his cause, so if the battle of Ṣiffīn had truly enjoyed divine sanction, God would surely have given ʿAlī victory.

Ibn Taymiyya was not the type of scholar to praise or entertain heresy. He was a man of staunch convictions who was imprisoned on multiple occasions on account of his beliefs. If he considered something praiseworthy, he did so because of its congruence with what he deemed orthodoxy. Why, then, does Ibn Taymiyya describe the arguments of the so-called *nawāṣib* in such detail in his *Minhāj*? He writes neither as a historian who merely notes their beliefs dispassionately nor as a theologian who seeks to refute them. Rather, he resurrects and argues in favor of certain anti-ʿAlid

[139] For *ḥadīth* condemning the rebels of Ṣiffīn, see ʿAbd al-Razzāq al-Ṣanʿānī, *al-Muṣannaf*, 11:240; Aḥmad b. Ḥanbal, *al-Musnad*, 4:197, 199; al-Bukhārī, *Ṣaḥīḥ*, 3:207; al-Ḥākim al-Naysābūrī, *al-Mustadrak*, 2:149–155/6; Ibn Abī Shayba, *al-Muṣannaf*, 8:723. For *ḥadīth* in which the Prophet curses Muʿāwiya, see Muslim, *Ṣaḥīḥ*, 8:207; al-Ṭabarī, *Tārīkh*, 8:185–186. For a collection of such reports, see al-Saqqāf, *Zahr al-rayḥān*.

[140] Ibn Taymiyya, *Minhāj*, 4:300–301. [141] Ibid., 4:494–495, 8:324–330.

[142] Ibid., 4:504.

views of history because he believes that Muʿāwiya was fully justified in going to war with ʿAlī. He endeavors to defend the political career of Muʿāwiya and his partisans because he is convinced that this can be done without bearing malice toward ʿAlī. He is sure that Muʿāwiya himself never hated ʿAlī.

Because of his certainty in the righteousness of the Companions, Ibn Taymiyya finds it impossible to accept pro-ʿAlid and Shīʿī claims that Muʿāwiya or other Companions disliked ʿAlī. In his view, the fact that some later Umayyads or ʿUthmānīs ended up hating ʿAlī is an unfortunate outcome of the civil wars that had engulfed the community, but it does not invalidate the legitimacy of their political grievances or actions against ʿAlī. In other words, although their hatred for ʿAlī can be condemned, their opposition to his accession and their criticisms of his decisions as caliph were all reasonable and lawful. For this reason, Ibn Taymiyya attempts to justify many of their perceptions of ʿAlī and the actions they took against him. In some cases, he deems their opinions correct; in others, he describes their actions as legally justified and valid, even if not necessarily correct. For example, he indicates that nonintervention would have been the better course of action, but he nonetheless defends the actions of the rebels and suggests that they were compelled to rebel by provocations from ʿAlī, his army, or heretical Shīʿīs.[143] His sympathy for anti-ʿAlids and his prejudice against pro-ʿAlids are obvious in much of his discourse on ʿAlī.

For many pro-ʿAlid Sunnīs as well as Shīʿīs, Ibn Taymiyya's willingness to resurrect and champion the views of anti-ʿAlids was shocking.[144] Although Ibn Taymiyya himself was confident that his defense of Muʿāwiya and the accompanying criticism of ʿAlī fell squarely within the bounds of orthodoxy, many viewed his statements about ʿAlī as heresy. It is in this context that we should read Ibn Ḥajar al-ʿAsqalānī's comment that some jurists deemed Ibn Taymiyya a hypocrite devoid of faith because he appeared to harbor antipathy for ʿAlī.[145]

Ibn Taymiyya generally criticized expressions of pro-ʿAlid doctrines among Sunnīs and Shīʿīs alike as objectionable. He considered special reverence for ʿAlī and his family contrary to the truth of the Prophet's message. Any belief in the special status of ʿAlī and his family was a sign that the believer had been taken in by fabricated pro-ʿAlid *ḥadīth*. In his

[143] Ibid., 4:316–317, 383–384.
[144] See ʿAbd al-Ḥamīd, *Ibn Taymiyya*, 216–220 and nn. 55–58 in this chapter.
[145] Ibn Ḥajar al-ʿAsqalānī, *al-Durar al-kāmina*, 1:155.

view, the case against ʿAli was, in truth, compelling, and it was thus perfectly reasonable for someone to withhold support from ʿAlī and back Muʿāwiya instead. Muʿāwiya had every right to ignore ʿAlī's political claims, and ʿĀʾisha, Ṭalḥa, and al-Zubayr had every right to raise an army against ʿAlī. All of the rebels' actions that led to the battles of the Camel and Ṣiffīn were justified. In Ibn Taymiyya's eyes, the Umayyads were likewise right to suppress the heresy of Shīʿism in Iraq. If anti-ʿAlid sentiment played a role in any of these events, it was only an unintended outgrowth of an otherwise acceptable political and religious platform that opposed the cult around ʿAlī. Further, according to Ibn Taymiyya, no contemporary of ʿAlī found his claims to the caliphate compelling, and his actions as caliph left much to be desired. In Ibn Taymiyya's depiction, therefore, ʿAlī's predecessors appear perfect in their conduct as caliphs, whereas ʿAlī is subpar. Since Ibn Taymiyya blames ʿAlī for the civil wars that occurred during his reign, he initially puts his critiques of ʿAlī in the mouths of phantom anti-ʿAlids, but it subsequently becomes apparent that these critiques represent Ibn Taymiyya's personal views when he makes the same points in gentler terms elsewhere. He says that ʿAlī's decisions did not represent the wisdom and example of the Prophet because (1) ʿAlī fought to secure the obedience of others, not for the sake of God or a prophetic commandment, (2) he led an assault against other Muslims when he could have refrained from war, and (3) those who fought against ʿAlī's army did so legitimately.

Pro-ʿAlids and Shīʿīs maintained that the Prophet foretold the civil wars of ʿAlī's caliphate, declared that ʿAlī's opponents would be in the wrong, and praised ʿAlī as rightly guided in his conduct. In one *ḥadīth*, the Prophet tells ʿAlī that the latter will fight three groups: oath-breakers (*nākithūn*); the wicked (*qāsiṭūn*); and heretics who "transgress the bounds" (*māriqūn*) of religion.[146] Pro-ʿAlids argued that this *ḥadīth* clarified the grounds on which ʿAlī fought each rebellious group that he confronted during his caliphate. ʿĀʾisha's army consisted of men (most prominently Ṭalḥa and al-Zubayr) who had pledged their allegiance to ʿAlī before rebelling against him; they were thus the prophesied party of oath-breakers. The members of Muʿāwiya's army were wicked and unjust, while the Khawārij transgressed the bounds of religion with their violent extremism and absolutism. ʿAlī was obliged to fight these factions to defend the civilians who had pledged allegiance to him and were either endangered or attacked by

[146] Al-Bazzār, *Musnad*, 2:215, 3:26; al-Ḥākim al-Naysābūrī, *al-Mustadrak*, 3:139–140; al-Iskāfī, *al-Miʿyār*, 37, 55; al-Ṭabarānī, *al-Muʿjam al-awsaṭ*, 8:213, 9:165.

these groups. In another *ḥadīth*, the Prophet specifically warns ʿĀʾisha that she will fight ʿAlī unjustly.[147] Al-Ḥillī cites both reports to defend ʿAlī's decision to fight his opponents, whereas Ibn Taymiyya rejects them as fabricated.[148]

Ibn Taymiyya also defends ʿĀʾisha against her critics by arguing that it had never been her intention to fight ʿAlī's army, but that a series of events beyond her control led to war. ʿĀʾisha left her home in Medina only because she saw a public good (*maṣlaḥa*) in using her status as a public figure to seek justice in the case of ʿUthmān's murder. In addition, she regretted her participation in the battle of the Camel, and this regret, for Ibn Taymiyya, indicates that she did not oppose ʿAlī unjustly, as the aforementioned *ḥadīth* about her asserts.

Ibn Taymiyya upholds a common Sunnī view that all of the participants in the battle of the Camel, including ʿAlī, regretted their participation in the war. This position combines mildly ʿUthmānī views about ʿAlī with mildly pro-ʿAlid views about his rivals. As I noted in Chapter 3, moderate pro-ʿAlids sought to exonerate ʿĀʾisha, Ṭalḥa, and al-Zubayr of culpability for the battle of the Camel by appealing to their remorse over their participation. This view contrasted starkly with that held by Shīʿīs, who believed that God would punish those who fought ʿAlī in that battle, including the commanders who were responsible for the war. Shīʿīs also rejected the claim that ʿAlī regretted fighting the rebels, because there were reports to the contrary. In these Shīʿī reports, ʿAlī is portrayed as a wise and just imām who patiently tried to reason with his adversaries but consistently met disdain and recalcitrance. According to these reports, after the battle of the Camel ʿAlī sternly addressed the corpses of his adversaries and showed no regret for his actions.[149]

Parallel to the pro-ʿAlid interpretations, there were both zealous and moderate ʿUthmānī theories about the battle of the Camel. Zealous ʿUthmānīs considered ʿAlī responsible for the death of ʿUthmān and thus saw war against him as justified. Moderate ʿUthmānīs deflected the blame for ʿUthmān's murder and the battle of the Camel from ʿAlī to a nefarious group of conspirators in his army (following the legendary heretic Ibn Sabaʾ). According to these moderate ʿUthmānīs, ʿAlī, ʿĀʾisha, and the other commanders reached an agreement on the day before the battle that ʿUthmān's killers were to be apprehended and punished on the

[147] Al-Bazzār, *Musnad*, 11:73; Ibn ʿAbd Rabbih, *al-ʿIqd*, 5:79.
[148] Al-Ḥillī, *Minhāj al-karāma*, 75, 93; cf. Ibn Taymiyya, *Minhāj*, 4:316, 6:112.
[149] Al-Mufīd, *al-Irshād*, 1:256.

morrow. However, in the middle of the night, a villainous group of fighters from ʿAlī's army attacked ʿĀʾisha's innocent soldiers, who were forced to defend themselves; the clash then escalated into the battle of the Camel. According to the moderate ʿUthmānī view, ʿAlī repented of his participation in the war, and ʿĀʾisha's army was ultimately fully justified in waging war against his army. Ibn Taymiyya narrates this version of history to support his claim that that the commanders of both armies were equally remorseful about their actions.[150] Each of them could have prevented the war by taking a different course of action, so ʿAlī possessed no moral superiority over his opponents. To reach this conclusion, Ibn Taymiyya must reject all pro-ʿAlid texts legitimizing ʿAlī's actions and embrace the moderate ʿUthmānī narratives that characterized the attack on ʿAlī's army as defensive. Ibn Taymiyya similarly relies on Umayyad narratives of history to undermine pro-ʿAlid narratives that legitimize the actions of al-Ḥusayn.

In sum, Shīʿīs and pro-ʿAlids believed that ʿAlī received moral support from the Prophet years before engaging in the civil wars of his caliphate. The Prophet's foretelling of the events makes them unavoidable. However, Ibn Taymiyya rejects this view as based on spurious reports because it completely delegitimizes the actions of the Companions and Umayyads who fought against ʿAlī. Instead, he argues that ʿAlī went to war because of his own personal interests and independent thinking (*raʾy*). Having portrayed ʿAlī's actions in this way, Ibn Taymiyya feels justified in criticizing ʿAlī's decisions and disagreeing with him.

In Defense of the Umayyads

Ibn Taymiyya is well aware that in Shīʿī historiography, the early caliphs and ʿAlī's political rivals are depicted as anti-ʿAlids, and he claims that the Shīʿīs extend this label to all Sunnīs.[151] Since he considers the accusation unfounded, especially when leveled against Companions, he sees no merit to the view that his own effort to justify the political careers of Muʿāwiya, Yazīd, and other Umayyads qualifies as an anti-ʿAlid endeavor.

Ibn Taymiyya treats pro-ʿAlid reports appearing in Sunnī historiography as Shīʿī material. For this reason, he doubts that Muʿāwiya poisoned al-Ḥasan b. ʿAlī, as some Sunnī sources report.[152] Nevertheless, he defends

[150] Ibn Taymiyya, *Minhāj*, 4:316–317. [151] Ibid., 2:607.
[152] Al-Balādhurī, *Ansāb al-ashrāf*, 1:404; Ibn ʿAbd al-Barr, *al-Istīʿāb*, 1:389; Ibn Saʿd, *Kitāb al-Ṭabaqāt al-kabīr*, 6:386; Maqrīzī, *Imtāʿ*, 5:361; Sibṭ Ibn al-Jawzī, *Tadhkirat al-khawāṣṣ*, 192; al-Ṭabarānī, *al-Muʿjam al-kabīr*, 3:71.

Mu'āwiya's killing of al-Ḥasan b. 'Alī, if it indeed occurred, by arguing that Mu'āwiya gave the order to poison him in circumstances of mutual hostility and war.[153] However, this claim is problematic since al-Ḥasan died after negotiating a peace settlement that entailed his abdication and recognition of Mu'āwiya as caliph.[154] Obviously, from the pro-'Alid and Shī'ī perspective, any attempt to justify the murder of 'Alids is blasphemous and anti-'Alid. Nowhere is the divide between pro-Umayyad polemicists and their anti-Umayyad interlocutors more conspicuous than in debates about al-Ḥusayn and Yazīd.

Ibn Taymiyya was not the first Sunnī or Ḥanbalī to defend Yazīd against his critics. In response to Shī'īs and many Sunnīs of the sixth/twelfth century who annually commemorated the martyrdom of al-Ḥusayn and denounced Yazīd as a villain during the month of Muḥarram, some prominent Sunnīs issued legal opinions discouraging condemnation of Yazīd. These scholars include al-Ghazālī (d. 505/1111), 'Abd al-Mughīth al-Ḥarbī (d. 583/1187), 'Abd al-Ghanī al-Maqdisī (d. 600/1203), and Ibn al-Ṣalāḥ (d. 643/1245).[155] Ibn al-Ṣalāḥ argued that it was the governor of Iraq, 'Ubayd Allāh b. Ziyād, who was to blame for al-Ḥusayn's death. According to al-Ghazālī and Ibn al-Ṣalāḥ, the claim that Yazīd ordered al-Ḥusayn's murder was not corroborated by any authentic reports. Ibn al-Ṣalāḥ added that even if it were the case that Yazīd ordered his death, faithful Muslims should nonetheless not damn Yazīd (*la'nuhu*) in their invocations.[156] The Damascene Ḥanbalī 'Abd al-Ghanī al-Maqdisī likewise contended that feeling love for Yazīd was not objectionable and that Muslims were free to venerate and love Yazīd if they so desired; by contrast, it was unlawful to attack his character or to condemn him if one did not love him.[157] 'Abd al-Ghanī's teacher, 'Abd al-Mughīth al-Ḥarbī, wrote a book about the merits of Yazīd, which prompted another prominent Ḥanbalī, Ibn al-Jawzī (d. 597/1201), to write an angry refutation.[158] Whereas 'Abd al-Mughīth declared it forbidden to condemn

153 Ibn Taymiyya, *Minhāj al-sunna*, 4:469–471. See also 'Abd al-Ḥamīd, *Ibn Taymiyya*, 371, 399.

154 *EI*², s.v. "(al-)Ḥasan b. 'Alī b. Abī Ṭālib" (L. Veccia Vaglieri).

155 Ibn Ḥajar al-Haytamī, *al-Ṣawā'iq al-muḥriqa*, 223; Ibn Ṭūlūn, *Qayd al-sharīd min akhbār Yazīd*, 57–60, 70.

156 Ibn Ḥajar al-Haytamī, *al-Ṣawā'iq al-muḥriqa*, 223.

157 Ibn Rajab, *al-Dhayl 'alā Ṭabaqāt al-Ḥanābila*, 4:34; Ibn Ṭūlūn, *Qayd al-sharīd min akhbār Yazīd*, 70. See also Cook, *Commanding Right*, 142 n. 199.

158 Al-Dhahabī, *Siyar*, 21:160; Ibn Ṭūlūn, *Qayd al-sharīd min akhbār Yazīd*, 70. See also Cook, *Commanding Right*, 142–143. Ibn al-Jawzī's refutation is still extant: see Ibn al-Jawzī, *Yazīd*.

Yazīd, Ibn al-Jawzī denounced Yazīd in the strongest terms and considered damning him for his crimes a pious deed.

Ibn Taymiyya joins the fray on the side of Yazīd. He argues that hatred of Yazīd can be traced to the Shīʿīs who cursed him and fabricated tales about him. According to Ibn Taymiyya, no one ever spoke ill of Yazīd or accused him of any impiety before the Shīʿīs began to spread lies about him.[159] He labels as false the accusations that Yazīd was a nonbeliever, despised religion, openly drank intoxicants, or ordered the murder of the Prophet's grandson: to the contrary, Yazīd never committed a crime that would have required a punishment (*ḥadd*) prescribed by Islamic law.[160] It is true that his army waged war against the Medinese Anṣār and their families in the Battle of Ḥarra, but it is slanderous to claim that he understood their deaths as vengeance for his forefathers who died fighting the Muslims at Badr and Uḥud.[161] Ibn Taymiyya further claims that far from rejoicing upon hearing the news of al-Ḥusayn's murder, Yazīd showed grief.[162] All of these defamatory claims about Yazīd, he concludes, can be traced to Shīʿī extremists (*ghulāt*) who desired to delegitimize his rule by slandering him. Ibn Taymiyya's ideological commitment to opposing Shīʿism thus leads him to deny any report that portrays Yazīd negatively.

Sunnīs who attempted to defend Yazīd's character while acknowledging the need to respect ʿAlī and his family faced the difficult challenge of balancing their Umayyad and ʿAlid allegiances in discussions of the history of conflict between these two houses. They sought to discredit Shīʿī historical grievances related to the treatment of ʿAlī and his progeny without denying the merits and tribulations of ʿAlids. To accomplish this, Ibn Taymiyya and other polemicists deflected blame for ʿAlid suffering away from their obvious political rivals (such as the Umayyads) to heretical Shīʿīs. The logic underpinning this argument was that since the Shīʿīs were obviously enemies of the rightly guided caliphs and other Companions, they must have been enemies of ʿAlī and his sons as well.

These Sunnī polemicists made two types of arguments about the treacherousness of Shīʿīs. First, some claimed that certain Shīʿīs (*rāfiḍa*) were secretly opposed to ʿAlī and his sons even while proclaiming love for them. This is the narrative employed in origin myths about Shīʿism that describe the *rāfiḍa* as individuals who betrayed the ʿAlid insurrectionist Zayd

159 Ibn Taymiyya, *Majmūʿ fatāwā*, 3:409. See also ʿAbd al-Ḥamīd, *Ibn Taymiyya*, 88.
160 Ibn Taymiyya, *Raʾs*, 207. See also ʿAbd al-Ḥamīd, *Ibn Taymiyya*, 372.
161 Ibn Taymiyya, *Majmūʿ fatāwā*, 3:409. 162 Ibn Taymiyya, *Raʾs*, 207.

b. ʿAlī (d. 122/740) and intentionally left him to die during his rebellion against the Umayyads.[163] This argument was also applied to the legendary Ibn Sabaʾ, who was depicted as the source of belief in *tafḍīl ʿAlī*, ʿAlī's divinity, his occultation, and Shīʿism in general, but who secretly conspired against ʿAlī once the latter became caliph.

The second line of argument assumed that Shīʿīs were dishonest and treacherous. Even if it was not their intention to cause al-Ḥusayn's death, they were culpable for it by (1) encouraging him to rebel against Yazīd, (2) inviting him to leave his home and come to Kūfa, and (3) failing to support him when he arrived in Iraq. The *rāfiḍa* were thus depicted as impious and cowardly.[164] To avoid direct criticism of al-Ḥusayn, the proponents of this argument discounted, if not entirely denied, his agency in his own political decisions, and transferred it to his Iraqi partisans. This move allowed them to criticize the rebellion against Yazīd as folly without directly condemning al-Ḥusayn. In this way, Sunnīs similarly diminished ʿĀʾisha's role in inciting an insurgency against ʿAlī. Days before the battle of the Camel, soldiers in ʿĀʾisha's army had convinced her to continue leading the march on to war when she desired to turn back.[165]

In the case of al-Ḥusayn, since the Shīʿīs of Kūfa misled him into insurrection, they were the real culprits in his death. According to pro-ʿAlid narratives, al-Ḥusayn was compelled to revolt by his personal conviction that Yazīd was completely unqualified to serve as caliph. But in his writings, Ibn Taymiyya rejects this narrative in favor of a theory in which al-Ḥusayn was deluded by Iraqi Shīʿīs and duped into rebelling against the caliph. Yazīd, meanwhile, was the rightful caliph and an innocent victim of Shīʿī slander.

The problem with pro-Yazīd narratives such as Ibn Taymiyya's is that they ignore the agency of al-Ḥusayn, the caliph, his army commanders, and his police force in the protracted conflict. In spite of Ibn Taymiyya's claim that the Shīʿīs of Kūfa betrayed al-Ḥusayn out of love for this material world (*dunyā*), the Kūfans in fact rose up against their governor under the leadership of al-Ḥusayn's cousin, Muslim b. ʿAqīl b. Abī Ṭālib (d. 60/680), though the governor successfully suppressed their revolt. The characterization of the Kūfans as acting solely from motives of expediency is untenable in view of the ruthlessness with which the governor imprisoned and executed anyone accused of providing support to al-Ḥusayn or his cousin. The governor also threatened to confiscate the

[163] Ibn Taymiyya, *Minhāj*, 1:34–35, 2:96, 4:64. [164] Ibid., 2:90–92.
[165] Spellberg, *Politics, Gender, and the Islamic Past*, 131–132.

property of any rebel and to punish members of his tribe in retaliation.[166] The same governor had made a spectacle of al-Ḥusayn's ambassadors to Baṣra and Kūfa by publicly executing them and crucifying their headless corpses.[167] After Muslim b. ʿAqīl's failed uprising, the public execution of al-Ḥusayn's Hāshimid cousin successfully discouraged the town's residents from continued revolt: if the governor was willing to execute a Hāshimid who possessed considerable social capital as a kinsman of the Prophet, then no one was safe. Pro-Yazīd narratives also ignore the role that Yazīd's police force played in seeking to arrest al-Ḥusayn and his partisans, as well as al-Ḥusayn's decision to send multiple ambassadors to Iraq and his desire to relocate there to avoid capture.

Ibn al-Zubayr and al-Ḥusayn are depicted as vowing to never recognize Yazīd as a legitimate successor to the Prophet.[168] Both left their homes in Medina in the middle of the night to flee Yazīd's police, who threatened to imprison and execute them.[169] In discussing this history, Ibn Taymiyya appears to downplay the desperation that Ibn al-Zubayr and al-Ḥusayn experienced under these circumstances. On multiple occasions, al-Ḥusayn stated that he was running for his life. He explained to well-wishers that whether he hid himself in Medina, in Mecca, or under a rock, the police would seize and kill him in order to eliminate all possible contenders to the caliphate and solidify Yazīd's rule.[170] When he learned that assassins had arrived in Mecca to kill him, al-Ḥusayn was forced to leave the city without completing his pilgrimage.[171] Such narratives portray al-Ḥusayn's purpose in traveling from Medina to Mecca and then to Iraq as not war, but as an attempt to escape violence and protect his family from imprisonment and execution.

Ibn al-Zubayr established himself in Mecca while al-Ḥusayn eventually decided to travel to Kūfa, the capital city of his father's government, where many residents had already pledged fealty to him. Ibn al-Zubayr and al-Ḥusayn made their political calculations in full awareness of the fact that they had become enemies of the state as soon as they refused to pledge allegiance to the new caliph. The two had become fugitives, and their actions indicate this.

166 Al-Balādhurī, *Ansāb al-ashrāf*, 2:81; Ibn Aʿtham al-Kūfī, *al-Futūḥ*, 5:38, 40, 50; al-Ṭabarī, *Tārīkh*, 4:277–279.
167 Ibn Aʿtham al-Kūfī, *al-Futūḥ*, 5:37.
168 Al-Dīnawarī, *al-Akhbār al-ṭiwāl*, 262–264; Ibn Aʿtham al-Kūfī, *al-Futūḥ*, 5:14.
169 Al-Ṭabarī, *Tārīkh*, 4:251–252.
170 Ibn ʿAsākir, *Taʾrīkh*, 14:216; al-Ṭabarī, *Tārīkh*, 4:289, 296.
171 Al-Yaʿqūbī, *Tārīkh*, 2:249; Ibn Ṭāwūs, *al-Luhūf*, 39–40.

For Ibn Taymiyya, however, al-Ḥusayn and Yazīd are both innocent victims of the machinations of one heretical group: the Shīʿīs. He sides with the Umayyads in condemning al-Ḥusayn's partisans in Kūfa for their rebellion against the caliph and the heresy of their Shīʿism. Despite his general sympathy for the Umayyad cause, Ibn Taymiyya is willing to gently criticize Yazīd's conduct in the civil strife. He concedes that Yazīd could have taken certain measures to ensure that al-Ḥusayn and his family were not harmed or killed by members of his state apparatus. He also acknowledges that Yazīd never sought justice for al-Ḥusayn's murder or held his killers accountable. Ibn Taymiyya rationalizes that since al-Ḥusayn was killed to safeguard Yazīd's sovereignty, the Umayyads may have considered al-Ḥusayn's murder justified under the circumstances.[172] Both Ibn Taymiyya and another anti-Shīʿī polemicist, al-Qāḍī Abū Bakr b. al-ʿArabī, note that the Umayyads likely portrayed al-Ḥusayn as a criminal engaged in an unlawful rebellion. The Umayyad soldiers who killed him may have considered it a religious duty to fight him because of statements attributed to the Prophet commanding Muslims to wage war against outlaws who cause strife in the community.[173]

As for al-Ḥusayn, Ibn Taymiyya argues that his decision to rebel was unsound (*raʾy fāsid*), because only very rarely do the positive consequences of a rebellion outweigh the evil (*sharr*) that results. In the case of al-Ḥusayn's revolt, he concludes, the harm that ensued was far greater than any benefit produced by the rebellion.[174] In fact, Ibn Taymiyya asserts that the revolt yielded not a single benefit (*maṣlaḥa*), worldly or religious. Had he quietly remained at home, all of the evil triggered by al-Ḥusayn's rebellion and subsequent murder could have been prevented.[175] He does not deny that al-Ḥusayn was killed wrongfully and that he became a martyr, but in contrast to the polemical lengths to which he is willing to go to exonerate ʿUthmān, Muʿāwiya, Ṭalḥa, al-Zubayr, and ʿĀʾisha, Ibn Taymiyya cannot bring himself to defend al-Ḥusayn's conduct, because he considers Shīʿī opposition to the Umayyads misguided. His outrage at the murder of ʿUthmān, the wickedness of his assassins, and the magnitude of their crime is boundless, and contrasts sharply with his near-silence on the fate of al-Ḥusayn.

In Ibn Taymiyya's view, al-Ḥusayn had been injudicious, like his father, and both were responsible for the bloodshed that occurred during their

172 Ibn Taymiyya, *Raʾs*, 207. See also ʿAbd al-Ḥamīd, *Ibn Taymiyya*, 383.
173 Ibn al-ʿArabī, *al-ʿAwāṣim*, 338; Ibn Taymiyya, *Minhāj*, 4:553.
174 Ibn Taymiyya, *Minhāj*, 4:528. 175 Ibid., 4:530.

respective political careers. He argues that ʿAlī and al-Ḥusayn alike chose to wage war even when it could have been avoided. In the case of al-Ḥusayn, a "hankering within his soul" (*hawāʾ khafī*) clouded his judgment and pushed him to act the way he did.[176] His reliance on Iraqi Shīʿīs was a further mistake, and his poor political strategizing led to the unfortunate circumstances that culminated in his death.

Ibn Taymiyya contends that al-Ḥusayn's rebellion and murder led to an increase in evil (*zād al-sharr*) in the world,[177] evident in the number of insurrections that followed al-Ḥusayn's murder. In addition to the uprising of the residents of Medina, Ibn al-Zubayr led a revolt in Mecca, the Penitents (Tawwābūn) led another in Iraq, and al-Mukhtār b. Abī ʿUbayd (d. 67/687) successfully orchestrated a coup in Kūfa. Ibn Taymiyya consistently advocates quietism under the Umayyads. He does not characterize any of these rebellions as righteous or sympathize with their aims. Ibn Taymiyya in certain ways is a pragmatist,[178] and it could be argued that his pragmatism prevented appreciation of the symbolic victories that the insurrectionists believed they had achieved by rebelling against the state. For Ibn Taymiyya, the tragedy of their deaths outweighed any perceived benefits.

Ibn Taymiyya also faults al-Ḥusayn's revolt for contributing to the ruin (*fasād*) of the world. He notes that God and the Prophet Muḥammad commanded the community to avoid the path of ruin and to follow the path that fosters the greater good (*ṣalāḥ*), and he identifies al-Ḥusayn's movement with the former path. In support of his argument, he cites reports in which multiple Companions advise al-Ḥusayn against rebellion for this reason.[179] By contrast, in pro-ʿAlid narratives the Companions seeking to dissuade al-Ḥusayn are motivated by his wellbeing and at no time accuse him of causing ruin. Al-Ḥusayn himself denies the accusation that his quest for justice will contribute to such ruin.[180] The accusation was likely propounded from Umayyad pulpits.

Further, Ibn Taymiyya cites *ḥadīth* in support of his claim that al-Ḥusayn's rebellion against Yazīd appeared to violate the Prophet's alleged advice to obey rulers and avoid political conflicts.[181] However, as noted earlier, this line of argument rests on ignoring the crisis al-Ḥusayn faced in Medina and Mecca that forced him to leave those cities fearing for his life.

[176] Ibid., 4:543. See also ʿAbd al-Ḥamīd, *Ibn Taymiyya*, 393.
[177] Ibn Taymiyya, *Minhāj*, 4:530. [178] Rapoport, "Radical Legal Thought," 209–221.
[179] Ibn Taymiyya, *Minhāj*, 4:530.
[180] Ibn Aʿtham al-Kūfī, *al-Futūḥ*, 5:21; al-Khuwārizmī, *Maqtal al-Ḥusayn*, 1:273.
[181] Ibn Taymiyya, *Minhāj*, 1:541–542, 4:553.

It is unlikely that either Ibn al-Zubayr or al-Ḥusayn could have remained peacefully in Medina once Yazīd became caliph. On one hand, both were steadfast in their refusal to offer oaths of allegiance to him. On the other hand, even if they became quietists, they were still his two most powerful rivals. The state had a clear interest in neutralizing the threat posed by al-Ḥusayn before he could establish himself in a location, amass sympathizers, and potentially launch an insurrection against the Umayyads. By failing to acknowledge the role that the state may have played in forcing al-Ḥusayn into flight and then into confrontation, Ibn Taymiyya falsely portrays al-Ḥusayn as having had a choice between virtuously staying in Medina, on the one hand, and following the "hankering in his soul" into a misguided rebellion, on the other.

Disparaging ʿAlid Imāms

As a Twelver Shīʿī, al-Ḥillī held that the Twelver imāms were infallible in their words and deeds. The purpose of God's appointment of infallible imāms, according to him, was to ensure the correct implementation of the sacred law, the preservation of all of the Prophet's teachings, and the community's continued protection from error. Al-Ḥillī argued that societies also need such imāms to serve as heads of state and to establish justice.[182] In his response to al-Ḥillī, Ibn Taymiyya acknowledges that the ʿAlid imāms were pious men but contends that most claims about their knowledge, particularly with regard to the imāms who succeeded Jaʿfar al-Ṣādiq, are exaggerated. Challenging the Shīʿī portrayal of the ʿAlid imāms as omniscient saints who were peerless in their knowledge of the religion, he claims that the imāms after al-Ṣādiq appear to have been men of little merit or knowledge.

Al-Ḥillī argued that the ʿAlid imāms saved the religion of Islam by teaching their followers correct theological and legal doctrines, while the members of other schools held false beliefs about God, prophets, the imāmate, and Islamic law.[183] Ibn Taymiyya considers this claim absurd using two modes of argumentation: First, he defends the legitimacy of the caliphs who succeeded the Prophet; then, second, the reputation of early Sunnī scholars. He points out that Islam was triumphant during the time of the first three caliphs, as shown by the conquests that took place during their reigns, whereas under ʿAlī community members fought each other in

[182] Al-Ḥillī, *Minhāj al-karāma*, 31, 113–114. [183] Ibid., *Minhāj al-karāma*, 36–66.

civil wars.[184] Ibn Taymiyya's implicit argument is that ʿAlī busied the community unnecessarily with his civil wars and did not allow its members to engage in conquests. Further, if ʿAlī (and al-Ḥasan) ruled the community but still failed to make Islam triumphant, how could one attribute such success to the subsequent Twelver imāms, who never became caliphs? For Ibn Taymiyya, true caliphs are those who wield real power and whom the people actually follow. They are not merely individuals who deserve to be followed because of some intrinsic quality. True leaders must establish justice, levy taxes, lead congregational worship, wage war, secure borders, and so on.[185] Against al-Ḥillī, he argues that the ʿAlid imāms cannot be said to have served Muslims as leaders when they did not fulfill any of these responsibilities. A key theme in Shīʿī narratives about the Twelver imāms is the machinations of caliphs who deprived them of their right to rule and assassinated them. Ibn Taymiyya turns this motif on its head by declaring that these ʿAlids could not have been the community's true leaders if they were indeed so powerless (*ʿājiz*), hindered (*mamnūʿ*), and helpless (*maghlūb*) their entire lives.[186]

As for the claim that the ʿAlid imāms were superior to their peers and taught the community correct doctrines to the exclusion of others, Ibn Taymiyya argues that the true leaders of the faith and experts in religious knowledge were the famous scholars who transmitted *ḥadīth*, offered legal opinions, and produced literature that the Sunnī community continues to rely on from generation to generation.[187] The contributions of these scholars drew the attention of other scholars, who judged them to be beneficial. By contrast, the ʿAlid imāms (especially after al-Ṣādiq) did not reach this stature and cannot be compared to the luminaries who were their contemporaries. Ibn Taymiyya makes his case by arguing, first, that none of the eponyms of the four Sunnī legal schools based their interpretation of Islamic law on the legal opinions of ʿAlī. Neither they nor any other imām of jurisprudence considered ʿAlī essential to understanding Islamic law.[188] Mālik and Medinese practice relied heavily on the legal opinions of ʿAbd Allāh b. ʿUmar; Ibn Masʿūd was a key figure for Abū Ḥanīfa's teachers in Kūfa; Aḥmad b. Ḥanbal and the *ahl al-ḥadīth* drew on the Companions collectively; and Meccan jurisprudence was based on the legal opinions of Ibn ʿAbbās, whom Ibn Taymiyya describes as an independent expert (*mujtahid*) and not, as the Shīʿīs portray him, someone

184 Ibn Taymiyya, *Minhāj*, 4:117, 513–514; Michot, "Ibn Taymiyya's Critique," 136–137.
185 Ibn Taymiyya, *Minhāj*, 4:112, 114; Michot, "Ibn Taymiyya's Critique," 133–134.
186 Ibn Taymiyya, *Minhāj*, 4:104–105; Michot, "Ibn Taymiyya's Critique," 126.
187 Ibn Taymiyya, *Minhāj*, 4:106–110, 7:529–530. 188 Ibid., 7:529–530.

who simply deferred to ʿAlī. Ibn Taymiyya claims that whereas Ibn ʿAbbās would refer to the legal opinions of various Companions and the precedents of Abū Bakr and ʿUmar, he never cited ʿAlī as an authority and, in fact, criticized ʿAlī on a number of matters.[189]

Second, rebutting al-Ḥillī's polemical claim that Sunnī jurisprudence is fundamentally indebted to the ʿAlid imāms,[190] Ibn Taymiyya retorts that jurists in the Sunnī tradition not only spurned ʿAlī as a legal authority but never relied on the Twelver imāms for knowledge either. Mālik, al-Shāfiʿī (d. 204/820), and Aḥmad b. Ḥanbal all turned to other experts because they found the ʿAlid imāms comparatively lacking in knowledge.[191] According to Ibn Taymiyya, after ʿAlī Zayn al-ʿĀbidīn, Muḥammad al-Bāqir (d. ca. 117/735), and Jaʿfar al-Ṣādiq, who were respected scholars, the ʿAlid imāms had little to no expertise in law or *ḥadīth*.[192] By contrast, the prominence of proto-Sunnī jurists can be attributed to the vast amounts of knowledge that they possessed, and this knowledge is the reason most Muslims prefer to follow the legal opinions of these jurists instead of the ʿAlid imāms. In particular, Ibn Taymiyya compares the merits and achievements of the Twelver imāms ʿAlī al-Hādī (d. 254/868) and al-Ḥasan al-ʿAskarī (d. 260/874) unfavorably to those of their Sunnī contemporaries.[193] In the eras of Mūsā al-Kāẓim (d. 183/799), ʿAlī al-Riḍā (d. 202/818), and Muḥammad al-Jawād (d. 220/835), most scholars and laymen also turned away from them to their contemporaries such as Mālik, al-Shāfiʿī and Aḥmad b. Ḥanbal, because they found such scholars more knowledgeable.[194] Even Hāshimids living in Medina regarded Mālik as more knowledgeable than Mūsā al-Kāẓim and thus would turn to the former for information about the Prophet and their religion.[195]

Ibn Taymiyya anticipates the Shīʿī response – namely, that the Twelver imāms might have used their discretion to conceal their knowledge from contemporaneous *ḥadīth* transmitters and scholars, sharing it only with their trusted disciples. He responds that even if this claim were true, their knowledge was of no benefit to the larger community, like concealed treasure that is never discovered.[196] However, Ibn Taymiyya is sure that the claim is false, because respected jurists and *ḥadīth* transmitters did in fact meet with al-Ṣādiq and his ancestors to obtain whatever knowledge that these ʿAlids possessed. After al-Ṣādiq, the fact that scholars

189 Ibid., 7:530. 190 Al-Ḥillī, *Minhāj al-karāma*, 162.
191 Ibn Taymiyya, *Minhāj*, 2:476, 4:108, 7:531–532. 192 Ibid., 2:470–473, 8:263.
193 Ibid., 2:470–473, 476, 3:402. 194 Ibid., 4:124–126, 5:164–165.
195 Ibid., 4:124; Michot, "Ibn Taymiyya's Critique," 143.
196 Ibn Taymiyya, *Minhāj*, 4:126; Michot, "Ibn Taymiyya's Critique," 145.

contemporaneous with his descendants mostly ignored them is evidence that the latter had nothing to add to al-Ṣādiq's teachings. Ibn Taymiyya refuses to consider the possibility that the ʿAlid imāms had disciples other than transmitters and scholars known to the Sunnī community.[197] He is obviously aware of Shīʿī *ḥadīth* collections, in which the imāms appear as teachers of a network of Shīʿī disciples, but he emphatically dismisses the trustworthiness of such literature.[198] Thus, rather than accept a history in which the Twelver imāms sat at the head of a crystallizing Imāmī community, Ibn Taymiyya opts to believe that the Twelver imāms (1) must have followed the doctrines and practices of the larger proto-Sunnī community, (2) deferred to the scholarship of proto-Sunnī jurists, (3) did not possess much knowledge in the case of al-Ṣādiq's successors, and, as a result, (4) failed to attract any disciples from the proto-Sunnī scholarly community.

Sunnī biographical dictionaries note the names of the disciples of the Twelver imāms and their predilection for Shīʿism. Many of them are identified as *rāfiḍa*, signifying their rejection of non-ʿAlid authorities. Ibn Taymiyya's determination to dissociate the ʿAlid imāms from Shīʿism and the *rāfiḍa* requires him to believe that Shīʿīs who attributed their doctrines (legal or theological) to the imāms were necessarily lying. However, an alternative explanation of their marginality in Sunnī literature is that the ʿAlids made claims to religious and political authority, attracted *rāfiḍa* as their disciples, and taught them doctrines preserved in Zaydī and Imāmī literature. Sectarian and political tensions between the ʿAlid imāms who made such claims, on the one hand, and caliphs who viewed them as subversive and proto-Sunnī scholars who considered their claims objectionable, on the other, would have led many Muslims to avoid associating with ʿAlids. Ibn Taymiyya chooses to ignore this possibility because it entails attributing heresy to the ʿAlid imāms and giving credence to Shīʿism's ʿAlid origins instead of the pre-Islamic and un-Islamic pedigree alleged by heresiographers.

Ibn Taymiyya did not consider himself an anthropomorphist or an anti-ʿAlid, nor would his admirers deem him guilty of either of these heresies. When one examines his statements, however, it becomes obvious why his detractors criticized him for relying on texts and arguments that appeared to support these two doctrines. Ibn Taymiyya, too, saw anthropomorphism and anti-ʿAlid sentiment as heresies, but his understanding of what positions qualified as anthropomorphist or anti-ʿAlid clearly differed from

[197] Ibn Taymiyya, *Minhāj*, 4:126–127; Michot, "Ibn Taymiyya's Critique," 145.
[198] Ibn Taymiyya, *Minhāj*, 1:8, 59, 2:467–468, 475–476, 4:127.

that of his critics. He was keenly aware that his own understanding of monotheism and history might be seen as heretical. In the case of anthropomorphism, he believed that his Ashʿarī rivals had mistakenly appropriated the assumptions and methodologies of innovators within the Islamic tradition, with the result that certain qurʾānic verses and *ḥadīth* now appeared anthropomorphic although they were not in fact so. His intransigence against his rivals in his numerous trials reflected his firm conviction that his beliefs correlated exactly with the religion that Muḥammad had preached. The same conviction inspired his near-complete rejection of pro-ʿAlid claims about ʿAlī and his progeny. He insisted that his critics were mistaken in accepting pro-ʿAlid *ḥadīth* of dubious authenticity and that, as a consequence, they were unintentionally supporting the heresy of Shīʿism. Even if his arguments appeared anti-ʿAlid to his critics, he was certain that he was, in fact, preserving the Prophet's true teachings about the Companions, Muʿāwiya, and ʿAlī with such arguments.

For Ibn Taymiyya, then, claims about ʿAlī's unique merits or criticism of the first three caliphs and ʿAlī's political rivals were all part of a matrix of falsehood associated with Shīʿism. Ibn Taymiyya's certainty in this belief empowered him to justify the actions of some anti-ʿAlid figures and to judge some of their claims to be well founded. By predicating his opinions about ʿAlī and his family on ʿUthmānī and Umayyad narratives about history, he effectively promoted the anti-ʿAlid doctrines that endured in these narratives. His ultimate objective was the refutation of Shīʿism, and in the service of this objective he had to erode the prestige that ʿAlī and his family had acquired through pro-ʿAlid literature that he believed to be fabricated. Ibn Taymiyya saw his refutation of such texts as a service to orthodoxy; however, his critics decried many of his arguments as anti-ʿAlid and heretical. Clearly, Ibn Taymiyya and his detractors were using different metrics.

6

The Rehabilitation of ʿAlī in Sunnī *Ḥadīth* and Historiography

The chapters above examined anti-ʿAlid sentiment in Sunnī, Muʿtazilī, and Ibāḍī literature. This final chapter considers the methods that *ḥadīth* specialists employed to reconcile expectations regarding ʿAlī's character and image in Sunnism with the vast number of disparate accounts about him. As a sect, Sunnism encompasses Muslims who differ considerably from one another doctrinally on the subject of ʿAlī and the *ahl al-bayt*. The previous chapter, for example, revealed the stark contrast between Ibn Taymiyya and his pro-ʿAlid interlocutors. Although Salafism in the late twentieth century has greatly enhanced Ibn Taymiyya's notoriety and prestige, both he and his interlocutors seem at times to reflect the boundaries of Sunnī Islam. Ibn Taymiyya's antipathy for Shīʿism leads him to reject reports exalting ʿAlī and Fāṭima that previous Sunnī scholars accepted as true. By contrast, other Sunnīs articulated their support for *tafḍīl ʿAlī* and granting the *ahl al-bayt* a unique status in the community.[1] But the most influential scholars of *ḥadīth* in Sunnī Islam tended to maintain a position somewhere in the middle. They were fonder of the *ahl al-bayt* than Ibn Taymiyya, but their love for ʿAlī did not mean support for *tafḍīl ʿAlī*.

Through the efforts of his admirers ʿAlī became a respected authority in both Sunnī and Shīʿī Islam within a few centuries of his death. However, his nearly universal portrayal as a pious authority obscures a centuries-long

[1] Al-Ghumārī, *ʿAlī ibn Abī Ṭālib Imām al-ʿārifīn*, 56; al-Ḥākim al-Ḥaskānī, *Shawāhid al-tanzīl*, 2:470–473; Ibn Abī 'l-Ḥadīd, *Sharḥ*, 1:7; al-Iskāfī, *al-Miʿyār*, 20–21, 63–78, 187, 206–254; al-Kanjī, *Kifāyat al-ṭālib*, 245, 246; al-Khuwārizmī, *al-Manāqib*, 106; al-Simnānī, *Manāẓir al-maḥāḍir*, 14–19.

process of contestation and rehabilitation.[2] The Umayyad state apparatus had facilitated the proliferation of ʿUthmānī and Umayyad portrayals of ʿAlī for close to a century. Nonetheless, after the fall of the Umayyads, ʿAlī's subsequent transformation from heretic to saint was neither immediate nor complete.

Beginning in the ninth century, the compilers of Sunni *ḥadīth* literature faced a great challenge in sifting through conflicting narratives regarding the legacy of ʿAlī. On the one hand, ʿUthmānī and pro-Umayyad scholars transmitted accounts that usually portrayed him as irreligious and immoral. On the other hand, transmitters, some described as Shīʿī and some not, narrated *ḥadīth* about his merits (*khaṣāʾiṣ*, *faḍāʾil*, *manāqib*) and the aid he provided to the Prophet as a pious member of the Muslim community. Over the centuries, Muslims transmitted such literature so widely that the popularity of the cult of ʿAlī and his admiration among poets, mystics, and soldiers transcended sectarian boundaries.[3]

Sunnīs with competing theological commitments, whether to pro-ʿAlid sentiment or anti-Shīʿī polemics, clearly dealt with the early source material differently. Pro-ʿAlids consistently accepted and transmitted *ḥadīth* that exalted ʿAlī, whereas early ʿUthmānīs and pro-Umayyads viewed him and his followers as a scourge of the community and as the source of sedition. These anti-ʿAlids transmitted *ḥadīth* that extolled the merits of ʿAlī's rivals. The narratives of the Kūfan storyteller Sayf b. ʿUmar reflect a slightly more moderate ʿUthmānī sentiment compared to that which was popular under the Umayyads. In Sayf's stories, ʿAlī is surrounded by criminals, and it is these criminal associates, not ʿAlī himself, who cause civil unrest and misguidance in the community. Sayf does not seem to recognize ʿAlī as a rightly guided caliph, instead portraying him as only one contender among many in a time of social turmoil.[4] The literary contributions of Sayf and other more temperate ʿUthmānīs nonetheless represent an important shift in the legacy of ʿUthmānī sentiment, since in their reports ʿAlī no longer appears as the arch-heretic but rather is depicted as a Companion who found himself in the company of heretics who venerated him, and fell victim to their machinations on numerous occasions. Both early Shīʿī and ʿUthmānī accounts portray ʿAlī as someone

[2] For key studies on historiography regarding ʿAlī, see *Encyclopaedia Islamica*, s.v. "ʿAlī b. Abī Ṭālib" (F. Manouchehri, M. Melvin-Koushki, R. Shah-Kazemi, et al.); Madelung, *Succession*; Petersen, *ʿAlī and Muʿāwiya*.

[3] Daftary, *Ismailis in Medieval Muslim Societies*, 183–203; Nasr, "Shiʿism and Sufism"; Rahim, "Perfection Manifested"; Yildirim, "Shīʿitisation of the Futuwwa Tradition."

[4] Anthony, *The Caliph and the Heretic*, 82–135; Crone, "Review: Kitāb al-ridda."

who disagreed with his predecessors and rivals on a number of issues.[5] The more moderate ʿUthmānīs, by contrast, circulated counter-reports in which ʿAlī appeared as a loyal partisan of the first three caliphs.[6] The ʿUthmānīs of the ninth century may have appropriated this image of ʿAlī from quietists, centrists, and ʿAlī's partisans who revered him and the first two caliphs together. Some, such as Abū 'l-Qāsim al-Saqaṭī (d. 406/1015), went further by claiming that ʿAlī and his family members in fact loved Muʿāwiya. In one report transmitted by al-Saqaṭī, al-Ḥusayn b. ʿAlī ascribes to Muʿāwiya the honorifics "scribe of the Qurʾān" and "uncle of the believers" (*khāl al-muʾminīn*) and asserts that the angel Gabriel had declared Muʿāwiya to be so pious that no true devotee of the Prophet's family could ever speak ill of him.[7]

Erling Petersen previously examined historiography regarding ʿAlī by comparing the interests and methods of ʿAbbāsid-era story-tellers, such as Sayf b. ʿUmar, who composed historical chronicles.[8] This chapter considers the work of influential scholars in the genre of *ḥadīth* to complement Petersen's work. In terms of prestige, the most venerated work of *ḥadīth* in Sunnī Islam would be *al-Jāmiʿ al-musnad al-ṣaḥīḥ* (The Collection of Authentic Transmissions) of al-Bukhārī.[9] Al-Bukhārī's *Ṣaḥīḥ* not only provides readers with the doctrines of its compiler, but also the views of an emerging group of *ḥadīth* scholars actively engaged in the formation and maintenance of orthodoxy. While al-Bukhārī is more circumspect in transmitting controversial material regarding ʿAlī, I occasionally contrast him with one of the most celebrated *ḥadīth* scholars of Baghdad, Aḥmad b. Ḥanbal. Aḥmad b. Ḥanbal consistently transmits material that provides the audience with greater context and additional commentary from transmitters. Although these two scholars and their students dedicated their

[5] On the matter of the caliphate, for example, ʿAlī voiced his dissatisfaction regarding the election of his predecessors according to a number of sources: see al-Ḥammūʾī, *Farāʾid al-Simṭayn*, 2:319–320; al-Kanjī, *Kifāyat al-ṭālib*, 386; al-Khuwārizmī, *al-Manāqib*, 313; al-Simnānī, *Manāẓir al-maḥāḍir*, 14–19. For reports in canonical collections that state that ʿAlī withheld his oath of fealty to Abū Bakr for six months, see al-Bukhārī, *Ṣaḥīḥ*, 5:82; Muslim, *Ṣaḥīh*, 5:153.

[6] For reports in which ʿAlī eagerly supports the candidacy of his predecessors and states his belief in their superiority to him, see al-Bayhaqī, *al-Sunan al-kubrā*, 8:143; al-Bukhārī, *Ṣaḥīḥ*, 4:195; al-Ḥākim al-Naysābūrī, *al-Mustadrak*, 3:76; Ibn Abī ʿĀṣim, *Kitāb al-sunna*, 555–561; Ibn Ḥajar al-Haytamī, *al-Ṣawāʿiq al-muḥriqa*, 60–65; Ibn Taymiyya, *Majmūʿ fatāwā*, 7:511–512; al-Samhūdī, *Jawāhir al-ʿaqdayn*, 248–250, 451–460; al-Ṭabarī, *Tārīkh*, 2:447.

[7] Ibn ʿAsākir, *Taʾrīkh*, 14:113–114.

[8] Petersen, *ʿAlī and Muʿāwiya*.

[9] On the canonization of the work, see Brown, *Canonization*.

lives to the collection and transmission of prophetic *ḥadīth*, the agency and predilections of each author becomes apparent in a comparative study.

Unlike their Muʿtazilī, Shīʿī, and Khārijī interlocutors, these proto-Sunnī scholars of *ḥadīth* were hopeful that all of the Prophet's Companions could be recognized as righteous figures in the literature they produced.[10] To achieve this objective, Aḥmad b. Ḥanbal transmitted many reports about the merits of the Companions embroiled in the early conflicts from their partisans.[11] ʿUthmānī, pro-Umayyad, and pro-ʿAlid *ḥadīth* all appear in Aḥmad b. Ḥanbal's *Musnad*. Although each of these factions contributes *ḥadīth* to al-Bukhārī's *Ṣaḥīḥ*, al-Bukhārī generally refrains from transmitting *ḥadīth* about ʿAlī's merits and the history of his caliphate. As I noted in Chapter 1, al-Bukhārī explains his position by citing the opinion of Ibn Sīrīn, who considered most reports about ʿAlī to be fabricated.[12] By contrast, Aḥmad b. Ḥanbal preserves and transmits hundreds of *ḥadīth* in praise of ʿAlī.[13]

Despite their differences in terms of methodology and receptiveness to pro-ʿAlid reports, the two scholars shared a concern for articulating orthodoxy through *ḥadīth* and their assessments of *ḥadīth* transmitters. Consequently, they sought to (1) condemn and suppress the legacy of anti-ʿAlid sentiment (*naṣb*), (2) discredit *ḥadīth* that undermined the superiority of Abū Bakr and ʿUmar (or explicitly upheld *tafḍīl ʿAlī*), and (3) appropriate ʿAlī as an innocuous member of the early community. The third objective resulted in these authors' acceptance of *ḥadīth* that depicted ʿAlī making mistakes and upsetting the Prophet or other Companions. In one case, ʿAlī refuses the Prophet's invitation to join him in worship,[14] and in another he leads a congregation in prayer while intoxicated.[15]

The compilers of Sunnī *ḥadīth* literature faced great challenges in sifting through the plethora of conflicting narratives about ʿAlī and reconciling them with their own vision of early Islamic history and what constituted orthodoxy. It appears that these scholars made use of their editorial privilege by transmitting selected versions of reports and omitting controversial material. Although the scholars sought to portray this process of

[10] For a comparative study of Muslim doctrines on the righteousness of Companions, see Lucas, *Constructive Critics*, 221–285.

[11] Ibid., 285. [12] Al-Bukhārī, *Ṣaḥīḥ*, 4:207–209.

[13] Aḥmad b. Ḥanbal, *Faḍāʾil Amīr al-Muʾminīn*.

[14] Aḥmad b. Ḥanbal, *al-Musnad*, 1:77, 91, 112; al-Bukhārī, *Ṣaḥīḥ*, 2:43, 8:155, 190; Muslim, *Ṣaḥīḥ*, 2:187.

[15] Abū Dāwūd al-Sijistānī, *Sunan*, 2:182; al-Bayhaqī, *al-Sunan al-kubrā*, 1:389.

selection as an objective one by relying solely on narrators who were trustworthy and avoiding those who were not, the reality was much more complex. *Ḥadīth* scholars clearly judged reports by their contents even when they cited problems in the chain of transmission as the principal reason for any negative assessment.[16] When confronting anti-ʿAlid *ḥadīth*, they responded in one of at least seven different ways.

REJECTION

In a number of cases, *ḥadīth* scholars rejected an anti-ʿAlid report outright, declaring it a fabrication. For example, claims that ʿAlī tried to physically injure or kill the Prophet or that the Prophet referred to him as the Korah (Qārūn) rather than the Aaron (Hārūn) of the community were systematically excluded from the canonical *ḥadīth* collections.[17] The transmitter of these claims, Ḥarīz b. ʿUthmān, was nevertheless considered trustworthy, so other reports that he transmitted appear in the collections of Aḥmad b. Ḥanbal, al-Bukhārī, and many others.[18] The prevalence of anti-ʿAlids in the chains of transmission in Sunnī *ḥadīth* literature is unknown, since biographers usually do not specify a transmitter's views on ʿAlī when the transmitter was pro-Umayyad or ʿUthmānī. Geographically, contempt for ʿAlī seems to have been ubiquitous among *ḥadīth* transmitters active in the pro-Umayyad Levant and ʿUthmānī Baṣra.[19] Scholars from these regions generally believed that there was no caliph during the tumultuous years in which ʿAlī ruled. It was Muʿāwiya who eventually followed ʿUthmān as the fourth caliph of the community.[20]

DEFLECTION

Scholars deflected accusations that ʿAlī committed serious crimes by acknowledging his culpability for minor sins, including that of keeping bad company. For example, the Marwānids accused ʿAlī of leading the

[16] Brown, "How we Know Early Hadīth Critics did Matn Criticism"; Brown, "The Rules of Matn Criticism."
[17] Al-Dhahabī, *Taʾrīkh*, 10:122; Ibn ʿAsākir, *Taʾrīkh*, 12:349.
[18] For example, see Abū Dāwūd al-Sijistānī, *Sunan*, 2:392; Aḥmad b. Ḥanbal, *al-Musnad*, 4:99, 105, 106; al-Bukhārī, *Ṣaḥīḥ*, 4:164; Ibn Māja, *Sunan*, 1:151; al-Tirmidhī, *Sunan*, 4:10.
[19] Al-Dhahabī, *Siyar*, 3:128, 15:476, 18:617; al-Ḥimyarī, *al-Ḥūr al-ʿayn*, 229–230; Ibn Taymiyya, *Majmūʿ fatāwā*, 3:408; al-Iskāfī, *al-Miʿyār*, 32.
[20] Ibn Taymiyya, *Minhāj*, 4:400–401.

hypocrites (*munāfiqūn*) in the slander of ʿĀʾisha in the *Ifk* incident. In the narratives found in the canonical collections (reported on the authority of al-Zuhrī), ʿAlī appears as an antagonist who does not assume ʿĀʾisha's innocence and encourages the Prophet to divorce her. However, he is not depicted as one of her slanderers.[21] When a Marwānid asked al-Zuhrī whether ʿAlī was a slanderer, he reportedly answered, "No . . . but ʿĀʾisha said, 'He behaved badly in my affair (*kāna musīʾan fī amrī*).'"[22]

While the Umayyads claimed that ʿAlī bore direct blame for the assassination of ʿUthmān,[23] Sunnī scholars tended to shift responsibility to ʿAlī's close associates.[24] Some Sunnīs portrayed ʿAlī as unwilling to surrender ʿUthmān's murderers because he was in need of their military and political support.[25]

Likewise, the heretical belief in ʿAlī's superiority to his predecessors was deflected away from ʿAlī to Ibn Sabaʾ, the legendary heretic in his army. According to this narrative, Ibn Sabaʾ was the real source of *tafḍīl ʿAlī*; ʿAlī himself strongly condemned this doctrine and punished Ibn Sabaʾ for holding it.[26] Ibn Sabaʾ came to serve as a figure to whom Sunnīs could attribute all crimes and heresies related to the memory of ʿAlī and the first civil war.[27] Ibn Sabaʾ was responsible not only for the death of ʿUthmān but also for the battle of the Camel and the birth of Shīʿism. Abbas Barzegar explains the significance of such historiography: "Through reliance on stories such as the infiltration of the community by the subversive Jew ʿAbd Allāh b. Sabaʾ, the responsibility for the events of the *fitna* in Sunni historical traditions are externalized, placed outside the space of the 'community.'"[28]

[21] Al-Bukhārī, *Ṣaḥīḥ*, 3:155, 5:58, 6:7, 8:163; Muslim, *Ṣaḥīḥ*, 8:115. See also Spellberg, *Politics, Gender, and the Islamic Past*, 69–70.

[22] ʿAbd al-Razzāq al-Ṣanʿānī, *Tafsīr al-Qurʾān*, 3:52; al-Bayhaqī, *Dalāʾil al-nubuwwa*, 4:73; al-Dhahabī, *Siyar*, 2:160; Ibn Shabba, *Taʾrīkh al-Madīna*, 1:337; al-Suyūṭī, *al-Durr al-manthūr*, 5:32.

[23] Al-Bayhaqī, *al-Sunan al-kubrā*, 8:189; Ibn ʿAbd Rabbih, *al-ʿIqd*, 5:81; Ibn Ḥajar al-ʿAsqalānī, *Tahdhīb al-Tahdhīb*, 8:411; Ibn Kathīr, *al-Bidāya wa ʾl-nihāya*, 7:288; Sibṭ Ibn al-Jawzī, *Tadhkirat al-khawāṣṣ*, 82; al-Ṭabarī, *Tārīkh*, 4:4, 30. See also Madelung, *Succession*, 156 (for Marwān b. al-Ḥakam's accusations), 189–190, 198–199 (for al-Walīd b. ʿUqba's poetry), 200–201, 205, 211 (for Muʿāwiya making such a claim).

[24] See al-Bukhārī, *al-Tārīkh al-ṣaghīr*, 1:104, 121; al-Dīnawarī, *al-Akhbār al-ṭiwāl*, 149; Ibn Shabba, *Taʾrīkh al-Madīna*, 4:1250. See also Madelung, *Succession*, 156; Yazigi, "Defense and Validation," 62–64.

[25] Al-ʿAynī, *ʿUmdat al-qārī*, 15:51; al-Dīnawarī, *al-Akhbār al-ṭiwāl*, 162, 170–171; Ibn ʿAbd Rabbih, *al-ʿIqd*, 5:83; Ibn Ḥajar al-ʿAsqalānī, *Fatḥ al-bārī*, 6:454, 13:448; Ibn Kathīr, *al-Bidāya wa ʾl-nihāya*, 7:288.

[26] Ibn Ḥajar al-ʿAsqalānī, *Lisān al-Mīzān*, 3:290.

[27] For a comprehensive study, see Anthony, *The Caliph and the Heretic*.

[28] Barzegar, "Remembering Community," 148.

Instead of accepting narratives in which Companions were responsible for discord and bloodshed, Sunnī heresiography and historiography mostly opted for a conspiracy theory that identified an outsider, a legendary black, Jewish scapegoat, as the cause for everything that went wrong in the community.

RECASTING: THE CURIOUS CASE OF "ABŪ TURĀB"

In at least one case, *ḥadīth* transmitters attempted to recast a derisive epithet that the Umayyads frequently used to refer to ʿAlī into an honorific nickname and a sign of distinction. ʿAlī possessed the unique distinction of having fathered the Prophet's descendants and was thus entitled to use the teknonym Abū 'l-Ḥasan in honor of al-Ḥasan, his eldest son, whose mother was Fāṭima, the Prophet's daughter. However, it was not in the interests of the Umayyads to remind their audiences of ʿAlī's close relationship to the Prophet every time they publicly disparaged or ritually cursed him. Consequently, according to abundant literary evidence in the Sunnī tradition, the Umayyads opted to refer to him as Abū Turāb, "the father of dust."[29] In letters between ʿUmar II (d. 101/720) and the Byzantine emperor Leo III (r. 717–741), preserved in Arabic as well as (non-Muslim) Armenian, Aljamiado, and Latin sources, Leo only knows ʿAlī by this epithet.[30] The Byzantine assumption that Abū Turāb was the name of ʿAlī was the result of a practice among leading Umayyads: Muʿāwiya,[31] Marwān b. al-Ḥakam,[32] al-Ḥajjāj b. Yūsuf,[33] and many other Umayyads reportedly called ʿAlī by this epithet. All of these anti-ʿAlid figures clearly used the epithet sarcastically. By the ninth century, however, Sunnī *ḥadīth* literature had firmly established a pious narrative in which the Prophet gave ʿAlī the nickname Abū Turāb. Some believed that ʿAlī received the name in the course of a battle,[34] whereas others said

29 Kohlberg, "Abū Turāb."

30 Hoyland, *Seeing Islam as Others Saw it*, 500–501; Jeffery, "Ghevond's Text," 292, 298.

31 Al-Dhahabī, *Taʾrīkh*, 3:627; al-Ḥākim al-Naysābūrī, *al-Mustadrak*, 3:108; Ibn Abī 'l-Ḥadīd, *Sharḥ*, 4:56–57; Ibn ʿAsākir, *Taʾrīkh*, 42:111; Muslim, *Ṣaḥīḥ*, 7:120; al-Nasāʾī, *Khaṣāʾiṣ*, 81.

32 Al-Bayhaqī, *al-Sunan al-kubrā*, 2:446; al-Ḥākim al-Naysābūrī, *Maʿrifat ʿulūm al-ḥadīth*, 211; Ibn ʿAsākir, *Taʾrīkh*, 42:17; Muslim, *Ṣaḥīḥ*, 7:123–124.

33 Al-Balādhurī, *Ansāb al-ashrāf*, 7:295, 13:365; al-Ḥākim al-Ḥaskānī, *Shawāhid al-tanzīl*, 1:121–122; Ibn Abī Ḥātim al-Rāzī, *Tafsīr*, 1:251; al-Jāḥiẓ, *al-Bayān wa 'l-tabyīn*, 200.

34 For example, see Aḥmad b. Ḥanbal, *al-Musnad*, 4:263; al-Ḥākim al-Naysābūrī, *al-Mustadrak*, 3:141; Ibn Maghāzilī, *Manāqib*, 27; al-Nasāʾī, *al-Sunan al-kubrā*, 5:153.

that he obtained it after a disagreement with his wife.[35] According to the reports that mention the marital dispute, ʿAlī himself considered Abū Turāb his most cherished nickname. Shīʿīs followed their Sunnī coreligionists in circulating many *ḥadīth* that recast Abū Turāb in positive terms.[36] The apparent agreement between the Sunnī and Shīʿī traditions leaves little room for challenging the shared narrative regarding the origins of the epithet. However, there is reason to believe that it was neither honorific nor commonly used by those who knew or venerated ʿAlī.

Linguistic Evidence

According to some lexicographers, variations of an invocation based on the verb *ta-ri-ba* were used in classical Arabic to damn someone. Examples include *taribat yadāk* (may your hands be soiled), *taribat yamīnuk* (may your right hand be soiled), and *taribat jabīnuk* (may your forehead be soiled).[37] The invocation *taribat yadāh* was understood to mean *lā aṣāba khayran*, "May he not find any bounty!"[38] Scholars also argued that like other curses, these invocations were used to express condemnation of someone, usually in response to words or deeds that the invoker considered objectionable, but they did not entail a wish for a literal outcome.[39] The phrases' literal meaning – "Your hands have become soiled" or "Your forehead has become soiled" – conveys the figurative message "You have become impoverished," "Your mind has become impoverished (and in need of knowledge)," or "You have lost everything (and become impoverished)."[40]

Evidence from Ḥadīth

As some lexicographers noted, *taribat yadāk* and its variants were commonly used in classical Arabic, and even appear in *ḥadīth*. Sometimes the Prophet is depicted chiding a Companion for saying something wrong or

[35] Al-Bukhārī, *Ṣaḥīḥ*, 1:114, 4:208, 7:119, 140; Ibn Maghāzilī, *Manāqib*, 28–29; Muslim, *Ṣaḥīḥ*, 7:124.
[36] Ibn Bābawayh, *ʿIlal al-sharāʾiʿ*, 1:155–157; Ibn Shahrāshūb, *Manāqib*, 2:305–306.
[37] Al-ʿAynī, *ʿUmdat al-qārī*, 2:211–212; Ibn Manẓūr, *Lisān al-ʿArab*, 1:229; al-Suyūṭī, *Tanwīr al-ḥawālik*, 1:71–72; al-Zabīdī, *Tāj al-ʿarūs*, 1:322.
[38] Al-Fīrūzābādī, *al-Qāmūs al-muḥīṭ*, 1:39; Ibn Manẓūr, *Lisān al-ʿArab*, 1:228; al-Zabīdī, *Tāj al-ʿarūs*, 1:231–232.
[39] Al-ʿAynī, *ʿUmdat al-qārī*, 3:237; al-Fīrūzābādī, *al-Qāmūs al-muḥīṭ*, 1:39.
[40] Al-Nawawī, *Sharḥ Ṣaḥīḥ Muslim*, 3:221; al-Suyūṭī, *Tanwīr al-ḥawālik*, 1:71–72.

rude.[41] On another occasion, he gives advice and concludes with a cautionary *taribat yadāk*.[42] The commentators understood the Prophet's use of the phrase to mean that ignoring his advice would lead to disastrous consequences.[43] Finally, when the Prophet reportedly said to someone, "Your forehead has become soiled," the phrase was interpreted to convey his desire that the addressee repent for his error with abundant prayers and prostration on the ground.[44]

Evidence from the Qur'ān and Its Exegesis

The Qur'ān refers to *turāb* (earth, soil, dust) as the fundamental origin of humankind in a number of verses.[45] The most relevant verse to this discussion is Q90:16, *aw miskīnan dhā matraba*, "Or a poor person in dire need." Exegetes understood *dhū matraba* literally as being covered in dust but also figuratively as being in abject poverty and in dire need of assistance.[46] Al-Ṭabarī provides a long discussion about the various possible interpretations of the phrase.[47] The term might refer to a person who has too many children and lives in poverty with them,[48] or to a homeless person who sleeps outside subjected to the elements and "possesses nothing but the dust that adheres to him."[49]

The Reception of the Epithet among ʿAlī's Disciples

A few reports indicate that those who personally knew ʿAlī, considered themselves his partisans, or lived in Iraq and respected his legacy refrained from using the name Abū Turāb to refer to him. In a number of cases, the Umayyads are depicted as calling ʿAlī by this name, to the confusion of his associates. In these cases, when the non-Umayyad interlocutor realizes that the Umayyads are referring to ʿAlī, he frequently interprets the epithet as

41 Abū Dāwūd al-Sijistānī, *Sunan*, 1:60; al-Bukhārī, *Ṣaḥīḥ*, 6:27, 7:110; Aḥmad b. Ḥanbal, *al-Musnad*, 6:33, 92, 201, 306, 309, 377; Ibn Māja, *Sunan*, 1:197; Muslim, *Ṣaḥīḥ*, 1:171–173, 4:163–164, 8:189.

42 Abū Dāwūd al-Sijistānī, *Sunan*, 1:454; Aḥmad b. Ḥanbal, *al-Musnad*, 2:428, 3:158, 302; al-Bukhārī, *Ṣaḥīḥ*, 6:123; Ibn Māja, *Sunan*, 1:597; Muslim, *Ṣaḥīḥ*, 4:175; al-Tirmidhī, *Sunan*, 2:275.

43 Al-Nawawī, *al-Majmūʿ*, 16:136.

44 Aḥmad b. Ḥanbal, *al-Musnad*, 3:144; Ibn Manẓūr, *Lisān al-ʿArab*, 1:229; al-Zabīdī, *Tāj al-ʿarūs*, 1:322.

45 For example, see Q18:37, 22:5, 30:20, 35:11, 40:67.

46 Al-Suyūṭī, *al-Itqān*, 1:373; al-Ṭabarī, *Tafsīr*, 30:258.

47 Al-Ṭabarī, *Tafsīr*, 30:256–259.

48 Ibid., 30:258–259.

49 Ibid., 30:257–258.

demeaning to ʿAlī. For example, in reports about the execution of ʿAlī's companion Ṣayfī b. Faṣīl (d. 51/671) one finds the following exchange involving Ṣayfī and the Umayyad governor of Kūfa, Ziyād b. Abīh:

Ziyād b. Abīh said, "O enemy of God! What is your opinion of Abū Turāb?"
"I do not know an Abū Turāb."
"Are you [really] unacquainted with him?"
"I do not know him."
"Do you not know ʿAlī b. Abī Ṭālib?"
"Of course I do."
"That man was Abū Turāb."
"No, that man was Abū al-Ḥasan and al-Ḥusayn."
Ziyād's police chief interjected, "The governor tells you that he is Abū Turāb and you [have the audacity to] say no?"
"When the governor says a lie, do you wish for me to lie and testify to falsehood as he has done?"
Ziyād answered, "This [insolence] shall be added to your original offense."[50]

Another report (previously referenced in Chapter 2) links the epithet to the Umayyad practice of cursing ʿAlī. In it, a man comes to Sahl b. Saʿd and informs him that the governor of Medina is disparaging ʿAlī from the pulpit and referring to him as Abū Turāb. In yet another report, a Kufan is brought before the Umayyad prince Muḥammad b. Hishām, who asks him whether or not he is a follower of Abū Turāb. The man responds, "Who is Abū Turāb?" The prince says, "ʿAlī b. Abī Ṭālib." The man responds, "Do you mean the cousin of God's messenger and the husband of his daughter Fāṭima? The father of al-Ḥasan and al-Ḥusayn?"[51] Likewise, when al-Ḥajjāj requested that al-Ḥasan al-Baṣrī share his opinion of Abū Turāb, al-Ḥasan asked for clarification: "Do you mean ʿAlī?"[52] All of these anecdotes suggest that Abū Turāb was an Umayyad epithet that Muslims who venerated ʿAlī never used. It is true that, according to both Sunnī and Shīʿī *ḥadīth*, the Prophet gave ʿAlī the nickname Abū Turāb. In Sunnī *ḥadīth*, the Prophet called him by this name jokingly upon finding him sleeping on the ground and covered in dust. However, the Umayyads applied the epithet disparagingly throughout their reign and even referred to the followers of ʿAlī as *turābīs*.[53] It is unclear why the Umayyads chose this particular

[50] Al-Balādhurī, *Ansāb al-ashrāf*, 5:251–252; Ibn ʿAsākir, *Taʾrīkh*, 24:259–260; Ibn al-Athīr, *al-Kāmil*, 3:477; al-Ṭabarī, *Tārīkh*, 4:198.
[51] Ibn ʿAbd Rabbih, *al-ʿIqd*, 5:348.
[52] Al-Balādhurī, *Ansāb al-ashrāf*, 2:147; al-Ḥākim al-Ḥaskānī, *Shawāhid al-tanzīl*, 1:122.
[53] Ibn Aʿtham al-Kūfī, *al-Futūḥ*, 5:143.

nickname. Perhaps they were aware of the version of the name's origin story that describes ʿAlī and Fāṭima experiencing marital strife and used the name to highlight alleged unhappiness in their marriage. The story could also be read to show the Prophet as giving ʿAlī the name Abū Turāb in dismay. In this case, the story would fall under a genre of anti-ʿAlid *ḥadīth* that were used to portray ʿAlī as a bad husband to Fāṭima. Another example of this genre is the famous report, narrated by al-Bukhārī and others, in which the Prophet allegedly censures ʿAlī for upsetting him and Fāṭima by considering the daughter of Abū Jahl as a second wife.[54] According to some accounts, the Prophet goes on to praise the fidelity of another son-in-law, Abū ʾl-ʿĀṣ b. al-Rabīʿ, who shared close kinship ties with the Umayyads.[55] In contrast to ʿAlī, this cousin of the Umayyads is described as a devoted husband. Thus, the topos of ʿAlī as a bad son-in-law that appears elsewhere in the *ḥadīth* literature may have something to do with the Umayyad use of Abū Turāb.

If Abū Turāb is tied to the phrases *taribat yadāh* or *dhā matraba*, then the Umayyads used the epithet to deride ʿAlī's appearance and to imply that he looked dirty and homeless. Whereas the Umayyads possessed great wealth and distributed it to their partisans, the figure of Abū Turāb was one of a pretender to the caliphate who commanded no such wealth. Pro-ʿAlid texts interpreted ʿAlī's modest means as a consequence of his principled refusal to use public funds to enrich himself or the aristocracy of his society,[56] but the Umayyads may have cast his poverty as a sign of failure or weakness. The epithet may have referred to the fact that ʿAlī had many children but remained poor, or it may have alluded to the wrathful invocation *taribat yadāh* as appropriate for someone who, in the Umayyads' view, had caused great misfortune with his many errors. Therefore, it is possible that the epithet Abū Turāb began as an anti-ʿAlid aspersion on ʿAlī but was subsequently recast and accepted as a merit.

ERASURE

Scholars of *ḥadīth* occasionally felt compelled to delete components of a report that were offensive to their sensibilities. In particular, *ḥadīth*

[54] See Chapter 1 Appendix, n. 46.

[55] Aḥmad b. Ḥanbal, *al-Musnad*, 4:326; al-Bukhārī, *Ṣaḥīḥ*, 4:212; Ibn Māja, *Sunan*, 1:644; Muslim, *Ṣaḥīḥ*, 7:142.

[56] Ibn Abī ʾl-Ḥadīd, *Sharḥ*, 7:37–40; Muḥammad b. Ṭalḥa al-Naṣībī, *Maṭālib al-saʾūl*, 178–188.

explicitly denigrating ʿAlī could not continue to circulate intact after the Umayyad period, since the ʿUthmāniyya gradually came to accept him as the fourth caliph. This development rendered problematic *ḥadīth* such as that transmitted by Abū Bakr b. al-ʿArabī and Ibn Abī ʾl-Ḥadīd on the authority of al-Bukhārī, in which the Prophet declares, "The family of Abū Ṭālib are no allies (*awliyāʾ*) of mine."[57] By the Mamluk period, extant copies of al-Bukhārī's *Ṣaḥīḥ* no longer identified the family of Abū Ṭālib as the rejected clan mentioned in the *ḥadīth*.[58] Nonetheless, Ibn Ḥajar al-ʿAsqalānī, in his assessment of the report, conceded that it had indeed originally named Abū Ṭālib's family: he had found a variant in Abū Nuʿaym al-Iṣbahānī's (d. 430/1038) *Mustakhraj* of al-Bukhārī's text that did not omit the family's name.[59] I examine this report's transmission in a few *ḥadīth* collections and their commentaries:

Aḥmad b. Ḥanbal, al-Bukhārī, and Muslim all narrate from Muḥammad b. Jaʿfar Ghundar (active in Baṣra, d. 193/809), who narrates from Shuʿba (Kūfa and Baṣra, d. 160/777), who narrates from Ismāʿīl b. Abī Khālid (Kūfa, d. 146/763), who narrates from Qays b. Abī Ḥāzim al-Aḥmasī (Kūfa, d. ca. 98/717), who narrates from ʿAmr b. al-ʿĀṣ that the Prophet announced openly, not privately, "The family of Abū *so-and-so* are no allies of mine. Rather, God and the righteous among the faithful are my allies."[60]

Al-Bukhārī's direct informant ʿAmr b. ʿAbbās (active in Baṣra, d. 235/849) notes that "there is a blank space (*bayāḍ*) in the book of Muḥammad b. Jaʿfar [Ghundar]."[61]

Al-Bukhārī adds, on the authority of the Umayyad ʿAnbasa b. ʿAbd al-Wāḥid (active in Kūfa, fl. early third/ninth century), who narrates from Bayān b. Bishr al-Aḥmasī (Kūfa, fl. second/eighth century), who narrates from Qays b. Abī Ḥāzim al-Aḥmasī, who narrates from ʿAmr that the Prophet continued, "but they have kinship ties that I will honor."[62]

Ibn Ḥajar transmits a report from al-Bukhārī as "The descendants of Abū _____ are no allies of mine."[63]

Al-Bukhārī's first report of this statement, transmitted by ʿAmr b. ʿAbbās, seems to have circulated in anti-ʿAlid Baṣra from at least the middle of the second/eighth century. Al-Bukhārī's second report comes from an Umayyad informant who narrates the *ḥadīth* on the authority of two transmitters belonging to the Aḥmasī clan in Kūfa. The chain of

[57] Ibn Abī ʾl-Ḥadīd, *Sharḥ*, 4:64; Ibn al-ʿArabī, *Aḥkām al-Qurʾān*, 3:461.
[58] Ibn Ḥajar al-ʿAsqalānī, *Fatḥ al-bārī*, 10:350–354; al-ʿAynī, *ʿUmdat al-qārī*, 22:94.
[59] Ibn Ḥajar al-ʿAsqalānī, *Fatḥ al-bārī*, 10:352. Al-Iṣbahānī's work is no longer extant.
[60] Aḥmad b. Ḥanbal, *al-Musnad*, 4:203; al-Bukhārī, *Ṣaḥīḥ*, 7:73; Muslim, *Ṣaḥīḥ*, 1:136.
[61] Al-Bukhārī, *Ṣaḥīḥ*, 7:73. [62] Ibid. [63] Ibn Ḥajar al-ʿAsqalānī, *Taghlīq al-taʿlīq*, 5:87.

transmission seems incomplete since only one person in it, Bayān, was active in the second/eighth century. Ibn Ḥajar and Badr al-Dīn al-ʿAynī (d. 855/1451) note in their respective commentaries on the Baṣran text that some copyists mistook a note about the deletion or blank space (*bayāḍ*) in the manuscript to stand for the name of a tribe, incorrectly reading the text to refer to the family of an "Abū Bayāḍ."[64]

Al-Bukhārī's *ḥadīth* appeared in three different forms, reflecting the varying sensibilities of its narrators. First, the earliest narrators transmitted the report in its complete form, explicitly naming the family of Abū Ṭālib (Text A). Sunnī *ḥadīth* scholars pointed to Qays b. Abī Ḥāzim and the Umayyad ʿAnbasa b. ʿAbd al-Wāḥid, both part of the report's chain of transmission, as anti-ʿAlids who might have fabricated the report.[65] Pro-ʿAlids, meanwhile, identified ʿAmr b. al-ʿĀṣ, a close confidant of Muʿāwiya, as the culprit.[66] ʿAmr is depicted as instrumental to Muʿāwiya's political victories, first as a rebel against ʿAlī and al-Ḥasan b. ʿAlī and finally as an Umayyad governor. ʿAlī reportedly denounced ʿAmr as sinful on repeated occasions and prayed for his punishment in supplications (*qunūt*) that he made in daily worship.[67] Most Sunnīs did not follow suit in censuring ʿAmr, since he was a Companion of the Prophet. However, some prominent Sunnīs, such as al-Nasāʾī and Abū 'l-Fidāʾ (d. 732/1331), refrained from venerating him because of his opposition to ʿAlī.[68] At least in the Umayyad period, transmitters generally identified Abū Ṭālib's family as the subject of the *ḥadīth*. However, scholars who read al-Bukhārī's *Ṣaḥīḥ* report that they frequently found Abū Ṭālib's name deleted from the *ḥadīth*. Since al-Bukhārī himself states that his informant found the clan's name omitted in his source, it is clear that deletions began to occur at least one generation before al-Bukhārī, though the precise point in time when copies of al-Bukhārī's *Ṣaḥīḥ* gained or lost the name cannot be pinned down. Extant copies of the work no longer contain Abū Ṭālib's name in full.

The testimony[69] of al-Bukhārī's informant suggests that Ghundar's book of *ḥadīth* once carried Abū Ṭālib's name in full, but either Ghundar or a copyist of his book deleted the second part of the name, leaving the

[64] Al-ʿAynī, *ʿUmdat al-qārī*, 22:94; Ibn Ḥajar al-ʿAsqalānī, *Fatḥ al-bārī*, 10:351.
[65] Ibn Ḥajar al-ʿAsqalānī, *Fatḥ al-bārī*, 10:352. [66] Ibn Abī 'l-Ḥadīd, *Sharḥ*, 4:64, 12:88.
[67] Al-Balādhurī, *Ansāb al-ashrāf*, 2:127, 352; Ibn Aʿtham al-Kūfī, *al-Futūḥ*, 4:201–202; al-Ṭabarī, *Tārīkh*, 4:34, 37, 52, 81.
[68] Al-Dhahabī, *Siyar*, 14:133; Abū 'l-Fidāʾ, *Tārīkh*, 1:186 (for a report from al-Shāfiʿī that identifies ʿAmr and three others as Companions whose testimonies are rejected).
[69] Al-Bukhārī, *Ṣaḥīḥ*, 7:73.

"Abū" intact (Text B). The person responsible for the deletion probably considered the *ḥadīth* anti-ʿAlid in tone and offensive to the Ṭālibids (the descendants of ʿAlī, ʿAqīl, and Jaʿfar b. Abī Ṭālib). As the Prophet's kinsfolk, the Ṭālibids possessed great social capital in early Islamic history, to the point that they threatened ʿAbbāsid claims to power.[70] Transmitters who sought to convey the report's lesson that allegiance to the faith should trump family ties, but had qualms about its anti-Ṭālibid tone, transmitted the text with either a lacuna or the anonymous "Abū so-and-so (*fulān*)." Neither Abū Bakr b. al-ʿArabī nor Ibn Ḥajar had problems in accepting the authenticity of this *ḥadīth*. The latter reasoned that it cut ties only between the Prophet and non-Muslim Ṭālibids.[71] As previously mentioned, pro-ʿAlids such as Ibn Abī 'l-Ḥadīd considered the *ḥadīth* an Umayyad fabrication.

Finally, in its third form (Text C), the report refers to the family of Abū Bayāḍ ("Father of blank space"). This version arose, as described earlier, from copyists' misreading of notes left in the text to indicate a lacuna (*bayāḍ*) after the word "Abū" and their conclusion that the Prophet spoke of a clan named Abū Bayāḍ. The three forms of the *ḥadīth* can be summarized thus:

Text A: the complete *ḥadīth*:
"The family of Abū Ṭālib are no allies of mine."
"The descendants of Abū Ṭālib are no allies of mine."[72]
Text B: a censored version:
"The family of Abū _____ are no allies of mine."
"The descendants of Abū _____ are no allies of mine."
"The family of Abū *so-and-so* are no allies of mine."
Text C: misreading of *bayāḍ* as a name:
"The family of Abū Bayāḍ are no allies of mine."

EMENDATION

Copyists and scholars emended *ḥadīth* that they considered objectionable in at least three ways: by obscuring the identity of a Companion; omitting reported speech; or emending key words. As for the first method, if a *ḥadīth* seemed to depict a Companion in a negative light, his identity

[70] Crone, *God's Rule*, 87–93; Elad, *Rebellion*; Zaman, *Religion and Politics*, 33–48.
[71] Ibn Ḥajar al-ʿAsqalānī, *Fatḥ al-bārī*, 10:352–354.
[72] Ibn Ḥajar claims to have found a variant in Abū Nuʿaym's *Mustakhraj* that had *banī Abī Ṭālib*: see Ibn Ḥajar al-ʿAsqalānī, *Fatḥ al-bārī*, 10:352.

might be obscured. For example, in the *ḥadīth* discussed in the previous section, the clan of Abū Ṭālib became "Abū so-and-so." In another case, ʿUmar b. al-Khaṭṭāb curses Samura b. Jundab for selling intoxicants.[73] In the recension of al-Bukhārī, Samura's name is omitted and the report consistently refers to him as "so-and-so" (*fulān*), giving no indication that the person selling intoxicants had been a Companion.[74] In a few anti-Umayyad *ḥadīth* in which the Prophet allegedly condemns Muʿāwiya as evil, Muʿāwiya's name is also replaced with "so-and-so."[75]

In another case previously noted in Chapter 2, Aḥmad b. Ḥanbal and Ibn ʿAsākir note that when Marwān b. al-Ḥakam became the governor of Medina, he would censure and ritually curse ʿAlī every Friday.[76] The name of this Umayyad governor (and future caliph) was omitted in other recensions where he commands others to join him in cursing ʿAlī. Al-Bukhārī included a heavily redacted version of the report in his *Ṣaḥīḥ*.[77] In al-Bukhārī's report, the name of the governor and his demand that others curse ʿAlī are omitted. Al-Bukhārī's redacted report is indicative of how denigrating statements in one version may be omitted elsewhere. Unlike the reports of Aḥmad b. Ḥanbal and Ibn ʿAsākir, which quoted the words of the governor directly, the governor's speech is fully excised in al-Bukhārī's account. Instead, a witness mentions only that the governor referred to ʿAlī as Abū Turāb. The *ḥadīth* is sanitized of its anti-ʿAlid historical context. Al-Bukhārī's proclivity for transmitting reports in which objectionable material is omitted can also be seen in cases where ʿAlī appears too Shīʿī for a Sunnī audience.

Multiple sources, including Muslim's *Ṣaḥīḥ* and ʿAbd al-Razzāq al-Ṣanʿānī's *Muṣannaf*, narrate ʿUmar's dismay that ʿAlī and ʿAbbās considered Abū Bakr and himself unjust (*ẓālim*) and sinful (*āthim*) in their decision to deny the Hāshimids their inheritance from the Prophet and convert the latter's estates into public endowments.[78] These two prominent Hāshimids are portrayed as holding opinions of the first two caliphs that would be considered quite offensive, Shīʿī, and incendiary to a Sunnī audience. Al-Bukhārī transmits versions of the report in which the views

[73] Aḥmad b. Ḥanbal, *al-Musnad*, 1:25. [74] Al-Bukhārī, *Ṣaḥīḥ*, 3:40.

[75] For the uncensored reports, see al-Balādhurī, *Ansāb al-ashrāf*, 5:126–127; Ibn Abī 'l-Ḥadīd, *Sharḥ*, 15:176; Ibn Ḥibbān, *Kitāb al-Majrūḥīn*, 1:157, 250. For reports in which Muʿāwiya's name is replaced with *fulān*, see Ibn ʿAdī, *al-Kāmil*, 3:419; Ibn ʿAsākir, *Taʾrīkh*, 59:155; Abū Nuʿaym al-Iṣbahānī, *Dhikr akhbār Iṣbahān*, 2:114.

[76] Aḥmad b. Ḥanbal, *al-ʿIlal*, 3:176; Ibn ʿAsākir, *Taʾrīkh*, 57:243; Ibn Kathīr, *al-Bidāya wa 'l-nihāya*, 8:284.

[77] Al-Bukhārī, *Ṣaḥīḥ*, 4:207–208. For more on this topic, see Chapter 2, nn. 54–61.

[78] ʿAbd al-Razzāq al-Ṣanʿānī, *al-Muṣannaf*, 5:470–471; Muslim, *Ṣaḥīḥ*, 5:152–153.

of ʿAlī and ʿAbbās are not explicitly stated; rather, it is vaguely noted that they used to claim "this and that" (*kadhā wa kadhā*) about Abū Bakr.[79] In another recension of al-Bukhārī, neither ʿAlī nor ʿAbbās voice any objection to the rule of Abū Bakr and ʿUmar. Their offensive views regarding the caliphs are completely omitted.[80]

In some cases, *ḥadīth* may have been emended so that negative words about a Companion were transformed into positive ones. ʿAlī benefited from this third type of emendation when early transmitters reported that ʿĀʾisha criticized ʿAlī's conduct in the *Ifk* incident. She reportedly said, "He behaved badly in my affair."[81] Some transmitters changed *kāna musīʾan* to *kāna musallaman*, with the effect that ʿĀʾisha now praised ʿAlī as free (*musallam*) of any wrongdoing in the matter.[82] Consequently, depending on the version they received and their own sensibilities, scholars taught al-Bukhārī's *Ṣaḥīḥ* with either version of the text. Published editions of al-Bukhārī's work contain the positive *musallam*, but many scholars in the medieval period still possessed copies in which ʿAlī was censured as *musīʾ*. The rehabilitation of ʿAlī played an important role in the gradual shift in the interpretation of this report. In the Umayyad period, an ʿUthmānī such as al-Zuhrī had no qualms in saying that ʿAlī had treated ʿĀʾisha unfairly in the *Ifk* incident, but centuries later, after ʿAlī's retroactive acceptance as an ʿUthmānī, it was unthinkable to acknowledge that he had ever been portrayed as an antagonist of Abū Bakr, ʿUmar, or ʿĀʾisha. Thus, later Sunnīs took for granted that ʿĀʾisha described ʿAlī as *musallam*, not *musīʾ*, in the *Ifk* incident.

CIRCULATION OF COUNTER-REPORTS

Sunnī *ḥadīth* collections included contributions from his partisans and detractors alike in their construction of an image of ʿAlī that was neither entirely evil nor fully pure. Rather, he appeared as a normal human being, subject to the same challenges and temptations as everyone else. This balancing effect may not have been coincidental: the content of certain reports suggests that when ʿAlī's detractors encountered a *ḥadīth* about his merits, they would narrate a counter-report to contradict it.

[79] Al-Bukhārī, *Ṣaḥīḥ*, 6:191, 8:147. [80] Ibid., 4:44; al-Tirmidhī, *Sunan*, 3:82.

[81] ʿAbd al-Razzāq al-Ṣanʿānī, *Tafsīr al-Qurʾān*, 3:52; al-Bayhaqī, *Dalāʾil al-nubuwwa*, 4:73; al-Dhahabī, *Siyar*, 2:160; Ibn Shabba, *Taʾrīkh al-Madīna*, 1:337; al-Suyūṭī, *al-Durr al-manthūr*, 5:32.

[82] Al-Bukhārī, *Ṣaḥīḥ*, 5:60; Ibn Ḥajar al-ʿAsqalānī, *Fatḥ al-bārī*, 7:336.

As noted earlier, some anti-ʿAlids, such as Ḥarīz b. ʿUthmān, cited Marwānids as their authorities for emending a famous *ḥadīth* that described ʿAlī as the Hārūn (Aaron) of the community; in the emended version, he became its Qārūn (Korah). In this case, it is clear that anti-ʿAlids were engaged in circulating a report that contradicted a well-known merit of ʿAlī. Other examples of counter-reports are slightly more subtle.[83] ʿAlī's partisans often portrayed him as a saint who worshiped God abundantly and greatly resembled the Prophet in his habits of worship.[84] But according to other reports, ʿAlī led prayers while intoxicated in the lifetime of the Prophet, and in a state of major ritual impurity as caliph.[85] Al-Bukhārī and others narrate a *ḥadīth* in which ʿAlī annoys the Prophet by declining his invitation to join him in prayer.[86] These reports appear to contradict the image of ʿAlī as a devout worshiper and support the Umayyad image of ʿAlī as someone who did not engage in daily worship.[87]

When ʿAlī married Fāṭima, the Prophet reportedly congratulated him for having been selected by God to marry his daughter.[88] Marriage to the Prophet's daughter was undoubtedly a great honor and an indication of ʿAlī's stature in the Prophet's eyes. Since Fāṭima was considered a woman of great piety, uniquely honored by God and her father, she required a spouse of equal caliber. Thus, some pro-ʿAlid *ḥadīth* assert that had it not been for ʿAlī, Fāṭima would never have found a suitable partner.[89] However, as the examples discussed earlier in this chapter indicate, there were counter-reports that depicted ʿAlī as a bad husband to Fāṭima.

According to some *ḥadīth*, the Prophet commanded everyone in his community to close their private entrances to his mosque.[90] The only exception was granted to ʿAlī, Fāṭima, and their two sons, who could

83 Hypothetically, texts could have circulated independently of one another or the less flattering reports about ʿAlī could be more ancient than the ones in his praise.

84 Al-Balādhurī, *Ansāb al-ashrāf*, 2:180; Ibn Shahrāshūb, *Manāqib*, 1:338–390; Muḥammad b. Ṭalḥa al-Naṣībī, *Maṭālib al-saʾūl*, 129 (where ʿAlī is compared to Christ in his worship).

85 Ḥabīb b. Abī Thābit appears to be a key transmitter of reports in which ʿAlī accidentally prays in a state of major impurity and another in which he leads prayer intoxicated: see ʿAbd al-Razzāq al-Ṣanʿānī, *al-Muṣannaf*, 2:350; al-Tirmidhī, *Sunan*, 4:305.

86 Aḥmad b. Ḥanbal, *al-Musnad*, 1:77, 91, 112; al-Bukhārī, *Ṣaḥīḥ*, 2:43, 8:155, 190; Muslim, *Ṣaḥīḥ*, 2:187.

87 Al-Ṭabarī, *Tārīkh*, 4:30 (where Syrians state that they had heard that ʿAlī did not pray).

88 Al-Haythamī, *Majmaʿ al-zawāʾid*, 9:204; Muḥibb al-Dīn al-Ṭabarī, *al-Riyāḍ al-naḍira*, 3:145–146; al-Ṭabarānī, *al-Muʿjam al-kabīr*, 10:156.

89 Al-Daylamī, *al-Firdaws*, 3:373 (read *li-Fāṭima* for *li-nā ṭayh*); al-Qundūzī, *Yanābīʿ al-mawadda*, 2:67, 80, 286.

90 Aḥmad b. Ḥanbal, *al-Musnad*, 4:369; Ibn Abī Shayba, *al-Muṣannaf*, 7:500; al-Nasāʾī, *al-Sunan al-kubrā*, 5:118–119; al-Ṭabarānī, *al-Muʿjam al-kabīr*, 12:78; al-Tirmidhī, *Sunan*, 5:305.

enter the mosque through their private entrance at any time, even in a state of major ritual impurity (*junub*).[91] Pro-ʿAlids and Shīʿīs understood these reports as further confirmation of the exceptional purity of the Prophet's household. The dispensation also offered a practical benefit: it allowed the family easy access to the Prophet's home. They could pass through the mosque even in a state of major ritual impurity without angering God or His Prophet.

As Hossein Modarressi has pointed out, the same merits that were ascribed to ʿAlī in pro-ʿAlid circles were also ascribed to the first three caliphs in ʿUthmānī circles.[92] Thus, in the *Ṣaḥīḥ* collections of al-Bukhārī and Muslim, the permission given to ʿAlī and Fāṭima to keep their entrance to the Prophet's mosque open was given to Abū Bakr instead.[93] The *ḥadīth* granting Abū Bakr the same privilege may thus be viewed as a counter-report to the *ḥadīth* about ʿAlī. In addition, ʿUthmānīs further narrated *ḥadīth* that portrayed ʿAlī as afflicted with frequent seminal discharge (*madhy*).[94] Reports about this malady may be understood as ʿUthmānī explanations for the dispensation he received to enter the Prophet's mosque even in a state of ritual impurity.

THE PRINCIPLE OF CHARITY

An ideological commitment to belief in the righteousness of all Companions led many scholars to either reject or charitably interpret texts that seemed to present any Companions in a negative light. Ibn Ḥazm, for example, argues that the man who killed the Prophet's revered Companion ʿAmmār b. Yāsir should receive a reward from God for his deed.[95] Ibn Ḥazm explains that the killer, Abū 'l-Ghādiya, had also been a Companion and, thus, his deed should be charitably understood as the error of an expert (*mujtahid*) engaged in religious hermeneutics.

In the case of ʿAlī, Sunnī canonical collections preserve reports that depict him as delaying his pledge of allegiance to Abū Bakr; however, these texts were reinterpreted to deny that ʿAlī ever questioned the first caliph's preeminence or challenged his candidacy. Accounts in which ʿAlī

[91] Al-Bayhaqī, *al-Sunan al-kubrā*, 7:65. [92] Modarressi, "Early Debates," 16–22.

[93] Al-Bukhārī, *Ṣaḥīḥ*, 4:254; Muslim, *Ṣaḥīḥ*, 7:108; al-Nasāʾī, *al-Sunan al-kubrā*, 5:35; al-Tirmidhī, *Sunan*, 5:270.

[94] ʿAbd al-Razzāq al-Ṣanʿānī, *al-Muṣannaf*, 1:155–157; Abū Dāwūd al-Sijistānī, *Sunan*, 1:53; Aḥmad b. Ḥanbal, *al-Musnad*, 1:80, 87, 108; al-Bukhārī, *Ṣaḥīḥ*, 1:42, 52; Ibn Abī Shayba, *al-Muṣannaf*, 1:115; Muslim, *Ṣaḥīḥ*, 1:169.

[95] Ibn Ḥazm, *al-Fiṣal*, 4:125.

complains about the succession of his predecessors never entered the canon and were largely rejected as forged.[96]

Both Muʿāwiya and ʿAlī benefited from the principle of charity and the tendency to defend all Companions as righteous. Influential scholars such as al-Nawawī proposed charitable reinterpretations for canonical *ḥadīth* that appear to show Muʿāwiya cursing ʿAlī or encouraging others to do so, while other scholars rejected such texts altogether.[97] The *ḥadīth* discussed above, "The family of Abū Ṭālib are no allies of mine," is another example: the text was read to refer hypothetically to non-Muslims in ʿAlī's family. Such generous interpretations were irrelevant to early ʿUthmānīs and pro-Umayyads who never recognized ʿAlī and his descendants as Muslims but rather condemned them as apostates and criminals. Consequently, charitable interpretations of the *ḥadīth* came to play a key role in safeguarding the honor of ʿAlī and his sons after their rehabilitation in Sunnism.[98]

FROM THREE CALIPHS TO FOUR

The early ʿUthmāniyya supported not only the caliphate of the first three caliphs but also the insurrection of ʿĀʾisha, Ṭalḥa, and al-Zubayr against ʿAlī. ʿUthmānīs such as Wurayza b. Muḥammad al-Ḥimṣī (d. 281/294) reportedly refused to recognize ʿAlī as a legitimate caliph because they believed that such recognition would necessarily entail opposition to and censure of the leaders who fought against him at the battle of the Camel.[99] The ʿUthmānī shift to accepting ʿAlī as a legitimate caliph probably began in Kūfa and Baghdad. Scott Lucas has argued for the possibility that early theologians who were Zaydīs or Baghdādī Muʿtazilīs "contributed to the profound respect for ʿAlī and his family found in the *Musnad* of Ibn Ḥanbal, *Muṣannaf* of Ibn Abī Shayba, and *Ṣaḥīḥ* of Muslim that seems stronger than the fourth-place status accorded him by [later] Sunnī doctrine."[100] It should be added that al-Maʾmūn played a key role in initiating public debates about the place of ʿAlī in Islamic history by

96 For representative examples, see al-Kanjī, *Kifāyat al-ṭālib*, 386; al-Khuwārizmī, *al-Manāqib*, 313; al-Simnānī, *Manāẓir al-maḥāḍir*, 14–19.

97 See al-Nawawī, *Sharḥ Ṣaḥīḥ Muslim*, 15:175–176; cf. Ḥammād, "Muʿāwiya raḍiya Allāh ʿanhu al-muftarā ʿalayhi."

98 For more on the concept of the principle of charity, see Brown, *Canonization*, 42–46.

99 Ibn Abī Yaʿlā, *Ṭabaqāt al-Ḥanābila*, 1:393. See also al-ʿUqaylī, *Muʿjam nawāṣib al-muḥaddithīn*, 46–47.

100 Lucas, *Constructive Critics*, 284.

proclaiming *tafḍīl ʿAlī* to be orthodoxy in 211/826, and once more the following year.[101] The caliph invited *ḥadīth* scholars and Muʿtazilīs who opposed *tafḍīl ʿAlī* to debate the issue with him in his court.[102] Al-Maʾmūn undoubtedly encouraged al-Jāḥiẓ, Abū Jaʿfar al-Iskāfī, and other theologians to discuss the issue of *tafḍīl ʿAlī* in their literary work. During the reign of al-Maʾmūn and in the years that followed, these scholars carefully considered evidence indicating ʿAlī's distinguished status. The same can be said about Aḥmad b. Ḥanbal, who made the conscious decision to locate and preserve hundreds of Kūfan *ḥadīth* about the merits of ʿAlī. All of these figures also resided in Baghdad, where they encountered each other's opinions. Aḥmad b. Ḥanbal may have accepted *ḥadīth* about ʿAlī's merits from pro-ʿAlid transmitters in Baghdad after conceding to the arguments of pro-ʿAlid theologians in the city. For example, probably to the dismay of the city's ʿUthmānīs, he reportedly agreed with proponents of *tafḍīl ʿAlī* that no Companion possessed more merits than ʿAlī.[103] Aḥmad b. Ḥanbal's decision to transmit hundreds of anecdotes in which the Prophet singles out ʿAlī for praise bears witness to his assessment.[104] He also reportedly began arguing for the need to accept ʿAlī as a legitimate fourth caliph among his ʿUthmānī peers.[105] Such advocacy would have involved some acceptance of the historical narratives of ʿAlī's partisans. Although Aḥmad b. Ḥanbal was not an outright proponent of *tafḍīl ʿAlī*, his acceptance of pro-ʿAlid *ḥadīth* led him to transmit reports associated with this doctrine.[106]

Sunnī scholars transmitted reports that explicitly articulated the merits of Companions both generally and specifically, but Lucas suggests that the most enduring achievement of Aḥmad b. Ḥanbal was an implicit polemic: the vindication of all Companions who participated in the civil wars that engulfed the community after the Prophet's death. By including them as important sources of *ḥadīth* in his *Musnad*, Aḥmad b. Ḥanbal acquitted these personalities of charges of impiety.[107] The inclusion in the *Musnad* of Companions who fought against ʿAlī indicated that despite reports that cast their political careers in a negative light, and despite the criticisms

[101] Al-Ṭabarī, *Tārīkh*, 7:188. See also *EI*², s.v. "al-Maʾmūn" (M. Rekaya).
[102] Ibn ʿAbd Rabbih, *al-ʿIqd*, 5:349–359.
[103] Ibn ʿAbd al-Barr, *al-Istīʿāb*, 3:1115; Muḥibb al-Dīn al-Ṭabarī, *al-Riyāḍ al-naḍira*, 3:188.
[104] For example, Aḥmad b. Ḥanbal, *Faḍāʾil Amīr al-Muʾminīn*.
[105] Ibn Abī Yaʿlā, *Ṭabaqāt al-Ḥanābila*, 1:393; Ibn Ḥajar al-ʿAsqalānī, *Fatḥ al-bārī*, 7:47. See also Madelung, *Der Imām al-Qāsim*, 223–228.
[106] Aḥmad b. Ḥanbal, *Faḍāʾil Amīr al-Muʾminīn*, 147; Aḥmad b. Ḥanbal, *Faḍāʾil al-ṣaḥāba*, 2:564, 671.
[107] Lucas, *Constructive Critics*, 285.

leveled against them by pro-ʿAlid theologians, these Companions were nonetheless trustworthy sources of information about the life of the Prophet and his teachings. By the middle of the ninth century, ʿAlī had also come to benefit from an emerging Sunnī orthodoxy that used the hermeneutical tools described in this chapter to delegitimize hostile depictions of him and appropriate him as the fourth caliph, extending the three-caliph model of the early ʿUthmāniyya. As others have noted, this acceptance of ʿAlī's fourth place (*tarbīʿ ʿAlī*) was an innovation for the ʿUthmāniyya of the ninth century.[108]

The image of ʿAlī b. Abī Ṭālib that appeared in Sunnī *ḥadīth* collections produced after the beginning of the ninth century was as complex and composite as the compilers' sources. Anti-ʿAlids viewed ʿAlī and his family with contempt, whereas to many pro-ʿAlids he was the most meritorious Muslim after the Prophet. A third group consisted of those who were ambivalent about ʿAlī's personality and considered him a Companion no different from his peers. For example, Ibn Taymiyya argued that ʿAlī possessed merits but also many shortcomings.[109] He forcefully argued that ʿAlī upset the Prophet and later waged war unnecessarily against his rivals.[110] Thus, ʿAlī was responsible for civil strife in the community, though he was not evil.

Whereas pro-ʿAlids remembered ʿAlī as someone who exercised independent judgment after the Prophet, later orthodoxy frequently portrayed him as agreeing with the positions of other authorities. ʿAlī's variant opinions on political and religious questions were gradually replaced in reports about him with answers that affirmed Sunnī orthodoxy.

Various caliphs, from Muʿāwiya to al-Maʾmūn, were clearly invested in shaping public perceptions about ʿAlī. While the Umayyads supported the circulation of tales that maligned him, al-Maʾmūn appears to have promoted ʿAlī's rehabilitation in the community. The case studies in this chapter indicate the ways in which Sunnī scholars made use of their editorial privilege to reshape ʿAlī's image: they selected those versions of reports that omitted what they saw as controversial material and obfuscated certain sensitive elements of the narratives they transmitted. In some cases, individuals resorted to outright deletion of particularly inflammatory words or passages when they were obliged to transmit such material. It is unclear to what extent copyists contributed to this revisionary process.

[108] Ibn Abī Yaʿlā, *Ṭabaqāt al-Ḥanābila*, 1:393. See also Afsaruddin, *Excellence*, 16–18; Melchert, *Ahmad ibn Hanbal*, 95–96; Zaman, *Religion and Politics*, 49–59, 169ff.; EI^2, s.v. "Imāma" (W. Madelung); "ʿUthmāniyya" (P. Crone).

[109] Ibn Taymiyya, *Minhāj*, 5:7. [110] Ibid., 4:255, 384, 389, 392.

Afterword

Clearly ʿAlī's legacy among Muslims was contested. The martyr and saint revered in Sunnī and Shīʿī literature was roundly condemned among Umayyads, ʿUthmānīs, and Khawārij. According to these factions, ʿAlī wrongfully waged war against other Muslims in pursuit of power and betrayed the values of his religion. This book documents the grievances of these early anti-ʿAlids and considers how some of their opinions about ʿAlī persisted in Muslim historiography long after the disappearance of these factions.

For those who revered him the most, ʿAlī personified justice and righteousness. He was the ideal imām and the accusations that his antagonists leveled against him were simply slander. Yet Sunnī *ḥadīth* scholars grappled with the conflicting narratives in nuanced ways to frequently produce an image somewhere in the middle. ʿAlī's many portrayals and the process of his rehabilitation over the centuries belies any notions that reverence for him among Muslims was ever static or universal. The story of ʿAlī's legacy was no less fraught with conflict than was his life.

ʿAlī's political career was a key subject that differentiated his admirers from his critics. By the middle of the ninth century, influential scholars in the fledgling Sunnī community aimed to venerate ʿAlī and his political rivals together and rejected historical narratives wherein the Prophet's Companions truly came to despise one another.[1] This nonpartisan commitment to all Companions became a quintessential Sunnī cultural and

[1] For example, Muʿāwiya was portrayed as revering ʿAlī and never doubting the legitimacy of his caliphate in these narratives: see Ibn Ḥajar al-ʿAsqalānī, *Fatḥ al-bārī*, 13:75; Ibn Ḥazm, *al-Fiṣal*, 4:124.

theological position. The nonpartisan culture that *ḥadīth* specialists promoted led to the rehabilitation of early caliphs and political figures who had previously been condemned in various geographic and factional rivalries. The memories of ʿUthmān, ʿAlī, and Muʿāwiya all benefited from this new Sunnī vision which sought to suppress and transcend partisan conflicts.[2] Thus, hagiography extolling the virtues of these rulers was included from ʿUthmānī, pro-ʿAlid, and pro-Umayyad sources, while literature attacking their deeds as rulers was largely rejected, censored, or charitably reinterpreted. As previously noted, censorship usually involved obfuscation of the Companion's identity or omissions in the parts of a report that transmitters considered objectionable.

While pro-ʿAlids, Umayyads, and ʿUthmānīs collectively recognized ʿAlī's tendency to act as an independent authority after the Prophet, later orthodoxy frequently portrayed him as deferring to others.[3] ʿAlī's variant opinions were gradually replaced with answers that avowedly affirmed Sunnī orthodoxy. In his rehabilitation, ʿAlī was shorn of his objectionable features and repackaged as an obedient and nondescript citizen who agreed with the views of his peers. He was neither a criminal, as anti-ʿAlids claimed, nor a Shīʿī imām. He became a virtuous Companion in the company of many others. ʿAlī the dissenter gave way to ʿAlī the conformist.

Anti-ʿAlid sentiment came to possess an erased history in Sunnī Islam. After enjoying some popularity in the Umayyad period, scholars of the ninth century largely ceased transmitting early ʿUthmānī reports that were hostile to ʿAlī. The erasure of anti-ʿAlid sentiment consisted not only of its disappearance, but also of a denial that it had ever existed. Sunnī polemicists came to deny that Muʿāwiya and Yazīd ever harbored any ill will toward ʿAlī or his family. Anti-ʿAlid sentiment was generally too unsettling for Sunnī scholars to keep as part of their own community's collective memory. Consequently, some externalized it as only a Khārijī phenomenon.[4] However, Sunnī canonical *ḥadīth* collections, biographical dictionaries, and historical chronicles all preserved reports in which respected Companions and *ḥadīth* transmitters articulated their aversion to ʿAlī.

The varied reception of *ḥadīth* about ʿAlī and his rivals reflects a negotiative process that has endured between Sunnīs of competing theological commitments down to the modern period. Pro-ʿAlids generally

[2] For the rehabilitation of ʿUthmān, see Keaney, *Medieval Islamic Historiography.*

[3] For the image of ʿAbd Allah b. ʿAbbās as a mentor to ʿAlī in pro-ʿAbbāsid literature, see Petersen, *ʿAlī and Muʿāwiya*, 75–78.

[4] Al-Zabīdī, *Tāj al-ʿarūs*, 2:436. See also al-ʿAwwād, *al-Naṣb*, 70.

accepted *manāqib* literature exalting ʿAlī and *mathālib* literature censuring his rivals while most Sunnīs committed to the maintenance of orthodoxy denied the historicity of such texts or charitably reinterpreted them.

The formation of orthodoxy in Sunnism appears as an intellectual and social endeavor that involved scholars in control of the teaching and transmission of texts. Scholars of *ḥadīth* made use of mechanisms that facilitated the censorship of objectionable material and the marginalization of their sources. This investigation of the declining popularity, contributions, and eventual disappearance of zealous *nawāṣib* emphasizes problems related to the politics of *ḥadīth* transmission and identity formation.

Maghan Keita writes that wars of identity and culture "are about epistemological construction and reconstruction. They are about exclusion and inclusion ... the excluded parties are regarded as being without culture: uncivilized ... without intellectual capacity."[5] In a sectarian milieu, the excluded "other" could not have a claim to true piety or share in God's grace. Thus, scholars avoided engaging or preserving the intellectual contributions of members of other sects and viewed them with suspicion, if not contempt. In composing their works, authors of foundational *ḥadīth* texts (i.e. compilations, commentaries, and biographical dictionaries) utilized their discretion to construct boundaries for their community in the imagined past based upon those that existed in their own lifetime. Pro-ʿAlid and anti-ʿAlid predecessors who did not fall within these later boundaries of Sunnī Islam were criticized and their contributions excluded *ex post facto*. Some *ḥadīth* transmitters and their narratives retroactively became too Shīʿī while others were considered too hostile to ʿAlī. Yet, as this survey of anti-ʿAlid literature has indicated, the process of exclusion and erasure was imperfect. One can glean vestiges of anti-ʿAlid historiography from later sources that discuss the contributions of Umayyad, ʿUthmānī, and Khārijī figures. The legacy of the *nawāṣib* endures in the writings of anti-Shīʿī polemicists who admire these figures and defend their opposition to ʿAlī.

In some cases, scholars claiming to revere ʿAlī but desiring to discredit Shīʿism accepted and sympathized with those accounts in which ʿAlī and his sons were the cause of civil unrest or disobeyed the teachings of the Prophet. In these cautionary tales, ʿAlī and his partisans commit misdeeds that the faithful should not emulate. After the ninth century, readers

[5] Keita, *Race and the Writing of History*, 11.

generally understood from such accounts that ʿAlī was prone to making honest mistakes. But when one considers the Umayyad and ʿUthmānī milieu from which such narratives emerged, it becomes apparent that the transmitters initially aimed to denigrate ʿAlī and his partisans. These stories were contributions of the *nawāṣib*.

Chapter 1 Appendix: Anti-ʿAlid Statements in Historical Literature

A few authors are credited with writing refutations of the beliefs of *nawāṣib*. In the Sunnī tradition, Najm al-Dīn al-Ṭūfī was imprisoned and paraded around the city of Cairo for allegedly writing such a work.[1] Like the writings of his Shīʿī counterparts, al-Ṭūfī's work probably offended Sunnīs by accepting the historicity of reports in which Companions (especially Umayyads) were depicted as *nawāṣib*. Twelver Shīʿī authors often included the term *nawāṣib* in the titles of works that were not primarily about *nawāṣib*. Instead, these texts aimed to establish ʿAlī's imāmate, his merits, and the legitimacy of Shīʿism. Frequently, Shīʿīs wrote these works as refutations of anti-Shīʿī books penned by Sunnī authors whom they identified as *nawāṣib*.[2] There seem to be no classical works specifically dedicated to cataloging anti-ʿAlid sentiment, but this appendix provides a survey of *naṣb* in Sunnī literature. At least three modern authors have also published surveys of *naṣb* in the Islamic intellectual tradition.[3]

TENSIONS IN THE TEXTS

Literary expressions of anti-ʿAlid sentiment fall into eight categories. Texts of the first three types reflect the beliefs of Muslims who were described as hostile to ʿAlids, whereas texts in categories 4 and 5 present views that were criticized as irreverent toward ʿAlids but were not necessarily motivated by personal antipathy to ʿAlī or his family. The attitudes expressed in texts of the fourth type were particularly prevalent among courtiers whose primary concern was to secure financial gifts from a caliph. Their poetry represents a form of state media and propaganda of the era. Poets and others who wished to please their anti-ʿAlid

[1] Ibn Rajab, *al-Dhayl ʿalā Ṭabaqāt al-Ḥanābila*, 4:368–369; al-Ziriklī, *al-Aʿlām*, 3:128.

[2] ʿAbd al-Jalīl al-Qazvīnī, *Kitāb al-Naqẓ*; Ibn Shahrāshūb, *Mathālib al-nawāṣib*; al-Tustarī, *Maṣāʾib al-nawāṣib*.

[3] Al-ʿAwwād, *al-Naṣb*; al-Muʿallim, *al-Nuṣb wa ʾl-nawāṣib*; al-ʿUqaylī, *Muʿjam nawāṣib al-muḥaddithīn*.

patrons would typically make anti-ʿAlid statements of types 1–4. In addition to seeking advancement within the bureaucracy, some courtiers may have felt coerced to make type-4 statements in order to show their loyalty to the state. It is quite possible that many people feigned animosity to ʿAlī because it was politically expedient to do so. Nevertheless, their statements reflect the beliefs that anti-ʿAlids publicly proclaimed and wished for the community to accept.

Texts of types 5 through 8 are characteristic both of anti-ʿAlid Muslims and of common Sunnī responses to Shīʿism. I have attempted to provide a gradation of texts that were clearly anti-ʿAlid (types 1–3) and to differentiate them from writings composed for anti-Shīʿī purposes (types 4–8). An individual whose statements were limited to categories 7 and 8 is likely to have been much more tolerant of pro-ʿAlid sentiments but to have been nonetheless anti-Shīʿī. Some polemicists such as Ibn Taymiyya expressed sentiments that ranged from anti-Shīʿī (types 5–8) to anti-ʿAlid (type 3). Sunnī polemicists who drew on the views of their anti-ʿAlid predecessors in their efforts to discredit Shīʿism typically contradicted their claim to revere members of the Prophet's Household by rejecting reports about their merits and accepting reports that seemed to belittle them or depict them unfavorably.

A systematic historical inquiry into the turbulent lives and beliefs of ʿAlids throughout the Umayyad and early ʿAbbāsid eras reveals the animosity that existed between the ʿAlids and their political and intellectual rivals.[4] Literature in the genre of history, biography, and *ḥadīth* describes these rivalries. While pro-ʿAlid scholars in the Sunnī tradition utilized pro-ʿAlid literature, anti-Shīʿī polemicists dismissed these reports as false and further used anti-ʿAlid elements in the Sunnī tradition to substantiate their claims. It should be acknowledged that the categories below allow for the possibility of an author to hold disparate views about ʿAlī and one of his descendants. The determining factor in the organization of texts was the nature of such criticism and not to whom it was directed. The framework below nonetheless suggests that criticisms about a particular ʿAlid may have reflected a larger trend of ʿAlid marginalization.

KEY THEMES OF ANTI-ʿALID TEXTS

The following eight types of expressions of contempt for ʿAlī and his family can be identified in the sources.

1 Defenses of Murder, Persecution, or Physical Attack Directed at ʿAlī or Members of his Household

ʿImrān b. Ḥiṭṭān was a Khārijī who had the distinction of being included as a *ḥadīth* transmitter in al-Bukhārī's *ḥadīth* collection.[5] He paid homage to ʿAlī's assassin, ʿAbd al-Raḥmān b. Muljam, with the following lines of poetry:

[4] See for example, Jafri, *Origins*; Madelung, *Succession*.

[5] Al-Bukhārī, *Ṣaḥīḥ*, 7:45, 65; al-Dhahabī, *Siyar*, 4:214–216. See also al-ʿUqaylī, *Muʿjam nawāṣib al-muḥaddithīn*, 362–366.

What a strike from the one who was God-conscious! He desired nothing
But to obtain the satisfaction of [God], The Enthroned
I remember him occasionally and deem him
The most loyal of God's creation when [all of mankind's deeds are] judged[6]

Ibn Ḥazm considered ʿAlī's assassination a consequence of *ijtihād*; thus, God would not punish Ibn Muljam for his deed.[7]

According to both Sunnī and Shīʿī sources, when Muʿāwiya's forces raised copies of the Qurʾān on spears and asked for arbitration at the battle of Ṣiffīn, ʿAlī initially ignored the request because he considered it a ploy to prolong hostilities. These sources portray proto-Khawārij as supporters of arbitration. If ʿAlī would not desist from fighting, they threatened to betray him, warning him, "We shall hand you over to these people or we shall deal with you as we dealt with ʿUthmān."[8]

A Khārijī attacked al-Ḥasan with a pickax for considering a peace treaty with Muʿāwiya, declaring, "You've become a polytheist like your father before you."[9]

Abū Rajāʾ al-ʿUṭāridī once heard a neighbor of the clan of Hujaym say, "Did you not see how God killed the criminal, son of the criminal, al-Ḥusayn b. ʿAlī?"[10] The speaker allegedly became blind thereafter.

Maysa bt. Siḥām al-Rubayʿī, the wife of Abū Bakra al-Thaqafī, said, "al-Ḥasan b. ʿAlī has died, so praise God who has relieved us of him!"[11]

Ibn al-Zubayr threatened to execute Muḥammad b. al-Ḥanafiyya if he continued to withhold his pledge of allegiance to him or to meet with Shīʿī pilgrims. Some reports claim that Ibn al-Zubayr had already gathered firewood to burn Ibn al-Ḥanafiyya alive at the time of his rescue.[12] It seems that Ibn al-Zubayr kept him confined to the Sacred Mosque in Mecca and under house arrest.[13]

2 Reports of Individuals Cursing or Disparaging ʿAlī or Members of his Family

A number of biographers mention Rabīʿa b. Yazīd al-Sulamī as a Companion of the Prophet who despised ʿAlī and would curse him.[14]

[6] Al-Baghdādī, *al-Farq bayn al-firaq*, 95; al-Dhahabī, *Siyar*, 4:215; Ibn ʿAbd al-Barr, *al-Istīʿāb*, 3:1128; Ibn ʿAsākir, *Taʾrīkh*, 43:495; Ibn Ḥazm, *al-Muḥallā*, 10:484.

[7] Ibn Ḥazm, *al-Muḥallā*, 10:484. See also Ansari, "Ibn Ḥazm selon certains savants shīʿites," 655.

[8] Ibn ʿAsākir, *Taʾrīkh*, 56:387; Ibn Aʿtham al-Kūfī, *al-Futūḥ*, 3:185–186; Ibn Shahrāshūb, *Manāqib*, 2:364 (citing Ibn Mardawayh); al-Shahrastānī, *al-Milal wa ʾl-niḥal*, 1:114; al-Ṭabarī, *Tārīkh*, 4:34–35.

[9] Al-Balādhurī, *Ansāb al-ashrāf*, 3:35. See also Madelung, *Succession*, 319.

[10] Ibn Saʿd, *Kitāb al-Ṭabaqāt al-kabīr*, 6:454. With slight differences, the report appears in Aḥmad b. Ḥanbal, *Faḍāʾil al-ṣaḥāba*, 2:574; al-Balādhurī, *Ansāb al-ashrāf*, 3:211; al-Dhahabī, *Siyar*, 3:313; al-Haythamī, *Majmaʿ al-zawāʾid*, 9:196; Ibn ʿAsākir, *Taʾrīkh*, 14:232; al-Mizzī, *Tahdhīb al-Kamāl*, 6:436; al-Ṭabarānī, *al-Muʿjam al-kabīr*, 3:112.

[11] Ibn Saʿd, *Kitāb al-Ṭabaqāt al-kabīr*, 6:395.

[12] Al-Balādhurī, *Ansāb al-ashrāf*, 3:280–285. [13] See Chapter 4.

[14] Some did not consider Rabīʿa to have been a Companion: see Ibn ʿAbd al-Barr, *al-Istīʿāb*, 2:493–494, 495; Ibn Ḥajar al-ʿAsqalānī, *al-Iṣāba*, 2:398; al-Ṣafadī, *al-Wāfī*, 14:60.

When al-Ḥasan b. ʿAlī surrendered to Muʿāwiya, some disgruntled men addressed him with the following epithets:

"O he who disgraced (*mudhill*) the Arabs!"[15]
"O he who disgraced the faithful!"[16]
"O he who dishonored (lit., blackened) the faces of the faithful!"[17]
"O he who brought shame to the faithful (*ʿār al-muʾminīn*)!"[18]

3 Public Denunciations of ʿAlī and his Kin as Sinful, Criminal, Guilty of Heresy, Causing Evil, or Intentionally Disobeying God or His Prophet

A Companion named Burayda b. ʿĀzib admitted to loathing ʿAlī during the lifetime of the Prophet. His hatred of ʿAlī led him to join Khālid b. al-Walīd in a plot to disgrace ʿAlī in the eyes of the Prophet by accusing him of unlawfully appropriating a female prisoner of war for himself. Instead, the Prophet became upset with Burayda for harboring malice toward ʿAlī.[19]

ʿAmr b. Yathribī al-Ḍabbī was a poet-warrior who boasted of killing three of ʿAlī's partisans during the battle of the Camel. He ridiculed these men for following the religion (*dīn*) of ʿAlī.[20] ʿAlī's rivals seem to have accused him of following his own misguided beliefs instead of the religion of the Prophet. ʿAmmār b. Yāsir eventually injured Ibn Yathribī in a duel and brought him to ʿAlī, who ordered his execution for his deeds.

In his exchange of letters with ʿAlī, Muʿāwiya argued that ʿAlī had been envious of the first three caliphs (*kullahum ḥasadta*) and that everyone knew this from the discontent ʿAlī showed upon their accession as caliphs.[21] Although various pro-ʿAlid Sunnī and Shīʿī texts noted ʿAlī's disgruntlement at the accession of his predecessors, ʿUthmānīs and Umayyads characterized ʿAlī specifically as envious of them.

According to a report praising ʿUmar b. al-Khaṭṭāb, ʿUmar criticized ʿAlī as inordinately covetous (*ḥarīṣ*) of the caliphate and argued that the position did not suit ʿAlī since he hankered for it.[22]

[15] Ibn al-Jawzī, *al-Muntaẓam*, 5:184; al-Ṭabarī, *Tārīkh*, 4:126.
[16] Al-Dhahabī, *Siyar*, 3:147; al-Ḥākim al-Naysābūrī, *al-Mustadrak*, 3:175; Ibn ʿAbd al-Barr, *al-Istīʿāb*, 1:387; Ibn ʿAsākir, *Taʾrīkh*, 13:279, 59:151; al-ʿUqaylī, *Kitāb al-ḍuʿafāʾ*, 2:175–176. See also Madelung, *Succession*, 323 n. 29.
[17] The person who said this was Sufyān b. al-Layl al-Ḥamdānī: see al-Dhahabī, *Siyar*, 3:272; al-Ḥākim al-Naysābūrī, *al-Mustadrak*, 3:170–171; al-Ṭabarī, *Tafsīr*, 30:330; al-Tirmidhī, *Sunan*, 5:115.
[18] Al-Dhahabī, *Siyar*, 3:145; Ibn ʿAbd al-Barr, *al-Istīʿāb*, 1:386; Ibn Abī Shayba, *al-Muṣannaf*, 8:631; Ibn ʿAsākir, *Taʾrīkh*, 13:261; Ibn Ḥajar al-ʿAsqalānī, *Fatḥ al-bārī*, 13:56.
[19] Al-Bukhārī, *Ṣaḥīḥ*, 5:110; al-Nasāʾī, *Khaṣāʾiṣ*, 102; Aḥmad b. Ḥanbal, *al-Musnad*, 5:350.
[20] Al-Balādhurī, *Ansāb al-ashrāf*, 2:244; al-Ṭabarī, *Tārīkh*, 3:526; Ibn ʿAsākir, *Taʾrīkh*, 43:464. For *dīn ʿAlī* see also Amir-Moezzi, *Spirituality*, 4–15.
[21] Al-Balādhurī, *Ansāb al-ashrāf*, 2:277–278. See also Madelung, *Succession*, 211. Specifically, he was accused of coveting (*ṭamʿ*) the caliphate: see Madelung, *Succession*, 271.
[22] Ibn Aʿtham al-Kūfī, *al-Futūḥ*, 2:325.

Some North African Mālikī jurists influenced by the Umayyads who ruled Andalusia reportedly held Muʿāwiya to have been a better Muslim than ʿAlī. They argued that "ʿAlī had no legal right to claim the imāmate and should not, therefore, have waged war against Muʿāwiya."[23] The pro-Umayyad Mālikīs substantiated their views by reporting Imām Mālik's disapproval of ʿAlī's decision to leave Medina for Kūfa and to engage in warfare with his rivals (at the battles of the Camel and Ṣiffīn).[24]

Some reports cast ʿAlī as responsible, either directly or indirectly, for the death of ʿUthmān.[25] Others claim that ʿAlī either encouraged or directed the sedition that ended in the death of ʿUthmān.[26] Still others fault him for refusing to surrender "the murderers of ʿUthmān" because he was in need of their military and political support.[27] For example, ʿUbayd Allāh b. ʿUmar b. al-Khaṭṭāb was a commander of

[23] Ibn Haytham, *The Advent of the Fatimids*, 29–30, 165–166. Ibrāhīm b. Muḥammad b. Birdhawn and Abū Bakr b. Hudhayl were two Mālikīs executed in 297/909 for reportedly rejecting ʿAlī's claim to the caliphate. Sunnī sources either remain silent regarding the reason for their executions or portray their deaths as a consequence of their refusal to recognize ʿUbayd Allāh al-Mahdī either as the Messenger of God or the new sovereign (depending on the source). Others noted their refusal to recognize the superiority of ʿAlī to the first three caliphs: see al-Dhahabī, *Siyar*, 14:216; al-Dhahabī, *Taʾrīkh*, 22:135; Ibn ʿIdhārī, *Akhbār al-Andalus wa ʾl-Maghrib*, 154–155, 282–283; al-Khushanī, *Ṭabaqāt ʿulamāʾ Ifrīqiya*, 215–216. Their refusal to recognize the sovereignty of al-Mahdī would have been a capital offense, but the alternative theological explanations for their executions do not seem credible in light of the history of the Fāṭimid empire. Generally, Sunnīs were not executed for refusing to become Ismāʿīlī. Ismāʿīlīs also did not consider the first three caliphs to have been pious for comparisons of merit to have been made. Although this study generally relies on the Sunnī intellectual tradition to understand Sunnism, I have mentioned Ibn al-Haytham's account since he was a contemporary eyewitness to the events. One could argue that since Ibn al-Haytham was a Zaydī who became Ismāʿīlī, his claim that these two Mālikīs were executed for refusing to recognize ʿAlī as a legitimate caliph is unattested in Sunnī literature. However, Ibn Taymiyya testifies to the existence of pro-Umayyads in Andalusia who considered Muʿāwiya the fourth caliph. Consequently, Ibn al-Haytham's account should not be discounted as unlikely: see Ibn Taymiyya, *Minhāj*, 4:400–401.

[24] ʿAbd al-Malik ibn Ḥabīb, *Kitāb al-taʾrīkh*, 115. See also al-Qāḍī al-Nuʿmān, *The Eloquent Clarification*, 11, 14.

[25] Al-Bayhaqī, *al-Sunan al-kubrā*, 8:189; Ibn ʿAbd Rabbih, *al-ʿIqd*, 5:81; Ibn Ḥajar al-ʿAsqalānī, *Tahdhīb al-Tahdhīb*, 8:411; Ibn Kathīr, *al-Bidāya wa ʾl-nihāya*, 7:288; Sibṭ Ibn al-Jawzī, *Tadhkirat al-khawāṣṣ*, 82; al-Ṭabarī, *Tārīkh*, 4:4, 30. See also Madelung, *Succession*, 156 (for Marwān b. al-Ḥakam's accusations), 189–190, 198–199 (for al-Walīd b. ʿUqba's poetry), 200–201, 205, 211 (for Muʿāwiya making such a claim).

[26] Al-Balādhurī, *Ansāb al-ashrāf*, 2:277–278, 5:551, 581; Ibn ʿAbd Rabbih, *al-ʿIqd*, 5:83; Ibn Aʿtham al-Kūfī, *al-Futūḥ*, 2:559; al-Mubarrad, *al-Kāmil*, 1:184. See also Madelung, *Succession*, 122 n. 209, 126, 134 n. 262.

[27] Al-ʿAynī, *ʿUmdat al-qārī*, 15:51; al-Dīnawarī, *al-Akhbār al-ṭiwāl*, 162, 170–171; Ibn ʿAbd Rabbih, *al-ʿIqd*, 5:83; Ibn Ḥajar al-ʿAsqalānī, *Fatḥ al-bārī*, 6:454, 13:448; Ibn Kathīr, *al-Bidāya wa ʾl-nihāya*, 7:288. Ibn Ḥajar is slightly inconsistent in explaining ʿAlī's conduct toward the claims of his rivals. In one place he alluded to the ʿUthmānī argument that ʿUthmān's assassins made up a large contingent of ʿAlī's army and he was unwilling to surrender them since he was in need of their support. In other places, Ibn Ḥajar principally argued that ʿAlī disregarded the claims of Muʿāwiya and the commanders of the army at

Muʿāwiya's army who proclaimed that the killers of ʿUthmān were the people of Iraq in general and ʿAlī's *anṣār* in particular.[28] Texts that defended ʿAlī clarified that the Umayyads accused ʿAlī's closest companions of killing ʿUthmān, but that he considered those accusations false.[29] The names of some of these accused companions are listed below in Section 8.

According to some reports, ʿAlī drank alcohol at a party and led a group of Companions in prayer while intoxicated.[30]

ʿAlī is also called an ass, a thief,[31] and the son of a thief.[32] When he rose to power, he reportedly confiscated items from ʿUthmān's residence that he considered public property.[33] Hearing of this, the Umayyads argued that ʿAlī had seized the property unlawfully. In lines of poetry, al-Walīd b. ʿUqba accused ʿAlī and the Hāshimids of killing ʿUthmān and looting his property in their efforts to usurp the caliphate.[34] When Marwānids described ʿAlī as a "thief, son of a thief," they may have been referring to the sentiments articulated by al-Walīd.

Finally, various reports claim that ʿAlī did not offer prayers,[35] that the Hāshimids were evil,[36] and that, according to Ibn al-Zubayr, the Prophet's kin were conceited.[37]

the battle of the Camel since they were not ʿUthmān's heirs and offered no admissible evidence to back their accusations that a particular person had killed ʿUthmān: see Ibn Ḥajar al-ʿAsqalānī, *Fatḥ al-bārī*, 6:454, cf. 7:84, 13:47, 13:448.

28 Al-Ṭabarī, *Tārīkh*, 4:24.

29 In letters attributed to ʿAlī, he considered Muʿāwiya's claim to be the avenger of ʿUthmān a diversion from his real wish to maintain power: see al-Dīnawarī, *al-Akhbār al-ṭiwāl*, 157; Ibn ʿAsākir, *Taʾrīkh*, 59:128; Ibn Aʿtham al-Kūfī, *al-Futūḥ*, 2:506. Al-Qurṭubī noted that there were no witnesses who were able to positively identify ʿUthmān's assassins under oath. It seems that only rumors and hearsay surrounded ʿAlī's compatriots, and that the actual assassins were unknown assailants who came from various parts of the empire: see al-Qurṭubī, *al-Tadhkira*, 1072, 1083.

30 Abū Dāwūd al-Sijistānī, *Sunan*, 2:182; al-Bayhaqī, *al-Sunan al-kubrā*, 1:389; Ibn Abī Ḥātim al-Rāzī, *Tafsīr*, 3:958; Ibn Ḥumayd, *al-Muntakhab*, 56; al-Ṭabarī, *Tafsīr*, 5:134; al-Tirmidhī, *Sunan*, 4:305. In other recensions, ʿAlī joined them in drinking and another Companion led the prayer intoxicated: see al-Ḥākim al-Naysābūrī, *al-Mustadrak*, 4:142; al-Ṭabarī, *Tafsīr*, 5:133. For more references, see al-ʿĀmilī, *al-Ṣaḥīḥ min sīrat al-imām ʿAlī*, 3:53–56.

31 Al-Balādhurī, *Ansāb al-ashrāf*, 8:82.

32 Al-Jāḥiẓ, *al-Bayān wa ʾl-tabyīn*, 317; Ibn Abī ʾl-Ḥadīd, *Sharḥ*, 4:58.

33 Abū ʾl-Faraj al-Iṣbahānī, *al-Aghānī*, 5:102; Ibn Abī ʾl-Ḥadīd, *Sharḥ*, 1:270. See also Madelung, *Succession*, 221.

34 Al-Balādhurī, *Ansāb al-ashrāf*, 5:598; Ibn ʿAbd al-Barr, *al-Istīʿāb*, 4:1557; Ibn Abī ʾl-Ḥadīd, *Sharḥ*, 1:270; Ibn ʿAsākir, *Taʾrīkh*, 1:270; al-Mubarrad, *al-Kāmil*, 3:21; al-Zubayrī, *Nasab Quraysh*, 139–140.

35 Al-Ṭabarī, *Tārīkh*, 4:30 (where Syrians state that this is what they have heard regarding ʿAlī). ʿAlī also refuses to pray when the Prophet invites him: see Aḥmad b. Ḥanbal, *al-Musnad*, 1:77, 91, 112; al-Bukhārī, *Ṣaḥīḥ*, 2:43, 8:155, 190; Muslim, *Ṣaḥīḥ*, 2:187.

36 Madelung, "Abū ʾl-ʿAmayṭar the Sufyānī," 332. Given the context, the taunt was probably directed toward the ʿAbbāsid caliphs who presented themselves as the chief representatives of the Hāshimids. An ʿAbbāsid accused the insurrectionists of rebelling against the "Banū Hāshim": see ibid., 336.

37 Al-Balādhurī, *Ansāb al-ashrāf*, 3:291, 5:317, 7:133.

*4 Denials that ʿAlī and his Family Members Possessed any Merits (*Faḍāʾil*)*

Since Shīʿī veneration of ʿAlī and his kin entailed belief in their right to the caliphate or the Shīʿī imāmate, political rivals often discredited claims to such authority by denying the merits of ʿAlids. Ibn al-Zubayr, for example, viewed Ibn al-Ḥanafiyya as a competitor for the caliphate because of al-Mukhtār b. Abī ʿUbayd al-Thaqafī's success in establishing a government in Ibn al-Ḥanafiyya's name in Kūfa and Ibn al-Ḥanafiyya's own refusal to pledge allegiance to Ibn al-Zubayr. Ibn al-Zubayr reportedly told a number of Ibn al-Ḥanafiyya's partisans, "[He] has never distinguished himself in spirituality, personal judgment, or intelligence. He has no right to this affair [the caliphate]."[38]

ʿAbd al-ʿAzīz al-Ṭabāṭabāʾī examines literature portraying early Muslims, including Companions, as refusing to discuss the merits of ʿAlī.[39] In one case, the person fears the repercussions that will befall him were al-Ḥajjāj b. Yūsuf, the ruthless Umayyad army commander in Iraq, to hear that he had discussed a merit of ʿAlī.[40] When someone asks ʿAbd Allāh b. ʿUmar to share what he knows about ʿAlī, he points to ʿAlī's home in Medina and says, "This is where he lived. This is the most I will say about him."[41] Pro-ʿAlids would point to ʿAbd Allāh b. ʿUmar's ʿUthmānī sensibilities as the reason for which he refrains to say more, while others would cite the Umayyad apparatus.

Under the Umayyads, ʿAlī became a man whose merits were obscured and forgotten. For example, one Companion had to assure a younger peer that indeed ʿAlī participated in the battle of Badr.[42] It became a common motif for someone to ask the Companions whether or not they had heard the Prophet say anything good about ʿAlī. They are all portrayed as living in a time and place in which most people assume the answer to be in the negative. Companions such as Abū Saʿīd al-Khudrī (d. 74/693), Zayd b. Arqam, and Saʿd b. Abī Waqqāṣ offer lengthy responses in which they recite the merits of ʿAlī.[43] The listener usually responds with disbelief and the Companion must swear that he heard the Prophet say these words about ʿAlī with his own two ears.

Under the ʿAbbāsids, some poets famously lampooned the ʿAlids to support ʿAbbāsid claims to power. They included Marwān b. Abī Ḥafṣa (d. 182/798), his grandson Abū al-Simṭ Marwān b. Abī 'l-Janūb (d. ca. 240/854), and Manṣūr b. Sulaymān al-Namarī (d. ca. 201/826). For example, Ibn Abī Ḥafṣa was financially compensated for the following lines:

Do you wish to efface the stars from the sky with your palms or conceal its crescent?
Or reject the words of your Lord that Gabriel conveyed to the Prophet and he then pronounced?

[38] Ibid., 3:280.
[39] Aḥmad b. Ḥanbal, *Faḍāʾil Amīr al-Muʾminīn*, 41–52. I am indebted to Sayyid Muhammad Rizvi for this reference.
[40] Ibid., 48; Ḥākim al-Naysābūrī, *al-Mustadrak*, 3:137.
[41] Aḥmad b. Ḥanbal, *Faḍāʾil Amīr al-Muʾminīn*, 45, 195.
[42] Ibid., 41; al-Bukhārī, *Ṣaḥīḥ*, 5:7.
[43] Aḥmad b. Ḥanbal, *Faḍāʾil Amīr al-Muʾminīn*, 41–43, 46, 244; al-Nasāʾī, *al-Sunan al-kubrā*, 5:121; al-Ṭabarānī, *al-Muʿjam al-kabīr*, 5:194.

The final verse of *Anfāl* bore witness to their inheritance! Now you all wish to negate it!
Leave the lions alone in their dens! Do not cause their cubs to lap up your blood . . .[44]

Ibn Abī Ḥafṣa argued that the last verse of Sūrat al-Anfāl (Q8:75), "those with blood relations are more entitled [to inheritance] in the Book of God," granted ʿAbbās b. ʿAbd al-Muṭṭalib, the only uncle (and closest agnate) to outlive the Prophet, the Prophet's inheritance, which included the imāmate or authority over the Muslim community. Since Fāṭima was a woman, she was not eligible to inherit such authority from her father, and consequently her descendants could not claim to be heirs to any authority from the Prophet through their kinship to her. Ibn Abī Ḥafṣa warned that if the ʿAlids began to challenge the ʿAbbāsids, they would be killed without hesitation and that ʿAbbāsid cubs – an allusion to the Abnāʾ, members of the ʿAbbāsid house and their clients – would relish their deaths.

Ibn Abī Ḥafṣa's grandson Marwān b. Abī 'l-Janūb also disparaged the political careers of ʿAlī and al-Ḥasan b. ʿAlī in a famous poem:

Your father ʿAlī was superior to all of you, but the electoral council rejected him, and they were men of great merit
He harmed the Messenger of God by upsetting his daughter with his proposal to the daughter of Abū Jahl, the damned
The Messenger of God publicly rebuked your father and [lamented] taking him as a son-in-law from the pulpit for reasons no one denies
In the case of your father, the two arbitrators judged that he should be divested and removed [from power] like sandals from one's feet
And his son Ḥasan certainly sold [the caliphate] after him. Therefore, both of them have rendered void your claims to it and your rope has become worn out
Indeed you withdrew from it when those who were undeserving possessed it and demanded it once those who were suitable obtained it[45]

The second and third lines refer to an incident in which ʿAlī is portrayed as angering Fāṭima and the Prophet for either considering or extending a marriage proposal to the daughter of Abū Jahl.[46] The story may have developed to counter reports which indicated that the prophetic *ḥadīth* "Fāṭima is a part of me; he who angers her, angers me as well" was historically relevant only in the

[44] Al-Dhahabī, *Taʾrīkh*, 12:391; Ibn ʿAsākir, *Taʾrīkh*, 57:291; al-Khaṭīb al-Baghdādī, *Taʾrīkh Baghdād*, 13:144–146.

[45] Abū 'l-Faraj al-Iṣbahānī, *al-Aghānī*, 23:150; Ibn Abī 'l-Ḥadīd, *Sharḥ*, 4:65; Ibn Manẓūr, *Mukhtār al-Aghānī*, 6:424.

[46] ʿAbd al-Razzāq al-Ṣanʿānī, *al-Muṣannaf*, 7:300–302; Abū Dāwūd al-Sijistānī, *Sunan*, 1:460; al-Bukhārī, *Ṣaḥīḥ*, 4:212, 6:158; Ibn Abī Shayba, *al-Muṣannaf*, 7:527; Aḥmad b. Ḥanbal, *al-Musnad*, 4:5, 326, 328; Ibn Māja, *Sunan*, 1:643–644; Muslim, *Ṣaḥīḥ*, 7:141–142; al-Tirmidhī, *Sunan*, 5:359–360.

case of Abū Bakr, who famously upset Fāṭima by disinheriting her and rejecting her claims to ownership of various estates that had belonged to the Prophet.[47] To defend Abū Bakr's honor, Ibn Kathīr argued that her anger was misplaced in this case since she was a woman and women were prone to volatile emotional states.[48] Ibn Taymiyya and Ibn Kathīr both claimed that she eventually realized her error and accepted Abū Bakr's opinion that a prophetic *ḥadīth* had already disinherited her.[49]

Some biographical sources describe Manṣūr al-Namarī as a poet who originally had anti-ʿAlid Khārijī sympathies but became an Imāmī after encountering Hishām b. al-Ḥakam in Kūfa.[50] Before his conversion, he composed pro-ʿAbbāsid poetry for the caliph Hārūn al-Rashīd. In the poem below, al-Namarī argues that the Ḥasanids and the Ḥusaynids contradict the Qurʾān by regarding themselves as descendants of the Prophet or considering him their father, since a verse in Sūrat al-Aḥzāb (Q33:40) states that "Muḥammad is not the father of any of your men." Al-Namarī urges them to desist from any ambitions to obtain power (or anything else) by virtue of their descent from Fāṭima.

They call the Prophet "a father," but a line from *Aḥzāb* forbids this
If they said: "(We are) the sons of a daughter!" and returned that which suits only the descendants of men, then this would be just
The sons of daughters do not inherit anything when paternal uncles are present; even the Psalms testify to this law
O sons of al-Ḥasan and al-Ḥusayn: Do the right thing!
Stay far from false hopes and desires! And dreams that promise only lies ...[51]

In their opposition to Shīʿī doctrines, authors dismissed the authenticity of reports that attributed unique merits (*khaṣāʾiṣ*) to ʿAlī and his progeny. Al-Jāḥiẓ, Ibn Ḥazm, Ibn Taymiyya, and Muḥammad b. Yaʿqūb al-Fīrūzābādī all wrote works that denied ʿAlī's possession of unique merits. Poets and authors generally revealed their partiality by promoting ʿUthmānī, Umayyad, or ʿAbbāsid theological and political claims.

47 ʿAbd al-Razzāq al-Ṣanʿānī, *al-Muṣannaf*, 5:472; Aḥmad b. Ḥanbal, *al-Musnad*, 1:6; al-Bayhaqī, *al-Sunan al-kubrā*, 6:300–301; al-Bukhārī, *Ṣaḥīḥ*, 4:42, 5:82, 8:3; Muslim, *Ṣaḥīḥ*, 5:153; al-Ṭabarānī, *Musnad al-Shāmīyīn*, 4:198.

48 Ibn Kathīr, *al-Bidāya wa 'l-nihāya*, 5:270, 310.

49 Ibid., 5:309; Ibn Taymiyya, *Minhāj*, 4:234. Although al-Bayhaqī cited a report which portrayed Fāṭima as becoming satisfied with Abū Bakr before she died, her opinion regarding the *ḥadīth* he narrated is not explicitly discussed: see al-Bayhaqī, *al-Sunan al-kubrā*, 6:301.

50 Al-Huṣrī, *Zahr al-ādāb*, 3:705; al-Tustarī, *Qāmūs al-rijāl*, 11:526. Others mentioned that he composed poetry with pro-ʿAlid sentiment, but concealed his beliefs due to the anti-ʿAlid feelings of Hārūn al-Rashīd: see Abū 'l-Faraj al-Iṣbahānī, *al-Aghānī*, 13:97–108; al-Khaṭīb al-Baghdādī, *Taʾrīkh Baghdād*, 13:67–70. See also al-Kaḥḥāla, *Muʿjam al-muʾallifīn*, 13:13.

51 Al-Huṣrī, *Zahr al-ādāb*, 3:705. Ibn Qutayba only transmits a small excerpt: see Ibn Qutayba, *al-Shiʿr wa 'l-shuʿarāʾ*, 2:847. See also al-ʿAwwād, *al-Naṣb*, 316.

5 Criticisms of the Actions and Opinions of ʿAlī and his Sons as Unwise or Mistaken

In sections 1–3 above, ʿAlī and his sons are portrayed as men of vice who invite criticism with their impiety. Despite some thematic overlap (i.e. Muslims criticizing ʿAlī), one key difference here is that *ḥadīth* transmitters may have circulated such stories under the assumption that ʿAlī unintentionally displeased God and His Prophet. Sunnīs generally understood such reports charitably, so that ʿAlī learned from his mistakes. Anti-ʿAlids considered ʿAlī to have been evil, so if they circulated these reports, it was to undermine his honor and criticize his character. In one example noted above, ʿAlī and Fāṭima refuse to join the Prophet in prayer. Other reports depict ʿAlī burning people alive,[52] leading prayer while intoxicated, and wishing to marry a second wife in the lifetime of Fāṭima.

When eighth- and ninth-century theologians criticized ʿAlī's political career and the way he dealt with challenges to his authority, the Baghdādī Muʿtazila accused them of belittling (*tanqīṣ*) ʿAlī.[53] These Muʿtazilīs asserted that some scholars unfairly avoided defending ʿAlī's conduct as caliph while offering generous interpretations of ʿUthmān's actions misdeeds or justifying Abū Bakr's war against those who refused to send him alms. They argued that ʿAlī's conduct as caliph could be vindicated on identical grounds.[54]

The governors of Syria would allegedly claim their lack of need for divorce or even marriage as a sign of their superior piety, while ʿAlī married ten times and left behind seventeen concubines upon his death.[55]

In some reports, ʿUmar and ʿAmr b. al-ʿĀṣ (d. 42/663) criticize ʿAlī as someone who was known to jest.[56]

Some texts claim that al-Ḥasan b. ʿAlī abdicated in favor of Muʿāwiya with the primary concern of obtaining large amounts of wealth for himself and his clan.[57] He is portrayed as a womanizer who married seventy, ninety, or even hundreds of women.[58]

6 Doubts about the Trustworthiness of ʿAlids as Transmitters of Religious Knowledge

Hundreds of ʿAlī's descendants narrated *ḥadīth*, exegetical reports, and legal texts over many centuries.[59] Sunnī *ḥadīth* scholars generally characterized the contents

52 Aḥmad b. Ḥanbal, *al-Musnad*, 1:282–283; al-Bukhārī, *Ṣaḥīḥ*, 4:21, 8:50; Ibn Abī Shayba, *al-Muṣannaf*, 7:658; al-Nasāʾī, *Sunan al-Nasāʾī*, 7:104; al-Shāfiʿī, *al-Umm*, 1:294. In some versions, ʿAlī cremates them after executing them: see al-Haythamī, *Majmaʿ al-zawāʾid*, 6:262; al-Ṭabarānī, *al-Muʿjam al-awsaṭ*, 7:140.

53 Al-Iskāfī, *al-Miʿyār*, 33–34. 54 Ibid., 34. 55 Al-Makkī, *Qūt al-qulūb*, 3:1621.

56 Al-Balādhurī, *Ansāb al-ashrāf*, 2:151, 10:344; Ibn ʿAbd al-Barr, *al-Istīʿāb*, 3:1119; Ibn Qutayba, *Taʾwīl mukhtalif al-ḥadīth*, 273 (Ibn Qutayba assumes the characteristic to be true of ʿAlī).

57 Al-Bukhārī, *Ṣaḥīḥ*, 3:170; Ibn ʿAsākir, *Taʾrīkh*, 13:271; al-Ṭabarī, *Tārīkh*, 4:22–23. See also Madelung, *Succession*, 329–330.

58 Al-Makkī, *Qūt al-qulūb*, 3:1621 (for the figures 250 and 300). See also Madelung, *Succession*, 380–387.

59 See al-Rajāʾī, *al-Muḥaddithūn min Āl Abī Ṭālib*.

and the transmitters of such reports as unreliable and Shīʿī. The Twelver imāms and their sons were sometimes criticized on these grounds. For example, ʿAlī b. Jaʿfar al-Ṣādiq is criticized for his narration of a pro-ʿAlid report.[60] According to Ibn Taymiyya, al-Bukhārī accepted Yaḥyā b. Saʿīd's negative judgment regarding the reliability of ʿAlī's father, Jaʿfar al-Ṣādiq, and refrained from narrating prophetic reports from this ʿAlid imām.[61] Abū Bakr b. Shihāb and Muḥammad b. ʿAqīl al-ʿAlawī considered the views of Yaḥyā b. Saʿīd and al-Bukhārī regarding al-Ṣādiq an affront to the Household of the Prophet.[62]

7 *Staunch Defenses or Endorsements of the Piety of Individuals who Fought against or Disagreed with the Household*

Some texts glorify Muʿāwiya as a righteous Muslim,[63] while others defend Yazīd as righteous and wrongly accused of misdeeds.[64] Frequently, nonpartisan Sunnīs who revered both ʿAlī and Muʿāwiya relied on pro-Umayyad literature to argue for the piety, salvation, and merits of Muʿāwiya and his descendants. Aḥmad b. Ḥanbal is quoted as explaining that "ʿAlī had many enemies who carefully searched for his vices but could not find any. Thus, they turned to excessively praising a man who waged war against him out of malice for ʿAlī."[65] Animosity for Muʿāwiya and the rejection of his alleged merits can be considered a criterion for differentiating a pro-ʿAlid Sunnī from a nonpartisan one. It is on this basis that some biographers considered the famous *ḥadīth* scholar al-Nasāʾī pro-ʿAlid.[66]

8 *Statements Condemning the Companions of ʿAlī as Evil*

Texts of this type criticize ʿAlī's disciples primarily for their opposition to ʿUthmān and ʿUthmān's governors before his assassination. The claim that ʿAlī's disciples were corrupt lent support to ʿUthmānī arguments about their role in causing sedition, bloodshed, and the emergence of political factions and sects. These texts condemned ʿAmmār as a murderer of ʿUthmān[67] and as someone who had

[60] Al-Dhahabī, *Mīzān al-iʿtidāl*, 3:117.
[61] Ibn ʿAdī, *al-Kāmil*, 2:131 (for Ibn Saʿīd's criticism of al-Ṣādiq); Ibn Taymiyya, *Minhāj*, 7:533–534.
[62] Muḥammad b. ʿAqīl al-ʿAlawī, *al-ʿAtb al-jamīl*, 37–39.
[63] For example, see Ibn Ḥajar al-Haytamī, *Taṭhīr al-janān*. See also Barzegar, "Remembering Community," 177–231.
[64] For example, see Ibn Taymiyya, *Majmūʿ fatāwā*, 3:409; Ibn Taymiyya, *Raʾs*, 207; Ibn Ṭūlūn, *Qayd al-sharīd min akhbār Yazīd*.
[65] Ibn Ḥajar al-ʿAsqalānī, *Fatḥ al-bārī*, 7:81; Ibn al-Jawzī, *al-Mawḍūʿāt*, 2:24. See also al-ʿAwwād, *al-Naṣb*, 599.
[66] See al-Dhahabī, *Siyar*, 14:133.
[67] Al-Dīnawarī, *al-Akhbār al-ṭiwāl*, 149; Ibn Shabba, *Taʾrīkh al-Madīna*, 4:1250. See also Madelung, *Succession*, 156.

been influenced by the infamous ʿAbd Allāh b. Sabaʾ and his cronies.[68] Abū Dharr[69] and ʿAmr b. al-Ḥamiq al-Khuzāʿī,[70] also Companions of the Prophet and ʿAlī, were similarly considered associates of Ibn Sabaʾ and enemies of ʿUthmān. Sayf b. ʿUmar linked ʿAmmār and Abū Dharr to Ibn Sabaʾ in order to discredit their criticisms of ʿUthmān and his Umayyad governors.[71] Ibn Sabaʾ was depicted as a covert Jew who was the source of civil unrest across the empire during the caliphate of ʿUthmān and the real cause of the battle of the Camel.[72] By portraying ʿAlī's disciples as associates of Ibn Sabaʾ, Sayf sought to discredit pro-ʿAlid sentiment, Shīʿism, and alternative historical reports that blamed ʿAlī's political rivals, such as ʿĀʾisha or the Umayyads, for these conflicts.

Other disciples of ʿAlī denounced in Sunnī historical narratives include Muḥammad b. Abī Bakr,[73] Ḥukaym b. Jabala,[74] Mālik al-Ashtar,[75] and many others. For example, in one report ʿĀʾisha curses ʿAlī's closest companions in a gathering. She names ʿAmmār, Mālik al-Ashtar, and her brother Muḥammad b. Abī Bakr.[76]

[68] Al-Ṭabarī, *Tārīkh*, 3:379. See also Anthony, *The Caliph and the Heretic*, 59 n. 138, 87–90, 93.

[69] Al-Ṭabarī, *Tārīkh*, 3:335. See also Anthony, *The Caliph and the Heretic*, 52–56; Madelung, *Succession*, 84.

[70] Al-Balādhurī, *Ansāb al-ashrāf*, 2:382, 5:272. See also Anthony, *The Caliph and the Heretic*, 96, 209.

[71] Al-ʿAskarī, *Maʿālim*, 1: 277–290; Keaney, *Medieval Islamic Historiography*, 38. In a famous study, al-ʿAskarī dismissed as fiction the alleged role of ʿAbd Allāh b. Sabaʾ in founding Shīʿism and instigating all of the conflicts that occurred during the caliphates of ʿUthmān and ʿAlī: see al-ʿAskarī, *ʿAbd Allāh ibn Sabaʾ wa asāṭīr ukhrā*.

[72] For example, see Ibn Kathīr, *al-Bidāya wa ʾl-nihāya*, 7:265–267.

[73] Al-Bukhārī, *al-Ḍuʿafāʾ al-ṣaghīr*, 1:104, 121. See also Anthony, *The Caliph and the Heretic*, 93, 98; Madelung, *Succession*, 156; Yazigi, "Defense and Validation," 62–64.

[74] Al-Ṭabarī, *Tārīkh*, 3:368, 457, 483. Sayf b. ʿUmar described him as a thief, someone who would curse ʿĀʾisha, a host of ʿAbd Allāh b. Sabaʾ, and one whom ʿUthmān had previously imprisoned: see also Anthony, *The Caliph and the Heretic*, 49–51, 122–126; Madelung, *Succession*, 144 n. 14.

[75] Al-Bukhārī, *al-Ḍuʿafāʾ al-ṣaghīr*, 1:121; al-Dīnawarī, *al-Akhbār al-ṭiwāl*, 149; al-Ṭabarī, *Tārīkh*, 3:561. See also Anthony, *The Caliph and the Heretic*, 32–33, 36, 43, 112, 128, 133.

[76] Al-Bukhārī, *al-Ḍuʿafāʾ al-ṣaghīr*, 1:121; Ibn ʿAsākir, *Taʾrīkh*, 56:381; Ibn Shabba, *Taʾrīkh al-Madīna*, 4:1244; al-Jāḥiẓ, *al-Bayān wa ʾl-tabyīn*, 359. See also Madelung, Succession, 160–161.

Chapter 2 Appendix: Reports about the Umayyads and the ʿUthmānīs

1 DEFENSES OF MURDER, PERSECUTION, OR PHYSICAL ATTACK DIRECTED AT ʿALĪ OR MEMBERS OF HIS HOUSEHOLD

A number of Sunnīs transmit reports that accuse Muʿāwiya of poisoning al-Ḥasan to facilitate Yazīd b. Muʿāwiya's succession.[1] Some reports cast Yazīd himself as the culprit.[2]

In one report, al-Ḥusayn warns his murderers in the Umayyad army that his death would violate the inviolability (*ḥurma*) of the Household of the Prophet.[3]

ʿUbayd Allāh b. Ziyād wrote to ʿUmar b. Saʿd b. Abī Waqqāṣ, his commander at Karbalāʾ, "Do not let al-Ḥusayn and his companions obtain any water. Prevent them from tasting a drop of it, just as they did to the pious ʿUthmān b. ʿAffān."[4]

In another letter, Ibn Ziyād wrote to ʿUmar:

> If Ḥusayn and his followers submit to my authority and surrender, you can send them to me in peace. If they refuse, then march against them. They are to be killed and decapitated for their actions. If Ḥusayn is killed, make the horses trample on his chest and back, for he is a disobedient rebel who splits the community and severs kinship relations. He is an evil and iniquitous man (*ʿāqq mushāqq qāṭiʿ ẓalūm*).[5]

1 Al-Balādhurī, *Ansāb al-ashrāf*, 1:404; Ibn ʿAbd al-Barr, *al-Istīʿāb*, 1:389; Ibn Saʿd, *Kitāb al-Ṭabaqāt al-kabīr*, 6:386; al-Maqrīzī, *Imtāʿ*, 5:361; Sibṭ Ibn al-Jawzī, *Tadhkirat al-khawāṣṣ*, 192; al-Ṭabarānī, *al-Muʿjam al-kabīr*, 3:71.

2 Ibn al-Jawzī, *al-Muntaẓam*, 5:226; al-Mizzī, *Tahdhīb al-Kamāl*, 6:253.

3 Al-Ṭabarī, *Tārīkh*, 4:322–323. See also Dakake, *Charismatic Community*, 88–90, 93–95.

4 Al-Dīnawarī, *al-Akhbār al-ṭiwāl*, 255; al-Khuwārizmī, *Maqtal al-Ḥusayn*, 1:346.

5 Al-Balādhurī, *Ansāb al-ashrāf*, 3:183; al-Ṭabarī, *Tārīkh*, 4:314; al-Ṭabarī, *The Caliphate of Yazīd*, 110. The phrase *qāṭiʿ* may refer to claims that al-Ḥusayn was "a highway robber" (*qāṭiʿ al-ṭarīq*). Such an interpretation rests on the fact that al-Ḥusayn and his followers took up arms and rebelled against the state. Jurists sometimes included rebels in the

Ibn Ziyād instructed Shimr b. Dhī ʾl-Jawshan, "If ʿUmar b. Saʿd acts according to my instructions, then heed him and obey him. However, if he refuses to fight them, then you are the commander of the people; attack Ḥusayn, cut off his head, and send it to me."[6]

Shimr reasoned that he fought and killed al-Ḥusayn because disobedience to rulers (who were appointed by God) made a person more wretched (*sharr*) than a donkey.[7]

When Ibn Ziyād met ʿAlī b. al-Ḥusayn Zayn al-ʿĀbidīn, he was confused and asked, "Wasn't ʿAlī b. al-Ḥusayn killed?" When Zayn al-ʿĀbidīn clarified that the army had killed a brother of the same name, Ibn Ziyād answered, "Rather, God killed him." Ibn Ziyād was invoking the belief that it was God's wish to destroy individuals who had incurred His wrath.[8]

Ibn Ziyād proclaimed, "Praise the Lord who made the truth manifest and those who follow it triumphant! He gave victory to the Commander of the Faithful Yazīd and his party and killed the liar, son of a liar, Ḥusayn b. ʿAlī and his partisans."[9]

ʿAmr b. al-Ḥajjāj, a commander of the Umayyad army at Karbalāʾ, addressed his soldiers in the following words: "O people of Kūfa, maintain obedience [to the caliph] and your allegiance to the greater community! Do not doubt the necessity of killing those who have rebelled against faith (*maraqa min al-dīn*) and opposed the imām (Yazīd)."[10]

After the massacre at Karbalāʾ the family of al-Ḥusayn b. ʿAlī was sent to the palace of Ibn Ziyād, who addressed Zaynab bt. ʿAlī thus: "Praise the Lord who disgraced you, killed you, and discredited your claims."[11]

2 REPORTS OF INDIVIDUALS CURSING OR DISPARAGING ʿALĪ OR MEMBERS OF HIS FAMILY

Muʿāwiya appointed Kathīr b. Shahāb as the governor of Rayy, and the latter frequently cursed ʿAlī from the pulpit.[12]

Ibn Ziyād disparaged ʿAlī, ʿAqīl b. Abī Ṭālib, and al-Ḥusayn before executing Muslim b. ʿAqīl.[13]

Ibn Ziyād ordered al-Ḥusayn's messenger to Kūfa, Qays b. Musahhar al-Ṣaydāwī, to damn al-Ḥusayn and his father ʿAlī from the pulpit. Ibn Ziyād executed Qays after he agreed to do so but damned Ibn Ziyād and his father instead.[14] In one recension, Ibn Ziyād commands Qays, "Ascend to the top of the palace and curse the liar, son of the liar [al-Ḥusayn, the son of ʿAlī]."[15] In another version, Ibn Ziyād

muḥāriba verse (Q5:33) and considered the death penalty to be a proper punishment for the sedition they caused: see Ibn Kathīr, *Tafsīr al-Qurʾān al-ʿaẓīm*, 2:53.

6 Al-Ṭabarī, *The Caliphate of Yazīd*, 110. 7 Al-Dhahabī, *Taʾrīkh*, 5:125–126.

8 Ibn Aʿtham al-Kūfī, *al-Futūḥ*, 5:123.

9 Ibn al-Athīr, *al-Kāmil*, 4:82–83; Ibn Ḥabīb, *Muḥabbar*, 480; al-Ṭabarī, *Tārīkh*, 4:350–351.

10 Al-Ṭabarī, *Tārīkh*, 4:331. 11 Ibid., 4:349. 12 Ibn al-Athīr, *al-Kāmil*, 3:413–414.

13 Al-Ṭabarī, *Tārīkh*, 4:283. 14 Ibid., 4:306 (transmitting from Abū Mikhnaf).

15 Ibid., 4:297.

tells Qays to damn al-Ḥusayn's brother, al-Ḥasan, as well. Instead, Qays publicly damns the caliph, Yazīd b. Muʿāwiya, and the Umayyad apparatus.[16]

As governor of Medina, Hishām b. Ismāʿīl (in office 84–87/703–706) would disparage ʿAlī b. Abī Ṭālib in his sermons although he was aware that ʿAlī b. al-Ḥusayn and his family considered his words hurtful.[17]

According to Ibn Ḥazm, al-Ḥajjāj b. Yūsuf and the preachers he employed would publicly damn (*yalʿan*) ʿAlī and Ibn al-Zubayr from the pulpit.[18] Other sources depict al-Ḥajjāj regularly disparaging ʿAlī, persecuting his former disciples, and punishing those who refused to curse ʿAlī.[19]

The brother of al-Ḥajjāj, Muḥammad b. Yūsuf al-Thaqafī, was the governor of Yemen, and he, too, would publicly damn ʿAlī from the pulpit.[20]

The Marwānid caliph al-Walīd b. ʿAbd al-Malik (r. 86–96/705–715) disparagingly referred to ʿAlī as a donkey.[21]

Al-Mubarrad (d. 285/898) reports:

> Khālid b. ʿAbd Allāh al-Qasrī, may God damn him, would damn (*yalʿan*) ʿAlī, may God have mercy on him, from the pulpit with the following words, "May God [damn][22] ʿAlī b. Abī Ṭālib b. ʿAbd al-Muṭṭalib b. Hāshim b. ʿAbd Manāf, paternal cousin to the Messenger of God, husband to his daughter, and the father of al-Ḥasan and al-Ḥusayn." Then he would turn to the audience and ask, "Have I properly mentioned [all of] his titles?"[23]

According to one source, Khālid al-Qasrī would refer to ʿAlī with words that "are not permissible" to repeat.[24] Yaḥyā b. Maʿīn described Khālid thus: "He was an evil man (*rajul sūʾ*) who would vilify (*yaqaʿu fī*) ʿAlī b. Abī Ṭālib."[25] Al-Dhahabī adds, "He was honest, but anti-ʿAlid, loathsome, and frequently unjust."[26]

After Khālid was removed from office and imprisoned in 120/738, he was subjected to long periods of torture until his death in 126/743. It seems that the governor of Iraq, Yūsuf b. ʿUmar al-Thaqafī, extracted a false confession from Khālid by means of torture. Khālid was forced to accuse some Hāshimids of agreeing to safeguard his wealth and to assist him in embezzling state funds. When one of the accused, Zayd b. ʿAlī b. al-Ḥusayn, came to Iraq to face his actual accuser (Yūsuf b. ʿUmar), both he and Khālid denied that any such agreement could

16 Al-Khuwārizmī, *Maqtal al-Ḥusayn*, 1:336.

17 Ibn Saʿd, *al-Ṭabaqāt al-kubrā*, 5:220; Sibṭ Ibn al-Jawzī, *Tadhkirat al-khawāṣṣ*, 1:295.

18 Ibn Ḥazm, *al-Muḥallā*, 5:64.

19 Al-Balādhurī, *Ansāb al-ashrāf*, 13:388; al-Dhahabī, *Siyar*, 4:267; al-Ḥākim al-Ḥaskānī, *Shawāhid al-tanzīl*, 1:121–122.

20 Ibn Kathīr, *al-Bidāya wa ʾl-nihāya*, 9:80.

21 Al-Balādhurī, *Ansāb al-ashrāf*, 8:82.

22 Out of respect for ʿAlī, copyists of al-Mubarrad's work amended *laʿana Allāh* to *faʿala Allah* to keep from actually pronouncing the invocation. Ibn Abī ʾl-Ḥadīd's copy reads *Allāhuma ʾlʿan*.

23 Ibn Abī ʾl-Ḥadīd, *Sharḥ*, 4:57; al-Mubarrad, *al-Kāmil*, 2:414.

24 Ibn ʿAsākir, *Taʾrīkh*, 16:160; al-Mizzī, *Tahdhīb al-Kamāl*, 8:116.

25 Ibn ʿAsākir, *Taʾrīkh*, 16:160; Ibn Ḥajar al-ʿAsqalānī, *Tahdhīb al-Tahdhīb*, 3:88; al-Mizzī, *Tahdhīb al-Kamāl*, 8:116.

26 *ṣadūq lākinnahu nāṣibī baghīḍ ẓalūm*: see al-Dhahabī, *Mīzān al-iʿtidāl*, 1:633.

have occurred, since Khālid was staunchly anti-ʿAlid. Zayd b. ʿAlī reportedly said: "How is it that he [Khālid] would ask me to safeguard his wealth when he curses my ancestors every Friday from the pulpit?" Then Zayd swore that he had never received any money from Khālid. Khālid was then summoned from prison to accuse Zayd again, but he only confirmed Zayd's testimony and said, "Why would I [give him my wealth] when I curse his father every Friday?"[27] When Zayd asked Khālid why he had initially implicated the ʿAlids, Khālid explained that he had accused them only under severe torture and had hoped for a settlement and his own release before any of them were summoned.[28]

Khālid b. ʿAbd al-Malik b. al-Ḥārith b. al-Ḥakam was an Umayyad governor of Medina (in office 114–118/732–736) and referred to Zayd b. ʿAlī as stupid (*safīh*) and encouraged another resident of Medina to address Zayd thus: "O son of Abū Turāb and son of Ḥusayn, the stupid one."[29]

Ḥadīth *Transmitters among the ʿUthmāniyya*

Abū Labīd Limāza b. Zabbār al-Baṣrī (d. ca. 80–9/699–708) was a prominent Follower (*tābiʿī*) and *ḥadīth* transmitter who fought ʿAlī at the battle of the Camel. He was famous for cursing ʿAlī. When asked if he loved ʿAlī, he responded, "How can I love a person who killed 2,500 members of my family in a single day?"[30]

Once, when the Kūfan Murra b. Sharāḥīl (d. 85/704) disparaged ʿAlī, he was asked how he could do so given that ʿAlī had been a Companion of the Prophet known for his good deeds. He replied, "What is my sin if his deeds preceded me and I experienced only evil from him?"[31]

Thawr b. Yazīd al-Ḥimṣī (d. ca. 153/770) was a prolific *ḥadīth* transmitter whose grandfather died fighting for Muʿāwiya at Ṣiffīn. Since he considered ʿAlī responsible for his grandfather's death, he would reportedly say, "I cannot love a person who killed my grandfather," whenever ʿAlī was mentioned in his presence.[32]

Ḥarīz b. ʿUthmān al-Ḥimṣī was a respected *ḥadīth* transmitter[33] who despised ʿAlī and blamed him for the deaths of his ancestors at Ṣiffīn. He reportedly claimed that ʿAlī had attempted to injure or kill the Prophet.[34] While most Muslims

27 Al-Balādhurī, *Ansāb al-ashrāf*, 9:118; Ibn al-Athīr, *al-Kāmil*, 5:230; Ibn Kathīr, *al-Bidāya wa 'l-nihāya*, 9:358; al-Ṭabarī, *Tārīkh*, 5:487.

28 Ibn al-Athīr, *al-Kāmil*, 5:230; al-Ṭabarī, *Tārīkh*, 5:487.

29 Ibn al-Athīr, *al-Kāmil*, 5:231; al-Ṭabarī, *Tārīkh*, 5:485. *Safīh* may have referred to someone who was legally incompetent: see Q4:5 and its exegesis.

30 Al-Dhahabī, *Taʾrīkh*, 6:538; Ibn ʿAsākir, *Taʾrīkh*, 50:305–306; Khalīfa ibn Khayyāṭ, *Tārīkh*, 140; al-Ṣafadī, *al-Wāfī*, 24:304.

31 Al-Fasawī, *al-Maʿrifa wa 'l-taʾrīkh*, 3:183.

32 Ibn ʿAsākir, *Taʾrīkh*, 11:186; Ibn Ḥajar al-ʿAsqalānī, *Tahdhīb al-Tahdhīb*, 2:30; Ibn Qutayba, *al-Maʿārif*, 505; Ibn Saʿd, *al-Ṭabaqāt al-kubrā*, 7:467.

33 For example, see Abū Dāwūd al-Sijistānī, *Sunan*, 2:161.

34 Ibn Ḥajar al-ʿAsqalānī, *Tahdhīb al-Tahdhīb*, 2:210; Ibn al-Jawzī, *Kitāb al-ḍuʿafāʾ*, 1:197. See also Kohlberg, "Some Imāmī Shīʿī Views on the *Ṣaḥāba*," 156 n. 69.

believed the Prophet had likened ʿAlī to Aaron in a famous *ḥadīth*,[35] Ḥarīz argued that they had misheard the *ḥadīth*: the Prophet had compared ʿAlī to the Biblical Korah (Arab. Qārūn), who rebelled against Moses, rather than to Aaron (Arab. Hārūn).[36] According to one source, Ḥarīz claimed that the Prophet, on his deathbed, had commanded the community to cut off ʿAlī's hand.[37]

Ibrāhīm b. Yaʿqūb al-Jūzajānī (d. ca. 259/873) was a prominent *ḥadīth* transmitter who reportedly considered ʿAlī guilty of killing more than twenty thousand Muslims.[38]

3 PUBLIC DENUNCIATIONS OF ʿALĪ AND HIS KIN AS SINFUL, CRIMINAL, GUILTY OF HERESY, CAUSING EVIL, OR INTENTIONALLY DISOBEYING GOD OR HIS PROPHET

An attitude common to conquerors in the ancient world was a sense of triumphalism and determinism in interpreting the world around them and explaining their own political ascendancy. The statements of pro-Umayyads and their various rivals reflect these sentiments. For example, Ibn Ziyād is reported to have said to Zaynab, the daughter of ʿAlī and Fāṭima, and other survivors of the massacre at Karbalāʾ, "God has relieved me of that terrible bully of yours (*ṭāghiyatiki*) and the disobedient rebels (*al-ʿuṣāt al-marada*) of your family."[39] Pro-Umayyad sources credit God with granting the Umayyad army military victories over disobedient rebels such as al-Ḥusayn b. ʿAlī, and they construed such victories as signs of divine validation and legitimacy for the regime. Thus, Yazīd b. Muʿāwiya reportedly argued that al-Ḥusayn had been killed because he had disregarded the qurʾānic verse 3:26, "Say: O God, possessor of sovereignty [or kingship]! You grant sovereignty to whom You please and remove sovereignty from whom You please. You honor whom You please and humiliate whom You please. In Your hand lies all that is good. You have Power over all things."[40]

Yazīd similarly appealed to the agency of God when he addressed ʿAlī b. al-Ḥusayn Zayn al-ʿĀbidīn, the only son of al-Ḥusayn to survive the massacre: "Your father was a man who cut kinship ties with me, was ignorant of my rights, and

[35] ʿAbd al-Razzāq al-Ṣanʿānī, *al-Muṣannaf*, 5:406, 11:206; Aḥmad b. Ḥanbal, *al-Musnad*, 1:170, 173, 175, 177, 179, 182, 184, 185; al-Bukhārī, *Ṣaḥīḥ*, 4:208, 5:129; Ibn Abī Shayba, *al-Muṣannaf*, 7:496; Ibn Māja, *Sunan*, 1:43, 45; Muslim, *Ṣaḥīḥ*, 7:120–121; al-Nasāʾī, *al-Sunan al-kubrā*, 5:44, 120–125; al-Tirmidhī, *Sunan*, 5:302, 304. See also al-Tustarī, *Iḥqāq al-ḥaqq*, 5:132–234, 16:1–94; al-Marʿashī al-Najafī, *Mulḥaqāt al-Iḥqāq*, 21:150–255, 22:333–408, 23:60–75.

[36] Al-Dhahabī, *Taʾrīkh*, 10:122; Ibn ʿAsākir, *Taʾrīkh*, 12:349; Ibn Ḥajar al-ʿAsqalānī, *Tahdhīb al-Tahdhīb*, 2:209; al-Khaṭīb al-Baghdādī, *Taʾrīkh Baghdād*, 8:262; al-Mizzī, *Tahdhīb al-Kamāl*, 5:577.

[37] Ibn Abī 'l-Ḥadīd, *Sharḥ*, 4:70; al-Jawharī, *al-Saqīfa wa Fadak*, 56 (this publication is based upon Ibn Abī 'l-Ḥadīd's citations).

[38] Ibn Ḥajar al-ʿAsqalānī, *Tahdhīb al-Tahdhīb*, 1:159. [39] Al-Ṭabarī, *Tārīkh*, 4:350.

[40] Ibid., 4:355.

contested my sovereignty. Thus, God did with him that which you have witnessed."[41]

Islamic law prohibits the enslavement of freeborn Muslims. When Zaynab bt. ʿAlī protested at the court of Yazīd that her household could not be enslaved unless the caliph and his entourage became apostates and followed another faith that permitted the enslavement of Muslims, Yazīd quipped, "Rather, it was your father and brother who already became apostates."[42] Yazīd is portrayed as upholding the common pro-Umayyad belief that ʿAlī, al-Ḥusayn, and their partisans were apostates and criminals guilty of causing sedition (*fitna*). Umayyad propaganda relied on a theological principle known as *qadr* to argue that it was divinely ordained for ʿAlī and his house to face military defeat because of their iniquities and false claims to authority and entitlement. Indeed, God was continuously discrediting their claims and exposing their vile nature by granting the caliph's armed forces repeated victories over them.

Another manifestation of this belief is Yazīd's statement, "As for [al-Ḥusayn's] claim that his father was superior to mine, my father disputed with his father and everyone knows in whose favor the dispute was resolved."[43] The statement implies divine approval of Muʿāwiya's rejection of ʿAlī's caliphate and claim to sovereignty, and it interprets the Umayyads' victories over ʿAlī and his house as signs of God's favor toward the Umayyads.

When the family of al-Ḥusayn was brought in chains to Yazīd's court, a soldier named Miḥfaz b. Thaʿlaba reportedly announced to the caliph that he had brought "vile and insolent criminals" (*al-liʾām al-fajara*) to the palace in Damascus.[44] In another recension, Miḥfaz, in possession of the head of al-Ḥusayn, announced from outside the palace gates, "I have the head of the most ignorant and disgraceful of men (*aḥmaq al-nās wa alʾamihim*)." Yazīd retorted, "Rather, the mother of Miḥfaz gave birth to someone more disgraceful and ignorant, but [al-Ḥusayn] was an unjust man who severed kinship ties (*qāṭiʿ ẓālim*)."[45]

Muslim b. ʿAmr al-Bāhilī believed that Muslim b. ʿAqīl b. Abī Ṭālib, al-Ḥusayn's cousin and messenger to Kūfa, was bound for hell because he had rebelled against the caliph, who was the deputy of God on earth. It follows that he also believed al-Ḥusayn and his associates to be doomed to hell. As Muslim b. ʿAqīl awaited his execution and requested some water, Muslim b. ʿAmr reportedly responded with relish, "Is that what you desire? That gives me great joy (*mā abradahā*)![46] No, by God, you will never taste a drop until you drink *ḥamīm* in the fires of hell."[47]

A soldier in the entourage of Shimr b. Dhī 'l-Jawshan is reported to have yelled at al-Ḥusayn and his associates that they were the ones described as foul and wicked (*khabīth*) in the Qurʾān (Q3:179). He declared, "I swear by the Lord of the Kaʿba,

[41] Ibid., 4:352. [42] *kharaja min al-dīn abūka wa akhūka*: see ibid., 4:353.
[43] Ibid., 4:355. [44] Ibid., 4:352.
[45] Ibid., 4:354. Alternatively, *qāṭiʿ* could refer to "a highway robber" (*qāṭiʿ al-ṭarīq*). Yazīd may have viewed Miḥfaz as uncouth for shouting from the palace gates to address the caliph.
[46] Lit., "nothing cools [the heart] more" (*mā abradahā ʿalā 'l-fuʾād*): al-Zabīdī, *Tāj al-ʿarūs*, 2:443.
[47] Al-Ṭabarī, *Tārīkh*, 4:281. *Ḥamīm* refers to a drink in hell: see Q6:70, Q10:4, and other verses.

we are the virtuous and pure while you are all foul and wicked! He has distinguished us from you!"[48] In the recensions of al-Ṭabarī and Ibn Kathīr the soldier is identified as Abū Ḥarb al-Sabīʿī.[49]

In another incident, al-Ḥusayn and his companions reportedly lit firewood around their tents at Karbalāʾ to keep the Umayyad army from attacking them from the rear. When Shimr rode to the tents, "he could not see anything except the fire blazing in the firewood. He began to ride back and called out at the top of his voice, 'Al-Ḥusayn, are you hurrying toward hellfire in this world before the Day of Resurrection?'"[50] Mālik b. Jarīra was another soldier who similarly mocked al-Ḥusayn.[51] Another soldier, ʿAbd Allāh b. Ḥawza al-Tamīmī, allegedly taunted al-Ḥusayn with "Good news! [You're going] to hell!"[52] Shimr and Muḥammad b. al-Ashʿath al-Kindī are also reported to have jeered at al-Ḥusayn with these words.[53]

Finally, according to one report ʿAlī b. Quraẓa b. Kaʿb said to al-Ḥusayn, "Liar! Son of a liar! You misled my brother and deceived him until you caused his death!"[54]

One of the most respected scholars of *ḥadīth* in Sunnī Islam is Abū Dāwūd al-Sijistānī (d. 275/889). Abū Dāwūd traveled great distances to collect oral traditions about the Prophet Muḥammad and the early community. Abū Dāwūd's son Abū Bakr (d. 316/928) followed in his father's footsteps, but was almost killed when he once related a scandalous story about ʿAlī. On the authority of al-Zuhrī and ʿUrwa b. al-Zubayr, Abū Bakr claimed that ʿAlī would secretly climb the walls of a home belonging to the Prophet's wife Umm Salama. He further explained that ʿAlī did this so frequently that his fingernails were reduced to stubs. After hearing this story, two descendants of ʿAlī took Abū Bakr to court and accused him of slandering their ancestor. Abū Bakr was initially found guilty and sentenced to death, but his conviction was overturned before the execution was carried out.[55]

48 Ibn Aʿtham al-Kūfī, *al-Futūḥ*, 5:199; al-Khuwārizmī, *Maqtal al-Ḥusayn*, 1:355.
49 Ibn Kathīr, *al-Bidāya wa 'l-nihāya*, 8:192; al-Ṭabarī, *Tārīkh*, 4:320.
50 Al-Ṭabarī, *Tārīkh*, 4:322; al-Ṭabarī, *The Caliphate of Yazīd*, 122.
51 Al-Khuwārizmī, *Maqtal al-Ḥusayn*, 1:352.
52 ʿAbd al-Razzāq al-Ṣanʿānī, *al-Muṣannaf*, 8:40, 633; al-Ṭabarānī, *al-Muʿjam al-kabīr*, 3:117; al-Ṭabarī, *Tārīkh*, 4:327–328.
53 Al-Balādhurī, *Ansāb al-ashrāf*, 3:193. 54 Al-Ṭabarī, *Tārīkh*, 4:330.
55 Abū 'l-Shaykh, *Ṭabaqāt al-muḥaddithīn bi-Iṣbahān*, 3:303; al-Dhahabī, *Taʾrīkh*, 23:517; Ibn ʿAdī, *al-Kāmil*, 4:266. In some versions of this report, the names of ʿAlī and Umm Salama are omitted: see al-Dhahabī, *Siyar*, 13:229; al-Dhahabī, *Tadhkirat al-ḥuffāẓ*, 2:771. In contrast to ʿĀʾisha, Umm Salama was a wife of the Prophet who was depicted as staunchly pro-ʿAlid and enjoying warm relations with ʿAlī: see al-Ḥākim al-Naysābūrī, *al-Mustadrak*, 3:119; al-Iskāfī, *al-Miʿyār*, 27–30.

Chapter 5 Appendix: Ibn Taymiyya's *Minhāj al-sunna*

In this appendix I compile, translate, and abridge key passages from Ibn Taymiyya's *Minhāj al-sunna* concerning ʿAlī and his family that pro-ʿAlids and Shīʿīs would consider heretical. Like al-Jāḥiẓ before him, Ibn Taymiyya presents the views of hypothetical anti-ʿAlids (*nawāṣib*) dialectically. He typically oscillates between condemning them as extreme and upholding them as sounder and less evil than the opposing Shīʿī position.[1] In other cases, he presents his own anti-Shīʿī position as representative of a consensus within Sunnism or among Muslims of the earliest generations. I have separated those claims that he attributes to *nawāṣib* from those he attributes to Sunnīs.

THE BELIEFS OF THE *NAWĀṢIB*

ʿAlī was not an imām to whom obedience was obligatory, because his authority as caliph was established neither through an official appointment nor through consensus.[2] Muʿāwiya carried out *ijtihād* (rationalized a valid legal opinion on the basis of the Qurʾān and prophetic practice) and was correct in rejecting ʿAlī's authority and going to war against him.[3] On the other hand, ʿAlī was mistaken in going to war against Muʿāwiya.[4] The Marwānids substantiated this belief with a number of arguments. For example, the Marwānids defended Muʿāwiya as the rightful guardian (or avenger) of ʿUthmān's spilled blood, since he was ʿUthmān's paternal cousin and the Umayyads, including ʿUthmān's sons, all acquiesced to his seniority and authority. Both Muʿāwiya and the Umayyads requested that ʿAlī either surrender ʿUthmān's murderers to them or give them the right, as a clan, to exact vengeance from the suspects. When ʿAlī rejected their requests, they

[1] Ibn Taymiyya, *Minhāj*, 4:400. For example, he argues that praise for ʿUmar b. Saʿd (who led the army against al-Ḥusayn b. ʿAlī) and considering him better than his father, is far less evil than considering Muḥammad b. Abī Bakr better than his father: see ibid., 2:65–68. In contrast to his father, Muḥammad b. Abī Bakr was an ardent partisan of ʿAlī and highly respected in Imāmī tradition: see Yazigi, "Defense and Validation."

[2] Ibn Taymiyya, *Minhāj*, 4:401. [3] Ibid., 4:391, 401. [4] Ibid., 4:401; 405.

refused to pledge allegiance to him but did not commit any acts of war against him.[5] ʿAlī, by contrast, initiated war with them, so they fought him in self-defense and in defense of their territories. This group claimed that ʿAlī was an unruly aggressor (*bāghī*) against them. Muʿāwiya, by contrast, possessed a greater right to the caliphate and was more meritorious than ʿAlī.[6] ʿAlī was either unable or unwilling to protect the Syrians from individuals in his army who wished to do them harm. Soldiers in ʿAlī's army were the aggressors and responsible for initiating the civil war.[7]

As for the *ḥadīth* in which the Prophet condemns the "transgressing party" (*al-fiʾat al-bāghiya*) that killed ʿAmmār b. Yāsir, some denied the authenticity of the *ḥadīth*, while others interpreted it differently. Some claimed that ʿAlī in fact represented the transgressing party since he and his party killed ʿAmmār "by practically throwing him upon our swords."[8] Others reinterpreted the adjective *bāghiya* positively to mean "seeking" rather than "transgressing," since Muʿāwiya's army sought to avenge ʿUthmān's blood.[9] The Marwānids and their partisans also argued that ʿAlī was a co-conspirator in the death of ʿUthmān. Some claimed that ʿAlī publicly ordered the murder, whereas others said that he did so clandestinely. Others still stated that ʿAlī only rejoiced and took satisfaction in ʿUthmān's assassination.[10]

Some claimed that Yazīd was a Companion, others said he was a rightly guided caliph, and yet others said he was a prophet.[11] Al-Ḥusayn was rightly killed because he wished to destroy the unity of the community. Furthermore, the army that killed al-Ḥusayn was obeying the Prophet, who ordered his followers to kill anyone who causes dissension after the authority of a ruler has been established.[12] Many

[5] Ibn Taymiyya notes elsewhere several reasons why ʿAlī could not acquiesce to these requests. For example, ʿAlī (and society at large) may not have known the precise identities of ʿUthmān's killers. Alternatively, ʿAlī may not have considered it permissible to execute multiple offenders for the death of one person: see ibid., 4:407.

[6] Ibn Taymiyya claims that most of Muʿāwiya's soldiers believed ʿAlī was greater in merit than Muʿāwiya. Only a few evil people believed Muʿāwiya was better than ʿAlī: see ibid., 4:383.

[7] Ibid., 4:383–384.

[8] Muʿāwiya is quoted as saying this: see Aḥmad b. Ḥanbal, *al-Musnad*, 4:199.

[9] Ibn Taymiyya, *Minhāj*, 4:405. Elsewhere, Ibn Taymiyya explains that *baghy* should be understood in this context as *ẓulm* and rejects any positive reinterpretations: see ibid., 4:418.

[10] Ibid., 4:406. Ibn Taymiyya considers these claims to be slanderous and defends ʿAlī as innocent of any wrongdoing in the death of ʿUthmān. He notes that it is narrated that some contemporaries of ʿAlī even committed perjury by swearing to the Syrian people that ʿAlī had been a participant in ʿUthmān's murder.

[11] Ibid., 4:559.

[12] Ibn Taymiyya and Abū Bakr b. al-ʿArabī mention this argument on behalf of Muslims who may have mistakenly killed al-Ḥusayn. The two authors never deny that al-Ḥusayn was wronged and died a martyr. See Ibn al-ʿArabī, *al-ʿAwāṣim*, 338; Ibn Taymiyya, *Minhāj*, 4:559. Ibn al-ʿArabī generally defends all Companions as pious individuals, including those Umayyads and their partisans who were infamously accused of crimes: see Ibn al-ʿArabī, *al-ʿAwāṣim*, 280–281, 289, 290, 340.

Umayyad partisans believed that their caliphs would face neither punishment nor accountability on the Day of Judgment.[13]

Some groups abused ʿAlī verbally and considered him blameworthy and reprehensible.[14] Different groups of *nawāṣib* claim variously that ʿAlī was an infidel (*kāfir*), that he was a criminal (*fāsiq*), or that he was unjust.[15] Compared to the claims advanced by the *rawāfiḍ* (*rāfiḍa*), the arguments of the *nawāṣib* are dialectically stronger; it is easier to doubt ʿAlī's conversion and faith or to consider his caliphate illegitimate because of the number of Companions who refused to pledge allegiance to him.[16] Those who went to war against ʿAlī were more righteous and closer to the truth than he was (*awlā bi'l-ḥaqq minhu*).[17] For a number of reasons, ʿAlī was unjust (*ẓālim*) and an unruly aggressor (*bāghī*) when he waged war against Muslims. He fought only to strengthen his own authority. He was the first to strike and initiate battle; he led an assault against Muslims (instead of fighting a defensive war); and, finally, he shed the blood of the community without a single benefit, either worldly or religious. His sword was sheathed against non-Muslims and unsheathed only against Muslims.[18] The Khawārij say that he was correct in the beginning of his reign but then committed *kufr*, became an apostate after arbitration, and died as an unbeliever.[19] The Marwānids say that ʿAlī was unjust, whereas Muʿāwiya was innocent of any wrongdoing.[20]

THE BELIEFS OF THE *AHL AL-SUNNA*

ʿAlī's caliphate neither strengthened nor ennobled the Muslim community.[21] The evidence that established the legitimacy of Abū Bakr's caliphate – the presence of a clear designation (*naṣṣ*) and consensus – is absent for the caliphate of ʿAlī. Nothing in the *Ṣaḥīḥayn* justifies his caliphate. Instead, some authors of *sunan* works transmit a report from Safīna (active 75/694) that some experts of *ḥadīth* have criticized as untrustworthy. As for consensus, its existence is impossible since around half of the community refrained from pledging allegiance to him or joining his army in his wars.[22] The Prophet designated Abū Bakr as his successor either explicitly or through numerous indications.[23] The Prophet died without a *waṣiyya* (last will and testament).[24] None of the Companions disagreed about Abū Bakr's and ʿUmar's superiority to ʿAlī in merit.[25] The scholars agreed on the good (*ḥasan*)

13 Ibn Taymiyya, *Minhāj*, 6:430. 14 Ibid., 4:400. 15 Ibid., 4:386, 401.
16 Ibn Taymiyya is responding to the Imāmī tendency to doubt or dismiss the faith of the first three caliphs and attack the legitimacy of their rule because there were Companions who opposed them: see ibid., 4:386–387.
17 Ibid., 4:400. 18 Ibid., 4:389.
19 Ibn Taymiyya held that all those who condemn ʿAlī are incorrect and misguided: ibid., 4:390.
20 Ibid., 4:390.
21 He believed the era of ʿAlī's caliphate could not be described as *ʿazīz* or possessing *ʿizz*: see ibid., 8:241.
22 Ibid., 4:388–389. 23 Ibid., 1:486 (for indications).
24 For more on Shīʿī claims about such a *waṣiyya*, see Ansari, "The *Kitāb al-Waṣiyya*."
25 Other Sunnī scholars disagreed: see al-Mīlānī, *Sharḥ Minhāj al-karāma*, 1:133.

behavior of Muʿāwiya after he became a Muslim.[26] It is reported that al-Shāfiʿī and others believed that there were only three [legitimate] caliphs: Abū Bakr, ʿUmar, and ʿUthmān.[27]

Some say that Muʿāwiya erred in his *ijtihād*, but that he will either receive a reward for his sincere effort or be forgiven for his error. Others say that ʿAlī and Muʿāwiya were both correct in their judgments.[28] Participation in the battle of Ṣiffīn was neither obligatory nor recommended according to Islamic law.[29] Leading Sunnī jurists such as Aḥmad b. Ḥanbal and Mālik believed that those who opposed ʿAlī were not the first to strike or to begin warfare. Thus, he was not legally obliged to fight them.[30] In fact, had ʿAlī abstained from war, it would have been better (*afḍal*), virtuous (*khayr*), and a greater good (*aṣlaḥ*).[31] ʿAlī fought his wars to consolidate worldly power (*riyāsa*). He shed the blood of Muslims in his quarrel with those who contested his claims until he was finally defeated. In the end, not a single benefit (*maṣlaḥa*), worldly or religious, came out of all of his fighting.[32]

Many Sunnī scholars of *ḥadīth* in Baṣra, the Levant (Shām), and Andalusia believed that ʿAlī was both superior in merit and closer to the truth than Muʿāwiya was, but that he never became a legitimate caliph. They call for God's mercy upon ʿAlī, but they maintain that there was no caliph in the period in which ʿAlī allegedly ruled; rather, there was only sedition and factionalism. A legitimate caliph is someone who receives the pledge of allegiance from the entire Muslim community, and ʿAlī never achieved this status. Consequently, when listing (and praising) the rightly guided caliphs, some of these scholars would intentionally exclude ʿAlī. Instead, they would name Muʿāwiya as the fourth caliph after ʿUthmān in their Friday sermons, since he received the pledge of allegiance without dissent.[33]

ʿUthmān was less deserving of murder than al-Ḥusayn. ʿUmar b. Saʿd's participation in the murder of al-Ḥusayn is analogous to the sin Muslims generally incur when they choose to disobey God. Al-Mukhtār al-Thaqafī, the Shīʿī, was worse than ʿUmar b. Saʿd, the *nāṣibī*.[34] Al-Ḥajjāj b. Yūsuf al-Thaqafī was better than Mukhtār, because he did not spill blood without just cause.[35]

[26] Ibn Taymiyya, *Minhāj*, 4:382. [27] Ibid., 4:404. [28] Ibid., 4:391–392.

[29] *Lā wājib wa lā mustaḥabb*: see ibid., 4:384. This claim obviously contradicts those pro-ʿAlid Sunnīs who believed that participation in the war under the command of ʿAlī was obligatory since he was God's rightly guided caliph: see al-Hararī, *al-Dalīl al-sharʿī*.

[30] Other reports identify the Khawārij as those who started the civil war: see Ibn Taymiyya, *Minhāj*, 4:390.

[31] Ibid., 4:389, 392. [32] Ibid., 7:454.

[33] Ibid., 4:400–401. Ibn Taymiyya mentions that Umayyads of Andalusia considered Muʿāwiya the fourth caliph, but this belief was upheld in other regions as well.

[34] He condemns Mukhtār for being a liar and allegedly claiming prophethood. In addition to praise for his deeds, criticism of Mukhtār also exists in Shīʿī *ḥadīth*, although Shīʿī scholars have debated the implications of these texts condemning him. For a discussion, see al-Khūʾī, *Muʿjam rijāl al-ḥadīth*, 19:102–110.

[35] Ibn Taymiyya, *Minhāj*, 2:70.

Al-Ḥasan and al-Ḥusayn may not have reached an age at which they could independently discern right from wrong in the Prophet's lifetime.[36] That which is narrated about Fāṭima claiming to have received Fadak as a gift, having individuals testify for her, or asking in a final will to be buried at night and to have none of them (Abū Bakr and his supporters) pray for her does not befit her (and is probably false). If it is true, it is considered a sin for which she shall be forgiven rather than a praiseworthy deed.[37] There is nothing praiseworthy in the anger of a person who is fully oppressed (*maẓlūman maḥḍan*) if the anger is for a worldly matter.[38] Indeed, God rebuked the hypocrites (*munāfiqūn*) when He said, "And among them are those who slander thee in the matter of the [distribution of] alms. If they are given a portion, they are pleased. If not, behold! They are indignant!" (Q9:58).... Does not someone who praises Fāṭima for bearing a resemblance to such people actually malign her?[39] If Abū Bakr upset her in this affair, he is nonetheless above reproach since he did so in obedience to God and His Messenger, in contrast to ʿAlī. ʿAlī upset Fāṭima by attempting to marry a second wife; he thus personally desired something that caused her pain (*lahu fī adhāhā gharaḍ*) and disturbed her (*rābahā*).[40] Since obedience to the ruler is obligatory and disobedience a major sin, ʿAlī's conduct (in allegedly supporting Fāṭima's claims against Abū Bakr) was far more objectionable (*aʿẓam*) than was Abū Bakr's conduct (in allegedly upsetting Fāṭima). ʿAlī's actions entailed disobedience to the Prophet's emirs, which entailed disobedience to the Prophet, which in turn entailed disobedience to God.[41]

As for Yazīd, all scholars agree that he did not order the murder of al-Ḥusayn or take any of his womenfolk captive. In fact, Yazīd was pained by the murder; he honored al-Ḥusayn's family and returned them safely to their homeland.[42] The evil that results from rebelling against a ruler is usually greater than any good deriving from it. In the case of those who rebelled against Yazīd (he cites the people of Medina and al-Ḥusayn), no good (*maṣlaḥa*) came from their actions, whether in

36 Ibid., 1:456. Ibn Taymiyya makes this claim despite the existence of *ḥadīth* which al-Ḥasan and al-Ḥusayn narrated from the Prophet. To verify that one had reached the age of discernment in the framework of *ḥadīth* scholars, a person only needed to show an ability to learn and transmit *ḥadīth*. Some Sunnīs required children to have reached the age of discernment for them to be considered Companions (see al-Mālikī, *al-Ṣuḥba wa 'l-ṣaḥaba*, 151–154). Sunnī *ḥadīth* collections include reports in which the Prophet's grandsons narrate from him; thus, pro-ʿAlid scholars would consider Ibn Taymiyya's comment offensive. For a selection of *ḥadīth* narrated by al-Ḥasan and al-Ḥusayn, see Aḥmad b. Ḥanbal, *al-Musnad,* 1:199–201.

37 Ibn Taymiyya, *Minhāj*, 4:243, 247, 248, 256, 257, 264. 38 Ibid., 4:245.

39 Ibid., 4:245–246. 40 Ibid., 4:255. 41 Ibid., 4:256.

42 Ibid., 4:472. Elsewhere Ibn Taymiyya admits that Yazīd continued to kill others in pursuit of establishing his rule and never punished those responsible for the death of al-Ḥusayn and his followers: see ibid., 4:506. Al-Mīlānī quotes numerous texts in which Yazīd ordered the death of anyone who refused his allegiance, including al-Ḥusayn. Al-Mīlānī claims that only *nawāṣib* defend the innocence of Yazīd (or specifically his innocence in the death of al-Ḥusayn): see al-Mīlānī, *Sharḥ Minhāj al-karāma*, 2:180–183, 191–192 (for Sunnī scholars who cursed Yazīd).

terms of this world or of the next one.[43] In the case of al-Ḥusayn, his revolt and murder led to great ruin (*fasād*) that would not have occurred had he remained at home.[44] He obtained none of the good that he desired and failed to repel any evil. In fact, his revolt and death resulted in an increase in evil. Thereafter, Satan brought into being two extremes, which become manifest every ʿĀshūrāʾ. The *nawāṣib* take great joy in the event and celebrate it, while another group mourns and recites eulogies and fictitious narratives. The members of the latter group curse Muslims of previous generations (including some Companions), attribute sins to innocent individuals, wail over calamities in the distant past in a manner that God has forbidden, and sow dissension in the community.[45]

Scholars of *ḥadīth* agree that most reports regarding ʿAlī's merits either are false or possess weak chains of transmission. The first three caliphs had not a single fault that was not matched or exceeded in ʿAlī.[46] The officials who worked for ʿAlī betrayed and disobeyed him more frequently than any previous governors did with ʿUthmān.[47] Marwān b. al-Ḥakam is wrongly portrayed as a villainous figure whom the Prophet exiled with his father; ʿUthmān was justified in allowing their return.[48] Abū Dharr criticized individuals who were blameless and obliged them to adhere to an asceticism that was beyond the obligatory commandments of God.[49] If the logical purpose of an infallible, divinely appointed imām is to ward off oppression, it is clear that ʿAlī did not occupy such an office, as God did not aid him in ending injustice. Historically, neither God nor any human aided any of the so-called (Twelver) imāms to successfully end oppression.[50]

The imāms of the Prophet's progeny, like the rest of the Muslim community, learned from the (proto-Sunnī) scholars of *ḥadīth*.[51] Unlike the Shīʿa, the ʿAlid imāms never denied predestination or that God could be seen. The Twelver imāms claimed neither that they were infallible nor that ʿAlī had been explicitly designated as caliph. There were scholars who were more knowledgeable than the ʿAlid imāms were, and more beneficial to the Muslim community.[52] In fact, the scholars agree that al-Zuhrī was more knowledgeable than was his contemporary Muḥammad al-Bāqir about the *ḥadīth* of the Prophet. After Jaʿfar al-Ṣādiq, the imāms evidently possessed neither useful knowledge nor any expertise that would have required scholars to seek their tutelage. ʿAlī al-Hādī and al-Ḥasan al-ʿAskarī were not scholars of religion. Even if these two figures issued legal opinions, it would be more appropriate and even obligatory for respected scholars in the (Sunnī) tradition to follow their own beliefs instead. It was incumbent on ʿAlī al-Hādī, al-Ḥasan al-ʿAskarī, and those of their ilk to defer to the likes of Mālik, al-Awzāʿī (d. 157/774), al-Thawrī (d. 161/778), Abū Ḥanīfa, Abū Yūsuf, al-Shāfiʿī, al-Buwayṭī

[43] Ibn Taymiyya, *Minhāj*, 4:528, 530.

[44] Those who defend al-Ḥusayn's actions would argue that such a belief is incorrect because his safety was predicated upon a pledge of allegiance, which al-Ḥusayn refused to give. As a result, he was safe neither in his home in Medina, which he was forced to flee, nor in the Sacred Mosque at Mecca.

[45] Ibid., 4:530. [46] Ibid., 5:6–7. [47] Ibid., 6:184. [48] Ibid., 6:268. [49] Ibid., 6:272.

[50] Ibid., 6: 393–394. [51] Ibid., 2:454.

[52] ibid., 6:387. Ibn Taymiyya cites the likes of Mālik b. Anas, al-Shāfiʿī, Aḥmad b. Ḥanbal, Layth b. Saʿd, al-Awzāʿī, Yaḥyā b. Saʿīd, Wakīʿ b. al-Jarrāh, ʿAbd Allāh b. al-Mubārak, Isḥāq b. Rāhawayh, and a few others: see ibid., 2:460.

(d. 231/846), al-Muzanī (d. 264/878), Aḥmad b. Ḥanbal, Abū Dāwūd al-Sijistānī, al-Bukhārī, and others of their caliber. Indeed, these figures were more knowledgeable of the religion of God and His Prophet than were al-Hādī and al-ʿAskarī.[53]

Those who follow reports with verified chains of transmission from the Prophet, his successors, his Companions, and the imāms from his household, such as Imām ʿAlī b. al-Ḥusayn Zayn al-ʿĀbidīn, his son Imām Abū Jaʿfar Muḥammad b. ʿAlī al-Bāqir, and his son Imām Abū ʿAbd Allāh Jaʿfar al-Ṣādiq, the shaykh of other scholars in the community, as well as the likes of Mālik b. Anas, Sufyān al-Thawrī, and their peers, will conclude that (the views of these authorities) are in complete agreement when it comes to the fundamentals of religion (*uṣūl al-dīn*) and the sacred law (*sharīʿa*).[54]

There was no reason for jurists revered in the Sunnī tradition to study under ʿAlī b. Mūsā al-Riḍā or the later ʿAlid imāms, because the latter had no substantive knowledge to share. Even if the ʿAlid imāms had some knowledge, nothing they taught contradicted or differed from the teachings of jurists within the Sunnī tradition.[55]

[53] He lists twenty-four famous scholars from the proto-Sunnī community whom he considered more knowledgeable than these two ʿAlid imāms. Greater knowledge and expertise relieved them of any need to refer to these ʿAlid imāms and prohibited them from deferring to their legal opinions: see ibid., 2:470–473.

[54] Ibn Taymiyya, *Jāmiʿ al-Masāʾil*, 3:87–88.

[55] Ibn Taymiyya, *Minhāj*, 4:29, 50–52, 63–64.

Bibliography

ARABIC MANUSCRIPTS

Hinds Xerox (Cambridge University Library, Or. 1402).
Kitāb al-Siyar (Sayyid Muḥammad b. Aḥmad b. Suʿūd Library, Sīb, Oman).

Majmūʿ al-Siyar (al-Sālimī Library, Bidiyya, Oman).

al-Siyar al-Ibāḍiyya (Aḥmad b. Nāṣir al-Sayfī Library, Nizwa, Oman).

PUBLISHED WORKS

ʿAbbād al-Badr, ʿAbd-al-Muḥsin, *al-Intiṣār li-ahl al-sunna wa ʻl-ḥadīth: fī radd abāṭīl Ḥasan al-Mālikī* (Riyadh: Dār al-Faḍīla, 2003).
ʿAbd al-Ḥamīd, Ṣāʾib, *Ibn Taymiyya: Ḥayātuhu wa ʿaqāʾiduhu* (Beirut: al-Ghadīr, 2002).
ʿAbd al-Jabbār, al-Qāḍī, *al-Mughnī* (Cairo: al-Dār al-Miṣriyya, 1965).
ʿAbd al-Jalīl Qazvīnī, *Kitāb al-Naqẓ = Baʿẓ-i maṣālib al-navāṣib fī naqẓ baʿẓ fażāʾiḥ al-Ravāfiẓ* (Tehran: Chāpkhānah-'i Sipihr, 1973).
ʿAbd al-Kāfī, Abū ʿAmmār, *Ārāʾ al-Khawārij al-kalāmiyya: al-Mūjaz*, ed. ʿAmmār Ṭālibī (Algiers: al-Sharika al-Waṭaniyya, 1978).
ʿAbd al-Malik ibn Ḥabīb, *Kitāb al-taʾrīkh* (Madrid: Consejo Superior de Investigaciones Científicas Instituto de Cooperación con el Mundo Arabe, 1991).
ʿAbd al-Razzāq al-Ṣanʿānī, Abū Bakr, *al-Muṣannaf*, ed. Ḥabīb al-Raḥmān al-Aʿẓamī (Beirut: al-Majlis al-ʿIlmī, 1970).
Tafsīr al-Qurʾān (Riyadh: Maktabat al-Rushd, 1989).
Ābī al-Azharī, Ṣāliḥ ibn ʿAbd al-Samīʿ, *al-Thamar al-dānī: sharḥ Risālat Ibn Abī Zayd al-Qayrawānī* (Beirut: al-Maktaba al-Thiqāfiyya, n.d.).

Abū Bakr ibn Shihāb, *Kitāb Wujūb al-ḥamiyya ʿan muḍār al-raqiyya* (Singapore: Maṭbaʿat al-Imām, 1910).

Abū Dāwūd al-Sijistānī, *Suʾālāt Abī ʿUbayd al-Ājurrī Abā Dāwūd Sulaymān ibn al-Ashʿath al-Sijistānī fī maʿrifat al-rijāl wa jarḥihim wa taʿdīlihim* (Mecca; Beirut: Maktabat Dār al-Istiqāma; Muʾassasat al-Rayyān, 1997).

Sunan Abī Dāwūd, ed. Saʿīd M. al-Laḥḥām (Beirut: Dār al-Fikr, 1990).

Abū Dāwūd al-Ṭayālisī, *Musnad Abī Dāwūd al-Ṭayālisī* (Beirut: Dār al-Maʿrifa, 1980).

Abū ʾl-Faraj al-Iṣbahānī, *al-Aghānī* (Beirut: Dār Iḥyāʾ al-Turāth al-ʿArabī, 1994).

Maqātil al-Ṭālibiyyīn, ed. Kāẓim Muẓaffar (Najaf: al-Maktaba al-Ḥaydariyya, 1965).

Abū ʾl-Fidāʾ, *al-Mukhtaṣar fī akhbār al-bashar = Tārīkh Abī ʾl-Fidāʾ* (Beirut: Dār al-Maʿrifa, 1919).

Abū Nuʿaym al-Iṣbahānī, *Dhikr akhbār Iṣbahān* (Leiden: Brill, 1934).

Maʿrifat al-ṣaḥāba (Riyadh: Dār Waṭan, 1998).

Tathbīt al-imāma wa tartīb al-khilāfa (Medina: Maktabat al-ʿUlūm wa ʾl-Ḥikam, 1987).

Abū Rayya, Maḥmūd, *Aḍwāʾ ʿalā ʾl-sunna al-Muḥammadiyya*, 5th ed. (Qum: Nashr al-Baṭḥāʾ, n.d.).

Abū ʾl-Shaykh, *Ṭabaqāt al-muḥaddithīn bi-Iṣbahān* (Beirut: Muʾassasat al-Risāla, 1987).

Abū Yaʿlā al-Mawṣilī, *Musnad Abī Yaʿlā al-Mawṣilī* (Damascus: Dār al-Maʾmūn li ʾl-Turāth, 1984).

Abū Yūsuf, al-Qāḍī, *Kitāb al-Āthār*, ed. Abū ʾl-Wafāʾ al-Afghānī (Beirut: Dār al-Kutub al-ʿIlmiyya, 1978).

Adem, Rodrigo, "The Intellectual Genealogy of Ibn Taymīya." Ph.D. thesis, University of Chicago, 2015.

Afsaruddin, Asma, *Excellence and Precedence: Medieval Islamic Discourse on Legitimate Leadership* (Leiden; Boston: Brill, 2002).

Aḥmad b. Ḥanbal, *Faḍāʾil Amīr al-Muʾminīn ʿAlī ibn Abī Ṭālib* (Qum: Muʾassasat al-Muḥaqqiq al-Ṭabāṭabāʾī, 2012).

Kitāb Faḍāʾil al-ṣaḥāba, ed. Waṣī Allāh M. ʿAbbās (Beirut: Muʾassasat al-Risāla, 1983).

Kitāb al-ʿIlal wa Maʿrifat al-rijāl (Beirut; Riyadh: al-Maktab al-Islāmī; Dār al-Khānī, 1988).

al-Musnad wa bi-hāmishihi muntakhab Kanz al-ʿummāl fī sunan al-aqwāl wa ʾl-aʿmāl (Beirut: Dār Ṣādir, 1969).

Aigle, Denise, "The Mongol Invasions of Bilād al-Shām by Ghāzān Khān and Ibn Taymāyah's Three 'Anti-Mongols' Fatwas." *Mamluk Studies Review* 11, no. 2 (2007): 89–120.

Ālūsī, Maḥmūd Shukrī, *Ṣabb al-ʿadhāb ʿalā man sabba al-aṣḥāb* (Riyadh: Aḍwāʾ al-Salaf, 1997).

Ālūsī, Shihāb al-Dīn Maḥmūd, *Rūḥ al-maʿānī fī tafsīr al-Qurʾān al-ʿaẓīm wa ʾl-sabʿ al-mathānī* (Beirut: Dār Iḥyāʾ al-Turāth al-ʿArabī, n.d.).

Āl Yāsīn, Rāḍī, *Ṣulḥ al-Ḥasan* (Beirut: Muʾassasat al-Nuʿmān, 1991).

Amaḥzūn, Muḥammad, *Taḥqīq mawāqif al-ṣaḥāba fī ʾl-fitna: min riwāyāt al-Imām al-Ṭabarī wa ʾl-muḥaddithīn* (Cairo: Dār al-Salām, 2007).

ʿĀmilī, Jaʿfar Murtaḍā, *al-Ṣaḥīḥ min sīrat al-imām ʿAlī: al-murtaḍā min sīrat al-Murtaḍā* (Beirut: al-Markaz al-Islāmī li ʼl-Dirāsāt, 2009).

Amīn, Muḥsin, *Aʿyān al-Shīʿa* (Beirut: Dār al-Taʿāruf, 1983).

Amīnī, ʿAbd al-Ḥusayn, *al-Ghadīr: fī ʼl-kitāb wa ʼl-sunna wa ʼl-adab* (Beirut: Dār al-Kitāb al-ʿArabī, 1977).

Amir-Moezzi, Mohammad Ali, *The Spirituality of Shiʿi Islam: Beliefs and Practices* (London: I. B. Tauris, 2011).

Amitai, Reuven, "The Mongol Occupation of Damascus in 1300: A Study of Mamluk Loyalties." In *The Mamluks in Egyptian and Syrian Politics and Society*, ed. Michael Winter and Amalia Levanoni, 21–41 (Leiden: Brill, 2004).

Ansari, Hassan, *Bar-rasīhā-yi taʾrīkhī dar ḥawzah-ʾi Islām va tashayyuʿ* (Tehran: Mōzeh va Markaz-i Isnād-i Majlis-i Shūrā-yi Islāmī, 2012).

"Ibn Ḥazm selon certains savants shīʿites." In *Ibn Ḥazm of Cordoba*, ed. Camilla Adang, Maribel Fierro, and Sabine Schmidtke, 645–661 (Leiden: Brill, 2013).

"The *Kitāb al-Waṣiyya* of ʿĪsā b. al-Mustafād: The History of a Text." In *Law and Tradition in Classical Islamic Thought: Studies in Honor of Professor Hossein Modarressi*, ed. Michael Cook, Najam Haider, Intisar Rabb, and Asma Sayeed, 67–79 (New York: Palgrave Macmillan, 2013).

Anthony, Sean W., *The Caliph and the Heretic: Ibn Sabaʾ and the Origins of Shiʿism* (Leiden: Brill, 2012).

"The Meccan Prison of ʿAbdallāh b. al-Zubayr and the Imprisonment of Muḥammad b. al-Ḥanafiyya." In *The Heritage of Arabo-Islamic Learning: Studies Presented to Wadad Kadi*, ed. Maurice Pomerantz and Aram Shahin, 3–27 (Leiden: Brill, 2015).

Ashʿarī, Abū ʼl-Ḥasan, *Maqālāt al-Islāmīyyīn wa ikhtilāf al-musạllīn* (Beirut: al-Maktaba al-Asṛiya, 1990).

ʿAskarī, Murtaḍā, *ʿAbd Allāh ibn Sabaʾ wa asāṭīr ukhrā*, 6th ed. (Tehran: Nashr Tawḥīd, 1992).

Aḥādīth Umm al-Muʾminīn ʿĀʾisha (Beirut: Majmaʿ al-ʿIlmī al-Islāmī, 1997).

Maʿālim al-madrasatayn (Beirut: Muʾassasat al-Nuʿmān, 1990).

Athamina, Khalil, "The Sources of al-Baladhuri's *Ansab al-ashraf*." *Jerusalem Studies in Arabic and Islam* 5 (1984): 237–262.

ʿAwwād, Badr, *al-Naṣb wa ʼl-nawāṣib: dirāsa taʾrīkhiyya ʿaqadiyya* (Riyadh: Maktabat Dār al-Minhāj li ʼl-Nashr wa ʼl-Tawzīʿ, 2012).

ʿAynī, Badr Dīn, *ʿUmdat al-qārī: sharḥ Ṣaḥīḥ al-Bukhārī* (Cairo: Idārat al-Ṭibāʿa al-Munīriyya, 1929).

Baghawī, al-Ḥusayn ibn Masʿūd, *Maʿālim al-tanzīl = Tafsīr al-Baghawī* (Beirut: Dār al-Maʿrifa, 1992).

Baghdādī, Abū Manṣūr ʿAbd al-Qāhir, *al-Farq bayn al-firaq* (Beirut: Dār al-Maʿrifa, 1994).

Kitāb Uṣūl al-dīn (Istanbul: Madrasat al-Ilāhīyāt bi-Dār al-Funūn al-Tūrkiyya, 1928).

Bāḥith, Abū ʿUmar. "Firyat amr Muʿāwiya ibn Abī Sufyān bi-sabb ʿAlī ibn Abī Ṭālib." *Mukāfiḥ al-shubahāt* (2014): https://antishubohat.wordpress.com/2014/01/29/sabtabary/ (accessed October 15, 2019).

"Firyat Muʿāwiya yanālu min ʿAlī ibn Abī Ṭālib." *Mukāfiḥ al-shubahāt* (2014): https://antishubohat.wordpress.com/2014/02/15/yanal/ (accessed October 15, 2019).

Baḥrānī, Yūsuf ibn Aḥmad, *al-Ḥadāʾiq al-nāḍira fī aḥkām al-ʿitra al-ṭāḥira* (Qum: Muʾassasat al-Nashr al-Islāmī, 1984).

Balādhurī, Aḥmad ibn Yaḥyā, *Ansāb al-ashrāf*: vol. 1, ed. M. Ḥamīd Allāh (Cairo: Dār al-Maʿārif, 1959); vol. 2, ed. Muḥammad Bāqir al-Maḥmūdī (Beirut: Mu'assasat al-Aʿlamī, 1974); vol. 3, ed. Muḥammad Bāqir al-Maḥmūdī (Beirut: Dār al-Taʿāruf li 'l-Maṭbūʿāt, 1977); vol. 4, ed. ʿAbd al-ʿAzīz al-Dūrī (Beirut: Orient-Institut der Deutschen Morgenländischen Gesellschaft, 1978); vol. 5, ed. Iḥsān ʿAbbās (Beirut: Orient-Institut der Deutschen Morgenländischen Gesellschaft, 1979); *Ansāb al-ashrāf = Kitāb jumal min ansāb al-ashrāf*, vols. 6–13, ed. Suhayl Zakkār and Riyāḍ Ziriklī (Beirut: Dār al-Fikr, 1996).

Balkhī, Abū 'l-Qāsim al-Kaʿbī, *Qabūl al-akhbār wa Maʿrifat al-rijāl* (Beirut: Dār al-Kutub al-ʿIlmiyya, 2000).

Bāqillānī, Qāḍī Abū Bakr, *Manāqib al-aʾimmat al-arbaʿa* (Beirut: Dār al-Muntakhab al-ʿArabī, 2002).

Barrādī, *al-Jawāhir* (Cairo: n.p., 1885).

Barzegar, Abbas, "Remembering Community: Historical Narrative in the Formation of Sunni Islam." Ph.D. thesis, Emory University, 2010.

Bāʿūnī, Muḥammad ibn Aḥmad, *Jawāhir al-maṭālib fī manāqib al-Imām ʿAlī ibn Abī Ṭālib* (Qum: Majmaʿ Iḥyāʾ al-Thaqāfa al-Islāmiyya, 1994).

Bayhaqī, Aḥmad ibn al-Ḥusayn, *Dalāʾil al-nubuwwa wa Maʿrifat aḥwāl ṣāḥib al-sharīʿa* (Beirut: Dār al-Kutub al-ʿIlmiyya, 1985).

al-Sunan al-kubrā (Beirut: Dār al-Fikr, 1999).

Bazzār, *al-Baḥr al-zakhkhār = Musnad al-Bazzār* (Medina: Maktabat al-ʿUlūm wa 'l-Ḥikam, 2009).

Bori, Caterina, "Ibn Taymiyya wa Jamāʿatuhu: Authority, Conflict, and Consensus in Ibn Taymiyya's Circle." In *Ibn Taymiyya and His Times*, ed. Yossef Rapoport and Shahab Ahmed, 23–52 (Karachi: Oxford University Press, 2010).

Borrut, Antoine, "Vanishing Syria: Periodization and Power in Early Islam." *Der Islam* 91, no. 1 (2014): 37–68.

Brown, Jonathan, *The Canonization of al-Bukhārī and Muslim: The Formation and Function of the Sunnī Ḥadīth Canon* (Leiden; Boston: Brill, 2007).

Hadith: Muhammad's Legacy in the Medieval and Modern World (Oxford: Oneworld Academic, 2018).

"How We Know Early Hadīth Critics Did Matn Criticism and Why It's So Hard to Find." *Islamic Law and Society* 15, no. 2 (2008): 143–184.

"The Rules of Matn Criticism: There Are No Rules." *Islamic Law and Society* 19, no. 4 (2012): 356–396.

Brown, Wendy. "Wounded Attachments." *Political Theory* 21, no. 3 (1993): 390–410.

Bukhārī, Muḥammad ibn Ismāʿīl, *al-Adab al-mufrad* (Beirut: Muʾassasat al-Kutub al-Thaqāfiyya, 1986).

al-Ḍuʿafāʾ al-ṣaghīr (Beirut: Dār al-Maʿrifa, 1986).

Ṣaḥīḥ al-Bukhārī (Beirut: Dār al-Fikr, 1981).

al-Tārīkh al-ṣaghīr (Beirut: Dār al-Maʿrifa, 1986).

Cobb, Paul, *White Banners: Contention in ʿAbbāsid Syria, 750–880* (Albany: State University of New York Press, 2001).

Cook, Michael, *Commanding Right and Forbidding Wrong in Islamic Thought* (Cambridge: Cambridge University Press, 2004).

Crone, Patricia, *God's Rule: Government and Islam* (New York: Columbia University Press, 2004).

"Review: Kitāb al-ridda wa 'l-futūḥ and Kitāb al-jamal wa masīr 'Ā'isha wa 'Alī. A Facsimile Edition of the Fragments Preserved in the University Library of Imām Muhammad Ibn Sa'ud Islamic University in Riyadh." *Journal of the Royal Asiatic Society* 6, no. 2 (1996): 237–40.

Crone, Patricia, and Fritz Zimmerman, *The Epistle of Sālim ibn Dhakwān* (Oxford: Oxford University Press, 2001).

Daftary, Farhad, *The Ismā'īlīs: Their History and Doctrines* (Cambridge: Cambridge University Press, 2007).

Ismailis in Medieval Muslim Societies (London: I. B. Tauris, 2005).

Dakake, Maria Massi, *The Charismatic Community: Shi'ite Identity in Early Islam* (Albany: State University of New York Press, 2007).

Dann, Michael, "Contested Boundaries: The Reception of Shī'ite Narrators in the Sunnī Hadith Tradition." Ph.D. thesis, Princeton University, 2015.

Dawraqī, Aḥmad ibn Ibrāhīm, *Musnad Sa'd ibn Abī Waqqāṣ* (Beirut: Dār al-Bashā'ir, 1987).

Daylamī, Abū Shujā' Shīrūya, *al-Firdaws bi-ma'thūr al-khiṭāb*, ed. M. Zaghlūl (Beirut: Dār al-Kutub al-'Ilmiyya, 1986).

Dhahabī, *Mīzān al-i'tidāl fī naqd al-rijāl* (Beirut: Dār al-Ma'rifa, 1963).

Siyar a'lām al-nubalā' (Beirut: Mu'assasat al-Risālah, 1993).

Tadhkirat al-ḥuffāẓ (Beirut: Dār Iḥyā' al-Turāth al-'Arabī, 1980).

Ta'rīkh al-Islām wa wafayāt al-mashāhīr wa 'l-a'lām (Beirut: Dār al-Kitāb al-'Arabī, 1998).

Dihlawī, 'Abd-al-'Azīz, and Maḥmūd Shukrī Ālūsī, *Mukhtaṣar al-Tuḥfa al-Ithnā 'ashariyya*, ed. Muḥibb al-Dīn al-Khaṭīb (Cairo: al-Maṭba'a as-Salafīya wa Maktabatuhā, 1967).

Dimashqiyya, 'Abd al-Raḥmān, "Ibṭāl da'wā 'l-rāfiḍa anna 'l-dawlat al-umawiyya wa ba'ḍ al-ṣaḥāba kānū yal'anūn sayyidanā 'Alī ibn Abī Ṭālib." *Shabakat al-difā' 'an al-sunna* (2013): www.dd-sunnah.net/forum/showthread.php?t=166704 (accessed October 15, 2019).

Dīnawarī, Abū Ḥanīfa, *al-Akhbār al-ṭiwāl* (Cairo: Wizārat al-Thaqāfa wa 'l-Irshād al-Qawmī, 1960).

Donner, Fred, *Narratives of Islamic Origins: The Beginnings of Islamic Historical Writing* (Princeton: Darwin Press, 1998).

El-'Aṭṭār, Jamāl, "The Political Thought of al-Jāḥiẓ with Special Reference to the Question of Khilafa (Imāmate): A Chronological Approach." Ph.D. thesis, University of Edinburgh, 1996.

El-Hibri, Tayeb, *Parable and Politics in Early Islamic History: The Rashidun Caliphs* (New York: Columbia University Press, 2010).

Elad, Amikam, *The Rebellion of Muhammad al-Nafs al-Zakiyya in 145/762: Ṭālibīs and Early 'Abbāsids in Conflict* (Leiden: Brill, 2016).

Fasawī, *Kitāb al-Ma'rifa wa 'l-ta'rīkh* (Beirut: Mu'assasat al-Risāla, 1981).

Fīrūzābādī, Muḥammad ibn Ya'qūb, *al-Qāmūs al-muḥīṭ* (Cairo: al-Hay'a al-Miṣriyya al-'Āmma li 'l-Kitāb, 1980).

al-Radd 'alā 'l-rāfiḍa = al-Qaḍḍāb al-mushtahar 'alā riqāb Ibn al-Muṭahhar, ed. 'Abd al-'Azīz b. Ṣāliḥ al-Maḥmūd al-Shāfi'ī (Cairo: Maktabat al-Imām al-Bukhārī li 'l-Nashr wa 'l-Tawzī', 2007).

Fīrūzābādī, Murtaḍā, *Faḍā'il al-khamsa min al-ṣiḥāḥ al-sitta wa ghayrihā min al-kutub al-mu'tabara 'inda ahl al-sunna wa 'l-jamā'a* (Beirut: Mu'assasat al-A'lamī li-'l-Maṭbu'āt, 1973).

Friedman, Yaron, "al-Ḥusayn ibn Ḥamdān al-Khasībī: A Historical Biography of the Founder of the Nuṣayrī-'Alawite Sect." *Studia Islamica* 93 (2001): 91–112.

"Ibn Taymiyya's Fatāwā against the Nuṣayrī-'Alawī Sect." *Der Islam* 82, no. 2 (2005): 349–363.

Gaiser, Adam, *Muslims, Scholars, Soldiers: The Origin and Elaboration of the Ibādī Imāmate Traditions* (Oxford: Oxford University Press, 2010).

"North African and Omani Ibādī Accounts of the Munāẓāra: A Preliminary Comparison." *Revue des mondes musulmans et de la Méditerranée* (2012): 63–73.

Shurāt Legends, Ibāḍī Identities: Martyrdom, Asceticism, and the Making of an Early Islamic Community (Columbia: University of South Carolina, 2016).

Gedi, Noa, and Yigal Elam, "Collective Memory: What Is It?" *History and Memory* 8, no. 1 (1996): 30–50.

Ghumārī, 'Abd Allāh ibn al-Ṣiddīq, *al-Qawl al-muqni' fī 'l-radd 'alā al-Albānī al-mubtadi'* (Tangier: Mu'assasat al-Taghlīf, 1986).

Ghumārī, Aḥmad ibn al-Ṣiddīq, *'Alī ibn Abī Ṭālib imām al-'ārifīn = al-Burhān al-jalī fī taḥqīq intisāb al-ṣūfiyya ilā 'Alī wa yalīh Kitāb Fatḥ al-Malik al-'Alī* (Cairo: Maṭba'at al-Sa'āda, 1969).

Fatḥ al-Malik al-'Alī bi-ṣiḥḥat ḥadīth bāb madīnat al-'Ilm 'Alī, ed. Muḥammad Hādī al-Amīnī (Isfahan: Maktabat al-Imām Amīr al-Mu'minīn al-'Āmma, 1983).

al-Jawāb al-mufīd li 'l-sā'il al-mustafīd, ed. Abū al-Faḍl Badr 'Imrānī (Beirut: Dār al-Kutub al-'Ilmiyya, 2002).

Haider, Najam, *The Origins of the Shī'a: Identity, Ritual, and Sacred Space in Eighth-Century Kūfa* (New York: Cambridge University Press, 2011).

The Rebel and the Imām in Early Islam: Explorations in Muslim Historiography (Cambridge: Cambridge University Press, 2019).

"The *Waṣiyya* of Abū Hāshim: The Impact of Polemic in Premodern Muslim Historiography." In *The Islamic Scholarly Tradition: Studies in History, Law and Thought in Honor of Professor Michael Allan Cook*, ed. Asad Q. Ahmed, Behnam Sadeghi, and Michael Bonner, 49–83 (Leiden; Boston: Brill, 2011).

Ḥākim al-Ḥaskānī, *Shawāhid al-tanzīl li-qawā'id al-tafḍīl fī 'l-āyāt al-nāzila fī ahl al-bayt*, ed. M. Bāqir Maḥmūdī (Tehran: Mu'assasat al-Ṭaba' wa 'l-Nashr, 1990).

Ḥākim al-Naysābūrī, Muḥammad b.'Abd Allāh, *Ma'rifat 'ulūm al-ḥadīth* (Beirut: Dār al-Āfāq al-Ḥadīth, 1980).

al-Mustadrak 'alā al-ṣaḥīḥayn wa bi-dhaylihī al-Talkhīṣ (Beirut: Dār al-Ma'rifa, 1986).

Ḥammād, Suhayla, "Mu'āwiya raḍiya Allāh 'anhu al-muftarā 'alayhi." *al-Madīna* (2012): www.al-madina.com/node/370002?risala (accessed October 15, 2019).

Ḥammū'ī, Ṣadr al-Dīn Ibrāhīm ibn Sa'd al-Dīn, *Farā'id al-Simṭayn: fī faḍā'il al-Murtaḍā wa 'l-Batūl wa 'l-Sibṭayn wa 'l-a'imma min dhurriyyatihim*, ed. M. Bāqir Maḥmūdī (Beirut: Mu'assasat al-Maḥmūdī, 1978).

Hararī, ʿAbd Allāh, *al-Dalīl al-sharʿī ʿalā ithbāt ʿiṣyān man qātalahum ʿAlī min ṣaḥābī aw tābiʿī* (Beirut: Dār al-Mashārīʿ, 2004).
al-Maqālāt al-sunniyya fī kashf ḍalālāt Aḥmad ibn Taymiyya (Beirut: Dār al-Mashārīʿ, 2004).
Harris, William, *Lebanon: A History, 600–2011* (Oxford: Oxford University Press, 2012).
Ḥasan, ʿAbd Allāh, *Munāẓarāt fī ʾl-imāma* (Qum: Anwār al-hudā, 1994).
Ḥaṭṭāb, *Mawāhib al-Jalīl li-sharḥ Mukhtaṣar Khalīl* (Beirut: Dār al-Kutub al-ʿIlmiyya, 1995).
Haythamī, Nūr al-Dīn, *Majmaʿ al-zawāʾid wa manbaʿ al-fawāʾid* (Beirut: Dār al-Kutub al-ʿIlmiyya, 1988).
Ḥillī, al-ʿAllāma, *Kashf al-yaqīn fī faḍāʾil Amīr al-Muʾminīn* (Tehran: Wizārat al-Thaqāfa wa ʾl-Irshād al-Islāmī, 1991).
Minhāj al-karāma fī maʿrifat al-imāma (Mashhad: Tāsūʿāʾ, 2000).
Nahj al-ḥaqq wa kashf al-ṣidq (Qum: Dār al-Hijra, 1986).
Ḥimyarī, Nashwān b. Saʿīd, *al-Ḥūr al-ʿayn* (Cairo: Maktabat al-Khānjī, 1948).
Hoffman, Valerie, *The Essentials of Ibāḍī Islam* (Syracuse: Syracuse University Press, 2012).
Hoyland, Robert, *Seeing Islam as Others Saw It: A Survey and Evaluation of Christian, Jewish, and Zoroastrian Writings on Early Islam* (Princeton: Darwin Press, 1997).
Husayn, Nebil, "Aḥkām concerning the *Ahl al-Bayt*." *Islamic Law and Society* 27, (2020), pp. 145–84.
"Scepticism and Uncontested History: A Review Article." *Journal of Shiʿa Islamic Studies* 7, no. 4 (2014): 385–409.
Huṣrī, Ibrāhīm ibn ʿAlī, *Zahr al-ādāb wa thamar al-albāb* (Beirut: Dār al-Jīl, 1972).
Ibn ʿAbd al-Barr, *al-Istīʿāb fī maʿrifat al-aṣḥāb* (Beirut: Dār al-Jīl, 1992).
al-Istidhkār (Beirut: Dār al-Kutub al-ʿIlmiyya, 2000).
al-Tamhīd (Rabat: Wizārat al-Awqāf wa ʾl-Shuʾūn al-Islāmiyya, 1967).
Ibn ʿAbd al-Hādī, *al-ʿUqūd al-durriyya min manāqib Shaykh al-Islām Ibn Taymiyya* (Cairo: al-Fārūq al-Ḥadītha, 2002).
Ibn ʿAbd Rabbih, *al-ʿIqd al-farīd* (Beirut: Dār al-Kutub al-ʿIlmiyya, 1983).
Ibn Abī ʿĀṣim, Abū Bakr, *Kitāb al-sunna*, ed. M. Nāṣir al-Albānī (Beirut: al-Maktab al-Islāmī, 1993).
Ibn Abī ʾl-Ḥadīd, *Sharḥ Nahj al-balāgha*, ed. Muḥammad Ibrāhīm (Qum: Muʾassasat Maṭbūʿātī-i Ismāʿīlīyān, 1983).
Ibn Abī Ḥātim al-Rāzī, ʿAbd al-Raḥmān, *Tafsīr al-Qurʾān al-ʿaẓīm* (Beirut: Dār al-Fikr, 2003).
Ibn Abī Shayba, *Muṣannaf Ibn Abī Shayba fī ʾl-aḥādīth wa ʾl-āthār*, ed. Saʿīd al-Laḥḥām (Beirut: Dār al-Fikr, 1989).
Ibn Abī Yaʿlā, *Ṭabaqāt al-Ḥanābila* (Beirut: Dār al-Maʿrifa, 1970).
Ibn ʿAdī, ʿAbd Allāh, *al-Kāmil fī ḍuʿafāʾ al-rijāl* (Beirut: Dār al-Fikr, 1988).
Ibn al-ʿArabī, al-Qāḍī Abū Bakr, *Aḥkām al-Qurʾān*, ed. ʿAbd al-Qādir ʿAṭṭā (Beirut: Dār al-Kutub al-ʿIlmiyya, 1988).
al-ʿAwāṣim min al-qawāṣim fī taḥqīq mawāqif al-ṣaḥāba baʿda wafāt al-Nabī, ed. ʿAmmār Ṭālibī (Cairo: Maktaba Dār al-Turāth, 1997).
Ibn ʿAsākir, *Taʾrīkh madīnat Dimashq* (Beirut: Dār al-Fikr, 1995).

Ibn A'tham al-Kūfī, *Kitāb al-Futūḥ* (Beirut: Dār al-Aḍwā', 1991).
Ibn al-Athīr, 'Izz al-Dīn 'Alī, *al-Kāmil fī 'l-tārīkh* (Beirut: Dār Ṣādir, 1965).
Usd al-ghāba fī Ma'rifat al-Ṣaḥāba (Beirut: Dār al-Kitāb al-'Arabī).
Ibn Bābawayh, Muḥammad b. 'Alī al-Qummī, *al-Amālī* (Qum: Mu'assasat al-Bi'tha, 1995).
'Ilal al-sharā'i' (Najaf: al-Maktaba al-Ḥaydariyya, 1966).
Kitāb al-Khiṣāl (Qum: Manshūrāt Jamā'at al-Mudarrisīn fī'l-Ḥawzat al-'Ilmiyya, 1983).
Kitāb man lā yaḥḍuruhu al-faqīh (Qum: Jamā'at al-Mudarrisīn fī 'l-Ḥawzah al-'Ilmiyya, 1983).
Ibn Biṭrīq, Yaḥyā ibn al-Ḥasan, *Khaṣā'iṣ al-waḥy al-mubīn* (Qum: Dār al-Qur'ān al-Karīm, 1996).
Ibn Fūrak, *Maqālāt al-Shaykh Abī al-Ḥasan al-Ash'arī* (Cairo: Maktabat al-Thaqāfa al-Dīniyya, 2005).
Ibn Ḥabīb, *Kitāb al-Muḥabbar* (Hyderabad: Maṭba'at Dā'irat al-Ma'ārif al-'Uthmāniyya, 1942).
Ibn Ḥajar al-'Asqalānī, *al-Durar al-kāmina fī a'yān al-mi'a al-thāmina* (Hyderabad: Maṭba'at Majlis Dā'irat al-Ma'ārif al-'Uthmāniyya, 1972).
Fatḥ al-bārī bi-sharḥ Ṣaḥīḥ al-Bukhārī (Beirut: Dār al-Ma'rifa, 1980).
Hady al-sārī: muqaddimat Fatḥ al-bārī bi-sharḥ Ṣaḥīḥ al-Bukhārī (Beirut: Dār Iḥyā' al-Turāth al-'Arabī, 1988).
al-Iṣāba fī tamyīz al-ṣaḥāba (Beirut: Dār al-Kutub al-'Ilmiyya, 1995).
Lisān al-Mīzān (Beirut: Mu'assasat al-A'lamī li 'l-Maṭbū'āt, 1971).
Tahdhīb al-Tahdhīb (Beirut: Dār al-Fikr, 1984).
Taghlīq al-ta'līq 'alā Ṣaḥīḥ al-Bukhārī, ed. Sa'īd 'A. Mūsā al-Qazaqī (Beirut; Amman: al-Maktab al-Islāmī; Dār 'Ammār, 1985).
Ibn Ḥajar al-Haytamī, Aḥmad, *Kitāb al-fatāwā al-ḥadīthiyya* (Cairo: al-Maṭba'at al-Taqqadum al-'Ilmiyya, 1927).
Kitāb Taṭhīr al-janān wa 'l-lisān 'an thalab Mu'āwiya ibn Abī Sufyān, ed. Abū 'Abd al-Raḥmān al-Miṣrī al-Atharī (Ṭanṭā: Dār al-Ṣaḥāba lli 'l-Turāth, 1992).
al-Ṣawā'iq al-muḥriqa fī 'l-radd 'alā ahl al-bid'a wa 'l-zandaqa, ed. 'Abd al-Wahhāb 'Abd al-Laṭīf (Cairo: Maṭba'at al-Qāhira, 1965).
Ibn Haytham, Ja'far ibn Aḥmad, *The Advent of the Fatimids: A Contemporary Shi'i Witness: An Edition and English Translation of Ibn al-Haytham's Kitāb al-Munāẓarāt*, ed. Wilferd Madelung and Paul Walker (London; New York: I. B. Tauris; in association with the Institute of Ismaili Studies, 2000).
Ibn Ḥazm, *Kitāb al-Fiṣal fī 'l-milal wa 'l-ahwā' wa 'l-niḥal* (Cairo: Maktabat al-Khānijī, 1904).
al-Muḥallā bi'l-āthār (Cairo: Idārat al-Ṭibā'a al-Munīriyya, 1928).
Rasā'il Ibn Ḥazm al-Andalusī, ed. Iḥsān 'Abbās (Beirut: al-Mu'assasa al-'Arabiyya li 'l-Dirāsāt wa 'l-Nashr, 1983).
Ibn Ḥibbān, *Kitāb al-Majrūḥīn min al-muḥaddithīn wa 'l-ḍu'afā' wa 'l-matrūkīn* (Mecca: Dār al-Bāz, 1970).
Ṣaḥīḥ Ibn Ḥibbān bi-tartīb Ibn Balbān, ed. Maḥmūd Ibrāhīm Zāyid (Beirut: Mu'assasat al-Risālah, 1993).
Ibn Hishām, *Sīrat al-Nabī*, ed. Muḥammad M. 'Abd al-Ḥamīd (Cairo: Maktabat Muḥammad 'Alī Ṣabīḥ, 1963).

Ibn Ḥumayd, *al-Muntakhab min Musnad ʿAbd ibn Ḥumayd* (Beirut: ʿAlām al-Kutub; Maktabat al-Nahda al-ʿArabiyya, 1988).

Ibn ʿIdhārī, Aḥmad ibn Muḥammad, *al-Bayān al-mughrib fī akhbār al-Andalus wa ʾl-Maghrib*, ed. G. S. Cohen and É. Lévi-Provençal (Beirut: Dār al-Thaqāfa, 1983).

Ibn al-Jawzī, *Kitāb al-ḍuʿafāʾ wa ʾl-matrūkīn* (Beirut: Dār al-Kutub al-ʿIlmiyya, 1986).

al-Mawḍūʿāt (Medina: al-Maktaba al-Salafiyya, 1966).

al-Muntaẓam fī taʾrīkh al-mulūk wa ʾl-umam (Beirut: Dār al-Kutub al-ʿIlmiyya, 1992).

al-Radd ʿalā ʾl-mutaʿaṣṣib al-ʿanīd al-māniʿ min dhamm Yazīd (Beirut: Dār al-Kutub al-ʿIlmiyya, 2005).

Ibn Kathīr, *al-Bidāya wa ʾl-nihāya* (Beirut: Dār Iḥyāʾ al-Turāth al-ʿArabī, 1988).

Tafsīr al-Qurʾān al-ʿaẓīm (Beirut: Dār al-Maʿrifa, 1993).

Ibn Khaldūn, *Tārīkh* (Cairo: Būlāq, 1867).

Ibn Khallikān, *Wafayāt al-aʿyān*, ed. Iḥsān ʿAbbās (Beirut: Dār al-Thaqāfa, 1968).

Ibn Maghāzilī, ʿAlī ibn Muḥammad, *Manāqib ʿAlī ibn Abī Ṭālib* (Qum: Intishārāt Sibṭ al-Nabī, 2005).

Ibn Maʿīn, Yaḥyā, *Tārīkh*, ed. ʿAbd Allāh Ḥasan (Beirut: Dār al-Qalam, 1990).

Ibn Māja, *Sunan*, ed. Muḥammad Fuʾād ʿAbd al-Bāqī (Beirut: Dār al-Fikr, 1954).

Ibn Manẓūr, *Lisān al-ʿArab* (Qum: Adab al-Ḥawza, 1984).

Mukhtār al-Aghānī fi al-akhbār wa ʾl-tahānī (Cairo: al-Dār al-Miṣriyya li ʾl-Taʾlīf wa ʾl-Tarjama, 1965).

Ibn Mardawayh, *Manāqib ʿAlī ibn Abī Ṭālib wa mā nazala min al-Qurʾān fī ʿAlī* (Qum: Dār al-Ḥadīth, 2001).

Ibn Qudāma, *al-Mughnī* (Beirut: Dār al-Kitāb al-ʿArabī, 1972).

Ibn Qutayba, ʿAbd Allāh ibn Muslim, *al-Ikhtilāf fī ʾl-lafẓ wa ʾl-radd ʿalā al-Jahmiyya wa ʾl-mushabbiha* (Riyadh: Dār al-Rāya, 1991).

al-Maʿārif (Cairo: Dār al-Maʿārif, 1969).

al-Shiʿr wa ʾl-shuʿarāʾ = Ṭabaqāt al-shuʿarāʾ (Cairo: Dār al-Ḥadīth, 2006).

Taʾwīl mukhtalif al-ḥadīth fī ʾl-radd ʿalā aʿdāʾ ahl al-ḥadīth (Beirut: Dār al-Kutub al-ʿIlmiyya).

ʿUyūn al-akhbār (Beirut: Dār al-Kutub al-ʿIlmiyya, 2003).

Ibn Rajab, *al-Dhayl ʿalā Ṭabaqāt al-Ḥanābila* (Beirut: Dār al-Maʿrifa, 1980).

Ibn Rustam al-Ṭabarī, Muḥammad, *al-Mustarshid fī imāmat Amīr al-Muʾminīn ʿAlī ibn Abī Ṭālib* (Qum: Muʾassasat al-Thaqāfa al-Islāmiyya li-Kūshānbūr, 1994).

Ibn Saʿd, *Kitāb al-Ṭabaqāt al-kabīr* (Cairo: Maktabat al-Khānjī, 2001).

al-Ṭabaqāt al-kubrā (Beirut: Dār Ṣādir, 1957).

Ibn Ṣalāḥ, ʿUthmān ibn ʿAbd al-Raḥmān, *Muqaddimat Ibn al-Ṣalāḥ fī ʿulūm al-ḥadīth* (Beirut: Dār al-Kutub al-ʿIlmiyya, 1995).

Ibn Shabba, ʿUmar, *Taʾrīkh al-Madīna al-munawwara*, ed. Fahīm Muḥammad Shaltūt (Qum: Dār al-Fikr, 1989).

Ibn Shāhīn, *Nāsikh al-ḥadīth wa mansūkhuh*, ed. Karīmah Bint ʿAlī (Beirut: Dār al-Kutub al-ʿIlmiyya, 1999).

Ibn Shahrāshūb, Muḥammad ibn ʿAlī, *Manāqib Āl Abī Ṭālib* (Qum: al-Maṭbaʿa al-ʿIlmiyya, 1959).

Mathālib al-nawāṣib (Baghdad: Dār al-Wifāq al-Waṭanī, 2016)
Ibn Taghrībirdī, *al-Nujūm al-zāhira fī mulūk Miṣr wa 'l-Qāhira* (Cairo: Wizārat al-Thaqāfa wa 'l-Irshād al-Qawmī; Dār al-Kutub al-Misriyya, 1970).
Ibn Ṭāwūs, Jamāl al-Dīn Aḥmad b. Mūsā, *Binā' al-maqāla al-Fāṭimiyya fī naqḍ al-Risāla al-'Uthmāniyya* (Beirut: Mu'assasat Āl al-Bayt li-aḥyā' al-Turāth, 1991).
Ibn Ṭāwūs, Raḍī al-Dīn 'Alī b. Mūsā, *al-Luhūf fī qatlā al-Ṭufūf* (Qum: Anwār al-Hudā, 1997).
al-Ṭarā'if fī Ma'rifat madhāhib al-ṭawā'if (Qum: Maṭba'at al-Khayyām, 1979).
Ibn Ṭayfūr, Aḥmad ibn Abī Ṭāhir, *Kitāb balāghāt al-nisā'* (Najaf: al-Maktaba al-Murtaḍawiyya, 1942).
Ibn Taymiyya, *Jāmi' al-Masā'il* (Mecca: Dār al-'Ālam al-Fawā'id, 2001).
Majmū' fatāwā shaykh al-Islām Aḥmad ibn Taymiyya, ed. 'Abd al-Raḥmān b. Muḥammad b. Qāsim (Medina: Majma' al-Malik Fahd, 1995).
Minhāj al-sunna al-nabawiyya, ed. Muḥammad Sālim ([Riyadh]: Jāmi'at al-Imām Muḥammad ibn Sa'ūd al-Islāmiyya, 1986).
Ra's al-Ḥusayn (Beirut: Dār al-Kitāb al-'Arabī, 1985).
Ibn Ṭūlūn, *al-A'immat al-ithnā 'ashar* (Beirut: Dār Bayrūt Dār Ṣādir, 1958).
Qayd al-sharīd min akhbār Yazīd (Cairo: Dār al-Ṣaḥwa, 1986).
Ījī, 'Aḍud Dīn 'Abd Raḥmān, *Kitāb al-Mawāqif* (Beirut: Dār al-Jīl, 1997).
Ījī, Aḥmad ibn Jalāl Dīn, *Faḍā'il al-thaqalayn min kitāb Tawḍīḥ al-dalā'il 'alā tarjīḥ al-faḍā'il*, ed. Ḥusayn al-Ḥasanī al-Bīrjandī (Tehran: al-Majma' al-'Ālamī li 'l-Taqrīb bayna al-Madhāhib al-Islāmiyya, 2007).
Iskāfī, Abū Ja'far, *al-Mi'yār wa 'l-muwāzana fī faḍā'il al-Imām Amīr al-Mu'minīn 'Alī ibn Abī Ṭālib, wa bayān afḍaliyyatihi 'ala jamī' al-'ālamīn ba'da al-anbiyā'* (Beirut: Maḥmūdī li-'l-Ṭibā'ah wa 'l-Nashr, 1981).
"Naqḍ al-'Uthmāniyya." In *al-'Uthmāniyya*, ed. 'Abd al-Salām Hārūn, 281–343 (Cairo: Dār al-Kitāb al-'Arabī, 1955).
Itlīdī, Muḥammad Diyāb, *Nawādir al-khulafā' = I'lām al-nās bi-mā waqa'a li 'l-Barāmika ma'a Banī al-'Abbās* (Beirut: Dār al-Kutub al-'Ilmiyya, 2004).
'Iyāḍ, al-Qāḍī, *al-Shifā bi-ta'rīf ḥuqūq al-Muṣṭafā* (Beirut: Dār al-Fikr, 1988).
Tartīb al-madārik wa taqrīb al-masālik li-Ma'rifat a'lām madhhab Mālik (Beirut: Dār al-Kutub al-'Ilmiyya, 1998).
Izkawī, Sirḥān b. Sa'īd, *Kashf al-ghumma al-jami' li-akhbār al-umma*, ed. Ḥasan al-Nābūdeh (Beirut: Dār al-Kutub al-'Ilmiyya, 2016).
Jackson, Sherman, "Ibn Taymiyyah on Trial in Damascus." *Journal of Semitic Studies* 39, no. 1 (1994): 41–85.
Jafri, S. Husain M., *The Origins and Early Development of Shi'a Islam* (Karachi: Oxford University Press, 2000).
Jāḥiẓ, 'Amr ibn Baḥr, *al-Bayān wa 'l-tabyīn* (Beirut: Maktabat al-ṭulāb, 1926).
"Istiḥqāq al-imāma." In *Rasā'il al-Jāḥiẓ: al-Rasā'il al-kalāmiyya*, 179–198.
"Kitāb Faḍl Hāshim 'alā 'Abd Shams." In *Rasā'il al-Jāḥiẓ: al-Rasā'il al-siyāsiyya*, 409–460.
Kitāb al-Ḥayawān (Beirut: Dār al-Kutub al-'Ilmiyya, 2003).
Rasā'il al-Jāḥiẓ: al-Rasā'il al-adabiyya, ed. 'Alī Abū Mulḥim (Beirut: Dār wa Maktabat al-Hilāl, 2002).

Rasā'il al-Jāḥiẓ: al-Rasā'il al-kalāmiyya, ed. ʿAlī Abū Mulḥim (Beirut: Dār wa Maktabat al-Hilāl, 2002).
Rasā'il al-Jāḥiẓ: al-Rasā'il al-siyāsiyya, ed. ʿAlī Abū Mulḥim (Beirut: Dār wa Maktabat al-Hilāl, 2002).
"Risālat al-ʿAbbāsiyya." In *Rasā'il al-Jāḥiẓ: al-Rasā'il al-siyāsiyya*, 467–470.
"Risālat al-awṭān wa 'l-buldān." In *Rasā'il al-Jāḥiẓ: al-Rasā'il al-siyāsiyya*, 99–122.
"Risālat al-Ḥakamayn wa taṣwīb Amīr al-Mu'minīn ʿAlī b. Abī Ṭālib fī fiʿlihi." In *Rasā'il al-Jāḥiẓ: al-Rasā'il al-siyāsiyya*, 339–399.
"Risāla fī 'l-Nābita." In *Rasā'il al-Jāḥiẓ: al-Rasā'il al-kalāmiyya*, 239–248.
"Risālat al-ʿUthmāniyya." In *Rasā'il al-Jāḥiẓ: al-Rasā'il al-siyāsiyya*, 129–328.
Jāḥiẓ, ʿAmr ibn Baḥr (attr.), *al-Maḥāsin wa 'l-aḍdād* (Beirut: Dār al-Hilāl, 2002).
al-Jamil, Tariq, "Cooperation and Contestation in Medieval Baghdad (656/1258–786/1384)." Ph.D. thesis, Princeton University, 2004.
"Ibn Taymiyya and Ibn al-Muṭahhar al-Ḥillī: Shiʿi Polemics and the Struggle for Religious Authority in Medieval Islam." In *Ibn Taymiyya and His Times*, ed. Yossef Rapoport and Shahab Ahmed, 229–246 (Karachi: Oxford University Press, 2010).
Jaṣṣāṣ, *Aḥkām al-Qur'ān* (Beirut: Dār al-Kutub al-ʿIlmiyya, 1994).
Jawharī, Abū Bakr Aḥmad, *al-Saqīfa wa Fadak*, ed. Muḥammad Hādī al-Amīnī (Beirut: Sharikat al-Kutubī, 1993).
Jeffery, Arthur, "Ghevond's Text of the Correspondence between ʿUmar II and Leo III." *Harvard Theological Review* 37 (1944): 269–332.
Juwaynī, Imām al-Ḥaramayn, *Kitāb al-Irshād ilā qawāṭiʿ al-adilla fī uṣūl al-iʿtiqād* (Cairo: Maktabat al-Khānjī, 1950).
Kaḥḥāla, ʿUmar Riḍā, *Muʿjam al-muʾallifīn: tarājim muṣannifī 'l-kutub al-ʿArabiyya* (Beirut: Maktabat al-Muthannā; Dār Iḥyā' al-Turāth al-ʿArabī, 1983).
Kanjī, Muḥammad ibn Yūsuf, *Kifāyat al-ṭālib fī manāqib ʿAlī ibn Abī Ṭālib wa yalīhi al-Bayān fī akhbār Ṣāḥib al-Zamān* (Tehran: Dār Iḥyā' Turāth Ahl al-Bayt, 1984).
Kansteiner, Wolf, "Finding Meaning in Memory: A Methodological Critique of Collective Memory Studies." *History and Theory* 41, no. 2 (2002): 179–197.
Kāshif, Sayyida Ismāʿīl, ed., *al-Siyar wa 'l-jawābāt li-ʿulamā' wa a'immat ʿUmān* ([Muscat]: Salṭanat ʿUmān Wizārat al-Turāth al-Qawmī wa 'l-Thaqāfa, 1986).
Keaney, Heather, *Medieval Islamic Historiography: Remembering Rebellion* (London: Routledge, 2015).
Keita, Maghan, *Race and the Writing of History: Riddling the Sphinx* (Oxford; New York: Oxford University Press, 2000).
Khalīfa ibn Khayyāṭ, *Tārīkh Khalīfa ibn Khayyāṭ*, ed. Suhayl Zakkār (Beirut: Dār al-Fikr, 1993).
Khallāl, Abū Bakr Aḥmad, *al-Sunna* (Riyadh: Dār al-Rāyah, 1989).
Khamīs, ʿUthmān, *Ḥiqba min al-tārīkh* (Alexandria: Dār al-Īmān, n.d.).
Khaṭīb Baghdādī, Abū Bakr, *Kitāb al-Muttafiq wa 'l-muftariq* (Damascus: Dār al-Qādirī, 1997).
Ta'rīkh Baghdād aw Madīnat al-Salām (Beirut: Dār al-Kutub al-ʿIlmiyya, 1997).
Khū'ī, Abū 'l-Qāsim, *Muʿjam rijāl al-ḥadīth wa-tafṣīl ṭabaqāt al-ruwāt*, 5th ed. (Tehran: Markaz Nashr al-Thaqāfat al-Islāmiyya, 1992).

Khushanī, Abū 'l-'Arab, *Kitāb Ṭabaqāt 'ulamā' Ifrīqiya*, ed. Mohammed Ben Cheneb (Paris: Dār al-Kitāb al-Lubnānī, 1915).

Khuwārizmī, Muwaffaq ibn Aḥmad Makkī, *al-Manāqib* (Qum: Mu'assasat al-Nashr al-Islāmī, 1993).

Maqtal al-Ḥusayn, ed. Muḥammad al-Samāwī (Qum: Dār Anwār al-Hudā, 1998).

Kitāb Sulaym ibn Qays al-Hilālī (Qum: Intishārāt-i Dalīl-i Mā, 2002).

Kohlberg, Etan, "Abū Turāb." *Bulletin of the School of Oriental and African Studies* 41 (1978): 347–352.

"Barā'a in Shī'ī Doctrine." *Jerusalem Studies in Arabic and Islam* 7 (1986): 139–175.

"Some Imāmī Shī'ī Views on the *Ṣaḥāba*." *Jerusalem Studies on Arabic and Islam* 5 (1984): 143–175.

Kulaynī, Muḥammad ibn Ya'qūb, *al-Kāfī* (Tehran: Dār al-Kutub al-Islāmiyya, 1968).

Kuthayrī, Muḥammad, *al-Salafiyya bayn ahl al-sunna wa 'l-imāmiyya* (Beirut: Markaz al-Ghadīr, 1997).

Laknawī, Muḥammad 'Abd Ḥalīm ibn Muḥammad Amīn Allāh, *Ḥall al-ma'āqid fī sharḥ al-'Aqā'id* (Lucknow: Sulṭān al-Maṭābi'; Maṭba'a al-'Alawiyya al-mansūba ilā 'Alī Bakhsh Khān, 1854).

Lalani, Arzina R., *Early Shī'ī Thought: The Teachings of Imām Muḥammad al-Bāqir* (London: I. B. Tauris in association with the Institute of Ismaili Studies, 2000).

Laoust, Henri, "Remarques sur les expéditions du Kasrawan sous les premiers Mamluks." *Bulletin du Musée de Beyrouth* 4 (1940): 93–115.

Lincoln, Bruce, *Theorizing Myth: Narrative, Ideology, and Scholarship* (Chicago: University of Chicago Press, 1999).

Lucas, Scott, *Constructive Critics, Ḥadīth Literature, and the Articulation of Sunnī Islam: The Legacy of the Generation of Ibn Sa'd, Ibn Ma'īn, and Ibn Ḥanbal* (Leiden; Boston: Brill, 2004).

Madelung, Wilferd, "Abū 'l-'Amayṭar the Sufyānī." *Jerusalem Studies in Arabic and Islam* 24 (2000): 327–342.

Der Imām al-Qāsim ibn Ibrāhīm und die Glaubenslehre der Zaiditen (Berlin: de Gruyter, 1965).

The Succession to Muḥammad: A Study of the Early Caliphate (New York: Cambridge University Press, 1996).

"The Sufyānī between Tradition and History." *Studia Islamica* 63 (1986): 5–48.

Madelung, Wilferd, and Abdulrahman al-Salimi, eds., *Ibāḍī Texts from the 2nd/8th Century* (Leiden: Brill, 2018).

Madkhalī, Rabī', "Bayān manāqib Mu'āwiya raḍiya Allāh 'anhu wa 'l-dhabb 'an *Ṣaḥīḥ Muslim*." *al-Mawqi' al-rasmī li-Rabī' ibn Hādī 'Umayr al-Madkhalī* (2012): www.rabee.net/ar/articles.php?cat=8&id=224 (accessed October 15, 2019).

Majlisī, Muḥammad Bāqir, *Biḥār al-anwār al-Jāmi'a li-durar akhbār al-a'immat al-aṭhār* (Beirut: Mu'assasat al-Wafā', 1983).

Makkī, Abū Ṭālib, *Qūt al-qulūb* (Cairo: Maktabat dār al-turāth, 2001).

Mālik, al-Imām, *Kitāb al-Muwaṭṭa'*, ed. Muḥammad Fu'ād 'Abd al-Bāqī (Beirut: Dār Ihyā' al-Turāth al-'Arabī, 1985).

Mālikī, Ḥasan ibn Farḥān, *Ma'a Sulaymān al-'Alwān fī Mu'āwiya ibn Abī Sufyān* (Amman: Markaz al-Dirāsāt al-Ta'rīkhiyya, 2004).

Naḥwa inqādh al-tārīkh al-Islāmī: qirāʾa naqdiyya li-namādhij min al-aʿmāl wa ʾl-dirāsāt al-Jāmiʿiyya (Riyadh: Muʾassasat al-Yamāma al-Ṣuḥufiyya, 1998).
al-Ṣuḥba wa ʾl-ṣaḥaba: bayn al-iṭlāq al-lughawī wa ʾl-tashkhīs al-sharʿī (Amman: Markaz al-Dirāsāt al-Tārīkhiyya, 2004).
Mamdūḥ, Maḥmūd, *Ghāyat al-tabjīl wa tark al-qaṭʿ fī ʾl-tafḍīl: risāla fī ʾl-mufāḍala bayna al-ṣaḥāba* (Abu Dhabi: Maktabat al-Faqīh, 2005).
Maqrīzī, Aḥmad ibn ʿAlī, *Imtāʿ al-asmāʿ bi-mā li ʾl-Nabī min al-aḥwāl wa ʾl-amwāl wa ʾl-ḥafada wa ʾl-matāʿ* (Beirut: Dār al-Kutub al-ʿIlmiyya, 1999).
Kitāb al-nizāʿ wa ʾl-takhāṣum fīmā bayna banī Umayya wa banī Hāshim (Cairo: Dār al-Maʿārif, 1988).
Marʿashī Najafī, Shihāb Dīn, *Mulḥaqāt al-Iḥqāq*, ed. Maḥmūd al-Marʿashī (Qum: Maktabat Āyat Allāh al-Marʿashī, 1988).
Masʿūdī, *Murūj al-dhahab wa maʿādin al-jawhar* (Qum: Manshūrāt Dār al-Hijra, 1984).
Māzandarānī, Muḥammad Ṣāliḥ, *Sharḥ Uṣūl al-Kāfī* (Beirut: Dār Iḥyāʾ al-Turāth al-ʿArabī, 2000).
Melchert, Christopher, *Ahmad ibn Hanbal* (Oxford: Oneworld, 2006).
"The Life and Works of Abū Dāwūd al-Sijistānī." *al-Qanṭara* 29 (2008): 9–44.
"The Life and Works of al-Nasāʾī." *Journal of Semitic Studies* 59 (2014): 377–407.
"The Rightly Guided Caliphs: The Range of Views." In *Political Quietism in Islam: Sunnī and Shīʿī Practice and Thought*, ed. Saud Sarhan, 63–79 (New York: I. B. Tauris, 2020).
"Sectaries in the Six Books: Evidence for their Exclusion from the Sunni Community." *The Muslim World* 82, no. 3–4 (2007): 287–295.
Michel, Thomas, ed., *A Muslim Theologian's Response to Christianity: Ibn Taymiyya's al-Jawab al-Sahih* (Delmar, NY: Caravan Books, 1984).
Michot, Yahya, "Ibn Taymiyya's Critique of Shīʿī Imāmology." *The Muslim World* 104, no. 1–2 (2014): 109–149.
Mīlānī, ʿAlī, *Sharḥ Minhāj al-karāma* (Qum: Markaz al-Ḥaqāʾiq al-Islāmiyya, 2007).
Mizzī, *Tahdhīb al-Kamāl fī asmāʾ al-rijāl* (Beirut: Muʾassasat al-Risāla, 1980).
Modarressi, Hossein, *Crisis and Consolidation in the Formative Period of Shiʿite Islam* (Princeton: Darwin Press, 1993).
"Early Debates on the Integrity of the Qurʾān: A Brief Survey." *Studia Islamica* 77 (1993): 5–39.
Momen, Moojan, *An Introduction to Shiʿi Islam: The History and Doctrines of Twelver Shiʿism* (New Haven: Yale University Press, 1985).
Mourad, Suleiman A., "Why did Ibn Taymiyya Hate Mount Lebanon?" In *In the House of Understanding: Histories in Memory of Kamal S. Salibi*, ed. Abdul Rahim Abu Husayn, Tarif Khalidi, and Suleiman A. Mourad, 373–388 (Beirut: American University of Beirut Press, 2017).
Muʿallim, Muḥsin, *al-Nuṣb* [*sic*] *wa ʾl-nawāṣib* (Beirut: Dār al-Hādī, 1997).
Mubarrad, Muḥammad ibn Yazīd, *al-Kāmil fī ʾl-lughat wa ʾl-adab wa ʾl-naḥw wa ʾl-taṣrīf*, ed. William Wright (Leipzig: Kreysing, 1864).
Mufīd, al-Shaykh, *al-Fuṣūl al-mukhtāra min al-ʿUyūn wa ʾl-maḥāsin* (Beirut: Dār al-Mufīd, 1993).
al-Irshād (Beirut: Dār al-Mufīd, 1993).

Muḥammad ibn ʿAqīl al-ʿAlawī, *al-ʿAtb al-jamīl ʿalā ahl al-jarḥ wa ʾl-taʿdīl*, ed. Ṣāliḥ al-Wardānī (Cairo: al-Hadaf li ʾl-iʿlām wal-nashr, n.d.).

al-Naṣāʾiḥ al-kāfiya li-man yatawallā Muʿāwiya (Qum: Dār al-Thaqāfa, 1992).

Taqwiyat al-īmān: bi-radd tazkiyat ibn Abī Sufyān (Beirut: Dār al-Bayān al-ʿArabī, 1993).

Muḥammad ibn Ṭalḥa al-Naṣībī, *Maṭālib al-saʾūl fī manāqib Āl al-Rasūl*, ed. Mājid ibn Aḥmad ʿAṭiyya (Beirut: Muʾassasat Umm al-Qurā, 2000).

Munajjid, Muḥammad Ṣāliḥ, "Lam yathbut ʿan Muʿāwiya sabb ʿAlī." *al-Islam suʾāl wa jawāb* (n.d.): http://islamqa.info/ar/219799 (accessed October 15, 2019).

Munāwī, ʿAbd Raʾūf, *Fayḍ al-qadīr sharḥ al-Jāmiʿ al-ṣaghīr min aḥādīth al-bashīr al-nadhīr* (Beirut: Dār al-Kutub al-ʿIlmiyya, 1994).

Murad, Hasan, "Ibn Taymiya on Trial: A Narrative Account of his Miḥan." *Islamic Studies* 18, no. 1 (1979): 1–32.

Muslim, *al-Jāmiʿ al-ṣaḥīḥ* (Beirut: Dār al-Fikr, 1974).

Najmī, Muḥammad Ṣādiq, *Aḍwāʾ ʿalā ʾl-Ṣaḥīḥayn* (Qum: Muʾassasat al-Maʿārif al-Islāmiyya, 1998).

Nasāʾī, *Khaṣāʾiṣ Amīr al-Muʾminīn ʿAlī ibn Abī Ṭālib*, ed. Muḥammad Hādī al-Amīnī (Tehran: Maktaba al-Nīnawā al-ḥadītha, 1969).

al-Sunan al-kubrā, ed. ʿAbd al-Ghaffār S. Bindārī and S. Kasrawī Ḥasan (Beirut: Dār al-Kutub al-ʿIlmiyya, 1991).

Sunan al-Nasāʾī (Beirut: Dār al-Fikr, 1930).

al-Nāshiʾ al-Akbar, ʿAbd Allāh ibn Muḥammad (attrib.), "Masāʾil al-imāma wa muqtaṭifāt min al-kitāb al-awsaṭ fī ʾl-maqālāt." In *Frühe Muʼtazilitische Häresiographie*, ed. Josef van Ess, 9–127 (Beirut: In Kommission bei F. Steiner, 1971).

Nasr, Seyyed Hossein, "Shiʿism and Sufism: Their Relationship in Essence and in History." *Religious Studies* 6, no. 3 (1970): 229–242.

Naṣr ibn Muzāḥim, *Waqʿat Ṣiffīn*, ed. ʿAbd al-Salām M. Hārūn (Cairo: al-Muʼassasat al-ʿArabiyya al-Ḥadītha, 1962).

Nawawī, *al-Majmūʿ sharḥ al-Muhadhdhab* (Cairo: Idārat al-Ṭibāʿa al-Munīriyya, 1925).

Ṣaḥiḥ Muslim bi-sharḥ al-Nawawī (Beirut: Dār al-Kitāb al-ʿArabī, 1987).

Noth, Albrecht, and Lawrence I. Conrad, *The Early Arabic Historical Tradition: A Source-Critical Study* (Princeton: Darwin Press, 1994).

Osman, Amr, "ʿAdālat al-Ṣaḥāba: The Construction of a Religious Doctrine." *Arabica* 60, no. 3–4 (2013): 272–305.

Petersen, Erling Ladewig, *ʿAlī and Muʿāwiya in Early Arabic Tradition: Studies on the Genesis and Growth of Islamic Historical Writing until the End of the Ninth Century* (Copenhagen: Munksgaard, 1964).

Pfeiffer, Judith, "Confessional Ambiguity vs. Confessional Polarization: Politics and the Negotiation of Religious Boundaries in the Ilkhanate." In *Politics, Patronage and the Transmission of Knowledge in 13th–15th Century Tabriz*, ed. Judith Pfeiffer, 129–168 (Leiden: Brill, 2014).

"Conversion Versions: Sultan Öljeytü's Conversion to Shi'ism (709/1309) in Muslim Narrative." *Mongolia Studies* 22 (1999): 35–67.

al-Qāḍī al-Nuʿmān, *The Epistle of the Eloquent Clarification Concerning The Refutation of Ibn Qutayba*, ed. Avraham Hakim (Leiden: Brill, 2012).

Sharḥ al-akhbār fī faḍā'il al-a'imma al-aṭhār (Qum: Mu'assasat al-Nashr al-Islāmī, 1988).

Qalhātī, Muḥammad ibn Sa'īd, *al-Kashf wa 'l-bayān* (Muscat: Wizārat al-Turāth al-Qawmī wa 'l-Thaqāfa, 1980).

Qalqashandī, Aḥmad ibn 'Alī, *Ma'āthir al-ināfa fī ma'ālim al-khilāfa* (Kuwait: Wizārat al-Irshād wa 'l-Anbā', 1964).

Qundūzī, Sulaymān, *Yanābī' al-mawadda* (Qum: Dār al-Uswa, 1995).

Qurṭubī, Abū 'l-'Abbās Aḥmad ibn 'Umar, *Kitāb al-Mufhim li-mā ashkala min Talkhīṣ Ṣaḥīḥ Muslim* (Beirut; Damascus: Dār ibn Kathīr; Dār al-Kalim al-Ṭayyib, 1996).

Qurṭubī, Abū'Abd Allāh Muḥammad ibn Aḥmad, *al-Jāmi' li-aḥkām al-Qur'ān = Tafsīr al-Qurṭubī* (Beirut: Dār Iḥyā' al-Turāth al-'Arabī, 1985).

Kitāb al-Tadhkira bi-aḥwāl al-mawtā wa umūr al-ākhira, ed. al-Ṣādiq ibn Muḥammad Ibn Ibrāhīm (Riyadh: Maktabat Dār al-Minhāj, 2004).

Rahim, Habibeh, "Perfection Manifested: 'Alī b. Abī Ṭālib's Image in Classical Persian and Modern Indian Muslim Poetry." Ph.D. thesis, Harvard University, 1989.

Rajā'ī, Mahdī, *al-Muḥaddithūn min Āl Abī Ṭālib* (Qum: Ma'had al-Dirāsāt li-Taḥqīq Ansāb al-Ashrāf, 2007).

Rapoport, Yossef, "Ibn Taymiyya's Radical Legal Thought: Rationalism, Pluralism and the Primacy of Intention." In *Ibn Taymiyya and His Times*, ed. Yossef Rapoport and Shahab Ahmed, 191–226 (Karachi: Oxford University Press, 2010).

Rassī, Qāsim ibn Ibrāhīm, *al-Radd 'alā 'l-rāfiḍa* (Cairo: Dār al-Āfāq al-'Arabiyya, 2000).

Rāzī, Fakhr al-Dīn, *Mafatīḥ al-ghayb = al-Tafsīr al-kabīr* (Beirut: Dār Iḥyā' al-Turāth al-'Arabī, 2001).

Sābi'ī, Nāṣir, *al-Khawārij: wa 'l-ḥaqīqa al-ghā'iba* (Muscat: n.p., 1999).

Sadeghi, Behnam, and Uwe Bergmann, "The Codex of a Companion of the Prophet and the Qurān of the Prophet." *Arabica* 57, no. 4 (2010): 343–436.

Ṣafadī, *Kitāb al-Wāfī bi-'l-wafayāt* (Beirut: Dār Iḥyā' al-Turāth al-'Arabī, 2000).

Saifullah, M. S. M, and 'Abdullah David, "The Codex of a Companion of the Prophet and the Qurān of the Prophet." *Islamic Awareness* (2007): www.islamic-awareness.org/History/Islam/Inscriptions/earlyislam.html (accessed October 15, 2019).

Saleh, Walid A., *The Formation of the Classical Tafsīr Tradition: The Qur'ān Commentary of al-Tha'labī* (Leiden: Brill, 2004).

"Ibn Taymiyya and the Rise of Radical Hermeneutics." In *Ibn Taymiyya and His Times*, ed. Yossef Rapoport and Shahab Ahmed, 123–162 (Karachi: Oxford University Press, 2010).

Sam'ānī, 'Abd-al-Karīm ibn Muḥammad, *al-Ansāb*, ed. 'Abd Allāh al-Bārūdī (Beirut: Dār al-Jinān, 1988).

Sam'ānī, Manṣūr ibn Muḥammad, *Tafsīr al-Qur'ān* (Riyadh: Dār al-Waṭan, 1997).

Samhūdī, Nūr al-Dīn 'Alī, *Jawāhir al-'aqdayn fī faḍl al-sharafayn: sharaf al-'Ilm al-jalī wa 'l-nasab al-Nabawī* (Beirut: Dār al-Kutub al-'Ilmiyya, 2003).

Sāmirī, Abū al-Fatḥ, *The Continuatio[n] of the Samaritan Chronicle of Abū 'l-Fatḥ al-Sāmirī al-Danafī*, trans. Milka Levy-Rubin (Princeton: Darwin Press, 2002).
Saqqāf, Ḥasan, *Majmū' rasā'il al-Saqqāf* (Beirut: Dār al-Imām al-Rawwās, 2007).
Ṣaḥīḥ sharḥ al-'Aqīda al-Ṭaḥāwiyya = al-Manhaj al-ṣaḥīḥ fī fahm 'aqīdat ahl al-sunna wa 'l-jamā'a ma'a al-tanqīḥ (Amman: Maktabat al-Imām al-Nawawī, 1995).
al-Salafiyya al-wahhābiyya : afkāruhā al-asāsiyya wa judhūruhā al-ta'rīkhiyya (Beirut: Dār al-Imām al-Rawwās, 2011).
Zahr al-rayḥān fī 'l-radd 'alā Taḥqīq al-bayān: al-ta'aqqub 'alā mā katabahu Qāsim ibn Nu'aym al-Ṭā'ī ḥawla Ibn Abī Sufyān (Beirut: Dār al-Imām Rawwās, 2009).
Sarakhsī, *Kitāb al-Mabsūṭ* (Beirut: Dār al-Ma'rifa, 1986).
Shāfi'ī, Muḥammad ibn Idrīs, *Kitāb al-Umm ma'a Mukhtaṣar al-Muzanī* (Beirut: Dār al-Fikr, 1983).
Shahrastānī, Muḥammad ibn 'Abd al-Karīm, *al-Milal wa'l-niḥal*, ed. Muḥammad Sayyid Kīlānī (Beirut: Dār al-Ma'rifa, 1975).
Sharaf al-Dīn, 'Abd al-Ḥusayn, *al-Fuṣūl al-muhimma fī ta'līf al-umma* (Tehran: 1964).
al-Murāja'āt (Beirut: al-Jam'īyat al-Islāmiyya, 1982).
Sharif, Mohd, "Baghy in Islamic Law and the Thinking of Ibn Taymiyya." *Arab Law Quarterly* 20, no. 3 (2006): 289–305.
Sharīf al-Murtaḍā, 'Alī Ibn Ḥusayn, *al-Shāfī fī 'l-imāma* (Tehran: Mu'assasat al-Ṣādiq, 1986).
Sharīf al-Raḍī and Muḥammad 'Abduh, *Nahj al-balāgha ... sharḥ al-ustādh al-imām Muḥammad 'Abdūh* (Beirut: Dār al-Ma'rifa, n.d.).
Sharon, Moshe, "Ahl al-Bayt: People of the House." *Jerusalem Studies in Arabic and Islam* 8 (1986): 169–184.
"Umayyads as Ahl al-Bayt." *Jerusalem Studies in Arabic and Islam* 14 (1991): 115–152.
Shawkānī, Muḥammad ibn 'Alī, *Nayl al-awṭār min aḥādīth sayyid al-akhyār* (Beirut: Dār al-Jīl, 1973).
Shaybānī, Muḥammad Ibn Ḥasan, *Kitāb al-Āthār*, ed. Abū 'l-Wafā' al-Afghānī (Beirut: Dār al-Kutub al-'Ilmiyya, 1993).
Sibṭ Ibn al-Jawzī, *Tadhkirat khawāṣṣ al-umma bi-dhikr khaṣā'iṣ al-a'imma* (Qum: Manshūrāt al-Sharīf al-Raḍī, 1998).
Simnānī, 'Alā' al-Dawla, *Manāẓir al-maḥāḍir li 'l-munāẓir al-ḥāḍir* (Cairo: Maktabat al-Thaqāfa al-Dīniyya, 1989).
Spellberg, Denise, *Politics, Gender, and the Islamic Past: The Legacy of 'A'isha bint Abi Bakr* (New York: Columbia University Press, 1994).
Stewart, Devin, *Islamic Legal Orthodoxy: Twelver Shiite Responses to the Sunni Legal System* (Salt Lake City: University of Utah Press, 1998).
"Popular Shiism in Medieval Egypt: Vestiges of Islamic Sectarian Polemics in Egyptian Arabic." *Studia Islamica* 84 (1996): 35–66.
Subkī, Taqī al-Dīn 'Alī ibn 'Abd al-Kāfī, *al-Sayf al-Ṣaqīl*, ed. Muḥammad Zāhid al-Kawtharī (Cairo: Maktabat al-Zahrān, 1937).
Suyūṭī, Jalāl al-Dīn 'Abd al-Raḥmān, *al-Durr al-manthūr fī 'l-tafsīr bi'l-ma'thūr* (Cairo: al-Maṭba'ah al-Maymaniyya, 1897).
al-Itqān fī 'ulūm al-Qur'ān, ed. Sa'īd al-Mandūb (Beirut: Dār al-Fikr, 1996).

Tanwīr al-ḥawālik: sharḥ ʿalā Muwaṭṭaʾ Mālik (Cairo: ʿĪsā al-Bābī al-Ḥalabī, 1934).
Ṭabarānī, Sulaymān ibn Aḥmad, *al-Muʿjam al-awsaṭ* (Cairo: Dār al-Ḥaramayn, 1995).
al-Muʿjam al-kabīr, ed. Ḥamdī ʿAbd al-Majīd Salafī (Beirut: Dār Iḥyāʾ al-Turāth al-ʿArabī, 2002).
Musnad al-Shāmīyīn (Beirut: Muʾassasat al-Risālah, 1996).
Ṭabarī, Muḥammad ibn Jarīr, *The History of al-Ṭabarī*, vol. 19: *The Caliphate of Yazīd b. Muʿāwiyah*, trans. I. K. A. Howard (Albany: State University of New York Press, 1990).
Jāmiʿ al-bayān ʿan taʾwīl al-Qurʾān = Tafsīr al-Ṭabarī (Beirut: Dār al-Fikr, 1995).
Taʾrīkh al-umam wa ʾl-mulūk = Tārīkh al-Ṭabarī (Beirut: Muʾassasat al-Aʿlamī, 1983).
Ṭabarī, Muḥibb al-Dīn, *al-Riyāḍ al-naḍira fī manāqib al-ʿashara* (Beirut: Dār al-Kutub al-ʿIlmiyya, 1984).
Dhakhāʾir al-ʿuqbā fī manāqib dhawī al-qurbā (Cairo: Maktabat al-Qudsī, 1937).
Ṭabrisī, Aḥmad ibn ʿAlī, *al-Iḥtijāj* (Najaf: Dār al-Nuʿmān, 1966).
Taftāzānī, Saʿd al-Dīn, *Sharḥ al-Maqāṣid fī ʿilm al-kalām* (Lahore: Dār al-Maʿārif al-Nuʿmāniyya, 1981).
Tahir-ul-Qadri, Muhammad, *The Ghadīr Declaration* (Lahore: Minhaj-ul-Qurʾan Publications, 2002).
Thaʿlabī, *al-Kashf wa ʾl-bayān = Tafsīr al-Thaʿlabī* (Beirut: Dār Iḥyāʾ al-Turāth al-ʿArabī, 2002).
Thaqafī, Ibrāhīm ibn Muḥammad, *al-Ghārāt* (Tehran: Anjuman Āthār Millī, 1975).
Tirmidhī, *al-Jāmiʿ al-ṣaḥīḥ = Sunan al-Tirmidhī* (Beirut: Dār al-Fikr, 1983).
Ṭurayḥī, Fakhr al-Dīn, *Majmaʿ al-baḥrayn* (Tehran: al-Maktaba al-Riḍawiyya, 1975).
Ṭūsī, Muḥammad b. al-Ḥasan, *al-Amālī* (Qum: Dār al-Thaqāfa, 1993).
Rijāl al-Kashshī = Ikhtiyār maʿrifat al-rijāl (Qum: Muʾassasat Āl al-Bayt, 1983).
Tahdhīb al-aḥkām: fī sharḥ al-Muqniʿa (Tehran: Dār al-Kutub al-Islamiyya, 1970).
Tustarī, Muḥammad Taqī, *Qāmūs al-rijāl* (Qum: Muʾassasat al-nashr al-islāmī, 1989).
Tustarī, Nūr Allāh, *Iḥqāq al-ḥaqq wa izhāq al-bāṭil*, ed. al-Sayyid Shihāb Dīn al-Marʿashī al-Najafī (Qum: Maktabat Āyat Allāh al-ʿUẓmā al-Marʿashī al-Najafī, 1982).
Maṣāʾib al-nawāṣib: fī ʾl-radd ʿalā Nawāqiḍ al-rawāfiḍ (Qum: Dalīl-i Mā, 2005).
al-Ṣawārim al-murhiqa fī naqd al-Ṣawāʿiq al-muḥriqa (Tehran: Nahẓat, 1948).
ʿUqaylī, ʿAbd al-Raḥmān, *Muʿjam nawāṣib al-muḥaddithīn* (Karbala: al-ʿUtba al-Ḥusayniyya al-Muqaddisa, 2014).
ʿUqaylī, Abū Jaʿfar Muḥammad b. ʿAmr, *Kitāb al-ḍuʿafāʾ al-kabīr*, ed. ʿAbd al-Muʿṭī Amīn Qalʿajī (Beirut: Manshūrāt Muḥammad ʿAlī Bayḍūn; Dār al-Kutub al-ʿIlmiyya, 1998).
van Ess, Josef, "Political Ideas in Early Islamic Religious Thought." *British Journal of Middle Eastern Studies* 28, no. 2 (2001): 151–164.
Wāḥidī, *Asbāb al-nuzūl* (Cairo: Muʾassasat al-Ḥalabī, 1968).
Wārjalānī, Abū Yaʿqūb Yūsuf, *Kitāb al-Dalīl li-ahl al-ʿuqūl li-bāghī al-sabīl* (Cairo: al-Maṭbaʿa al-Bārūniyya, 1888).

Wolf, Kenneth, *Conquerors and Chroniclers of Early Medieval Spain* (Liverpool: Liverpool University Press, 2011).
Yazigi, Maya, "Defense and Validation in Shi'i and Sunni Tradition: The Case of Muḥammad b. Abī Bakr." *Studia Islamica* 98/99 (2004): 49–70.
Ya'qūbī, *Tārīkh* (Beirut: Dār Ṣādir, 1960).
Yāqūt al-Ḥamawī, *Mu'jam al-buldān* (Beirut: Dār Ihyā' al-Turāth al-'Arabī, 1979).
Yildirim, Riza, "Shī'itisation of the Futuwwa Tradition in the Fifteenth Century." *British Journal of Middle Eastern Studies* 40, no. 1 (2013): 53–70.
Yūnus, Ṣāḥib, *Mu'āwiya ibn Abī Sufyān fi 'l-kitāb wa 'l-sunna wa 'l-tārīkh* (Beirut: Dār al-'Ulūm, 2002).
Zabīdī, Muḥammad Murtaḍā, *Tāj al-'arūs min jawāhir al-Qāmūs* (Beirut: Dār al-Fikr, 1994).
Zaman, Muhammad Qasim, *Religion and Politics under the Early 'Abbāsids: The Emergence of the Proto-Sunnī Elite* (Leiden: Brill, 1997).
Zarandī, Muḥammad ibn Yūsuf, *Naẓm durar al-simṭayn fī faḍā'il al-Muṣṭafā wa 'l-Murtaḍā wa 'l-Batūl wa 'l-Sibṭayn* (Najaf: Maṭba'at al-Qaḍā', 1958).
Ziriklī, Khayr al-Din, *al-A'lām: qāmūs tarājim li-ashhar al-rijāl wa 'l-nisā' min al-'Arab wa 'l-musta'ribīn wa 'l-mustashriqīn* (Beirut: Dār al-'Ilm li 'l-Malāyīn, 1980).
Zubayrī, Muṣ'ab b. 'Abd Allāh, *Kitāb Nasab Quraysh* (Cairo: Dār al-Ma'ārif, 1982).
Zurqānī, Muḥammad ibn 'Abd al-Bāqī, *Sharḥ al-Zurqānī 'alā Muwaṭṭa' al-Imām Mālik* (Cairo: al-Maṭba'ah al-Khayriyya, 1892).

Index

Other Titles in the Series

Revealed Sciences: The Natural Sciences in Islam in Seventeenth Century Morocco, Justin K. Stearns
Agricultural Innovation in the Early Islamic World: The Diffusion of Crops and Farming Techniques, 700–1100, Andrew M. Watson
Muslim Tradition: Studies in Chronology, Provenance and Authorship of Early Hadith, G. H. A. Juynboll
Social History of Timbuktu: The Role of Muslim Scholars and Notables 1400–1900, Elias N. Saad
Sex and Society in Islam: Birth Control before the Nineteenth Century, B.F. Musallam
Towns and Townsmen of Ottoman Anatolia: Trade, Crafts and Food Production in an Urban Setting 1520–1650, Suraiya Faroqhi
Unlawful Gain and Legitimate Profit in Islamic Law: Riba, Gharar and Islamic Banking, Nabil A. Saleh
Men of Modest Substance: House Owners and House Property in Seventeenth-Century Ankara and Kayseri, Suraiya Faroqhi
Roman, Provincial and Islamic Law: The Origins of the Islamic Patronate, Patricia Crone
Economic Life in Ottoman Jerusalem, Amnon Cohen
Mannerism in Arabic Poetry: A Structural Analysis of Selected Texts (3rd Century AH/9th Century AD–5th Century AH/11th Century AD), Stefan Sperl
The Rise and Rule of Tamerlane, Beatrice Forbes Manz
Popular Culture in Medieval Cairo, Boaz Shoshan
Early Philosophical Shiism: The Ismaili Neoplatonism of Abu Ya'qub Al-Sijistani, Paul E. Walker
Indian Merchants and Eurasian Trade, 1600–1750, Stephen Frederic Dale
Palestinian Peasants and Ottoman Officials: Rural Administration around Sixteenth-Century Jerusalem, Amy Singer
Arabic Historical Thought in the Classical Period, Tarif Khalidi
Mongols and Mamluks: The Mamluk-Ilkhanid War, 1260–1281, Reuven Amitai-Preiss
Knowledge and Social Practice in Medieval Damascus, 1190–1350, Michael Chamberlain
The Politics of Households in Ottoman Egypt: The Rise of the Qazdağlis, Jane Hathaway
Hierarchy and Egalitarianism in Islamic Thought, Louise Marlow
Commodity and Exchange in the Mongol Empire: A Cultural History of Islamic Textiles, Thomas T. Allsen
State and Provincial Society in the Ottoman Empire: Mosul, 1540–1834, Dina Rizk Khoury
The Mamluks in Egyptian Politics and Society, Thomas Philipp and Ulrich Haarmann (eds.)
The Delhi Sultanate: A Political and Military History, Peter Jackson
European and Islamic Trade in the Early Ottoman State: The Merchants of Genoa and Turkey, Kate Fleet

The Ottoman City between East and West: Aleppo, Izmir, and Istanbul, Edhem Eldem, Daniel Goffman, and Bruce Masters
The Politics of Trade in Safavid Iran: Silk for Silver, 1600–1730, Rudolph P. Matthee
The Idea of Idolatry and the Emergence of Islam: From Polemic to History, G. R. Hawting
A Monetary History of the Ottoman Empire, Şevket Pamuk
Classical Arabic Biography: The Heirs of the Prophets in the Age of Al-Ma'mun, Michael Cooperson
Empire and Elites after the Muslim Conquest: The Transformation of Northern Mesopotamia, Chase F. Robinson
Poverty and Charity in Medieval Islam: Mamluk Egypt, 1250–1517, Adam Sabra
Culture and Conquest in Mongol Eurasia, Thomas T. Allsen
Christians and Jews in the Ottoman Arab World: The Roots of Sectarianism, Bruce Masters
Arabic Administration in Norman Sicily: The Royal Diwan, Jeremy Johns
Law, Society and Culture in the Maghrib, 1300–1500, David S. Powers
Revival and Reform in Islam: The Legacy of Muhammad al-Shawkani, Bernard Haykel
Tolerance and Coercion in Islam: Interfaith Relations in the Muslim Tradition, Yohanan Friedmann
Guns for the Sultan: Military Power and the Weapons Industry in the Ottoman Empire, Gábor Ágoston
Marriage, Money and Divorce in Medieval Islamic Society, Yossef Rapoport
The Empire of the Qara Khitai in Eurasian History: Between China and the Islamic World, Michal Biran
Domesticity and Power in the Early Mughal World, Ruby Lal
Power, Politics and Religion in Timurid Iran, Beatrice Forbes Manz
Postal Systems in the Pre-Modern Islamic World, Adam J. Silverstein
Kingship and Ideology in the Islamic and Mongol Worlds, Anne F. Broadbridge
Justice, Punishment and the Medieval Muslim Imagination, Christian Lange
The Shiites of Lebanon under Ottoman Rule, 1516–1788, Stefan Winter
Women and Slavery in the Late Ottoman Empire, Madeline Zilfi
The Second Ottoman Empire: Political and Social Transformation in the Early Modern World, Baki Tezcan
The Legendary Biographies of Tamerlane: Islam and Heroic Apocrypha in Central Asia, Ron Sela
Non-Muslims in the Early Islamic Empire: From Surrender to Coexistence, Milka Levy-Rubin
The Origins of the Shi'a: Identity, Ritual, and Sacred Space in Eighth-Century Kufa, Najam Haider
Politics, Law, and Community in Islamic Thought: The Taymiyyan Moment, Ovamir Anjum
The Power of Oratory in the Medieval Muslim World, Linda G. Jones
Animals in the Qur'an, Sarra Tlili
The Logic of Law Making in Islam: Women and Prayer in the Legal Tradition, Behnam Sadeghi

Empire and Power in the Reign of Süleyman: Narrating the Sixteenth-Century Ottoman World, Kaya Şahin
Law and Piety in Medieval Islam, Megan H. Reid
Women and the Transmission of Religious Knowledge in Islam, Asma Sayeed
The New Muslims of Post-Conquest Iran: Tradition, Memory, and Conversion, Sarah Bowen Savant
The Mamluk City in the Middle East: History, Culture, and the Urban Landscape, Nimrod Luz
Disability in the Ottoman Arab World, 1500–1800, Sara Scalenghe
The Holy City of Medina: Sacred Space in Early Islamic Arabia, Harry Munt
Muslim Midwives: The Craft of Birthing in the Premodern Middle East, Avner Giladi
Doubt in Islamic Law: A History of Legal Maxims, Interpretation, and Islamic Criminal Law, Intisar A. Rabb
The Second Formation of Islamic Law: The Hanafi School in the Early Modern Ottoman Empire, Guy Burak
Sexual Violation in Islamic Law: Substance, Evidence, and Procedure, Hina Azam
Gender Hierarchy in the Qur'an: Medieval Interpretations, Modern Responses, Karen Bauer
Intellectual Networks in Timurid Iran: Sharaf al-Din 'Ali Yazdi and the Islamicate Republic of Letters, Ilker Evrim Binbaş
Authority and Identity in Medieval Islamic Historiography: Persian Histories from the Peripheries, Mimi Hanaoka
The Economics of Ottoman Justice: Settlement and Trial in the Sharia Courts, Top of Form Metin Coşgel and Boğaç Ergene
The Mystics of al-Andalus: Ibn Barrajan and Islamic Thought in the Twelfth Century, Yousef Casewit
Muhammad's Heirs: The Rise of Muslim Scholarly Communities, 622–950, Jonathan E. Brockopp
The First of the Modern Ottomans: The Intellectual History of Ahmed Vasif, Ethan Menchinger
Non-Muslim Provinces under Early Islam: Islamic Rule and Iranian Legitimacy in Armenia and Caucasian Albania, Alison Vacca
Women and the Making of the Mongol Empire, Anne F. Broadbridge
Slavery and Empire in Central Asia, Jeff Eden
Christianity in Fifteenth-Century Iraq, Thomas A. Carlson
Child Custody in Islamic Law: Theory and Practice in Egypt since the Sixteenth Century, Ahmed Fekry Ibrahim
Ibadi Muslims of North Africa: Manuscripts, Mobilization and the Making of a Written Tradition, Paul M. Love Jr.
Islamic Law of the Sea: Freedom of Navigation and Passage Rights in Islamic Thought, Hassan S. Khalilieh
Law and Politics under the Abassids: An Intellectual Portrait of al-Juwayni, Sohaira Z. M. Siddiqui
Friends of the Emir: Non-Muslim State Officials in Premodern Islamic Thought, Luke B. Yarbrough

The Crisis of Kingship in Late Medieval Islam: Persian Emigres and the Making of Ottoman Sovereignty, Christopher Markiewicz
Collective Liability in Islam: The ʿĀqila and Blood Money Payments, Nurit Tsafrir
Arabic Poetics: Aesthetic Experience in Classical Arabic Literature, Lara Harb
The Sufi Saint of Jam: History, Religion and Politics of a Sunni Shrine in Shiʿi Iran, Shivan Mahendrarajah
Opposing the Imām: The Legacy of the Nawāṣib in Islamic Literature, Nebil Husayn